ForeEdge
An imprint of University Press of New England
www.upne.com
Manufactured in the United States of America
Designed by Eric M. Brooks
Typeset in Fresco Plus Pro by Passumpsic Publishing

First ForeEdge paperback edition 2018
Paperback ISBN 978-1-5126-0318-7

LIBRARY OF CONGRESS CATALOGING-IN-PUBLICATION DATA
Names: Thornton, Jerry.
Title: From darkness to dynasty : the first 40 years of the New England
    Patriots / Jerry Thornton ; foreword by Michael Holley.
Description: Lebanon NH : ForeEdge, [2016] | Includes bibliographical
    references and index.
Identifiers: LCCN 2016009535 (print) | LCCN 2016050546 (ebook) | ISBN
    9781611689747 (cloth) | ISBN 9781512600018 (epub, mobi & pdf)
Subjects: LCSH: New England Patriots (Football team)—History.
Classification: LCC GV956.N36 T56 2016 (print) | LCC GV956.N36
    (ebook) | DDC 796.332/640974461—dc23
LC record available at https://lccn.loc.gov/2016009535

5 4 3 2 1

FROM DARKNESS TO **DYNASTY**

FROM DARKNESS

JERRY
THORNTON

DARKNESS

THE FIRST 40 YEARS of the
NEW ENGLAND PATRIOTS

TO

DYNASTY

★ ★

Foreword by
Michael Holley

ForeEdge

To my beguiling Irish rose, Anne.
My singer and actress who has always
insisted we gamble on ourselves,
even when there was a safer, easier path.
And who, during all those hours I
spend obsessing over a football team,
has raised our Marine and our musician
to follow their passions as well.
Love is not a big enough word.

CONTENTS

★   *Illustrations appear following page 142.*

FOREWORD

Maybe you've never met Jerry Thornton personally, but you already know him. He's one of those guys, your guys, a familiar voice from the neighborhood who watches the Patriots game and feels the same way you do about it.

Jerry is from your section of the stadium. He's your buddy from the gym. He's the comedy-loving friend who can be in the audience appreciating the comic, or on the mic as the comic. He's even comfortable being the nerd who crushes world geography, politics, and '80s pop at the local bar's trivia night.

More than anything, though, Jerry is an always-on-the-job Patriots ambassador. When he was growing up near Boston, on the South Shore, he probably didn't realize that, just by being himself, he was establishing his credentials as a historian and a comic. It's easy to see now how intertwined the two passions are. There was a time in Patriots history when an exceptional sense of humor was a requirement. Otherwise, what did you have?

This was the team that spent the first ten years of its existence trying to find a permanent home stadium, and when it found that brand-new home in 1971, the discount building was immediately out of date. Its toilets overflowed the first time they were ever used, and the bathroom experience got worse from there. It had parking issues. Its primary tenant led the National Football League in bad PR and heartbreak. The Patriots that Jerry grew up watching taught lessons, lessons that you didn't necessarily want to learn on Sunday afternoons at one o'clock.

They had the hope of young, strong, Heisman trophy-winning quarterback Jim Plunkett in 1971. But it took him a decade to win a Super Bowl, and when he did it he was long gone from New England, three thousand miles away in Oakland. There always seemed to be a trap door built into Patriots fanhood, a "Yeah, but . . ." on the other side of the celebration. The 1976 season alone makes the case for cynicism and paranoia. In the spring of that year, a teenaged Jerry watched as his team, with the fifth overall pick in the draft, made one of the most astute choices in franchise history with cornerback Mike Haynes. In the fall the Patriots, with Haynes and other stars, looked like the best team in football. They went into Pittsburgh and scored 30 points on a Steel Curtain defense that allowed an average of just 10 points per game. They hosted the Raiders and put 48 points on them. Yet in the postseason, in Oakland, an official mistook a virtual love tap for a roughing penalty, and the result was the same as it always was back then: someone else got to exalt at the end of the year. The Raiders won the Super Bowl and, years later, welcomed Haynes to help them win another one.

It always seemed that someone was out to get the Patriots, whether it was a misguided official, a coach with wanderlust, drunk fans carrying a goalpost down Route 1, cash-strapped management, or management with plenty of cash and zero emotional investment in New England.

I promise you that Jerry sees it that way. Yes, he's the ambassador, but with one caveat: it's not really a traditional job for him. This is his life. The team's joy is his as well; the names of their critics are forever in his back pocket. One of the best things about Jerry's Patriot observations is that he was there with them, there with you, for every creative letdown that the team authored, but he was able to hover alongside the hopelessness. He was the stenographer along for the ride, alternately devastated and bemused by the actions of the old Patriots, but never sacked by their incompetence. To that end, the biggest surprise from Patriots history is not the Jacksons' Victory Tour putting the team's future in peril, nor is it the attempted moves to Jacksonville and St. Louis. The heartening takeaway just might be Jerry and thousands of fans like him emerging from the dark days as optimists.

That's one of the reasons Jerry is perfect for this story. He loves the region, he loves football, he loves the team, and he loves to laugh. Those are the necessary elements to truly put this organization into perspective. Who better to do it than a man whose wardrobe consists primarily of Patriots t-shirts and sweatshirts? We're talking about someone whose idea of summer beach reading is a book on football theory. He seems to enjoy the fact that part of his job entails scanning the Internet for anyone who is not properly bowing down to the current Patriots and then blogging about the lost soul. He debates the Patriots in print, on the air, even on boats far out on Lake Champlain in Vermont. (True story: that was a stress-relieving vacation for him last summer.)

When you finish this book, you'll undoubtedly understand Jerry better. He has grown with this team, which used to reside on the margins of New England sports. It searched for credibility when the Celtics were winning eight NBA titles in a row. It begged for respectability when the Bruins commanded respect, and instilled fear, in the NHL in 1970 and 1972. It wanted to be at the table, to be taken seriously, in the 1980s when the Red Sox sometimes wished that their fans weren't so serious, scrutinizing every move of every game, convinced that—due to moronic management—they would die without a championship. The Patriots have now gotten everything they hoped for and more, and Jerry personally guides you through their unlikely discard-to-diamond journey.

You won't just learn about Jerry, though. He and his stories are so familiar that, in the end, you will feel that you've seen glimpses of your self-portrait.

Michael Holley

FROM DARKNESS TO DYNASTY

INTRODUCTION

★ ★

What do you do when your real life exceeds your dreams?
TOM GRUNICK, *Broadcast News*

It's human nature to look at every great success story and just assume that good times and prosperity always existed. We forget that every story of triumph involves a humble backstory, of hard times that had to be endured and adversity that needed to be overcome before greatness was attained. When we're celebrating achievements, we tend to forget all about the struggles.

It's like the old saying: no one wants to hear about your labor pains, just show us how cute the baby is.

Bill Gates didn't just come out of the womb writing software code, crushing the competition and filling his diapers with money; he had to endure years of looking awkward in his gym uniform and getting stuffed into lockers on his way to the top. Einstein was a Swiss patent clerk before he came up with all those formulas we pretend to understand. When Jesus would walk into a room and leave the door open behind him—and one of the Apostles would say, "Hey! Do you mind shutting that thing? What were you, born in a barn?"—he could truthfully say, "Well, now that you mention it . . ."

Our ancestors spent eons scurrying around in the bushes, evading predators, and eating berries out of dinosaur poop. And we would still be doing so if an asteroid hadn't come along and conveniently wiped out the top ninety percent of the food chain for us. But we still managed to write ourselves an origin story in which we were created with the snap of some Almighty fingers and given dominion over all living things in our first day on the job.

So when the New England Patriots beat the Seattle Seahawks to win Super Bowl XLIX, in what was arguably the best and most dramatic football game ever played, the world could be forgiven if it thought this was the norm for them. After all, that win was the Patriots' fourth championship in only 14 seasons, to go with six Super Bowl appearances and a remarkable eight trips to their conference championship game. When an obscure, undrafted rookie

1

out of the relatively unheard-of University of West Alabama named Malcolm Butler intercepted a potentially game-winning pass at the goal line to seal the win for New England, he didn't just cement several legacies at once. He encased them in that protective, impenetrable, blast-proof, steel-reinforced concrete they build nuclear missile silos out of. Butler's pick preserved the game's most valuable player award for Patriots quarterback Tom Brady. It was his third award—tying Joe Montana's record—and established him as one of the most successful QBs in NFL history. The championship was New England head coach Bill Belichick's sixth, including four while running the Pats and two in his earlier stint as the defensive coordinator for the New York Giants. It made the two of them—Brady and Belichick—the winningest QB/coach combo in the history of pro football and the most recognizable duo since Abbott and Costello. And it inducted team owner Robert Kraft—on his seventh trip to the Super Bowl since saving the franchise 21 years earlier—into the pantheon of the most important owners since the NFL was founded nearly a century earlier.

So sure, it's understandable if casual fans and millennials make the mistake of thinking it was ever thus, that life for the Patriots and the football fans of New England has always been a steady stream of good times and unforgettable wins, one right after the other. A never-ending playlist of highlights set to shuffle mode. The period from 2001 to 2015 saw 10 trips to the AFC championship game (five of them in a row), 13 AFC East division titles, and an incredible 14 seasons with 10 or more wins. In a modern NFL where the system is set up to help teams at the bottom, in order to minimize repeated, long-term success, 15 years at or near the top of the league is practically an eternity. So there's no shame in assuming the previous 40 years of the Patriots' existence was all superhero quarterbacks, diabolically brilliant coaches, and titans-of-industry owners, accompanied by a constant string of trophy presentations, confetti showers, and parades.

But nothing could be further from the truth.

I know, because I lived it.

I grew up the youngest of five kids in a Patriots-first household in the Boston suburb of Weymouth, Massachusetts. Meaning that, in an era when the Red Sox, Celtics, and Bruins took turns dominating the sports landscape where we lived, I was raised to care more about the Patriots than those other more successful and popular teams. At the time, this was the equivalent of telling people your favorite Stooge was Shemp. So I can tell you firsthand that the Patriots of my formative years raised failure to an art form. They weren't just another unit rolled off the assembly line at the Loser Sports Franchise factory. They were uniquely bad. Comically atrocious. Ridiculously terrible. No other team was ever as consistently and irredeemably gawdawful as the Patriots I grew up loving.

The Boston/New England Patriots of the 20th century weren't content to just be garden-variety bad. Mostly unsuccessful on the field, they were laughingstocks off of it. Nineteen times in their first 40 years of existence, they finished with six or fewer wins. In their first quarter-century as a franchise, they won a grand total of one playoff game, and even that one was in the old American Football League, before it became part of the National Football League. The few times they did manage to put together a winner and offer hope for future success, the optimism quickly unraveled in controversy, scandal, or disgrace. It took them a full decade just to get a stadium of their own to play in, and from the day it opened, Schaefer Stadium was an obsolete dump. Along the way they made more headlines for lawsuits, arrests, power struggles, drug problems, and inept, bizarre, borderline-insane behavior from players, coaches, and owners than for anything they ever did on the field.

The Patriots of the last century may not have invented the downtrodden, hopeless sports franchise, but they did make First Team All-America in that category.

Worse still, the Boston/New England Patriots committed a more egregious sin than being just a bunch of failing, snake-bitten losers, one that is unpardonable under any circumstances.

For long periods of time, they were irrelevant.

There were stretches of futility when they couldn't sell out home games, so they were blacked out on local TV. The Patriots of my childhood were so unpopular that tickets to their games were always available. My older brothers took me to see them a dozen or so times before I'd ever set foot in Fenway Park to see a Red Sox game or entered the Boston Garden to watch the Celtics or Bruins. The Pats were so far off most people's cultural radar when I was a kid that when I wore their helmet and uniform for Halloween, a grown man in my own neighborhood had no idea who the hell I was supposed to be. That moment traumatized me for years. While the other, more well-adjusted kids were outside doing well-adjusted kid things, I'd be holed up in my room listening to games on the radio like it was the 1940s and FDR was coming on for a fireside chat. In the lead-up to Christmas every year, I used to pore through the kids' Holy Bible of the time, the Sears Wish Book, picking out the stuff I was going to put on my list. A good two dozen or so pages of the catalog were dedicated just to pro football merchandise I wanted. Sweatshirts. Posters. Pennants. Even back then you could have outfitted your entire room from bedspread to wastebasket to wall coverings in your team's gear, if your team happened to be one of the 20 or so most popular franchises. Invariably, the best swag would be listed with a footnote at the bottom in agate type: "Not available in the following teams: Patriots . . ."

And never mind being able to pick out the gear of any of their individual players. I mean, they might have sometimes listed the jersey of the Pats' starting quarterback. But typically, whoever had the job was a threat to be benched, so instead they'd offer you three different Dallas Cowboys jerseys or four different Pittsburgh Steelers jerseys, instead of wasting precious space on a shirt no parent would waste money on.

It honestly felt at times like the Patriots weren't in the actual NFL, instead belonging in some sort of junior varsity that didn't really count. Never mind rooting for them to win championships; my most realistic dream was that someday they'd just *matter*.

So it's surreal to sit here, with the Patriots sitting atop the North American professional sports world, the model franchise and the gold standard for winning in the modern era, and think about how far they've come. Not only about how they've managed to make that turnaround, build a dynasty, and sustain it, but also how their rise to the top has affected my own life as a guy raised to be a fan.

By the time the Patriots were winning Super Bowls, the kid with the Patriots Halloween costume and the non-Patriots bedecked bedroom who only wished he'd get to see them be relevant someday was doing things he never dreamed possible.

In 2004 I started writing about the Patriots for Boston's upstart *Barstool Sports*, a free biweekly newspaper. A few years later, Barstool became a daily online blog, opened branches in other cities, exploded into a sports, sex, pop culture, humor, and lifestyle phenomenon, and basically took over the Internet. Then, just a few months prior to the Patriots-Seahawks epic in Arizona, I left Barstool and my unrelated day job of 17 years to start a full-time career with WEEI, a regional sports radio powerhouse I had been listening to since forever. So in the span of one lifetime, I'd gone from caring about a team almost no one else did to covering them while they won their fourth Super Bowl. From sitting alone in my room listening to them lose games on my clock radio to talking about them for a living. From hoping I'd live long enough to see them matter to the rest of America to interviewing the likes of Brady and Belichick while they were at the center of the sports universe.

The word "surreal" doesn't suffice. It feels dreamlike, like I'm going to snap out of this fugue state I've been in and find out I'm still 13 years old, freezing my ass on the metal bleachers in their crappy old stadium, breathing the beer-and-Marlboros breath of the drunk next to me and realizing I've just imagined the last decade and a half as the Patriots drop another game by three touchdowns.

Granted, the Patriots are by no means the only team to go from terrible to dynastic. But I'll argue that no franchise in pro sports has suffered as many decades of such complete and hilarious futility and then achieved so many years of sustained dominance. For generations, they set the standard for dysfunction, mismanagement, and failure, and now they're the model of success. They are the polar opposite of what they once were. And their turnaround has been so extreme it's unthinkable. The same New England Patriots team that can arguably claim to have the best quarterback in the history of football once had a franchise quarterback who walked out of training camp and then sued them, just because his agent was trying to establish a legal precedent.

They got Brady with the 199th pick of the draft, but over the years have had the top overall pick five times. One of those picks was a success, one they traded to a team that was building a dynasty, and the other three were complete disasters.

Today, their scouting system is the standard the rest of the NFL aspires to. But the first franchise player they ever drafted worked off his rookie contract in their ticket office. They once used a first-round pick on a player who was having knee surgery they didn't know about. And they once came very close to drafting a dead guy.

Now they unquestionably have the most successful coach of the modern era. But they once had a head coach who suffered a nervous breakdown, another one who had his general manager rooting for him to lose so he could fire him, and twice had coaches build championship-caliber rosters only to get caught working for other teams.

That's right, twice.

They lost the best coach they'd had to that point to a hated rival in an ugly, protracted legal battle. Then they got an even better coach from the same team in another ugly, protracted legal battle. Their owner is one of the most powerful and influential figures in all of pro sports. But their first owner bought the team with vacation cottage money, lost the franchise when his son blew every nickel the family had promoting a Michael Jackson concert tour, and then sold it to a businessman who became one of the most hated men in America.

Today, the Patriots play in a state-of-the-art facility. But in years past their stands once burned down in the middle of a game, they opened a stadium with no working toilets, and even played "home" games in San Diego and

Birmingham. Their home crowds were so insanely rowdy that the team was banned from *Monday Night Football*, and fans were almost killed after stealing the goal posts from Sullivan Stadium.

These days, their personnel department produces bottom-of-the-roster players like Super Bowl hero Butler. But on one occasion, the team was left so shorthanded they pulled a half-drunk ex-player out of the stands and suited him up.

They have won four of the six Super Bowls they've been to in the 2000s, but they lost their first two championship games by a combined score of 97–20.

That first Super Bowl win in 2001 followed a series of bizarre, tragic, historic, and coincidental moments, without any one of which the first championship —and quite possibly the three that followed—might never have happened.

The purpose of this book is to tell the story of the Boston/New England Patriots the way it has never been told. But I also want this book to be of benefit to non-Patriots fans. For you poor creatures who have had the misfortune of growing up in other parts of the country, rooting for other teams, my wish is that this book gives you hope. Because no matter how downtrodden your particular team might be, there's no way you have it worse than we once did. (Hello, Cleveland.) And if this stunning, unfathomable turnaround from misery to sustained excellence happened here, then truly, anything is possible. Because that crap my mother could never order for me because the league didn't bother to make it is now among the best-selling merchandise the NFL offers. Those years of blackouts have been replaced by record TV ratings. And that team that almost backed up the moving trucks is now worth over a billion dollars.

And every second of the ugly past was worth it. Because sure, it's easy to admire a team that's an internationally recognized symbol of excellence and success. But if you could love the New England Patriots from 1960 to 2000, then you really know what true love is.

All the peculiar, dysfunctional, offbeat, horrible, and sometimes tragic stories make this era of unprecedented success that much harder to fathom. I write from the perspective of the fans who were there for most of it, suffering through the terrible times, laughing at the weird moments, and sharing in the triumph—with millions of other New England football lovers—when it finally all turned good.

This story is for them.

Go Patriots.

1

THE FOOLISH CLUB

★ ★ ★ ★ ★ ★ ★ ★ ★ ★ ★ ★ ★ ★ ★ ★ ★ ★ ★

BILLY SULLIVAN AND THE AFL

Great moments are born of great opportunities.
HERB BROOKS, *Miracle*

I got to meet Billy Sullivan once. That would be *the* Billy Sullivan, founder and owner of the Boston Patriots. The man who single-handedly brought professional football to New England.

To most people who grew up in Massachusetts, this would be a throw-away story, one that's told in a casual, "Guess who I met today," kind of way, repeated once or twice and then quickly forgotten. But to me, this was as big a deal as big deals get. I grew up as a football fan first in a football-first household on the South Shore of Boston at a time when almost no one in New England was a football fan first. So you bet meeting the man who gave birth to the franchise I loved and dedicated years of my life to was a big deal for me. Picture a political science major getting to meet the president. Or a jazz fan being introduced to Miles Davis. Picture a 30-year-old virgin in a Lieutenant Worf Starfleet uniform meeting Gene Roddenberry and you'd have gone too far, but not by much.

I wasn't expecting a lot; the Sullivan-owned Patriots were without a doubt the worst-run organization in all of sports. At this time, I was in my late twenties and the Patriots of my formative years were almost always laughingstocks. For their first 40 years, they were as bush-league and incompetent off the field as they were bumbling and inept on it. In a popularity contest among the four Boston pro teams, the Pats couldn't make the medal stand. The region always belonged to (at different times) the Celtics, Red Sox, or Bruins. I'd call the Patriots of the 60s through the 90s an afterthought, if I didn't think that would be a slur against afterthoughts.

I was introduced to Billy by my father-in-law on a summer morning in the mid-90s, when he took me for a round of golf at the country club he belonged to on Cape Cod. It's one of those exclusive private courses where you need to be an invited guest of a member to even make it through the gates. There were a lot of new-money members there, dot-com millionaires and so forth. But they still had a lot of the old guard guys like my father-in-law, a World War II vet who went to school on the GI Bill, made a decent living, and joined the club a generation ago when it was still somewhat affordable.

I'd known that Billy Sullivan was also a club member, but on the few occasions I'd been on the property I'd never seen him. But I'd always hoped to. After all, he was the man who founded the football team I loved. And who owned and ran the franchise most of my life, for better or worse. And it was mostly "worse."

The impression I always had of the Sullivan Family—one that virtually every Patriots fan shared—was that when it came to owing a professional sports organization, they were in way over their heads. That they had no football savvy and even less business acumen, and that you wouldn't trust them to run a snack bar at the beach, much less an NFL franchise.

So on this particular day, I was loosening up near the starters shed and waiting to be sent up to first tee when my father-in-law called me over because there was someone he wanted me to meet. It was Billy Sullivan. A lifetime of preconceived notions prepared me to be unimpressed.

And the life lesson I learned from the meeting was, no matter how low your expectations of anything are, you can still walk away from it disappointed.

Billy Sullivan was a very nice man. Friendly, gregarious. An affable old Irishman with a lilt in his voice and a loud laugh. The kind of guy pubs, offices, and golf courses around Massachusetts are lousy with. And a man it was impossible not to like. Someone very much like my wife's father, only with the baggage of being the undisputed Worst Owner in Sports.

And that's where the crushing disappointment hit. As I was standing there shaking the old boy's hand and listening to the two of them bust each other's chops about their golf games, it struck me that these could be any two old bucks I'd ever met. There's a pair of guys like them sitting at the bar in every Knights of Columbus in New England, talking over one another and laughing at their own jokes. It hit me that, while I wasn't expecting more out of Billy Sullivan, I was expecting, well . . . *more*.

Part of me wanted to feel like I was meeting a titan of industry. A business giant with power oozing out of every pore. An NFL owner is one of the great icons of American culture. So on some level I wanted to see something befitting a powerful man. An entourage, maybe? A security detail of sinister guys in mirrored shades wearing earpieces and talking into their cufflinks? I guess I would've just settled for him driving around Al Czervik-at-Bushwood style, in a Rolls Royce with a horn that plays "We're in the Money." Instead, I got this unassuming, genial old man.

As fate would have it, a couple of decades later and under vastly different circumstances, I'd get to meet Robert Kraft, a much more successful Patriots owner. Kraft would give off the same casual friendliness as Sullivan, but with an air of business savvy and power his predecessor lacked.

There is no more impressive and powerful a figure in modern society than the owner of a pro football team. None. Maybe 150 years ago it was railroad barons and industrialists, and I suppose for most of the 20th century it was politicians. They always said that the U.S. Senate is the most exclusive men's club in the world, but there are 100 Senators. There are 32 NFL owners. And as they've proven thousands of times over, any nitwit can get elected. It takes real influence to buy a football team. So forgive me for thinking that anyone who owned a team would be larger than life; that, as Shakespeare said of Caesar, an NFL owner would bestride the narrow world like a colossus.

And Billy Sullivan should've been even more than that. Because he wasn't just some Lucky Spermer who was born rich and got to own Daddy's team. This man was a pioneer. A founder of the American Football League. One of the dreamers who dared to believe they could found a league to rival the NFL, take on the behemoth and beat it at its own game. Those original AFL guys were visionaries. Real men of thought and action who made million-dollar deals over a steak, a cigarette, and a highball, then sealed it with a handshake. The kind of men that are a dying breed but whose names will live forever in the game because they're cast in bronze on the Lamar Hunt Trophy and chiseled in granite at Ralph Wilson Stadium. You don't expect to find legends like that standing around in baggy shorts and a big sun hat giving your father-in-law a ration of shit about his backswing. You expect more of them. It's a bit like meeting James Bond as he leaves the men's room stall in a Wendy's, and he says, "You do NOT want to go in there, Chief." It's more ordinary than you're ready for.

Unless, of course, you happen to be a New England Patriots fan. At least, a Pats fan who remembers the bad old days. If you were following them back then, before all the Super Bowl championships and the dynasty talk and the new stadium, when every season was a struggle for even minimal respectability, then the Billy Sullivan I met—that run-of-the-mill, garden-variety, charming but not terribly impressive old Irishman—was exactly what you'd expect the founder of the Pats to be.

THE PIPE DREAM

There's only one thing America loves better than a great success story. And that's a great success story that has humble beginnings. And as beginnings go, the birth of the Patriots is about as humble as they come.

There have been hundreds of great accounts of how the American Football League was founded. It really is one of the great success stories in the history of U.S. business: the way a group of entrepreneurs and investors threw together a fly-by-night operation that nearly took down the all-powerful NFL is part of the lore of the sport. Today, in a time when franchises are bought by billionaires and giant corporate conglomerates as a tax dodge, it sounds almost too good to be true.

And the story of how Billy Sullivan got a team into the AFL is the best of them all. Because the Patriots were created almost by accident. The footnote under an asterisk following an afterthought.

Major League Baseball was still the most popular sport in the United States in 1959. But there was no doubting that the National Football League was beginning to challenge baseball to be the king of the national sports hill. They were certainly starting to figure out the fine art of hype and self-promotion. The 1958 NFL Championship Game from Yankee Stadium was televised nationally on NBC and drew a record audience. The Baltimore Colts beat the New York Giants in overtime for the title, and the league wasted no time dubbing it "The Greatest Game Ever Played," the name it still goes by, even half a century and hundreds of better games later.

The NFL of the time had 12 teams spread across the country, from San Francisco to New York. Two of those teams were in Chicago, but only one—the seven-time champion Bears, who were run by the legendary George Halas—had any merit. Struggling in the Bears' shadow were the Chicago Cardinals; it was no secret to anyone that financially the Cards were the weakest team in the league, and, like the weak animal in a herd, they drew the attention of hungry predators.

Buying an interest in the Cardinals was seen as an entry into the league by a slew of wealthy businessmen, not the least of whom was Lamar Hunt, the heir to the fortune of Texas oil millionaire H.L. Hunt. Lamar approached NFL commissioner Bert Bell about buying the club and moving them to Dallas. And there were others interested as well:

★ Bud Adams of Oklahoma, another oil tycoon's kid, the son of the head of Phillips Petroleum;

★ Max Winter, who made his money with a Minneapolis restaurant that specialized in turkey, of all things, and also owned the Lakers of the then-National Basketball League; and

★ Bob Howsam, a Denver-based minor league baseball owner/troublemaker who specialized in being a pain in the ass to the Major Leagues, hitting them with anti-trust lawsuits.

For various reasons, Commissioner Bell essentially told all these guys to go piss up a rope; the Cards were not for sale. A year later, the franchise was relocated to St. Louis, but the Hunts, Adamses, Winters and Howsams would still not be part of the NFL. Undeterred, the men took another run at Bell. If they couldn't buy one team, they asked, how about letting them start their own? But Bell wanted no part of that, either. The NFL was onto something good. They were gaining popularity, putting out a good product, and he was reluctant to mess with a good thing by watering it down with expansion.

This disappointment might have defeated a lesser man than Hunt, but instead it serves as one of those instructive moral tales that successful men get paid $50,000 per speech to tell to hotel conference rooms full of executives. It would've been easy for Hunt to just accept the rejection. But legend has it that, after being told no by the league, Hunt made the decision to start his own rival league on the flight back to Dallas. And the football world would never be the same.

Upon landing, Hunt got in touch with other rejected suitors for the Cardinals and pitched them the idea of starting their own football league. A meeting took place in March of 1959 between him and Adams. They agreed that Hunt would put a team in Dallas and Adams would put one in Houston, so the infant league would have a natural geographic rivalry. Howsam, of course, would put one in Denver. Winter's would be in Minneapolis/St. Paul. They got a commitment out of Harry Wismer, a radio sportscaster who'd owned pieces of some NFL teams, to put a club in New York. Barron Hilton, whose family at that time was still famous for their hotel chain and not his skanky granddaughter and her pioneering work in celebrity sex tapes, agreed to field a team in Los Angeles.

That gave the fledgling league six charter members, and they held their first owners' meeting in Chicago in August of that year. It was there that they decided they would officially call it the American Football League—but in the conference room, behind closed doors and over some Chesterfields and Rob Roys, they called themselves "The Foolish Club," because nobody in their right mind would try to do what they were about to. Even they acknowledged that trying to compete against the NFL was a financial suicide mission.

The people running the NFL, though, didn't seem to agree. The commissioner's office contacted the owners of the upstart league and backpedaled faster than any defensive back ever had. In not so many words, they said, "When we said we didn't want to expand, what we meant to say was of course we'd love to expand! We're all for it! And we have just the cities in mind! Minneapolis/St. Paul, Dallas, Houston . . ." and began offering all the AFL teams expansion franchises. But the upstart new owners held their ground.

In the midst of it all, the AFL recruited Ralph Wilson, who owned a piece of the Detroit Lions, to add a seventh team in Buffalo. They therefore needed an eighth city, and the likely choice seemed to be Boston, a big sports town with no NFL franchise to compete with. But there was no obvious, deep-pocketed investor there to turn to.

Yet somehow, inexplicably, they found one of the least likely men imaginable. A man with no rich dad, no oil fortune or hotel chain, but a guy with enough cash for the down payment on a summer cottage and big dreams.

Billy was born William Hallissey Sullivan, Jr. in Lowell, Massachusetts, one of those small, blue-collar, working-class cities that did well back when America still had a manufacturing base. But when the factory jobs went overseas, its chief industries became Section 8 housing, government assistance, and "Checks Cashed Here" businesses. Sullivan's father was a sportswriter for the *Boston Globe*, a classic Irish parent who raised his kid to know the value of hard work. "NINA," which is shorthand for "No Irish Need Apply," was a common sign in the windows of Boston that gave generations of Irishmen—including Billy Sullivan Sr.—a massive chip on their shoulders they never took off.

Billy Junior went to Boston College in the mid-1930s and took a job doing publicity for the athletic department, before becoming the school's first full-time sports information director upon graduation. BC legend Frank Leahy coached the Eagles to the Cotton Bowl in 1939, a season he followed with an 11-0 run for "The Team of Destiny," which included a win against Georgetown in front of 41,000 fans at Fenway Park, in a game sportswriting legend Grantland Rice called one of the best football games ever played. That season ended with BC beating Tennessee in the Sugar Bowl, though they weren't voted national champions in any of the approximately 720 national polls taken at the time.

By all accounts, Billy took his old man's lessons about hard work to heart, and he drew the attention of some in the school administration. When Leahy left BC for his alma mater Notre Dame after the Sugar Bowl victory, he took Sullivan with him and gave him the made-up title of "special assistant," which basically included publicity and some recruiting. When World War II broke

out, Sullivan joined the Navy, and by the end of the war was handli
information duties for Naval Academy football, defeating the Axis Po
press release at a time.

After the war, he came back to Boston and landed a job running the
department for the then-Boston Braves of baseball's National League, and was
damned good at his job. It suited Sullivan, who had a fair amount of carnival
barker in his soul. Among his accomplishments, he produced promotional
films for the club. He's credited with the idea of taking some of the worst seats
in the house, fixing them up a little bit and selling them as premium, high-
priced "sky boxes" to big-moneyed high rollers. Today we regularly tear down
perfectly good stadiums to build new ones, just so owners can squeeze in more
luxury suites. But in the 1940s it was unheard of, until Billy Sullivan invented it.

But the single greatest accomplishment of Sullivan's days with the Braves,
and the lasting legacy for which he doesn't get nearly the credit he deserves,
is being the driving force behind getting the Braves to back the Jimmy Fund,
which is widely recognized as the world's leading charity in battling cancer in
children. It has helped millions. And when the Braves moved to Milwaukee
years later, Sullivan convinced the Red Sox to take the Jimmy Fund over as
their official club charity. But without Billy Sullivan's involvement, it might
have died on the vine sixty years ago.

In the long run, National League baseball in Boston was doomed. Braves
Field was an armpit, the owners were bleeding money and couldn't compete
with the Sox, and they played their last game in Boston in 1952. Sullivan
kicked around to a few different jobs, including one in Los Angeles working
with Leahy producing sports films, before moving back to Boston to become,
of all things, president of an oil company. It's a safe bet that he wasn't pulling
in the kind of money Hunt and Adams were from the job, since being an oil
exec from Boston is more or less equivalent to owning the best lobster boat in
Oklahoma. But it kept him in touch with a lot of his old contacts and cronies
from the church and the sports world. And just as importantly, it kept him in
contact with his relatives. Because it was a cousin of Billy's who stepped in
one day and changed not only his life, but the course of pro sports in Boston.

Anybody who has spent any time in Massachusetts will know that the place
is overrun with Sullivans. Just teeming with them. Walk into any bar in eastern Mass and yell, "Hey Sully!" and at least three guys in Scally caps will say,
"Yeah?" In Scituate, a tiny coastal town on Boston's South Shore (dubbed by
some as "a drinking village with a fishing problem"), there are 40 Sullivans
listed in the phone book. By comparison, Indianapolis, the sixth largest city in
the United States, has a total of four. It's as if all the Sullivan ancestors came

.cross from Ireland, made landfall in Massachusetts, and decided to just take a load off, grab a pint, and make a home here while all the other immigrants kept moving west and south, where the good weather and jobs were.

Billy's cousin Bob Sullivan, who ran an ad agency that had Willimansett, Massachusetts–based Hampden-Harvard brewing company as a client, came to him with a proposal. Hampden-Harvard was interested in bringing National League baseball back to Boston, and he was hoping Billy could use his sports connections to help make it happen. Billy thought the idea was nuts; National League baseball had failed miserably in Boston. The Braves' attendance was a fraction of what the Red Sox drew. Plus, his old boss with the Braves, Lou Perini, had taken massive criticism for letting the team leave town. Perini was a contractor and as politically wired in as anyone in the city. There's a saying that goes, "the most popular pastimes in Boston are sports, politics, and re-venge," and Perini was good at all three. Sullivan knew he wouldn't just sit back and let someone else bring a team and make him even more hated among the great unwashed masses, so he'd pull strings to see to it that no National League team was brought in.

What interested Sullivan, though, was Hampden-Harvard's concept for a ballpark. They wanted to build a domed stadium in downtown Boston. Bear in mind, this was 1958. The Houston Astrodome wouldn't open for another seven years. And even when it did, it was called "The 8th Wonder of the World." This was still the age of wooden bleachers. Hell, baseball had only broken the color barrier 10 years earlier. The idea of playing baseball under a dome must have sounded like flying cars or rockets to the moon or computers that will let you watch Barron Hilton's granddaughter's sex tape.

Sullivan hated the baseball idea but loved the stadium, and suggested the company try for an NFL expansion franchise. At that point, Boston was still the largest market in the country without a football team, and he assumed that the league owners would jump at the chance to put a team there, especially with a ballpark that seemed to them like something out of Buck Rogers.

And he wasn't planning just a domed stadium. The place Sullivan was pro-posing would come with extras including, but not limited to:

★ a convention center
★ a 350-room hotel
★ upper-level "apartment boxes," complete with kitchens
★ an upscale, 2,500-seat restaurant.

This was the equivalent of holding a 1950s rotary phone in your hands and talking about building an iPhone. So sure, Billy Sullivan was a man of vision.

Whether his were the Steve Jobs kinds of visions or the visions of a delusional mental patient is all in how you look at it.

This is an exact quote from the original AFL press guide in 1959: *"The Boston plan is no pipe dream. It has been announced and will be ready . . . for the 1962 season."*

But of course it was a pipe dream. And ten years later when they finally opened the dump that was Schaefer, it was fair to ask what they were smoking in that pipe.

The notion of building it downtown didn't survive long. As a future Pats owner would find out for himself decades later when he tried to move them to the city, you've got a better chance of building a space station than a football stadium in Boston. Instead, the project turned to Norwood, a suburb south of the city that sits at the intersection of Route 128 and Route 1 and is only semi-famous for a six-lane sprawl of car dealerships, motor lodges, and speedburger places called "The Automile." But to Sullivan and the brewery, Norwood offered cheap land and highway access that they could sell to potential tenants—not the least of whom would be the Red Sox.

Billy worked quietly behind the scenes to bring the Red Sox on board with this little Xanadu they were planning. And the Sox were interested. A commonly held misconception in the greater sports world is that Fenway Park is a baseball shrine, what John Updike called a "lyric little bandbox." A precious jewel of historic American architecture. Or, in the copyrighted slogan of the current Sox owners, "America's Most Beloved Ballpark." But the fact of the matter is that Fenway is, by and large, obsolete, in spite of all the mythologizing and waxing poetic about it. It has terrible sight lines. Thousands of seats don't even face the infield, so it's hard to watch the pitcher and batter without needing corrective spinal surgery. There are still hundreds of seats stuck behind posts. My guess is the seats were cramped even by the standards of 1912, when the place was built. So in today's world of cheese-stuffed-crust pizza and high-carb craft beers, they can be a form of torture.

To give credit where it's due, the Sox have made significant upgrades to the park in the 2000s, but the place remains an antiquated tourist trap. So in 1958, one can only imagine it was more run down and a lot hell-hole-ier, because owner Tom Yawkey and GM Joe Cronin (Baseball Hall of Famers, both) wanted out.

Cronin listened to Sullivan's pitch about a 55,000-seat state-of-the-art dome in the suburbs and was intrigued, but only under the condition that the whole operation remain a secret until they had a deal in place. Sox management didn't want to commit to leaving Fenway only to have the project fall through, then have to face the political fallout when they came crawling back.

Sports, politics, revenge.

The old PR director knew the score, and Sullivan promised Cronin he'd keep a lid on everything.

For some reason, there's nothing that rich, visionary businessmen love more than little architectural models of the mega-projects they're about to build. And the people behind this dome project were no exception. The problem for Sullivan was that he needed one built without word getting around. He couldn't just ask anyone to do it. So he hired an artsy-craftsy neighbor to do it.

Sullivan had the architectural plans all set. He had his model. He had his investors. He had the Red Sox as tenants ready to play 77 games a year in the dome, and the possibility of luring an NFL franchise there as well. All he needed to keep the deal alive was to keep it from leaking out in the press or else the whole house of cards would end up on the floor.

So naturally, the brewery decided to throw a cocktail party to announce the plan, show off the model, and congratulate themselves for their vision and ingenuity.

And they invited the press.

The next morning it was all over the radio and in all five of Boston's major daily newspapers. The date was April 1.

Some of the papers treated it like an April Fool's Day gag. But they ran pictures of the model, and the Red Sox' name was attached to the project. Sullivan was horrified. He scrambled as best he could to spin the whole thing as just an idea in the early planning stages, with no deal in the works. But it was no use. There was no unringing that bell. The Red Sox were just breaking spring training camp down in Sarasota, Florida, and Sullivan frantically worked the phones trying to talk to someone in Sox management, so he could damage-control this deal and keep it from collapsing. He finally got hold of team Treasurer Joe Comisky and apologized for the leak. He assured Comisky he'd done everything he could to keep a lid on the story.

"Well then, you have been spectacularly unsuccessful," Comisky replied.

In the manner of the Cowboys' trademarked "America's Team" and the Raiders own "Commitment to Excellence," Billy could have made "Spectacularly Unsuccessful" his franchise's copyrighted slogan right then and there.

The Red Sox were officially done with their involvement and the whole scheme was starting to look increasingly hare-brained, but it wasn't dead yet. The investors still felt that the stadium out in the suburbs could be a money-maker by attracting other events: college football games, conventions, circuses, and the like. And Sullivan was still working the NFL angle. He had a huge backer in Commissioner Bell, who was giddy over the concept of weather-free football played indoors—especially in the biggest television market in the country that still didn't have an NFL team. The league owners had a meeting scheduled the following January, and he promised Billy he'd go to bat for him.

Sullivan had another potential supporter in New York Giants owner Tim Mara, one of the most influential figures in pro football history. In that era, without a team of their own, most New England football fans pulled for the Giants. If Mara was willing to hand all those customers over to a Boston-based team, who were the other NFL owners to argue? Having Mara in his corner would all but lock up a team for Sullivan.

On February 18, 1959, Billy flew down to New York to meet with Tim Mara to seal the deal. His plane was delayed taking off, so when he landed in LaGuardia, he went to a pay phone and called the Giants office to say he was running late. The secretary who answered the phone was in tears. Mara had died during the night.

Sullivan didn't give up hope. Bert Bell still loved the notion of a team playing under the roof in Norwood. And he was still committed to pitching the idea at the league meeting, once the season was over. That is, until October of that year, when Bell also dropped dead.

Sullivan might have retired the All-Time Understatement Trophy when he later said, "I began to feel that I wasn't meant to have an NFL franchise."[1]

Bell's death was the final straw. Tim Mara's son Jack told Billy that, with the commissioner gone, every owner in the league considered himself to be the one running the show. And without Bell's leadership, there's no way they'd agree on anything, much less putting a team in a town without a stadium or an oil-rich owner. To put it in movie terms, Bell dying was like Vito Corleone's death in "The Godfather," with the rest of the Five Families struggling for control. Maybe once the mob war was over and all the family business was settled they'd address Sullivan's proposal, but not now.

Enter the AFL.

Billy had heard about how Hunt, Howsam, Adams, and their group were forming a rival league and he thought that might work as a Plan B. Jack Mara told him, as a friend, that he had to be out of his cotton-picking mind. First of all, he said, the planned AFL team in New York—the most important franchise, for obvious reasons—was doomed to fail. He told Sullivan that Harry Wismer, the sportscaster and prospective owner of the New York team, was a con artist with a long history of stiffing his creditors and bouncing checks. Mara promised Billy that with crooks like Wismer involved, the AFL would fold before they ever played a game. Hampden-Harvard agreed. The buy-in for a seat at the AFL's poker table was $25,000. After checking with people who'd done business with Wismer, the brewery owners told Sullivan, "If there's a worse investment than a franchise in the American Football League, we don't know what it is." And with that, they backed out.

But it wasn't like Billy Sullivan to let a little thing like having no investors stop him. He may have had no money, no backers, no stadium, no franchise, and no support from anyone, but like so many great men of vision, he also had no common sense. So he pressed on, undeterred.

His connection to the AFL wannabe owners was Leahy, who had been hired by Hilton to get his Los Angeles Chargers off the ground. With the franchises in LA, New York, Dallas, Houston, Denver, and Minneapolis-St. Paul, the Buffalo team recently awarded to Ralph Wilson made seven, and that meant that they needed an eighth team to round things out.

Sullivan's main competition for the eighth franchise appeared to come from Bob Carpenter of Philadelphia. Carpenter owned the Phillies, which not only meant he had a stadium all ready to go, but also experience running a sports team, all the staff and resources he'd need, plus a bottomless pit of cash at his disposal. The only downside of a bid from Carpenter was that Philly already had the Eagles, whereas in Boston Sullivan would have no NFL team to compete with.

Billy had two other things working in his favor. One, he was one of the all-time great schmooze artists. And two, he had Leahy on his side. At a meeting to pick the eighth team, Leahy put on a full-court charm offensive on Boston's behalf, trying to convince a group of bright, wealthy, successful businessmen to choose a guy with no money and no place to play over . . . well, a bright, wealthy, successful businessman. Before they put it to a vote, though, Carpenter rescinded his bid, and the league awarded the final team to Boston. Hunt called Sullivan and told him he was in, provided he had the 25 large deposited in the league's bank account by the close of business the next day.

To that point, the only liquid cash Sullivan had was eight grand he and his wife had been saving to buy a vacation house on Cape Cod. The rest of the money came from a group of investors he scrambled to put together. Among them were some Boston construction magnates, one of the former owners of the Braves, Billy's uncle Joe Sullivan (who ran a printing company in Lowell), and ex-Red Sox centerfielder Dom DiMaggio.[2]

The $25,000 was deposited, and on November 16, 1959, Sullivan became the proud owner of a football team.

He wanted to get the word out as soon as possible, but didn't have an office, much less a PR staff or the paper and printing presses he'd need to issue a press release. So he got his hands on some old football programs, wrote an announcement himself, and handed it all off to Uncle Joe to print off. He then got in touch with an old contact at one of the Boston papers to tip him off to the pending good news, so they could run an exclusive in the late edition.

You can imagine what great news this was for a football-starved city. Boston had been home to two previous, short-lived NFL franchises. The Redskins actually played their first five seasons in Boston before moving to Washington in 1937, and the Boston Yanks were formed during World War II, only to become the New York Bulldogs in 1949. And after all those years without pro football, Boston was about to be in on the ground floor of a league that would revolutionize the game. So naturally, the press and the public were delirious at the news.

Just kidding. The headline of the "exclusive" the next day said:

NO PLACE TO PLAY
But Boston Gets Franchise
In Shaky New League

Billy Sullivan, the sportswriter's kid from Lowell, had investors, $25,000 in debt, and a piece of paper that said he owned the Boston franchise in an American Football League that didn't exist yet. What he didn't have was a staff, an office, a place to play, equipment, coaches, a team name or, for that matter, a team. The first priority was stocking every team's rosters with players. And to that end, the first meeting of all eight AFL owners was held in Minneapolis.

In attendance were the press, family members, business partners, and corporate sponsors, probably about 200 people in all. Their first order of business was to hammer out the league bylaws and vote on a commissioner. The commissioner's job went to Joe Foss, a former brigadier general who'd fought at Guadalcanal before becoming governor of South Dakota.

One of the most significant things they voted to do involved their television broadcast deal. The AFL had negotiated a five-year deal with ABC to broadcast 37 games a year that paid the league $2,125,000 annually. And the owners adopted the revolutionary idea that they split all the TV money equally. That would level the playing field and make it easier for small-market teams to compete financially with the ones in the big cities. Years later, the NFL would adopt the same plan, and it's credited with making it the world power that it has become. But at that time, the arrangement was groundbreaking.

The problems for Billy Sullivan started right off the bat when the Minnesota ownership group, led by Max Winter, questioned Boston's right to a franchise.

Their argument went that the league couldn't offer new franchises without the unanimous approval of the other owners. Sullivan went into five-alarm panic mode and pulled Hunt aside, begging him to do something. Hunt gave him the 1960 businessman's equivalent of "I got this," arguing to the Minnesota group that unanimous approval only applied to any expansion franchises beyond the "original" eight. And to prove it, he asked Barron Hilton to call his lawyer, who was upstairs drafting the bylaws, to confirm it. Hilton got on the phone with his lawyer's room, mumbled into the phone for a while, and a few minutes later the attorney came down and announced to everyone that . . . well whaddaya know! . . . the language was in there and the Boston franchise was in. Sullivan didn't grow up in Massachusetts without learning a thing or two about sketchy business deals and bald-faced lies. "If that provision wasn't in the bylaws before Hilton's call, it certainly was afterwards," he said later.

But the Minnesota group was far from done with monkey-wrenching the works. With the whole crowd of reporters and high rollers assembled, New York owner Wismer came crashing in, one of those moments that only happen in old movies where everyone wears fedoras and talks fast. He was waving around the latest edition of the local newspaper, which was reporting the NFL had decided to put an expansion franchise in Minneapolis-St. Paul, and screaming, "This is it! It's the Last Supper for the AFL in Minneapolis!!!" The NFL had reportedly awarded the Minnesota franchise to Max Winter's group. The older league was trying to kill the upstart league in the nest by buying people off.

All hell broke loose. Middle-aged men in suits and ties were screaming at each other. Wismer tried to strangle Winter and had to be physically restrained by Frank Leahy. We live in a time where we can't even put a Lehman Brothers' executive in jail for bankrupting the country, but these guys were doing business the old school way: grown men lying, backstabbing, and trying to kill each other. The way it was meant to be done.

Winter and his people denied that there was any truth to the report, but Sullivan, a bullshitter's bullshitter, smelled a rat. And he was right; it wasn't much longer before the Minnesota group did, in fact, pull out and join the NFL. And in short order, the AFL agreed to award their eighth franchise to a pair of California businessmen by the unlikely names of F. Wayne Valley and Chet Soda, who stepped in and agreed to put a franchise in Oakland, so that the AFL still had teams in eight cities. (The original idea was to call their team "The Oakland Senores," before cooler heads prevailed and they agreed to go with the Raiders.)

For his part, Sullivan always assumed that the subterfuge with Minnesota was orchestrated by George Halas, the legend who owned the Bears. Even after the AFL and NFL merged and he and Halas became colleagues and friends, Sullivan believed Halas was behind it all, because he knew the Boston market was too important to give to an upstart league. And when it comes to conniving, underhanded, back-room shenanigans, Boston has nothing on Chicago.

2 A MOUNTAIN OF MATCHSTICKS

★★★★★★★★★★★★★★★★★★★★★★★

I got a good deal on those boys. The scouts said they showed a lot of promise.
MCGRATH, *Slap Shot*

For as long as I can remember, I've always had a bizarre fascination with sports history. Don't get me wrong; growing up, I had other interests, too. Normal stuff, toys and playing outside and video games and music my parents hated and numbing my brain with crappy television, things every kid likes. In time, I'd have that "Eureka!" moment—like when Phoebe Cates comes out of the pool in slow motion in *Fast Times at Ridgemont High*—and discover girls. But for whatever reason, I always remember being more interested and more versed in old sports trivia than all the other kids. It was an interest bordering on fixation. It felt like a birthday or Christmas never went by without someone gifting me some coffee table book like *On and Off the Court* by Red Auerbach or *Bobby Orr and the Big, Bad Bruins*. Or it would be some enormous cinder block like the latest edition of *The Baseball Encyclopedia*, which I'd get lost in for hours.

The early history of the Patriots was always a little murkier. It took more work to find out about those days. There was less written about it. I almost never saw film from those early years. Just a few posed black-and-white photos of players who didn't look nearly as athletic as the superhumans I was watching on TV every Sunday in the 70s. To me, those early Patriots always looked kind of . . . I hesitate to say it . . . dumpy. Barrel-chested and small and slow-footed. I'm sure they were great athletes in their time and were tough as a steak from the Waffle House. But most of them looked more like my gym teachers than professional athletes.

Though, to be fair, the Patriots were a start-up team in a league that had just come into existence and had to fill a roster in short order amid a system that was chaotic, to put it mildly.

In its inaugural season, the AFL didn't hold a draft in the way we commonly picture one. Instead, players' names were literally drawn out of the hotel meeting room's wastebasket. The league had put together a scouting committee that graded all the top amateur players in the country. Their names were then grouped by position, thrown in the basket, and the owners pulled names out, one position at a time. So the new professional league that was formed to challenge the mighty NFL for the heart, mind, and wallet of the American sports fan began with a player selection system that was 1/100th as sophisticated as your last fantasy football draft, and a hundred times more random.

THE AFL DRAFT

The AFL draft came after the NFL's draft. So each club had to factor in their ability to sign anyone they selected. Whether it made sense to try to outbid the NFL for a player's services or to play it safe and only go after guys who were undrafted (and presumably less talented) was all part of the mental calculus when building a roster.

The AFL drafts were done in a messy, unwieldy manner. The league owners had decided going into the first draft that each franchise be allowed one "territorial pick," a player from their region that each team could call dibs on, ostensibly for the publicity and to boost local interest. After the territorial picks were sorted out, players were drafted by position. After an order of selection was determined, teams had a quarterback draft, followed by a running back draft, and so on. In this high school booster club's 50/50 raffle drawing that the AFL called a draft, there were 33 rounds in all, for a total of 264 players between the eight teams.

One immediate problem they ran into was that Minnesota jumped ship *after* the draft, meaning one-eighth of the players had been selected by a team that was no longer in the league. Rather than just give the rights for all the Minnesota draftees to Oakland, the owners decided to treat the Raiders like you do your buddy who shows up late for your fantasy football draft because his wife had him doing chores. Which is to tell him, "Tough shit." The other owners swooped down like seagulls on a trash pile and signed up all they could of the Minnesota draftees. They then offered Oakland a so-called "allocation draft," which was AFL shorthand for "build a team out of everyone else's scraps, unwanteds, and undrafted nobodies and good fricking luck to you." Each of the other seven teams were allowed to "protect" 11 of their own players, and Oakland had to build a roster out of their choice of the best 24 of the unprotected ones.

Every lifelong Patriots fan grows up hearing the story of how the team selected Ron Burton, a halfback out of Northwestern, as their first-ever draft pick. The choice of Burton paid off, as he would go on to a great career and represent the team well as a pillar of the community. But that's not the whole story. As a matter of fact, it's more like one of those half-truths they tell to make history simpler and more interesting, like Columbus being the only one who believed the world was round (it was common knowledge from the time of Pythagoras), or Paul Revere being the only one who warned the Colonial Militia that the British were coming (William Dawes and Israel Bissel rode much farther but were cursed with names that didn't rhyme with "hear").

Make no mistake, Burton was a solid player and a great humanitarian. He had a five-year AFL career and averaged a not-to-be-sneezed-at 3.6 yards per carry. Having grown up poor in Springfield, Ohio, Burton raised money for children of poverty, ran free football camps for underprivileged youth, and became a leader in the Boy Scouts of America, for which he was awarded national honors. The half-truth is the part about him being the Patriots first-ever draft pick; he was designated so after the fact.

Sullivan designated Burton as the club's "official" first pick in part for the good PR. Burton had also been selected ninth overall in the NFL draft by the Philadelphia Eagles, and it certainly didn't hurt the team's credibility to build their team around a player who was that highly regarded. But if you want to get technical, Boston's real first draft choice was Gerhard Schwedes, a halfback out of Syracuse.

And Schwedes seemed as good a choice as any. The book on him coming out of college was that he was one of those versatile guys who would line up all over the field for the Orangemen, someone a pro team could build around because he could do so many things.

Unfortunately, while he may have been able to do them all, he couldn't do any of them especially well. And to make matters worse, Schwedes had also been selected in the NFL Draft by the Baltimore Colts in the fourth round, so in order to lure him away from the Colts, Sullivan offered him a guaranteed no-cut two-year deal. But before the end of Schwedes' first training camp, his coaches had already surmised that he couldn't help them. By the time the deal ran out, Gerhard Schwedes, a player signed to be the cornerstone of the Patriots franchise, was working off his contract in the team's ticket office. By way of contrast, Dallas' territorial pick was SMU quarterback Don Meredith, who went on to greatness with the NFL's Cowboys. Houston claimed the rights to Billy Cannon, the national Player of the Year with LSU, who set a slew of the AFL's early records, both at running back and tight end. Boston's choice was answering phones and counting ticket stubs.

It was Billy Sullivan's first major, costly blunder. It wouldn't be his last.

Sullivan and his brain trust understood the situation they were in. All the

AFL teams were competing against a rival league that was established, successful, and had far more resources than they did. They didn't have the operating capital to win too many bidding wars for the football talent that was out there against the deep pockets of the NFL owners. And Sullivan's team was the poorest in the AFL. So the task facing them was to fan out across the country and find as many able-bodied unemployed football players as they could.

But first, they needed a coach.

LOU SABAN

In the evolution of NFL football, the players have changed, the equipment has changed, the rules have changed, and strategies have changed. Even the ball and the field have been tweaked. The one true constant in the history of the game has been the coaches. The NFL is a coach-dominated enterprise like no other professional league. Coaches have always been the NFL's headliners. From the first day tickets went on sale 90 years ago to the last time a big name was hired to boost luxury suite sales, coaches have been the ones who put asses in the seats. You can argue that people want to see quarterbacks too, and you'd be right. But if an expansion football team were a concert, the coach would be the headliner and the QB's name would be at the bottom of the ticket stub, after "Also with . . ." and just above "No Refunds."

The great NFL dynasties have all had great coaches—without exception, and right from the beginning. Believe it or not, that same George Halas who was the turd in the AFL's punchbowl at that Minnesota meeting in 1960 was already coaching the Bears in 1922. Curly Lambeau was running the Green Bay Packers. It's hard to imagine the league without them. It's as if they weren't so much contacted, interviewed, and hired like mortal men, but instead they sprang up out of the earth like gods in a Greek myth. And all the great coaches of all the future dynasties descended in one way or another from them.

The search for the Next Great Coach has made and broken NFL owners since the league crawled out of the primordial ooze. It has been the difference between having a taxpayer-funded stadium built for you and being humiliated in front of your gold-digging trophy wife by some jackasses wearing t-shirts that demand you sell the team.

And finding that guy was Billy Sullivan's next crucial order of business.

Sullivan was an oil company executive who used to issue press releases for a failed baseball team. He was now charged with putting together the management team of a professional football operation, going through the mental contact lists of all the people he knew or had ever met and then thinking about whom he'd call for a job interview.

One of the people Billy had a personal history with was the Boston College Eagles' head coach, Mike Holovak. Holovak had been on Leahy's undefeated 1940 team, as a two-way, 60-minute fullback/linebacker. He had also served on PT boats in World War II, then come back and played three years in the NFL before returning to BC to coach freshman ball. And when Leahy left BC for Notre Dame, Holovak was given the head job and held it throughout the 50s.

By 1959, Holovak (like the vast majority of guys in his profession) was under fire from the school's alumni. BC was about to play their last game of the year against Holy Cross, their archrival at the time. Holovak was feeling the heat and knew it was probably his last game. So he was happy to be handed a note in his office from Billy Sullivan explaining that he was looking to hire people to run his new team and that, if the worst should happen to Holovak at BC, a job would be available for him.

What Holovak didn't know was that one of the angry, dissatisfied alumni who were demanding he be canned was that same Billy Sullivan.

To the surprise of no one—especially Sullivan himself—Holovak was pink-slipped and became the Boston AFL franchise's first employee. The first question Billy faced was what job to give him. Holovak was a humble, soft-spoken, intelligent man. There are those who have always believed that the job of football coach is best done by obsessive, maniacal nutjobs, and Sullivan must have felt the same way, because he didn't give Holovak the head job. In addition, he needed to make a profit and probably didn't think a marketing campaign built around "Holovak: A Failure at a Local College but Ready to Kick Ass in the Pros" would be great for ticket sales. So he made him head of scouting.

Another ex-BC guy that Sullivan was familiar with was Ed McKeever, a Texas Tech grad and one of Leahy's assistants at Chestnut Hill. McKeever's sole claim to fame was a 12–2 record as interim coach at Notre Dame while Leahy was on active duty in the war. He was also loud, preternaturally confident, and probably a little obnoxious. A ten-gallon hat and a couple of six shooters away from being the perfect Texas stereotype. But that only made him the ideal counterpoint to the quiet, cerebral Holovak. Sullivan hired him to be his first general manager.

The third club employee was another buddy of Sullivan's, a guy named Jack Grinold, whose first assignment was to come up with a name for the Boston football club. And the old public relations director in Sullivan wasn't about to miss the chance to get some free marketing out of the deal. So Grinold set up a fan contest to come up with a name.

Some suggested "Boston Pilgrims," but there wasn't a lot of support for naming a football team after a bunch of judgmental, uber-religious buttinskis who saw to it that for 400 years Massachusetts liquor stores couldn't open on Sundays. So the three finalists were "Minutemen," "Bulls," and "Patriots." To further bang the PR drum on this one, the club got the superintendent of Boston schools, Bill Ohrenberger, to organize an essay contest in which school kids explained what they thought the name should be and why. We can only speculate about how many of those essays suggested "Dicks" and "Poopheads," though as a former schoolboy myself, my educated guess would be "lots." In the end, "Patriots" it was.

Meanwhile, the search for a head coach continued. One of the first people Sullivan considered was Schwedes' coach at Syracuse, Ben Schwartzwalder. And he must have been determined to restrict the search to members of the Funny Name Society, because the other candidates were Georgia's Wally Butts and Penn State's Rip Engle. (A bit of trivia: At the time, Engle was grooming his successor, a young assistant coach/future icon/eventually disgraced pedophile-enabler by the name of Joe Paterno.)

Another decidedly less silly name was that of Otto Graham, the former Cleveland Browns QB who to this day is considered one of the ten best ever to play the position. But Graham considered his job coaching at the Coast Guard Academy to be a much better prospect than one in an upstart league that was likely to fold in its first year, so he turned it down.

One name that kept coming up in the search was Lou Saban. He'd coached at Northwestern and was coming off an undefeated season at Western Illinois. More importantly, he'd played under Paul Brown in Cleveland. Brown was the innovative coaching giant who is credited with inventing, among other things, the coaching playbook. (What teams wrote their plays down on before that, whether it was papyrus scrolls or scratched in the dirt with a stick or scrimshawed into whale's teeth, will forever remain a mystery.) But Brown came up with the idea of mimeographing them and putting them in whatever passed for a Trapper Keeper in those days. Even more importantly than that, Saban seemed to have the temperament they were looking for.

In other words, he was a driven, intense lunatic.

He was also highly intelligent. In the war, he worked for the OSS, which was the precursor to the CIA. He was stationed in China and trained to be fluent in the language, which makes him probably the only coach in the history of football to speak more Mandarin Chinese than you'll find on a Szechuan takeout menu.

Recommendations for Saban came from several sources. The GM of the Buffalo team said that if there hadn't been a coach in place before he was hired, Saban would've been his guy. Eventually, someone on the Patriots staff with a connection to Paul Brown called Brown and asked his opinion, and Brown leveled with him. "I think Lou is ready to be a head coach in professional football." That was good enough for Billy, and on February 8, Lou Saban was named the first head coach in Patriots history.

Today, NFL teams have entire staffs in their scouting departments that make a decent living doing nothing but keeping tabs on unsigned players, those guys that TV pundits like to call "street free agents" in order to sound cool. Teams hold workouts 52 weeks out of the year in order to be ready for any contingency, from all three quarterbacks on the roster getting hurt at once to the whole offensive line getting food poisoning to their punter getting deported back to whatever former Communist hellhole he comes from. And all that info is kept ready so that an emergency backup can be brought in in a matter of hours if the worst should happen. The Patriots had nothing of the sort. Their scouting method didn't so much resemble the 21st-century NFL as it did casting calls for *American Idol*. Saban described it in a 1994 interview with the *Boston Globe*: "We had tryouts in the city of Boston from one end to the other. We had carpenters, we had bricklayers, we had stoker men. You name it, we had it. We had 125 helmets in one tryout camp and we put a head in every helmet. I remember our first real camp we had at the University of Massachusetts out there in Amherst. I couldn't tell you how many players we had out there. We must have had 350."[3]

But the search wasn't limited to just Boston. The team's staff, such as it was, fanned out to as many cities as they could, inviting players to come to UMass Amherst and try out. Saban took a trip to Minneapolis-St. Paul to visit with some of his old Northwestern players and assorted other ex-Big Ten guys who lived in the area and recruit them. Looking back, it was actually a stroke of genius, proof that maybe Saban was playing chess when everyone else was playing checkers. The Minnesota team that went to the NFL instead of the AFL would've scooped up a lot of out-of-work players from the region; why not invite them to try out for Boston instead? It was the equivalent of casting your line where no one else is fishing. Or trying to pick up women at the fabric store. Hunting in a place where you're the only predator increases your chances. Fortunately for the franchise he worked for, Saban's trip was not a waste of time. As a matter of fact, he struck gold. Because even though he didn't find anyone else, Saban met a player who had been out of organized football for five full years and was now tending bar. But in one of those bazillion-to-one shots that almost make you believe in the power of fate, that bartender not only made the club but went on to be synonymous with the Patriots franchise for the next 50 years.

GINO CAPPELLETTI

There are pro athletes who you'll always associate with one particular team, and vice versa. Ernie Banks and the Cubs. Bobby Orr and the Bruins. John Elway and the Broncos. But there are very few guys who spend their entire careers with that team, and there are even fewer who were with the organization from their inception right up until the present day. But one player who does fit that description is Gino Raymond Michael "Duke" Cappelletti. He was an all-purpose, multi-dimensional player in their first season, and he broadcast their games until his retirement in 2012. From their first training camp in 1960 to him reading excruciatingly awkward in-game ads for condoms (which was like having your dad interrupt the game to have "the talk" with you) in the 2000s, you can make a case that until recently, the Patriots had never played a down in their history that he hadn't witnessed.

Cappelletti played at the U of Minnesota. His natural position was halfback, but they had an All-American there named Paul Giel, so in order to get playing time he moved to quarterback. And while that may sound like a step up, it wasn't. The Golden Gophers played a single-wing offense, in which the QB pretty much handed off and blocked, and only occasionally ran it himself. But as he'd show later on, Cappelletti was hungry to play football and was willing to do anything and play anywhere to stay on the field, including placekicker. After graduation, he only had one shot at the pros, and that was an invitation to try out with Detroit. Unfortunately for him, the Lions were stacked at quarterback with Hall of Famer Bobby Layne, future league MVP Earl Morrall, and Harry Gilmer. Cappelletti got little chance to prove what he could do and was shown the door so fast he never even got to ask if he could try out as a kicker.

After a stint in the army where he played some, Gino went to Canada, where he got the proverbial cup of coffee before getting cut a couple of months into his rookie year. A lesser man might have given up. But as in any instructive, inspirational tale or 80s arena rock song, Cappelletti didn't stop believing. Talk of a new football league forming and putting a team in Minnesota gave Gino some hope his chance at a pro career wasn't dead yet. But when that deal fell through, he found himself tending bar and his playing limited to the tavern's touch football team. Then he heard from some ex-teammates that Saban had been in town looking for players to come try out for Boston, and he wanted in. Cappelletti and Saban had never met, so he asked mutual acquaintances to call on his behalf and put in a good word for him.

If you've ever been a man in your early twenties and asked your best friends to do something that could change your life forever and make all your hopes and dreams come true, then you know what Gino's friends did for him: promised they'd help, then forgot all about it and did nothing.

So Cappelletti placed the call himself. And two weeks later, Saban called back to say he had all the faith and confidence in the world in him. That he'd seen something in Gino that convinced him this was a young man who could achieve anything in this world he set his mind to.

Or he would have, if real life was a Disney movie.

In reality, what he said was, "Well, I guess you've got as good a chance to make this team as anyone." The contract negotiations were also a ringing endorsement: "I'm sending you the minimum contract: $7,500. See you July fourth." Click.

But still, Gino Cappelletti had his shot at playing professional football. And while no one knew it at the time, the Patriots' first great player was on his way to his first training camp. He knew he didn't have the arm to make it as a quarterback. If he was going to make it, it would have to be elsewhere, so he told the coaches he was a defensive back. He'd played a little there in college and liked to hit. He knew throwing his body around and drilling people was the fastest way to get the coaches' attention. He figured that if he could last until they started looking for kickers, he could try out there as well. He figured correctly, and started the season as a defensive back as well as the team's placekicker.

The problem for Cappelletti was that he wasn't fast, which became evident once the season started. He showed good instincts and ball skills and made some interceptions, but he also got burned repeatedly on long passes by wideouts he couldn't catch. And if there's one shortcoming no coach can overlook, it's lack of speed. In prehistoric times, the first football coach to sprout legs and crawl out of the primordial sea no sooner stepped onto dry land before he raised his head and said, "You can't teach speed." And every coach that has ever existed since has said the same thing, Saban included.

As the season wore on, Cappelletti became increasingly worried about his job. Then at practice one day with about three weeks to go in the season, the offense was running a passing drill. Without saying anything, Gino jumped into the formation and ran the next play. As fate would have it, it was a pass play intended for him. Cappelletti made a nice break on the ball and a tough catch. Holovak pulled him aside to ask where he learned that. Cappelletti explained how as a single-wing quarterback he sometimes caught passes. The way the team operated was so fly-by-night that Holovak immediately made him a wide receiver, and that's where he stayed for his career.

As for the man who threw him that fated pass . . .

Walpole is a fairly nondescript suburban Massachusetts town. For a long time, it was mostly known for having a Massachusetts Correctional Institution in it, until residents got tired of seeing their property values plummet from being associated with a maximum security prison and got the state to change its name from MCI Walpole to the much friendlier, more vague, more Thomas the Tank Engine-y "MCI Cedar Junction." Beyond that, Walpole is semi-famous for being the town you drive through to get to a Patriots game, its powerhouse high school football program, and being the birthplace of arguably the most unlikely first starting quarterback any pro team has ever had.

As schoolboy athletes go, Butch Songin was a legend. Just one of those naturally gifted kids who seemed to be able to do anything, he was a standout in three sports. He was recruited by Major League teams, but turned down signing bonuses in order to go to Boston College. While at BC he started at quarterback for the Eagles and was considered by some to be the best American-born hockey player ever, but for a pro career, he chose quarterbacking. Tryouts with Philly and Cleveland didn't pan out for him, and eventually he found himself playing in Canada.

Songin's Canadian career was a success. You could say he was almost too successful, since he outperformed his contract, and when he asked for a raise was basically told that if he didn't like it, he could lump it. So he quit football and moved back to Massachusetts. That was 1954; by the time the Patriots were searching for players, Butch Songin had been out of football for six years. He was working as a parole officer with side gigs coaching high school ball part-time and playing on a semi-pro team for 50 bucks a game. He was also 36 years old.

The only reason he ended up in Lou Saban's camp was at the suggestion of a sportswriter who thought Songin would be worth having "for old time's sake." You couldn't have blamed Saban if he couldn't have been bothered to deal with the hassle of having a local legend in his camp. A couple of years earlier, Red Auerbach had chapped the ass of every basketball fan in New England when he said he didn't want the distraction of "some local yokel" on the Celtics. And that yokel just happened to be Bob Cousy. But Saban had looked at a dozen or more quarterbacks by that point and hadn't liked what he saw, so out of either common courtesy or (more likely) desperation, he was willing to look at Songin too.

Details on Songin's practices with the team are scarce. He could have very well been the football equivalent of Roy Hobbs in *The Natural*, when he takes his first batting practice with the Knights, with Saban as Pop Fisher, telling Songin, "People don't start playin' ball at your age. They retire." But then Butch starts slinging balls all over the field while the guys half his age stop what they're doing to watch in amazement. And after practice he tells his coach, "It took me sixteen years to get here. You play me, and I'll give ya the best I got." On the other hand, it could also have been that every other QB in camp just plain sucked. Saban's best QB prospect up to that point was Tommy Greene, whom they'd gotten from the Chargers in exchange for the rights to tackle Ron Mix, a future Hall of Famer. Regardless, not only did Songin make the club, Saban announced he'd won the starting job.

The Patriots were heading into their inaugural season in a brand new league —one that could make or break their future as a viable business venture—led by a quarterback who was only two years younger than the head coach.

In addition to Ron Burton, Cappelletti, and Songin, the club managed to find some other decent talent. Jim Colclough, another BC grad, was a wideout they'd signed out of the Canadian League. They drafted fullback Larry Garron, one of Saban's Western Illinois players, who was tough enough to hold rank in six different martial arts disciplines. They swiped linebacker Tommy Addison off the Philadelphia Eagles practice squad and he, along with safety Ross O'Hanley, made first team All-AFL. Standout defensive end Bob Dee and guard Charles Leo made second team.

During the season, Ed McKeever got tipped off by a friend in the NFL that the Cardinals had cut Jim Lee "Earthquake" Hunt, a massive rookie defensive tackle who was injured but had potential to help the Pats down the road. McKeever called Hunt at his home in St. Louis on a Friday morning and offered him a contract. Hunt landed in Boston at 7:40 p.m., got a crash course from the coaches, and was in uniform for that night's game. He'd play ten years for the Pats and set the AFL record for fumble recoveries. So while the Patriots roster wasn't stocked with talent, there were some diamonds in there.

The coaching staff was in place. The roster was taking shape. The season was about to start. The AFL was divided into two divisions, with the Houston Oilers, New York Titans, Buffalo Bills, and the Patriots in the Eastern Division, and the Dallas Texans, Denver Broncos, Oakland Raiders, and Los Angeles Chargers in the Western Division. The schedule and playoff format were remarkably simple: they would play a 14-game regular season, with every club playing each of the seven others twice, home and away. Then the first-place team in each division at the end of the year would meet in a championship game.

Now the only tiny detail to work out was where the Patriots were going to play, since they didn't have a stadium of their own. It was an issue that would haunt their dreams for the next 12 years. And given the way that search for a home played out, the condition of the place when they finally got one, and the financial ruin that resulted from owning it, it's a miracle the Billy Sullivan I met all those years later was sitting in a golf cart at a country club and not in a wheelchair in some mental institution.

3

THE BEGINNING OF THE END . . .
AT THE BEGINNING

★ ★

If you start out depressed, everything's kind of a pleasant surprise.
LLOYD DOBLER, *Say Anything*

In the life of every boy, as he treads the weary path to manhood, there are certain milestone moments. Learning to ride a bike. Seeing your first R-rated movie. Getting your driver's license. Your first time getting drunk, followed by your first hangover. The first time you kiss a girl. Getting to second base. Getting to third base (etc., etc.). Graduation Day. And so on. And no rite of passage is more universally all-American than a boy going to his first-ever professional sporting event.

I'm embarrassed to say I never set foot in a professional sports stadium until I was 13 years old. This is especially weird because I was one of those kids who watched every game of every Boston team, then re-watched the highlights on the local news, then devoured the recap in the sports page the next day.

And mostly, I begged to go to a game.

But my parents just weren't into taking me to these things. I'm the youngest of five, so by the time I came along my dad had pretty much adopted a philosophy of "Been there/done that already with your older brothers." My mom, bless her, was terrified of the idea of me getting lost in the crowd, which was especially odd given that my older brothers used to take the subway to Red Sox games from our house in Dorchester when Jack was eight and Bill was seven. I guess that even though we were in the same family, we somehow managed to be products of a different time.

But finally, when I hit 13, Jack and Bill took pity on me. (Or more likely, had an extra ticket and couldn't get anyone else to go. But I won't quibble.) I'm sure I was still the annoying little brother to them, but at that age I'd grown tolerable enough that they agreed to take me to a game. They and our cousin Phil and their buddies Mike and Tom had gotten Patriots season tickets, and one was available for a late-season game against the New Orleans Saints. Finally, after all the years of waiting and hoping, I was finally going to an actual, for-real, live, in-person professional sporting event.

And this wasn't just any event. This was the National Football League. The En Eff frigging L. The biggest of the big time. Back then it wasn't common practice to medicate kids (the preferred method for treating hyperactivity at the time was a loud "Shut up!" administered with a smack in the head), but that week they could've shot me full of elephant tranquilizers and it wouldn't have calmed me down.

The Patriots were playing in Schaefer Stadium, their still spanking-new venue in Foxboro. This was 1976, and Schaefer had opened in 1971, so all I could picture was a sparkling, state-of-the-art palace, still with that new stadium smell. I was prepared to be dazzled.

I'd always heard from friends who'd been to Red Sox games what a cool feeling it was when you first walk into Fenway and see the place in person. And I will never, ever forget that feeling of coming out from under the stands at Schaefer, walking up the ramp, and looking out at the stadium for the first time. I'm pretty sure my exact words were:

"This . . . is . . . kind of a *dump*, isn't it?"

It most certainly was. To mangle a phrase from Ned Beatty when he first walks into Notre Dame Stadium in *Rudy*, Schaefer Stadium was the least beautiful sight these eyes had ever seen. It was a dreary, low-rent, slapped-together collection of concrete slabs. I certainly hadn't been around much, but I'd seen enough to know that this was what buildings looked like in Eastern Bloc countries. It was "Foxborostan."

Schaefer looked nothing like the megabowls and ultradomes I saw on TV every week. It was four separate sections of bleachers that weren't connected in any way. The seats were aluminum benches everywhere, except for the lower sections between the 30-yard lines that had red, white, and blue wooden seats that looked to be the size of kindergarten chairs (and were as comfortable as sitting on a picket fence). Behind the stands opposite us was the press box, a four-story metal office building that could have once housed the Foxborostan Ministry of Agriculture. And the whole place was perched on top of a hill and surrounded by a 15-foot-high chain-link fence to give it that prison-y touch.

And yet, as bad as Schaefer Stadium was, as horrible and unrewarding as the fan experience there was, we all knew one thing. Every football fan in New England, all the media, players, and the owner all knew it. Hell, even I knew it, and I was just a kid. We understood that as ugly, uncomfortable, and obsolete as that tenement slum of a stadium was, it was the best we could do. You could even argue it was the best the Patriots could ever have hoped to do.

From their inception in 1960 through the 1970 season, the Patriots didn't even have that. Billy Sullivan had been awarded a franchise—in spite of the fact that his stadium situation was such a mess—strictly because the AFL wanted to tap into the Boston TV market. But the pressure was on from the day of that first league meeting in Minneapolis for the Patriots to build a stadium and get their literal house in order.

NICKERSON FIELD, BOSTON UNIVERSITY

Yet for 11 full seasons, the Patriots had no place to call their own. Prior to the opening of Schaefer in '71, the Patriots had four official home stadiums, none of which belonged to them. On two occasions they were forced to hold "home" games on fields thousands of miles from Boston. And Billy Sullivan spent the entire decade of the 1960s doing battle in the bloodsport of Massachusetts politics to get a stadium built, all the while struggling just to find a place to play from one season to the next, since the Boston real estate listings weren't exactly filled with "Pro Football Venue for Rent" ads.

To find a stadium where his team could play in that initial 1960 season, Billy Sullivan went with the place he knew best: Braves Field. When the Braves left town in 1953, the ballpark was deeded over to Boston University and renamed Nickerson Field. The problem was that by 1960 the place was even more of a rat trap than when the Braves had played there. To make matters worse, the university had no interest in letting the Pats use it.

One thing that has always been true of Boston is that the mayor of the city rules with absolute power. Ever since the first Puritan settler of the New World said, "This'll be a great place to build a house once I run those Indians out of here," the man in charge has gotten whatever he wanted. At the time, the mayor was John Collins, and Sullivan convinced him to convince the university to let the Patriots play at Nickerson. Possibly, His Honor reasoned with them and impressed upon them how much the city would benefit from having a pro football team. But more likely, he told them that if they ever wanted the snow removed or the trash picked up again they'd shut their mouths and do what they were told.

Whatever it was, it worked, and on April 1 (there's that date again) it was announced that the Patriots first home would be BU. It was good for public confidence; prior to the announcement, the running joke around the sports editors' desks in town was that the team's official slogan was "An announcement will be made in 10 days."

Finding a stadium didn't necessarily mean they were all set, as Nickerson was in no condition to host a football game. Major repairs were needed, including to the stands. Fortunately for Sullivan, the Philadelphia Phillies had just finished improvements to Shibe Park. Not too proud to accept another team's hand-me-downs, he bought their old stands and had them trucked up to Boston. He also had the field re-sodded with grass hauled down from Canada, on the logic that it would stand up to New England winters. In all, the project cost $325,000, and GM Ed McKeever called it "the greatest reconstruction job since the Civil War." To pay for it, Sullivan had passed the collection plate to the same partners who'd helped him put up the league entry fee. They had all kicked in with more working capital, and the club now had $250,000.

Sullivan also came up with a scheme to raise even more money, based on the way the Green Bay Packers operate. The Packers are, to this day, a publicly held company. Billy thought that if his team sold non-voting stocks, fans would snatch up the shares and it would be the easiest money he had ever made.[4] The thinking was that people would pay to get a certificate saying they owned a piece of the Patriots. They'd buy them as souvenirs, frame them as conversation pieces, give them out as gifts for Father's Day or whatever. It was certainly legal, and all Billy would have to do was pay them some dividends every once in a while. The rest of his time he could spend swimming in the giant piles of cash on the floor of his walk-in vault and laughing maniacally, or whatever it is successful businessmen do with their ill-gotten fortunes.

And it would not only bring in cash, it would generate fan interest, under the assumption that if a guy owns a piece of a team, he's going to want to come see them play.

A fat lot of good that did him. The scheme raised money all right, but did nothing for ticket sales. Most of the stock sales ended up being to Wall Street investors who had zero interest in coming to a game. And, because of a mention of the stock offering in *Stars and Stripes*, a lot of the remaining stock was bought up by active-duty soldiers stationed in Germany, none of whom were exactly available to pop into Nickerson to watch football.

In all, the public offering brought in $540,000, selling 139,000 shares to 1,600 investors. Years later, Sullivan bought them out, and doing so cost him over $2 million. It wouldn't be the last time a financial deal would blow up in the Sullivan family's face like a cartoon cigar.

But hey, at least the team had a place to play as their first-ever training camp approached.

TRAINING CAMP

The Patriots' inaugural training camp was held at the University of Massachusetts in Amherst. And it was exactly what you'd expect from a franchise that had essentially been making it all up as they went along. "Mass confusion" was how Cappelletti described it in an interview years later: "The Patriots were trying to do everything as first-class as possible, but they were new at this."

Even though the final roster would have only 35 players, they had 10 times that many players when camp opened on July 4, 1960. The 350 invitees were simply too many to manage at the same time, so players were divided into three groups: one that was on the field, one that had just left, and one that was up next. The prospects who flew into Boston's Logan Airport were shuttled back and forth from Boston to Amherst, which on a good day is a two-hour drive from Boston. And there is never a good day. The driver making all those trips was Billy Sullivan's kid Chuck, who at the time was a ball boy but would later become team counsel and vice president.

Among the 350 invitees were dozens, scores, if not hundreds who had no business trying out for a pro football team. It seemed like the only requirement for trying out was having a heartbeat. Like that old joke about Massachusetts state workers that says a perfect score on the hiring exam is a 98.6. Cappelletti recalled one guy who'd been cut and four days later the coaches spotted him standing in line at the cafeteria, waiting to get fed. He'd stuck around, unnoticed, just for the free food, like the Pats were running a soup kitchen.

The players ranged from the young-and-untalented to the old-and-no-longer-talented. One of the old timers was a retired linebacker named Hardy Brown, who was tiny but had a huge reputation as a bloodthirsty headhunter who saw blindsiding, vicious hits as being his ticket to a steady paycheck.

In keeping with Sullivan's philosophy to build the team around the funniest-named people he could find, someone had invited a guy named Gunnar Gatski, who supposedly was once a great center for the Browns but by now looked like someone's grandfather. Saban liked having the older guys around to show the younger guys how it was done in the pros. But as camp wore on he weeded them out, and for the most part chose the young guys who couldn't play over the old guys who couldn't.

Another silly-namer was Sarafine Fazio, a huge rookie center from Pitt. One story goes that after dinner one night, Fazio had put *Gunsmoke* on the TV in the lounge and a couple dozen players were watching it with him. After a few minutes, another massive offensive lineman, Jack Davis from Maryland, got up, walked over to the TV, turned the knob to another station (note: if you're under the age of 40, google "TV knob" and it'll explain everything) without saying a word and went back to his seat. For the others in the room, it was that part in a prison movie where the two biggest, toughest guys start challenging each other for alpha male status. Fazio got up, said nothing, and turned the knob back to *Gunsmoke*. Silence filled the room, mixed with the smell of fear. Now both guys walked to the TV. Davis reached for the knob. Fazio reached for him. They grabbed each other, started grappling, and hit the deck. Chairs flew everywhere and everyone else jumped back to a safe distance. The two started rolling on the floor while everyone else stood there, dumbstruck, waiting for them to kill one another, until the silence was broken with . . . giggling. Coming from the two on the floor. It turned out that Fazio and Davis knew each other from working side gigs on the professional wrestling circuit and staged the whole thing to mess with everyone's heads. Mission accomplished.

During that first camp, one of the gimmicks they used to drum up publicity for the new franchise was to hold practices in different towns around the state. One weekday they were using an elementary school in Lexington. They were running through plays, installing their offense, and working on calls when the bell rang and hundreds of students came pouring out of the school onto the practice field. "The students would be getting into our huddles," Saban said. "We tried to shoo them away. A teacher came over and said the school grounds belonged to the kids and not to us and when it was recess time, it was the kids' time." So every time the recess bell rang, the players had to clear the field for fear of being bitched out again.

Even under the best of circumstances, talent evaluation is hard. And this was far from the best circumstances for Saban. He had to cut 90 percent of the roster before the season began. And with too many players in camp for Saban to meet with them all personally, roster cuts were announced the old-school way, by being posted on the bulletin board. Between managing his personnel, the logistics of all the traveling around, and fending off attacks from angry school teachers, the last thing he needed was another distraction. But that's exactly what he got.

FIRST PRESEASON

Boston got the honors of playing in the AFL's first exhibition game, at Buffalo on July 30. The plan was to introduce the sport of pro football to western New York with a massive parade the night before the game that would drum up interest and move tickets. It half worked; 100,000 people lined the parade route, 16,000 went to the game. Saban was ripped, because not only did the parade nonsense disrupt his practice schedule, War Memorial Stadium in Buffalo was still under construction, reducing the Pats to prepping for the game in a public park. But he couldn't complain about much else, since they won 28-7.

Only two out of the five Boston papers even bothered to cover the game, but the win still generated some fan buzz. That Sunday, McKeever went into the

Patriots office, which was located in a basement space in downtown Boston, to catch up on some work. People walking by, seeing someone in the office, kept banging on the door looking to buy tickets. McKeever said he moved 400 bucks' worth that morning alone.

By the time of the Pats' first home preseason game, Nickerson Field wasn't ready either. Billy managed to twist enough cardigan-sweatered, leather-elbow-patched Ivy League arms to get the use of what would be the second field the Patriots would call home, Harvard Stadium, for the first preseason game against Dallas. It would be history in the making: pro football coming to Boston. And the first ever professional game ever held at that ancient, revered, gridiron shrine.

All that history-making must have been more than the people of Boston could bear, because only 11,000 of them bothered to show up.

SEASON ONE, 1960

But the Pats would get another crack at making history, as they got to do the honors of hosting the first regular season game against Denver. The AFL thought it wise not to try to compete head-to-head with either the NFL by playing on Sundays or college football by playing Saturdays, so they scheduled their games for Friday nights, like high school games, with the first one taking place on September 9, 1960.

Once in a while these days, on special occasions, the NFL will honor those original eight American Football League franchises by having them play in their throwback uniforms from that inaugural season. And if we can glean anything from the history lessons, it's that good taste was in short supply in 1960, because so many of those uniforms were atrocious. For every retro-cool, stylish color scheme, like the powder blue jerseys the Los Angeles Chargers rocked back then, there was the hideousness of the New York Titans (now the Jets), whose brown jerseys and brown, logoless helmets made the players look like turds.

But for sheer ugliness, no team has ever competed with the Denver Broncos. As they did against the Patriots in 2010 to honor the AFL's 50th anniversary, Denver took the field for that very first game wearing socks with brown and yellow vertical stripes that looked kind of like those jars of Smuckers that have both the peanut butter and jelly in them together. An abomination. And one they corrected the following year by holding a public ceremony where they burned the damned things.

Somehow, though, in a rare display of good judgment, the Patriots avoided the Hideous Uniform Embarrassment of '60. They sported red jerseys and white helmets that bore the logo of a simple blue tri-cornered hat. The look we all know and love, the "Pat Patriot" logo of a Minuteman hiking a football, was a cartoon drawn by *Boston Globe* artist Phil Bissell and didn't become their official symbol until their second season.

That's how the two most unlikely, cash-strapped teams in football took the field to introduce Planet Earth to the new American Football League. And for Billy Sullivan, the night was a success. Maybe not a competitive success, as they lost 13–10 on a 76-yard punt return. And maybe it wasn't a financial success, since they only drew 21,597 fans. But it was real football in a real league in front of live human beings paying real money to watch it. And for a guy who had no business owning a sports franchise, he had every reason to feel good about getting off to a solid start.

It's funny now, funny in the "ironic foreshadowing" kind of way, not "ha ha" funny, that the Patriots, who would spend the next 50 years mired in controversy and scandal, would take all of one game to get involved in both.

The controversy came when Saban benched his starting quarterback. After one game that was lost on a special-teams play, he decided he couldn't trust Songin to be his starter, so he made the switch to Tommy Greene for their second game of the season, at New York. But with the Pats down 24–7, Saban changed his mind again, benching Green and putting Songin back in. The move worked; Songin led them to 21 unanswered points and the win. As quarterback controversies go, it wasn't the tumultuous kind that tears a team apart. But the fact that the franchise was two games old and had already made three changes at the position didn't exactly instill confidence in either the QB or the coach who was calling the shots.

The "scandal" came on the last play of the game, a 52-yard fumble return for a touchdown by defensive back Chuck Shonta that won Boston the game. Some of the Titans players complained that linebacker Jack Rudolph illegally kicked the ball to Shonta, but the refs didn't call it. For the team that would later introduce the world to scandals like the Snow Plow Game (in the 1980s), Spygate (the 2000s), and DeflateGate (2015), it would also not be their last allegation of cheating.

The 1960 Patriots also wasted very little time establishing themselves as one of the worst teams in the American Football League. After managing a three-game winning streak that brought them to 5–5, they dropped the last four games of the season by a combined score of 133–45 to finish in last place in the Eastern Division, only a half game ahead of Denver for the worst record in the league.

BOB DEE

The highlight of the year came, appropriately enough, in a blowout loss to the Chargers at Nickerson. The Chargers, leading 45–14 and running out the clock, fumbled the ball in their own end zone. As the ball rolled free, several people went after it, including players from both teams and a little kid who had run out onto the field. As the sweaty mass of enraged humanity converged on the ball, Patriots defensive end Bob Dee hurled himself on the kid instead of the ball, saving him from getting crushed under a tsunami of blubber and testosterone. Dee, a U.S. Marine who came to the Patriots out of Quincy, Massachusetts, by way of Holy Cross and the Washington Redskins, eventually had his number retired by the club after a great 12-year career. But as far as anyone knows, that was the only life he ever saved on a football field.[5]

Sullivan and his investors could also count on their one-eighth share of the money from the TV contract with ABC, which worked out to over a quarter of a million dollars, guaranteed annually. But even that didn't happen without lawyers getting involved. Late in the year, the Pats had a road game in Dallas, and ABC tried to weasel out of having to show it. But the league had a contract, threatened the network with a lawsuit, and the show went on. How Billy Sullivan and Lamar Hunt felt about having to force their broadcast partners to broadcast them we can't be sure, but it's likely comparable to being the bride at a shotgun wedding. You're glad to be going through with it, but it can't make you feel good about yourself.

Or the groom.

Sullivan's group was losing money, but it was nothing a new business venture couldn't handle. The team and the league survived the first year. The games were on TV. He had a core group of solid players to build around.

Now headed into the offseason, the major problem facing Billy was the fact that the man he trusted to run his franchise might be nuts.

All football coaches are nutbags to some extent. It's one of those jobs where you just *have* to be a little bit off your rocker to do it. The hours are incredible. You have to live, eat, sleep, and breathe the job. The rewards are meager. Everyone in the world thinks they know better than you and every other coach in the universe is trying to work harder than you in order to out-think you and take your job away. It's just not a job for a normal, well-adjusted man. Coaching a football team is a horribly stressful, unforgiving business, and not many are cut out for it. Remember what Alec Baldwin says to the real estate sales guys in *Glengarry Glen Ross*? "Nice guy? I don't give a shit. Good father? Fuck you! Go home and play with your kids. You wanna work here—close!" That's the life of a head coach in a nutshell.

Lou Saban was a good guy and a family man. His second cousin Nick has coached in the NFL and won three NCAA National Championships and competed for a few more. So there's that. But during that first year running the Patriots it became increasingly clear to everyone involved that he wasn't cut out for the job. For starters, Saban was too indecisive. His assessments of his players changed by the minute. He cut guys on a whim. That decision to bench Songin after one game was only the tip of the iceberg. If it's true what they say about a team being a reflection of its coach (something I've always believed), then the entire Patriots team was nervous to the point of being unstable. Mercurial almost to the point of paranoia.

There's another old saying that I agree with: just because you're paranoid doesn't mean someone isn't out to get you. And for the players, that someone was Coach Saban. Gino Cappelletti kicked the field goal that recorded the first points ever scored in the AFL. And he later described how frozen with fear he was as he lined up the kick. "It wasn't because these would be the first points ever scored in the AFL. We had no sense of history in those days. It was more a feeling of survival," he said. "The way things were, I knew if I blew it, they'd probably try someone else."

The players weren't worried about how much money they made. The money was crap and they knew it. They were just happy to earn a living playing football and were terrified about the prospect of getting cut and having to go find real jobs. And Saban's unpredictability made the atmosphere around the club so tense, it was almost impossible to function, much less worry about team-building or winning. Every day felt like they were back in camp at UMass, fighting for a roster spot. The players were so used to seeing teammates replaced without warning that it almost became routine. One time they were sharing a practice field with West Point. And when the Army players came out to start warm ups, linebacker Jack Rudolph yelled "Jesus Christ! This time he's brought in a whole team!"

As great a line as that was, most Patriots players were too busy desperately clinging to their jobs to see the humor in it.

After that first year, the Patriots had a fairly decent offseason. They swung a trade with Oakland for Babe Parilli, who quickly established himself as their franchise quarterback. They made another deal with the Houston Oilers that landed them 270-pound defensive lineman Houston Antwine. They drafted corner Don Webb, who'd have five interceptions (two for touchdowns) for them as a rookie.

SEASON TWO, 1961

When the second season started, on September 9, 1961, it became more and more obvious that Saban was going to make more snap judgments, keep creating roster turmoil, rule with fear and paranoia, and generally just go all Captain Queeg on everyone. And the owner was getting worried.

After one particularly tough loss, a 37-30 heartbreaker to the Titans in New York, Sullivan sat with his coach on the train ride back to Boston. "I don't have to look at the film," Saban said, "I know right now who I have to cut." He then proceeded to rattle off the names of half the guys on the 35-man roster. Sullivan was horrified and suggested in the politest possible terms that maybe if all the players that Saban wanted to cut deserved it, then maybe, just maybe, it was his selection process that sucked. To the surprise of no one, Saban didn't see it that way.

Things finally came to a head when Billy got a call from Lamar Hunt in Dallas. It seemed Saban had called him offering them Ron Burton for two bozos the Texans would just as soon live without. One of them was a drunk and the other was a fat, slow, disgruntled clubhouse cancer type. It's a testament to the legend that is Lamar Hunt that, rather than swindle the Patriots, he decided to alert Sullivan to the fact that his coach had gone completely banana sandwich and needed to be stopped. (There's a lesson for all you kids out there. Putting the greater good of the league ahead of the needs of your own team is how you get the modern-day American Football Conference Championship trophy named after you. Good life tip.)

Sullivan approached Saban and asked him about the deal, reminding him that Burton could not only play, he was a good guy and a credit to the organization. Saban reminded the boss that he had the power to make deals, which Sullivan conceded. But they left it like this: they'd wait a week and see. Billy suggested the two players Saban wanted in the deal would probably be put on waivers anyway. And he was right; they were. But just to demonstrate how unstable the coach was becoming, Saban didn't put in a claim for either one of them. He had tried to trade one of his best for two guys he didn't want even when they were sitting at the end of the driveway wearing "FREE PLAYER" signs taped to them. That pretty much sealed his fate with the Patriots. After five weeks and a record of 2-3, Billy wanted to fire Saban.

Years later, Sullivan recounted the conversation to author Larry Fox, and there aren't enough "a"s and "w"s in the word "awkward" to describe how awkward it must have been. According to his recollection, the discussion went as follows.[6]

Lou: "We had a great workout today. Our best of the year! You know, Friday night is my birthday, and I think the boys are ready to give me a great present."

Billy: "Um . . . Lou? I want to talk to you about some changes in the staff."

Lou: "Well, I'm not going to let any of them go, particularly your friend Holovak. He's been sensational."

Billy: "No, Lou. The person I'm talking about is you."

Saban was dumbfounded, and didn't take it well. He accused McKeever of undermining him and stabbing him in the back. Sullivan assured Saban the decision was all his and in the best interest of the team. But Billy was enough of a standup guy that, in order to cushion the blow, he promised Saban he wouldn't miss a paycheck. He'd be paid in full for the year and Billy would pull strings to get him a job in TV. Of course, it didn't hurt that if Saban could find work elsewhere, the Patriots wouldn't have to pay him. So with that financial motivation, Billy sent out a heartfelt letter to the network and to every owner in the league saying what an unbelievable asset Lou was and what a great representative he'd be for the league on television. Ralph Wilson up in Buffalo read the letter and allegedly said, "If this guy's so good, maybe we ought to hire him." Which he promptly did.

Now the Patriots weren't even halfway through season No. 2, but they were already on head coach No. 2.

4 HOME FOR LITTLE WANDERERS

★ ★

Do I really look like a guy with a plan? You know what I am?
I'm a dog chasing cars. I wouldn't know what to do with one
if I caught it! You know, I just . . . do things.
THE JOKER, *The Dark Knight*

It might have been Sullivan's first coaching change, but he went right to the Pro Sports Franchise Owner's Manual to make his choice. Since time immemorial, owners have been replacing coaches with their exact opposite. If you fire an angry, overbearing taskmaster, you replace him with a positive, reassuring player's coach. The logic being that the change of personality lightens the mood, takes the pressure off the players, and the hope is that they respond by playing better. Then typically over time they begin to tune out Coach Kumbaya, take advantage of his good nature and walk all over him. In which case you fire him and bring in another angry, overbearing taskmaster to wake them up. Lather, rinse, repeat.

And that's exactly how Sullivan played his first regime change.

MIKE HOLOVAK

Lou Saban was the hard-skulled coach the players didn't respond to, so Billy replaced him with the more relatable assistant Mike Holovak, and it worked out better. He promoted Holovak, the good cop to Lou Saban's bad cop. The Anti-Saban. And the players loved him for it. Cappelletti especially was grateful for the change. He'd been walking on eggshells with Saban for a year and a half, plus he had a personal connection with Holovak. Not only had he made Gino a receiver and jumpstarted his career, he'd once probably saved Cappelletti's spot on the team by covering for him when he was sick.

In that first off-season, Cappelletti came down with hepatitis and lost a ton of weight. He reported to camp not only still sick, but with a mountain of hospital bills from months of treatment. He had no other option but to make the club. Camp opened with Saban running the squad through his usual torturous drills, trying to whip them into shape. Cappelletti was in no condition for any of it and spent a good amount of time on the sidelines puking his guts out. When Holovak came over to check on him, Cappelletti fessed up, but begged him not to say anything to Saban because he knew he'd be on the next bus back to Minnesota if he was ever found out. Holovak kept it to himself, in one of those tender bonding moments that two people share forever, like two coworkers covering for each other so no one gets in trouble with the boss.

Once he was in the driver's seat, Holovak wasted no time making his first gawdawful decision, when he opted to rotate the quarterbacking duties between Butch Songin and Babe Parilli. It has been tried since, most notably by Tom Landry in the early 70s when he'd alternate between Roger Staubach and Craig Morton, and in the 90s by Lloyd Carr at Michigan, who swapped his QB every quarter, giving one quarter to Drew Henson and the next one to some skinny kid named Tom Brady. (More on him later.) The system has failed every time it has ever been tried. Players hate it. There's no continuity or chance for the quarterback to establish leadership of the offense. And for the '61 Pats, it was even more unsettling, because Holovak tried swapping Songin and Parilli between plays. It was quickly scrapped, and eventually Parilli won the full-time job.

Still, the Patriots players were happy to play for the new guy. Cappelletti wasn't the only one who responded well to Holovak. Sullivan got the bounce he was looking for, and the team started playing better immediately. After a 2–3 start for Saban, they tied their first game under Holovak and then rattled off seven wins in their last eight games and ended the season with a four-game winning streak. Holovak was a player's coach, the kind the boys enjoy playing for, and the team responded to his mild temperament with some success.

But there was more to the Patriots bounce in that second season of 1961. They also added some players who, once they settled into pro football, began not only to win games, but to do something else the club desperately needed: attract a following. They drafted a player who would not only go on to anchor their defensive line at the end opposite Bob Dee for years to come but who would also become known for being just as crazy off the field as he was on it—the one they called "The Wild Man" has become a staple of Patriots lore.

LARRY EISENHAUER

By way of background, and just to inject a little bit of autobiography here, my father died when I was nine years old. So, while he was home every night, I never really got to know him, grown man to grown man. As far as I can tell, John "Bud" Thornton was a good guy. A blue-collar Irishman who was close enough to his family to move his wife and kids out of the city and into the house directly across the street from his own brother and his family. But to the extent I understood him, he was a man of few words who was always sort of a mystery to me.

Except for one thing. Later in life I found out that my father's favorite athlete was Patriots defensive end Larry "Ike" Eisenhauer. While I never saw Eisenhauer play, everything I've come to learn about him since tells me my dad was a guy I could have enjoyed hanging out with had God had it in mind.

Eisenhauer was yet another product of Boston College who made his way onto the Patriots roster when they took him in the sixth round of the 1961 AFL draft. He was six foot five, 250 pounds, and by all accounts hit like a cement mixer with the brake lines cut and was absolutely fearless, on and off the field. Eisenhauer was exactly the kind of hilarious, unpredictable, borderline nutjob who, were he playing today, would have 3 million Twitter followers and fill half the daily content of TMZ Sports.

A typical Larry Eisenhauer story is the time he spotted teammate Jim Colclough wearing an offensively loud sport coat. Eisenhauer came up behind him and said, "Colclough! That's the ugliest fucking coat I've ever seen in my life," grabbed it from the bottom and tore it in half right up the back. His pregame ritual typically involved jacking himself up by slamming his head off the metal doors of his locker or smashing his forearms through the drywall in the locker room. He was also not above getting his teammates pumped up on the sidelines by getting a running start and bashing full speed into one of them. And on a few occasions during pregame introductions, he walked up to the goalpost, got up a full head of steam, and crashed his head into it to psych out the other team. "I was always known as a guy that got himself very emotionally motivated before games," he said.

Meaning he was also a master of understatement.

But his greatest locker-room move ever was before a game in Kansas City, on a freezing cold day with the field covered in snow. Eisenhauer ran out of the locker room and up the tunnel wearing nothing but his cleats, helmet and jock. "Nobody in the stands could see me," he said. "It was a big game for us and I did it just to loosen everybody up. Guys were laughing."

Patriots management was plenty familiar with Eisenhauer's wilder side, so when the club reached the AFL Championship game in 1963, they wanted to rein in his activities off the field. For the title game, they had to face the Chargers in San Diego, the city that the Chargers had moved to after one season in Los Angeles.

In his 2011 book "The Games That Changed the Game: The Evolution of the

NFL in Seven Sundays," former quarterback-turned-NFL analyst Ron Jaworski discussed that game with Eisenhauer, who explained his team's frame of mind going in. "After we beat the Bills, we got back to Boston and had a fabulous party. I think it went on for two days," he said. "Well, San Diego is a great area with beaches and all the other places to go. Maybe we got a little distracted."

Yeah, you could say that. In order to pump the brakes on Eisenhauer's party train, management thought it would be a good idea to bring in his father, Dutch, to be his roommate for the week. In fact, it was the worst possible idea. Dutch Eisenhauer was basically an older, 350-pound version of his son.

The club was staying at the Stardust Hotel in Mission Valley. The place was a mecca for the party crowd, partly for the weather, partly because it was so close to the border with Mexico and Tijuana. The older Eisenhauer met Larry and some of his teammates at the hotel, in a bar called The Reef Lounge. The back wall of the bar was a massive window whose other side was under the surface of the hotel swimming pool. Every night at nine, they put on an underwater ballet show for the bar patrons, consisting of hot girls in bikinis doing synchronized swimming. Dutch was hot and exhausted from the plane flight, so Larry suggested he take a swim to cool off and relax. "Just don't go until nine, though," he told the old man, "because they're putting chlorine in the pool."

"Sure, son," Dutch said, and went off to change. With that, Larry tipped off his teammates that they didn't want to miss the nine o'clock show, and he left too.

Exactly at nine, a crowd gathered in the bar and the mermaid show started. At about 9:05, the show came to an abrupt halt when a huge fat, middle-aged man cannonballed into the middle of the pool and the performers swam away screaming, nose clips flying in all directions. A few seconds later, Larry jumped in after Dutch and the two of them swam around for the horrified bar crowd while the Patriots players pissed themselves laughing.

Billy Sullivan's son Patrick was 10 years old at the time, and he tells the story of how the hotel manager tracked down Billy to tell him one of his players was ruining his mermaid show. "I immediately said to my dad, 'It's got to be Ike.' And when we arrived there, sure enough, there's Ike Eisenhauer in the pool." According to legend, as Sullivan and the hotel manager were dragging the Eisenhauers out of the water, Dutch turned to Larry and said, "Did it seem to you like everyone was watching us?"

It's hard for anyone under the age of say, 30, to believe, but in the days before cable TV, every city had its own, locally produced kids' shows. It's hard to fathom in an age when you can go to any city in America and watch the exact same TV lineup, but with the exception of PBS shows and Captain Kangaroo, every market had their own kids programming. Boston had several of its own Krusty the Klown types, the most popular of which was Rex Trailer, a cowboy-sheriff type who sang songs, taught kids life lessons, called them "Pardner" and stuff like that. Picture a live-action and incredibly un-PC version of Sheriff Woody from *Toy Story*.

Rex Trailer had an offensive Mexican-stereotype sidekick named Pablo. (Later replaced with a boring cavalry guy named Sgt. Billy. Thanks again, Fun Police.) Pablo talked with a thick, semi-racist Mexican accent, wore a giant sombrero, and was always trying to sneak off to take a siesta—he basically personified every stereotype short of sneaking his pregnant wife across the border to drop an anchor baby. Pablo was pretty bad.

Someone at the *Rex Trailer* show thought it would be funny to film a bit of Pablo practicing with the Patriots. The team happily went along for the free publicity and the chance to attract young football fans. The bit they taped was Pablo taking a handoff and running through the Pats defense. As he ran, the players would come running up, dive for him, and miss, and Pablo would scamper in for the touchdown.

There was just one thing they didn't count on.

Larry Eisenhauer.

Pablo made it through ten guys, but the 11th would have none of it. Ike came charging in at full throttle, drilled him into the dirt, and came up screaming, "Nobody gets across our goal line! Not even a clown!"

Poor, hapless Pablo lay on the turf, gasping for breath. The TV crew stood there for a second trying to process what they'd just witnessed before regaining their composure, running to their fallen comrade's aid, and demanding to know what in the hell the Wild Man was thinking. Years later, an older, wiser Eisenhauer admitted, "I'm kind of ashamed of it now. But I just couldn't stand to see anybody score on us if there was a chance I could stop him. He was slow, so it wasn't any trick catching him. I didn't really hurt him. I just sort of jumped on his back. Why give the guy a free touchdown?" Eisenhauer quickly established himself as the face of the franchise, even if that face was crazy enough to almost kill an actor on a kids' TV show. Any publicity is good publicity.

By the Pats' second season in 1961, football was catching on in Boston, with attendance at Nickerson Field averaging 19,500 per game. But the franchise was still very much flying by the seat of their pants in a lot of ways. During a mid-October home game against Buffalo on a Friday night, a storm was barreling up the coast, and Sullivan was in a panic about having a game scheduled in the middle of a major weather event. Possibly because he was concerned about people's safety, but more likely because he was worried about that other natural disaster: low ticket sales. At the last minute, he got AFL commissioner Joe Foss to push the game back from Friday to Sunday.

The Bills, to put it mildly, were thrown for a loop. They were prepared for a one-night stay in Boston, and the possibility of being stuck there longer had never been discussed. None of the players or staff had packed extra clothes, so by the time they flew home they'd been wearing the same clothes for an entire weekend and the plane stank like an open sewer. For all that trouble, the game still sold fewer than 10,000 tickets and the Patriots blew Buffalo out, 52–21.

Perhaps no story of those early Patriots is more preposterous, more misunderstood, or more fitting than what became known as The Man in the Trench Coat.

THE MAN IN THE TRENCH COAT

For their second-to-last home game against the Dallas Texans in '61, the Patriots drew an overflow crowd, with 5,000 standing-room-only tickets sold. The problem with having a lot of fans with nowhere to sit—especially Boston Patriots fans—is that it's just asking for trouble. Today it's popular in football to refer to the home crowd as "The 12th Man," as in "The 12th Man helped us win today." It's just an expression, and one meant to be taken figuratively. But for the game against Dallas, it was literally true.

Breaking probably every fire code in the book as well as all standards of common sense, the Patriots allowed the standing-room-only fans to watch the game from the field, and a mob of them ringed the sidelines. The Patriots were leading 28–21 and Dallas was driving with under a minute to play. With the clock ticking down and only seconds left, the Texans' wideout Chris Burford caught a 40-yard pass before getting knocked out of bounds on the Patriots' two-yard line. The scoreboard clock showed 0:00, so the thousands standing around rushed onto the field to celebrate. Usually, running onto the field was reserved for walk-off, game-winning World Series home runs and drunken douchebags acting on dares from their idiot buddies, not an early November victory that represented only the Pats' fifth win of the season. But what else could you expect from people standing right along the sidelines? The only ones who couldn't see this coming were the people running the show.

The problem for all involved was that the referees overruled the timekeeper and asked for time to be put back on the clock, giving the Texans one more chance to tie the game. It took some doing, but the officials managed to restore order, clear the field, and push everyone back to the sidelines.

That is to say, almost everyone.

As Dallas lined up for the last play, one fan in the back of the end zone slipped back onto the field. In one of those odd historical inaccuracies that take on a life of their own, it has always been said that the guy was wearing a trench coat. But film of the play is readily available on YouTube. And you don't need to break it down like it's the Zapruder film to see what happened.

A fat guy in a windbreaker slithers into the end zone. The Patriots are loaded up for the run, with a six-man line and no linebackers. Windbreaker Guy sneaks up behind the line and at the snap of the ball crouches down behind the Pats' defensive tackles at the goal line. Dallas QB Cotton Davidson goes back to pass and looks for Burford running a crossing route across the back of the end zone with a step on his coverage. But Windbreaker Guy slides to his right, gets a hand on the pass and knocks it down. Game over.

The historically inaccurate version is that Trench Coat Man then ran back into the crowd, everyone denied seeing anything, like witnesses to a Mob hit, and he was never seen again. There's even one version where The Trench Coat Man is Billy Sullivan himself. But watch the video; Windbreaker Guy just takes a victory lap like it was the most normal thing in the world, the Patriots celebrate, and the Texans fly home to Dallas to start work on the invention of the instant-replay challenge flag. Sadly for them, it would come decades too late to help.

While no one could have known it at the time, the Man in the Trench Coat incident set a tone for the Patriots; for the rest of their existence, this would be a franchise that would never do things the conventional way.

The first order of business going into that season was to find a new place to play, because in no one's opinion was Nickerson Field cutting it as a home stadium. Despite the occasional big crowd, the team couldn't draw consistently. For example, one game drew fewer than 8,500 people, and a good chunk of that crowd was there because a supermarket promotion had given them free tickets. And besides, there was something about playing in a college stadium that made the whole Patriots operation feel amateurish.

Looking back, it's odd that BU was their first choice, because there was a pro sports venue in the city that had been hosting football since 1915. BU, BC, and Dartmouth had all played there, as had the Boston Redskins and Boston Yanks. The place was not only available, it was known around the world: Fenway Park. And in the winter of '63, Billy Sullivan struck a deal with Red Sox owner Tom Yawkey to make it the Patriots' "permanent" home.

FENWAY PARK

As rundown as Fenway Park was, the Patriots' players loved playing there. They saw Fenway as their first truly professional home stadium, and it made them finally feel like pros. As Gino Cappelletti put it, "We felt like we were legitimate because it was a major league venue."[7]

Barely suited for baseball, Fenway was an awkward setup for football, to say the least; one end zone ran up the third-base line and the other was out by the right-field bleachers, which meant that one sideline ran along the grandstands on the first-base side. Temporary bleachers were set up in front of the Green Monster's left-field wall. One problem they ran into was that the best seats in the house, the first-base-side lower box seats, were at ground level, so that players and coaches on the sidelines would block the view of the people in those seats. The solution was something that has likely never been tried before or since in gridiron history: the Patriots put both benches on the left-field sidelines. And there's a reason that setup has never been tried again. Any three-year-old could figure out that it's an obviously terrible idea.

"That led to some crazy things," Cappelletti said. "We could wander over near their bench and eavesdrop on their play-calling. I remember Hank Stram calling for screen passes and us yelling to our defense about what was coming."

Another problem with the layout of Fenway was that the playing surface itself could barely contain a football field. The proximity to the fans along both sidelines and the back of the end zones just invited chaos, and chaos graciously accepted.

There was so little room between the sidelines and the Green Monster's bleachers that fans in the stands could tap players on the shoulder and talk to them. The Patriots' tackle Tom Neville, who'd played at Mississippi State, had never seen anything like it. "They would want to know why we weren't throwing the ball more often," he said. "We would be trying to have meetings on the bench and they would be leaning over making suggestions. It wasn't exactly what I was used to in the SEC."

Every extra point and field goal led to a scrum of people fighting for the ball. Crowd control was almost nonexistent. In 2012, on the 100th anniversary of Fenway Park, NFL Films did a tribute to the Patriots' time playing there that includes a clip of a game against San Diego from 1966, in which Pats backup quarterback John Huarte throws a pass intended for J.D. Garrett into a crowd of about two dozen fans roaming free on the field. The pass falls incomplete, then takes one bounce before getting scooped up by a fan who puts a head fake on the one woefully outnumbered cop on duty and runs out of the garage door in the center field wall without breaking stride.

But again, the players loved Fenway. Cappelletti described to NFL Films the excitement of looking for Ted Williams' locker and the feeling that the franchise had finally hit the big time.[8] The fans loved the proximity to the players, the utter lack of security, and the free footballs it provided. It was pandemonium, but it was a great show.

But with those great shows came some gigantic headaches. To cite just a few examples:

★ **Fenway Park, 1964.** The night before the last game of the season, against Buffalo, a winter storm blasted the city and dumped a foot of snow on it. Many of the streets of Boston hadn't been cleared, and those that had been plowed were gridlocked. As the afternoon wore on, it occurred to everyone on the Patriots that Cappelletti hadn't been heard from; he was stuck in traffic and couldn't make it to the stadium. One saving grace was that, due to the fact that Buffalo was 11-2 and the Patriots were 10-2-1, the kickoff had been moved back an hour for prime-time TV, buying the Pats some extra time. But still, as game time approached, no Gino. The coaches were in a state of panic, worrying if he was stranded or seriously injured somewhere . . . or worse. The official time of the kickoff came and went and still no Gino.

But this time, the Pats benefited from their own incompetence. The grounds crew had thought to cover the field with a tarp, but the thing was so piled with snow, no one could figure out how to get it off the field. While they were figuring it out, Cappelletti made it through the traffic to the ballpark. Eventually the crew brought snowplows onto the field to clear the tarp, Gino suited up, and was ready for the opening kick. The football fans of America benefited as well, as they were treated to the kind of entertainment that only watching plows clearing snow off a tarpaulin for an hour can bring. The Bills won, 21-14.

★ **Jack Murphy Stadium, San Diego, California, 1967.** For all of Fenway's shortcomings as a football stadium, there was one thing the Patriots could count on: any scheduling conflicts that might arise from sharing a park with the Red Sox would be over by September, as that's when baseball's regular season ended. (The Red Sox of the 1960s were assumed to have no chance of making the postseason.) The Sox were so consistently gawdawful that by '67, an entire generation of New Englanders had been born, raised, and grown to adulthood since the last time the Sox had been in the World Series. The year before, they'd finished a half game out of last place in the 12-team American League and were 100-1 long shots to win the pennant.

So the Patriots had every reason to believe that they'd have three weeks of games, four tops, when the Red Sox schedule would be an issue, after which they'd have the place all to themselves. But then, a miracle happened. Or in the syrupy, shamelessly overblown rhetoric of the Boston baseball press of the day, an "Impossible Dream" happened. The Red Sox won the American League pennant on the last day of the season and made it to the World Series for the first time in 21 years. To this day it stands as one of the all-time Cinderella stories in the history of sports. It made legends out of a host of Sox players. It transformed the whole culture of the region. It turned Boston into a baseball town for generations. It was a great moment for everyone in New England.

Except, naturally, the Patriots.

The Pats were scheduled to play the Chargers at home on October 8, which conflicted with game four of the Series. Since this was a possibility that no one in the Patriots organization had even remotely considered, no contingency plans had ever been made. So they scrambled to find the next closest viable location where the game could be held. And they found it in San Diego; in other words, on a continent that's lousy with football stadiums from one end to the other, they chose the one that was the farthest distance away from their fans. *And* they chose to play it in front of their opponents' home crowd. And so it was that the Patriots played against San Diego in San Diego, in a stadium filled with San Diegans, and called themselves the "home" team. Somehow, they managed to fight their way to a 31–31 tie.

Back in Boston they might've called it the Improbable Dream, except no one was paying attention.

★ **Legion Field, Birmingham, Alabama, 1968.** In '68, the Red Sox returned to form and didn't make the postseason. But the Patriots remained totally consistent in their inability to solve stadium scheduling problems. Their home game against the Jets on September 22 conflicted with a Sox game, again forcing them to scramble to find an alternate site. And again, they came up with the worst possible solution. While this time they didn't literally give the Jets the home field, they might as well have. They did the next worst thing: they gave the home field to the face of the Jets franchise, Joe Namath. Namath came to national prominence quarterbacking the Crimson Tide, and in Alabama his return was being treated as if he were de Gaulle liberating Paris. Unlike the year before, this time the Pats "home field" disadvantage cost them dearly. To the delight of the locals, Namath lit the Patriots up and cruised to a 47–31 win.

So, already on their third official home stadium, the Patriots had twice run into situations where the landlord needed the place and they were left with no choice but to be the "home" team in games played thousands of miles out of town. The situation was such a chaotic mess that, for some of those seasons, the club had to send the few season ticket holders they had three different sheets of tickets, because they didn't know for sure where they'd be playing.

Yet, in spite of it all, the Patriots saw immediate results on the field the moment they fired Lou Saban and replaced him with Mike Holovak in the middle of that 1961 season. Holovak installed an aggressive, blitz-heavy attacking defense that the players loved. And they rewarded him with a record of 7-1-1 down the stretch. In '62, Holovak installed Babe Parilli as the full-time quarterback, and the team went 9-4-1, good enough for second place in the AFL East. But it was the following season that the club got its first taste of postseason success.

In 1963 the Pats regressed to a record of 7-6-1, but that was good enough to put them atop their division, tied with Buffalo. Under the league's postseason structure, that meant a playoff game, with the winner going to the AFL Championship game. Holovak's swarming defense dominated the game, holding the Bills to just seven yards on 12 rushing attempts and only 19-for-45 through the air, with their lone score coming on a 93-yard touchdown pass. Meanwhile, the Patriots offense managed two touchdown passes from Parilli and four Gino Cappelletti field goals to cruise to a 26-8 win and a trip to the championship game in San Diego. That's when Larry Eisenhauer and his teammates began the premature celebration that started in Buffalo, moved back to Boston, and lasted all the way to the hotel pool bar. Which you could argue was smart of them, because there would be nothing at all worth celebrating once the game started.

The Chargers' coach was Sid Gillman, the brilliant tactician and innovator who was in the process of fathering what we all recognize now as the modern passing game. Gillman was at least a generation ahead of his time, meeting with mathematicians in order to develop efficient passing routes that would gain the maximum number of yards while throwing the ball the shortest distance possible. Even in the pass-happy AFL, the Chargers' attack stood alone, outscoring the second-best offense in the league by 36 points. The Patriots' defense under Holovak countered it with the blitz. And . . . the blitz. It's all they had. And it was useless. The game was a slaughter.

The Patriots managed to keep it a close game for less than a quarter. San Diego took a 21-7 lead into the second before throwing into overdrive. The Patriots just kept blitzing. It was the football equivalent of a dogfight between a World War I fighter plane and an F-14. The Chargers not only threw for 300-plus yards, they ran for over 300 as well on their way to a 51-10 thumping. The final score of the game came on a late one-yard TD run by San Diego's backup quarterback John Hadl. That score wouldn't really be significant to Patriots fans for another 22 years. Then, when we'd see them get blown out again in similar fashion in a championship game, we'd at least have the comfort of knowing that the 1963 beat-down was slightly more humiliating. But more on that later.

They won 10 games in '64 and 8 in '66, but those would be the last decent seasons they'd have under Holovak. And the front office continued to show a genius for screwing up personnel decisions.

NICK BUONICONTI

It is not a stretch to say that perhaps the best player the Patriots had in their first 40 years of existence was linebacker Nick Buoniconti. Drafted out of Notre Dame in 1961, the Patriots grabbed him in the 13th round. He was considered small for the NFL, but in one of those classic "you can't measure heart" scenarios, he quickly proved that he played a lot bigger than his actual size. Just two games into his rookie season, he was installed as a starter and never relinquished the spot. Just as importantly for a guy who was considered too small to play pro ball, he never left the field. He played in all 14 games in each of his first five seasons and in his sixth year only missed one.

Nick Buoniconti was everything they could've hoped for. He made all the plays. He was an underdog. He was tough. He was relentless. He set a tone for the entire defense. Nabbing him with the 102nd pick in the draft was like finding a wad of cash in the street.

But they just wouldn't have been the Patriots if they didn't pick up the money, walk half a block, and blow it all on the first rip-off arcade claw-machine game they came upon.

In '67, Buoniconti finally suffered an injury serious enough to keep him out of the lineup for a significant period of time, and he only played eight games that season. Whether the club thought this was a sign of his undersized body finally wearing out from the punishment he took or whether they just said, "Hey, we haven't done anything really stupid in a while. Let's get rid of our best player!" is uncertain. But they traded him to the Miami Dolphins for what basically amounted to some pizza coupons.

Buoniconti went on to be the heart and soul of one of the greatest football units ever assembled, the Dolphins' "No Name" Defense of the 70s. In '72 he was the captain of the only undefeated team in history. To this day, he's considered one of the best middle linebackers of all time and is an NFL Hall of Famer. And as for the Patriots management that gave up on him in 1968, in the end, it turned out they were right. He eventually did have to retire. Seven seasons after the trade.

THE LOST ROOKIES

More typical of the type of players the roster was filled with by 1968 were rookie wideouts Bill Murphy and Aaron Marsh. The book on Murphy was that he had great hands, but was not only too slow to get open, he also had terrible eyesight and couldn't see a ball thrown his way. Marsh's problems were the opposite. He was fast, a terrific route-runner with great vision, but he couldn't catch the ball to save his life.

On one occasion, the Pats were set to play a road game in the Houston Astrodome. On the day before the game, the team held a workout in the stadium. The players finished practice, showered, dressed, and went back to the hotel. What no one noticed was that their rookie receivers were nowhere to be found, and no one knew what had become of them. That is, until the hotel switchboard got a frantic, panicky call from someone asking to speak to anyone with the Patriots. It was Murphy and Marsh on the line, calling from inside the stadium. They'd wandered off, somehow managed to get lost, and couldn't find their way out. The joke among the writers was that an Astrodome security guard saw them and tossed them the keys, but Marsh dropped them and Murphy couldn't find them.

DENNIS BYRD

By 1968, the NFL and AFL had merged and held one draft. The Patriots were coming off a terrible '67 season in which they went 3-10-1 and were sitting pretty with the sixth overall pick. By most accounts, the '68 draft class was deep, and there would be plenty of solid, blue-chip, can't-miss, building-block-type players when the Patriots' turn came. They had made it clear they had their eye on Dennis Byrd, a highly regarded defensive end out of NC State.

If Hollywood ever gets around to greenlighting "Boston Patriots: The Motion Picture," the ideal opening scene would be this one particular magical moment from their 1968 draft. It's the perfect establishing shot to illustrate just how bungling, amateurish, and inept team management was in those early days. The scene opens with a shot of what passed for an NFL draft war room in those days. Always looking for a chance at some positive press, the Pats had invited the entire Boston sports media to be there when they picked. A handful of reporters are gathered around the conference room along with GM Ed McKeever, Holovak, and the rest of the Patriots front office, scouting, and coaching staffs. When their turn comes, Byrd is still on the board, and they waste no time making the pick. Now beaming at the prospect of having Byrd to build their defense around, they place a call to his house and put it on speakerphone for the assembled media to hear:

Holovak: "Is Dennis there, please?"
Answer: "He's not."
Holovak: "This is Mike Holovak, the coach of the Boston Patriots, and I'd
    like to get in touch with him. Do you know where I can reach him?"
Answer: "The hospital."
Holovak: "Hospital? What's he doing in the hospital?"
Answer: "He's just had a knee operation."[9]

Byrd would end up lasting all of one season before a combination of injury and ineffectiveness ended his career. Believe it or not, it almost gets worse.

Jump cut to one of the later rounds. The Patriots are on the clock. Still stung from the Dennis Byrd fiasco, McKeever informs the rest of his staff he wants to take a certain highly touted wide receiver prospect. Until one of his scouts informs him that the kid has one major drawback: he's dead. He'd been killed in a car crash weeks earlier.

As is usually the case, though, when it came to managing the team into the ground, Holovak had plenty of help. And it wasn't just limited to McKeever drafting guys who were lying on operating tables or in coffins. In addition to bad drafts and signing sociopaths, the Pats repeatedly let quality players slip through their fingers.

As much as it pained Sullivan to do it, he had no choice but to make another coaching change. Ironically, the two men he had in mind—neither of whom would end up signing with the team—would go on to change the way we look at coaching.

VINCE LOMBARDI

One of them was none other than Vince Lombardi. The one who's synonymous with success. The Vince Lombardi the Super Bowl trophy is named after. The architect of modern football. The inventor of the unstoppable Power Sweep. The star of every NFL Films documentary ever made, with his classic "What the hell's going on out here?!" line. The one who said, "Winning isn't everything; it's the only thing." *That* Vince Lombardi. In the early part of 1969, Lombardi was one stroke of the pen away from being hired by Billy Sullivan as Patriots head coach.

After winning Super Bowls I and II with the Green Bay Packers, Lombardi had retired from coaching and was now just a team executive. But the worst-kept secret in the football world was that front office work wasn't cutting it for him. Lombardi missed the competitiveness of coaching. He missed the action and excitement. He also likely missed the ability to wave your arms like a maniac and scream, "What the hell's going on out here?" too, since even in the "Mad Men" era, pre-sexual harassment lawsuit days of the 60s, you couldn't do that in an office and get away with it. Lombardi wanted to get back to the sidelines, as God intended.

Sullivan had already fired Holovak. And Lombardi, understandably, was his first, last, and only choice to take Holovak's place. For a decade, the Boston media had been merciless in pointing out how amateurish and incompetent an operation the Patriots were, and hiring Lombardi would give the franchise instant credibility they couldn't get any other way.

Sullivan and Lombardi spent quite a lot of time together discussing NFL events in the week leading up to Super Bowl III. The Patriots wanted Lombardi for all the obvious reasons, and he was from Brooklyn, so the move back to the northeast had some appeal for him.

And Sullivan was making it worth his while. He offered to make him the highest paid coach in football, give him total control over all personnel moves, and give him 30,000 shares of non-voting Patriots stock. Lombardi liked the offer, and just before the game told Sullivan he was very interested. All he'd need was the chance to run it by his attorney before he'd sign it.

Super Bowl III, January 12, 1969, was a historic, earth-shattering upset; the New York Jets upset the 17-point favorite Baltimore Colts, instantly cementing the AFL's credibility and causing the Patriots' stock price to rise by three dollars a share immediately after the game. As Sullivan pointed out, if Lombardi had signed the deal before the kickoff, "he would've made ninety thousand dollars without lifting a finger." And there's no telling how much higher the stock could've gone. "Just the announcement we were hiring Vince would've put a quarter of a million dollars in his pocket," Sullivan said.

Now all that was needed was for Lombardi's lawyer to sign off on the deal. Unfortunately for Billy, that lawyer was a Washington power broker by the name of Edward Bennett Williams. Williams at one time owned the Baltimore Orioles, who were always ridiculously overloaded with pitching, hitting, defense, and the best coaches in baseball to make life miserable for the Red Sox.

But at this particular time, Williams happened to be part owner of the Washington Redskins.

See if you can guess where this is going.

Williams instead signed Lombardi to coach the 'Skins, right out from under

Sullivan's nose. As payment, Lombardi would receive a 7 percent chunk of the team. Williams insisted he didn't do anything wrong or unethical, which speaks volumes about his ethics, because you rarely see a conflict of interest where the conflicted interest is so bloody obvious. He claimed that if Vince had taken the Patriots offer, he would've have been fine with it. Lombardi, for his part, claimed that Sullivan's deal would have been better for him financially, but that what his decision ultimately came down to was the chance to be a celebrity in DC. "I'll get to golf with the President," he told Billy. "Imagine, me, a kid from Brooklyn, golfing with the President!"

Lombardi only lasted one season in Washington, going 7-5-2. He died before the start of the next season. The president he got to golf with was Richard Nixon. In the long run, Nixon didn't fare much better.

CHUCK NOLL

The next coach the Pats missed out on was none other than Chuck Noll.

Football historians will tell you it's hard to overstate how big a deal that Jets-Colts Super Bowl was. It not only gave legitimacy to the AFL teams and the respect they sorely lacked, it was probably the exact moment that pro football overtook all other sports to become America's national pastime. It gave the country its first great baby boomer, crossover-appeal superstar in Joe Namath. That one game made Namath the face of football and an instant media sensation. It put him on the cover of Time magazine, had the press following him all over town as he squired models and actresses around, and gave him the enduring moniker "Broadway Joe." The bottom line is that the effects of that game on the entire nation were profound.

And the effect of Super Bowl III on the Patriots was, like seemingly every other human endeavor of the time, horrible and debilitating. A game they didn't even play in managed to set the club back years in their struggle for respectability.

Billy Sullivan had considered one Plan B contingency in the event he couldn't land Vince Lombardi. There were two highly regarded head-coaching prospects working that Super Bowl: one was the Colts' defensive backs coach, Chuck Noll, and on the other sideline was the Jets' receivers coach, Clive (rhymes with "sleeve") Rush.

Both came highly recommended. Billy heard raves about Noll from Sid Gillman, Oakland team president Al Davis, and Noll's boss, the Colts' Don Shula.

Rush got a ringing endorsement from Namath himself, who told Sullivan he had the brains, the demeanor, and the respect from players to be a great head coach.

It would be nice to be able to say that Billy rejected the advice of three of the greatest minds ever to run an NFL franchise and took the word of the future star of *C.C. & Company*, who wore fur coats and got drunk at Toots Shor's every night. But that wouldn't be true. In fact, it was fate that stepped in and made the decision for him.

Once the Jets pulled off the biggest upset in the history of American pro sports, there was no way Sullivan could come back to Boston with a coach from the losing team. As it was, the sharks in the press were in a feeding frenzy, and announcing that the Pats' new coach was coming from the team that just got humiliated in the Super Bowl would be like opening Chuck Noll's jugular and throwing him in the water. So Billy gave the job to Clive Rush.

Granted, there were some concerns. Rush had been an assistant under some great college coaches like Bud Wilkinson at Oklahoma and Woody Hayes at Ohio State. But his only experience as a head guy was at the University of Toledo, where he had never won more than three games in a season and, more ominously, fought with his athletic director.

Still, the Super Bowl upset decided it. Rush got the job.

In typical Patriots fashion, of course, Noll went to Pittsburgh to become the legend who won four Super Bowls, and Rush became perhaps the single biggest human train wreck in team history.

5

BREAKDOWNS

★ ★

I don't gripe to you, Reiben. I'm a captain. There's a chain of
command. Gripes go up, not down. Always up. You gripe to me,
I gripe to my superior officer, so on, so on, and so on. I don't gripe
to you. I don't gripe in front of you. You should know that . . .
  CAPT. MILLER, *Saving Private Ryan*

CLIVE RUSH

Establishing shot: the Patriots are holding a press conference. Team brass and assembled media fill a conference room. It's Clive Rush's second day with the club. He'd met with the Boston media on his first day and now the team has called this press conference to introduce their new GM George Sauer, whom they'd hired to replace Ed McKeever. For the last eight years, Sauer had also been with the Jets as director of player personnel, so Rush has the honor of introducing him.

Rush steps to the podium, grabs the mic stand and . . .

BZZZZZZZ!!!

The new head coach of the Patriots is standing before the world with 120 volts of electric death running up his arm. Everyone looks on, jaws open, frozen in horror, not knowing how to react. Through some bizarre wiring mishap, the microphone was connected to a wall outlet. Fortunately for Rush (and for whatever insurance company handled the Pats' workman's comp claims), one man keeps his wits about him: team director Danny Marr pulls the plug and probably saves Rush's life in the process.

Rush takes a moment, regains his composure, goes back to the podium, and in one of those grace-under-fire moments says, "I heard the Boston press was rough. But I had no idea they'd be *this* rough." *Rimshot!*

Scene.

The Live Mic Incident might have been the biggest omen for how bizarre Rush's career with the Patriots would be, but it wasn't the first. Rush was supposed to have flown up from New York for that introductory presser, but a severe blizzard grounded every plane in the Northeast Corridor. Even God, it seemed, was against this unholy marriage. Rush had no choice but to take the train to Boston. "It's the first time I ever heard of someone being ridden *into* town on a rail," he said.[10] *That was Clive Rush, everyone! He'll be here all week . . .*

It didn't take long for people around the team to figure out that, to put it politely, Clive Rush wasn't playing with a full deck. *Boston Globe* beat writer Will McDonough told a story about requesting a lunch meeting during Rush's first training camp. An interview was set up and he was told he could meet Rush in his dorm room at Phillips Academy Andover. When McDonough walked in, he found the coach sitting behind his desk, buck naked except for a towel around his neck. And the room was unbearably cold. Rush had two massive air conditioning units in his room and had been running both on full blast for hours and the place was freezing. Then Rush began the interview by saying he was battling a cold that for some reason he just couldn't seem to shake. "Wonder why?" McDonough thought to himself.

The whole Clive Rush Era (Error?) in Boston sounds like those stories you hear about the last days of the Nixon White House, all full of paranoia, delusions, rapid mood swings, fits of rage, everything short of Rush making Henry Kissinger pray with him and talking to the paintings on the wall. The only real difference was that Nixon was disgraced out of the most powerful office in the world and Rush was coaching a football team. That, and the fact that it took Nixon years to come unglued and Rush pretty much lost his marbles the moment he got the job.

Though, like I've already mentioned, just because you're paranoid doesn't mean people aren't really out to get you. And in Rush's case, those people were the Boston press. One of the major themes of Ted Williams' autobiography was how the baseball writers hounded him and made his life miserable. Ripping Teddy Ballgame sold papers, so they did it every chance they got. If the greatest hitter who ever lived wasn't immune, the coach of a struggling football franchise had absolutely no chance at getting a fair shake. And unfortunately for Clive Rush, he was singularly unfit to handle the criticism.

One of the old line of veteran media hatchet men was Clif Keane. Williams singled him out as one of the writers who was especially vicious toward him. Keane was well known as a crotchety, surly old fart on the radio. *Clif & Claf* was a show he did with another bomb-tosser named Larry Claflin, and the two of them were the sports-talk equivalent of Statler & Waldorf sitting up in the balcony telling the Muppets how much they suck. Keane wasted no time getting under Clive Rush's fingernails. The coach was making wholesale changes to the roster, and Keane said something along the lines of, he can make all the changes he wants, but until they get an influx of talent, they'll still be the same old Patriots. That's pretty tame stuff, actually, but it was more than Rush could handle. He went into a tirade and tried to have Keane banned from the premises. Which, if you're as thin-skinned as Rush and trying to curry favor with the press, isn't exactly the best way to go about it.

And it got worse. There's an old saying that you shouldn't pick fights with people who buy ink by the barrel, but apparently Rush had never heard it. One of the beat writers did a report where he quoted backup quarterback Tom Sherman as saying he wanted more playing time and he felt like he wasn't getting a fair chance to win a job. Rush responded by cutting Sherman the next day, which you can justify, and then blowing his stack at the reporter, which you can't. Predictably, it only made matters worse.

Rush didn't save his psychosis for just the ink-stained wretches in the press. He was always worried about how he was perceived by his players. After his pep talks to the team, he'd pull a veteran or two aside and ask them, "How was I?" Which, when you're trying to lead men, gain their confidence, and get them to fight for you, isn't exactly the way Patton would've done it. Rush also became convinced someone was bugging the meeting room to steal his game plans. So he took to playing it up for whomever he thought was listening by giving fake game plans while shaking his head and pantomiming "No . . ."

Rush's players did what any grown men would do when they realize that an authority figure might be struggling with irrationality: they exploited it for cheap laughs.

Well, one guy did at least.

Word got around that Rush was afraid of snakes. Not just a good, macho, Indiana Jones–like hatred, but a real phobia. So one veteran, who was already in Rush's doghouse, packed a rubber snake into his luggage on a team flight. As soon as the plane reached altitude and the coach was relaxing in the front row, he threw the snake down the aisle at his feet. Rush understandably freaked out, jumped up on the seat, and screamed bloody murder for someone to come get rid of the damned thing. Good times.

GENE THOMAS

There were times when Clive Rush was not even the crazy one. Consider the running back the club saddled him with in 1968. Years earlier, when Lamar Hunt's franchise was the Dallas Texans, he bailed Billy Sullivan out of a terrible decision when Lou Saban tried to trade Ron Burton for two of Hunt's worst players. By '68, he'd moved the team to Kansas City, renamed them the

Chiefs, started winning, and was apparently feeling less charitable, because he unloaded a nutjob named Gene Thomas on the Patriots like he was dumping toxic waste.

The main reason being that Thomas had once pulled a gun on a Chiefs teammate. He'd been in the league for two years by the time he came to Boston, but the writers quickly determined that the whole no-pulling-guns-on-your-teammates policy wasn't the only concept he was unclear on.

On one road trip, the team bus was taking everyone from the airport to the hotel. A few of the writers spent that time asking Thomas a few questions, getting to know him. When the bus pulled up to the hotel, they all got out, went to the luggage storage, grabbed their suitcases, and made their way to the lobby. About halfway to the door Thomas, who was walking with them empty-handed, turned to them and said, "Hey! How come you guys aren't bringing in my bags? Isn't that how it's supposed to work?" It would be his last season in pro football.

And Clive Rush's understanding of "how it's supposed to work" wasn't much better. Early in the '69 season, before a game against a powerhouse Kansas City Chiefs team that would go on to win the Super Bowl, Rush decided to shake up his offensive line. But not by replacing anyone, just keeping the same five players and shuffling them all around to different positions. It made no sense on any level. They could barely hold their blocks as it was, never mind putting all five of them in positions they'd never played before. At practice they all lined up at their new spots, giving each other the kind of looks your family does when Grandma starts calling everyone by the wrong name. But Rush was ready to try it for real. It wasn't until just before game time that the assistant coaches were able to talk him out of it and everyone went back to their normal spots.

Every week it seemed Rush had another run-in with somebody. One time some kids were heckling from behind the bench, so he left the sidelines mid-game to scream at them. In a game against Buffalo he got into it with a Bills assistant coach. Then when he didn't like an official's call, he pulled his team off the field until he got an explanation.

In the early November game against Miami, the halftime show was canceled due to heavy rain. One fan who was drunk, bored, and attention-whore-y enough went out onto the empty field and slid around in the mud to the cheers of the few people still in the stands. Late in the game, the Patriots scored a touchdown to pull within one point, but rather than kick the extra point for the tie, Rush made the call to go for the two-point conversion and the win. The attempt failed and the Pats lost. In the postgame press conference, Rush refused to talk about the decision to go for two, which is all anyone was interested in. Instead, he chose to rant and rave about the muddy drunk guy and his "desecration of the game."

Things came to a head after a game in San Diego late in the season. The Patriots lost to the Chargers, 28-18, but what Billy Sullivan couldn't accept was that, in the first half alone, Rush had taken two bench penalties for running out onto the field to argue calls. They were his sixth and seventh such penalties of the season, and Billy went to the locker room at halftime to tell Rush he had to knock it off, because his temper was costing the team. The next morning at the team hotel, at the crack of dawn, the reporters covering the team all got calls from the front desk telling them, "Coach Rush has scheduled a major announcement." The writers, some still in their pajamas, bleary-eyed and no doubt hung over from newspaper-expense-account gin, shuffled their way into the conference room to find Rush waiting for them.

He didn't have a major announcement. In fact, he didn't have an announcement of any kind. What he did have was a bone to pick with each and every one of them. He'd been up early, called back to Boston where, because of the three-hour time difference, the early edition newspapers were already on sale, and he found out what negative things they'd all written about him. He then proceeded to harangue the lot of them for as long as they'd sit there and listen.

Still, for all of Clive Rush's general instability, and despite a 4-10 record, he managed to survive the 1969 season.

ALUMNI STADIUM, BOSTON COLLEGE

After the season, the Patriots once again found themselves relocating to a new "permanent" home, this time to Boston College's Alumni Field. But there was a growing sense of urgency that they would need a stadium of their own in order to survive as a franchise.

The arrangement among AFL teams was that they split all gate revenue, with the home team keeping 60 percent and the visitors getting 40. And since the Patriots spent those early years playing in tiny, mostly dilapidated ballparks, and their home gate receipts were so low, they were actually making more money playing road games than they made at home.

And some of Sullivan's fellow owners saw it as the equivalent of welfare. Sonny Werblin of the New York Jets made it clear that he, for one, resented it. "Billy, I think this love affair you have with Boston is terrific," he said. "But don't ask me to keep paying for that affection." So Billy's problem was twofold. He needed to build a stadium of his own with no money and no land or else risk being forced to sell his franchise. But he couldn't just worry about the long term, because he was constantly scrambling to be sure he had a place to play next season, and in some instances, next week.

Probably no modern pro sports team ever had less operating capital than the Boston Patriots. The cheapness of the organization is legendary. Their practice facility for most of the '60s was a dirt lot at Phillips Academy high school in Andover, Massachusetts. They had no weight room and no whirlpool. To this day, players tell stories of film sessions held in an equipment shed, with a bed sheet hung over a rusty water pipe used as a movie screen while they sat on boxes and milk crates. It was even worse on rainy days. "The roof leaked and I remember the coach kept a bunch of light bulbs in his pocket," guard Lennie St. Jean said. "Water would come through the roof, hit the projector bulb and burn it out. We'd have to wait while he replaced it."

Not that the film sessions were of much use anyway, as the AFL had no rule regarding home and road uniforms. So often times both teams would dress in dark shirts, which was fine for the people at the game, but on the black-and-white game film they were indistinguishable.

MUTINY ON THE BEDSPREAD

On one Patriots road trip to Buffalo, the plan was for the team to fly in the day of the game and then fly home right after, rather than spring for an overnight stay at a hotel. They'd go right from the airport to the stadium with just enough time to eat, get suited up, and take the field for warm-ups. The problem was that the time of the flight to New York was changed to much earlier in the day. So, the team would have hours to kill and no place to do it. Patriots director Paul Sonnabend's family happened to own a motel in Buffalo, and he made arrangements so that the players could get rooms for the afternoon. But the Pats had also made a deal with the manager: no messing up the beds. Players could lie down on top of the bedspread, but they couldn't sleep in the beds because he didn't want to have to pay the chambermaids to come in later to make them up again. Any player who pulled back his covers would be fined ten bucks.

Now, this was 40 years before *Dateline:* NBC and CSI would shine black lights on hotel bedspreads and show us that they all basically look like Jackson Pollack paintings from all the bodily fluids and DNA all over them. Nevertheless, most of the players simply refused to cooperate, just on general principle. A mini-uprising took place in which the players ripped back their covers and took their nappies between the nice, clean sheets, like free men.

It's not clear how much the Bedspread Rebellion cost ownership. But the players knew they had struck a blow against tyranny, oppression, and skinflintiness, like true patriots.

The Patriots were like a married couple saving up for a place of their own while living in substandard housing and moving every time their lease was up. Sullivan was looking for a home for his team while barely having enough for first month/last month/security deposit. To do so, he had to battle landlords, the elements, his fellow owners, local politicians, and sometimes his employees. He was constantly putting out fires.

Figuratively and literally.

In the middle of a preseason game against the Washington Redskins on August 16, 1969, a fire broke out in the grandstand.[11] Not under the stands. Not adjacent to the stands. Literally the wooden bleachers themselves burst into flames. While fans scrambled out of their seats and ran for their lives down the steps onto the field, the flames quickly spread and the air was choked with thick black clouds of smoke. There are no reports of anyone getting hurt in the chaos, and details on what actually started the blaze are murky. But it's hard to imagine a more perfect symbol for the state of the franchise. I like to imagine that the fire marshal inspecting the damage wrote in his report, "Suspected Cause of Fire: Metaphor."

The combination of a mentally unstable coach and a cramped, run-down stadium worked out about as badly as you'd expect. The crowds at BC were notoriously rowdy and abusive, a bad situation for a mercurial, thin-skinned crackpot like Rush. He repeatedly got into it with hecklers, which (to the surprise of no one but Rush) created a vicious cycle of more heckling. The school's administration was furious. Billy Sullivan was mortified. He pulled Rush aside and explained to him that the Pats were barely hanging on financially and it was only because Boston College was willing to do them a favor that they had a place to play at all. Besides, he said, pretty soon it wouldn't be their problem. He explained to his coach that he'd been talking with Harvard about moving into their stadium the following year. The deal wasn't done and he was telling Rush this in the strictest confidence, and asked him not to mention it to anyone until everything was finalized. Rush publicly apologized to BC, and the controversy died down.

At least for a few days, which is how long Rush kept his mouth shut. With the team leaving for its next road game, he kicked the entire press corps off the team plane because he had something super-secret to tell his players. When the press was gone, he announced to the team that he'd been talking personally to the president of Harvard and worked out a deal to move the Patriots there. But he ordered the players not to mention it to reporters or tell anyone else until after the season was over. When the press was allowed back on board, they found out immediately what Rush had said.

From the flight attendant.

For the 1970 season, the Patriots succeeded in relocating to Harvard, but not much else. The one story from that season that made its way into New England lore to be passed down from generation to generation really isn't about anything the team accomplished. But it might be the most quintessentially Patriots story ever told. It's the legend of Bob Gladieux.

HARPO

Bob "Harpo" Gladieux was a standout halfback for Notre Dame during part of Ara Parseghian's glory years. He also had the distinction of being the only Patriots player to get a mention in the movie *Rudy*, during the bar scene where Rudy is sucking back giant mugs of draft beer and hitting on Mary from the booster's club before he spills it to her that he's not an ND student. But Gladieux's college skills didn't advertise him as much of a pro prospect. He was the Patriots eighth-round draft pick in 1969 and hung on with them as a special teams player and rarely used backup running back. At the end of his second training camp, Harpo was cut. The news didn't sit well with him, but the team told him to stick around because more cuts might be coming, and if they did, he'd get the call. So he stayed around Boston, spending the next few days knocking back drinks at every dive in the South End and wallowing in his own misery.

The Pats opened the season, and Gladieux and one of his friends decided, "To hell with it," they'd just go. So they filled a cooler, grabbed a few packs of cigarettes, drove to Harvard Stadium and tailgated out of Harpo's AMC Gremlin. (Note: I have no idea what kind of car he drove. I'm claiming the literary license to make it a Gremlin because it's the worst car of all time.)

Half-drunk, Gladieux and his buddy bought tickets and found their seats. What they didn't know was that Patriots Larry Carwell and John Charles were beefing with the team over money and refused to sign contracts. So the Patriots, desperate to fill the roster spots, took a chance. Over the PA system, they made an announcement: "Will Bob Gladieux please report to the trainer's room?" Gladieux's friend was off buying beer. Harpo had no idea what to do. After a moment or two of confusion, he went down to the locker room to find out why he had been paged; they told him to suit up, he was going in. His buddy came back to the seats, beers in hand, but Gladieux was nowhere to be found.

But it didn't take long to locate him.

At the end of the opening kickoff, the call came over the PA from the announcer: "Kick returned by Jake Scott. Tackle on the play by No. 24, Bob Gladieux . . ."

The Patriots managed to pull off an upset over Miami in the opener, but things went downhill fast from there. They lost their next five games, then faced a home game against Buffalo. During pregame warmups, Rush complained of feeling lightheaded and dizzy. The team doctor, Burton Nault, checked Rush's vitals and found he was suffering from tachycardia, which is doctor-speak for an abnormally fast heartbeat. After calling around, they found a bed for him at a hotel up the street. Nault gave him a sedative and ordered him to rest. Sullivan asked Offensive Coordinator John Mazur to step in and coach the team on an emergency basis. But Rush refused to follow the doctor's orders. Even in a sedated stupor, he managed to get hold of his personal doctor and get his OK to coach. So by halftime, Rush reappeared on the Boston sidelines. In the turmoil, the Pats got thumped, 45–10.

The Patriots medical and coaching staffs warned Sullivan and the team's directors that Rush was coming unraveled and that they had to step in before he destroyed himself. The directors met with Rush's doctor, then went to the coach's house to talk to him personally. The talks went on until 2:00 a.m. In a rare understatement, Billy called it, "a tough night."

Sullivan and the board agreed to do the decent thing. There was no way Rush could coach anymore. He was clearly a man in crisis, sick both physically and emotionally. So they offered to give him a leave of absence, with full pay, so that he could get back on his feet and not have to worry about providing for his family. They promoted Mazur to head coach. Stand-up guy that he was, Mazur was reluctant to take the job under the circumstances, but Billy reminded him that he was under contract; besides, Rush was gone regardless of Mazur's decision. The next day, Rush addressed his players to give his side of the story, and one who was there remarked what a pathetic sight he was: "It was like watching a man die before you." The club then held a press conference so Sullivan could explain the reason for the coaching change to the public, while respecting Rush's privacy and not giving away too much about his condition.

Then the other bomb dropped. The assembled media got word that Clive Rush was holding his own press conference immediately afterward. He told them he was refusing the club's offer. "I have resigned effective Monday at midnight. That release they sent out about a leave of absence is inaccurate." He then went off on an angry diatribe at every member of the media and the team who he felt had ever done him wrong, including Danny Marr, the guy who'd saved his life a year and a half earlier in the electrified mic incident. In order to save face and not appear like he was coming unraveled, Clive Rush instead chose professional and financial suicide. Sullivan's people, realizing they were dealing with a sick man, refused to take the cheese and said nothing. And the most bizarre episode in the very bizarre history of the team was over.

A few footnotes about Clive Rush's career. First, his former boss from the Jets, Weeb Ewbank, tried to do a solid for an old colleague by getting him another job in coaching. Knowing that Rush wasn't fit for any kind of stress, Ewbank lined up just about the most low-pressure football job one could imagine, at the U.S. Merchant Marine Academy in King's Point, New York. Still, Rush couldn't hack it. He was unable to make it through his first year before he resigned.

Footnote No. 2 involves Woody Hayes of all people, the Ohio State coaching legend whose career went up in flames in a nanosecond on national television when he socked a Clemson player on the jaw in the Gator Bowl. The day after Hayes got fired in disgrace, an army of media descended on his house in Columbus to find that he wasn't home. But Clive Rush was there. He'd come for a visit because he figured his old coach could use some advice from someone who knew a thing or two about life after you've destroyed your career.

And finally, Clive Rush's contribution to the sport of football will always be defined by his one, almost-brilliant, practically groundbreaking, near-innovation. Great football minds are known for the systems they developed. The aforementioned Sid Gillman and the modern passing offense. Vince Lombardi perfected the Power Sweep. Buddy Ryan's 46 Defense and Bill Walsh's West Coast Offense. Rush's legacy is the brief, shining moment when he gave the world the worst concept ever.

THE BLACK POWER DEFENSE

In the 1960s and 70s, racial tensions in America were arguably at their highest point since the Civil War. The Civil Rights Act of 1964 and the Voting Rights Act of 1965 put an end to Jim Crow laws. Malcolm X and Martin Luther King were assassinated in 1965 and 1968, respectively. The Watts Riots in Los Angeles in 1965 left 34 dead and did $40 million of damage. At the 1968 Olympics, two black American athletes created a firestorm when they raised their fists during the national anthem. In 1974, a federal judge would order the forced busing of public school kids in Boston to desegregate the schools, and the city would explode in racial upheaval. And it was in that climate that Clive Rush decided to sit on top of the powder keg and start playing with matches. During that 1969 season, he got it in his head to motivate his team by creating an all-black defensive unit. The idea was to inspire the team by appealing to his black players' sense of pride. He called it the Black Power Defense.

There were two problems with it. The first was that it was a terrible (and inherently racist) idea. The second, more practical problem is that he didn't have 11 black defensive players. But he was so gung-ho about the idea that he swapped some black offensive players over to defense. No one but Rush thought it was a good idea, but he was the boss, so they went along.

The BPD got its chance in week eight of the season, in a game against the Houston Oilers. The Pats were losing 0-7, and Rush was getting increasingly desperate and anxious to try his new scheme. He even tipped off a reporter, and news of it made it into the papers the morning of the game. Early in the first half, the Patriots regular defense sacked Oilers QB Don Trull on second down, setting up a third and long.

Now was the time to make some history. Rush called for the BPD and they took the field. Trull went back to pass again and spotted a Houston receiver wide open down the middle of the field, which is understandable given that a handful of the defenders had never played defense a day in their lives. Trull hit his open man for a long gain and a first down, at which point Rush sent his regular unit back out and the Black Power Defense was never heard from again.

On the subject of race relations, even when the Patriots did something right, they did it wrong. No intention was so noble that it was beyond the club's ability to screw it up.

ROMMIE LOUDD

Rommie Loudd was originally a linebacker and tight end for the Patriots. And in 1966, in the midst of all the racial tension in a city where the Red Sox were the last Major League team to integrate, the Patriots made Loudd the AFL's first black assistant coach. They later promoted him to director of player personnel and then director of pro scouting. Loudd then went on to become the first black owner of a pro sports franchise, when he founded the Florida Blazers of the short-lived World Football League.

On the other hand, you can make a case that Rommie Loudd was the last kind of guy you want to have pioneering *anything*. When Branch Rickey decided to break baseball's color barrier, he tabbed Jackie Robinson, a man of strength of character and impeccable moral fiber. When the Pats chose Loudd to tear down the barriers of Injustice, break through the glass ceiling of Discrimination and open the window of Opportunity, they managed to crash through the patio door of Habitual Criminal Behavior.

For starters, he had a criminal record long before he ever came to Boston. In 1957, when Loudd was 24, he and two companions were charged with various "moral offenses" involving three boys aged 12, 13, and 15, and were later convicted of "sexual misconduct." What exactly happened is unknown, but with charges like that, there's hardly a best-case scenario. In 1975, when Loudd was running the Blazers, he was convicted again, this time to two concurrent 14-year sentences for conspiracy and delivery of cocaine. That was the bad news; the good news is that those convictions got prosecutors to drop charges that Loudd had embezzled state sales-tax revenues.

He served three years in jail before being paroled, became a church pastor, and—as they say—turned his life around. There's no disputing that Loudd had a successful career with the Patriots and served them well, or that the team deserves credit for breaking the coaching color barrier. But Jackie Robinson this guy was not.

The Patriots found themselves in a legal entanglement right at the start of the 1970s. But it didn't involve criminal charges. Instead, they found themselves in the uniquely Patriots position of being abandoned and then sued by their most important player.

JOE KAPP

In 1970 the Patriots' general manager was George Sauer, who stumbled upon a deal to land a potential franchise player in former Canadian star turned Minnesota Vikings Super Bowl quarterback Joe Kapp. But what Sauer got instead was a legal nightmare. The equivalent of thinking you've hooked a tuna, but when you haul it onto the boat it's a shark.

Kapp had been drafted out of California in 1959. In a long and complicated story, he played in both Canada and in the NFL and proved himself in both countries by leading teams to the Grey Cup and the Super Bowl. But he wasn't being paid like one, mostly due to rules in both leagues that restricted player movement.

Kapp spent the summer of 1970 without a team. Billy Sullivan was particularly smitten with him. Kapp was a handsome Mexican-American household name with the bona fides of a proven winner who could put butts in seats. So Sauer swung a trade for him, contingent on the club signing him to a contract.

There was one thing Sullivan, the Patriots, and the entire NFL didn't see coming, though: Joe Kapp's agent, John Elliot Cook.

Cook, like any self-respecting, blood-sucking sports agent, was hell-bent on getting his client the maximum money he could. That was no surprise to Sullivan, who willingly forked over a three-year, no-cut, $600,000-a-year contract, which he called "the biggest contract in football today, coach or player." But Cook had bigger goals than just lining Joe Kapp's pockets; he was doing what grifters call "playing the long con." His ultimate goal was to bring down the whole NFL system that bound players to teams. He was angling to hit the league with an anti-trust lawsuit, and Kapp was going to be his test case. He wanted *Kapp v. the Boston Patriots* to set a legal precedent. *That* was the can of worms Billy Sullivan unwittingly opened when he made the Kapp deal.

Sullivan and Cook worked out the parameters of a deal and signed a "memo of agreement," which basically stated that they agreed to a deal in principle, pending the signing of a detailed, formal contract, which would then supersede the memo. It was standard operating procedure, and Kapp was allowed to report to the Patriots.

The first sign that something was wrong—terribly, terribly wrong—came when the NFL headquarters contacted the Patriots asking where Kapp's contract was. The way this works is kind of like closing on a house: the contract is signed by the team and sent to the player. He then signs it and sends it to his agent. Once the agent signs it, he sends it to the league office. And once that circle is closed, the contract is binding. The Pats had sent it to Kapp, and he claimed he'd sent it to Cook. But apparently that was as far as it went. Commissioner Pete Rozelle's office kept asking for the contract. The Patriots, fearing they'd lose their starting quarterback, kept stalling. GM Sauer did what any red-blooded American does whenever a bill collector calls; he lied through his teeth and told them "It's on the way," and that they'd get it any day. That ruse managed to keep the wolves away for the entire 1970 season.

By May of 1971, Rozelle told all parties involved that if there wasn't a legit contract by the start of training camp, Kapp wouldn't be allowed to report. When he did, Cook told him to leave. Billy Sullivan was crushed. He liked Kapp, and actually helped him carry his luggage to his car.

But whatever feelings Sullivan was feeling, they weren't important enough for him to share with John Mazur. Apparently, Billy's notion of a need-to-know basis didn't extend to his head coach, because all that time Mazur had no idea what was going on. He'd heard some vague mention of "contract problems" with his quarterback. If his key player was trying to set labor law precedent, it was news to him. He went out to the start of practice, found out that his quarterback had left without saying so much as "goodbye," and the two literally never saw each other again.

The headlines in the Boston papers the next day said "KAPP QUITS!" He never played another down of football in his life.

Cook, on behalf of Kapp, filed suit against the Patriots, Sullivan, the NFL, and basically everyone involved in professional football (short of the cheerleaders and the kid who runs on the field after a kickoff to pick up the kicking tee), seeking $12 million in damages. But a jury couldn't wrap their brain around how a guy making $200,000 a year could be "damaged," so they gave him the old "You'll get nothing and like it."

There are several weird footnotes to Kapp's career. First, that he went into acting for awhile. He made appearances in movies like *Semi-Tough*, *Two Minute Warning*, and the classic *The Longest Yard*. Eventually, though, he returned to football, where his major claim to fame was being the winning coach in the most famous ending in college football history, the game where Cal ran the game-winning kickoff return through the Stanford band. Later, he went back to Canada, where as the GM of the BC Lions, he signed Boston College quarterback Doug Flutie, who became one of the great players in CFL history and eventually retired as a member of the Patriots. It's a Circle of Life kind of thing.

CARL GARRETT

One player of that era who Mazur was able to keep tabs on was Carl Garrett, a running back the club drafted in 1969 out of that noted football factory, New Mexico Highlands University. When Garrett arrived, Mazur was still the backfield coach. He took Garrett under his wing and told the kid if he worked hard and stuck with the program, Mazur would make him rookie of the year. And he succeeded. "The Road Runner" averaged 5.0 yards a carry, was voted second team All-AFL and won the ROTY over the No. 1 overall pick, a guy named O.J. Simpson.

It didn't take much time for the Patriots to realize what kind of a humanitarian the man was. Garrett quickly established that he was going to be one of those classic cases of a guy who's a coach's dream on the field but a nightmare off it. Mazur once said that in a review of game films to grade each player, he counted only four mental errors Garrett had committed in an entire 14-game season. But in the locker room, he was surly and unapproachable, ubersensitive with a hair-trigger temper. Anything they said to him stood a good chance of being taken either as criticism or racist or both. Garrett was also legendary for pulling late nights out on the town with women who weren't named "Mrs. Carl Garrett," a practice that in a simpler time was referred to as "a clubhouse distraction."

Another problem was that Garrett was always in danger of being shipped off to Vietnam. The only thing keeping him from active military duty was his National Guard commitment, which required him to do nothing more than attend meetings. Still, even the prospect of a two-year tour of the Ho Chi Minh Trail wasn't enough to stop Garrett from regularly blowing off those meetings. So Mazur sat him down for a heart-to-heart. And to get the point across, told Garrett he was fining him 1500 bucks and asked him, "If you were me, what would you have done?" Garrett thought about it a second and said, "I'd have fined the sucker two thousand dollars."

Eventually, Mazur was promoted to head coach in the middle of the 1970 season, but it only made matters worse. The two men were close, owing a lot of their individual professional successes to each other. This not only bred resentment among Garrett's teammates and charges of favoritism, it encouraged Garrett to walk all over the coach. He routinely blew off meetings. He skipped practices, allegedly for "personal reasons," with Mazur's blessing. The dissension was threatening to rip the club apart. Once it became clear that Mazur was the only one in the organization who wasn't fed up with Garrett's act, management decided to cut their losses and in the offseason traded him to the Dallas Cowboys for another talented-but-troubled coach-killing headache, Duane Thomas.

For his part, Garrett reacted to the deal by taking the high road, if by taking the high road you mean he demeaned his ex-teammates publicly and made it clear that he thought Thomas would hate playing in Boston. "Thomas is gonna find a *big* difference when he gets to the Patriots," he said. "He's gonna miss all those blockers he had in Dallas." To the Patriots' humiliation, the quote was picked up and included in every wire-service story about the transaction.

Unfortunately for him, Garrett would go on to share one other trait with O.J. Simpson, one related to how they treated the ladies when their playing days were done. In 1985, he was convicted of rape and sentenced to nine years in jail. He later failed to register as a sex offender, had his bail revoked, and in 2005 he was sent back to jail for another two years.

Patriots historians have always called this era "The Nomad Years," but that's not entirely accurate. Nomads *want* to move around; it's their culture. Nomads aren't looking to settle down. They're rolling stones, and wherever they lay their hat is their home. The Patriots of the 1960s were more like the Israelites, wandering in the wilderness for years in search of a promised land and pretty much being treated like crap wherever they pitched their tents.

6

BUILDING AND LOAN

★ ★

George, it's deep in the race for a man to want his
own roof and walls and fireplace. And we're helping
him get those things in our "shabby little office."
POP BAILEY, *It's a Wonderful Life*

The Patriots were homeless drifters, shuttling from borrowed stadium to borrowed stadium like a moveable hobo camp, and pressure was mounting on the team to fix their situation by building a stadium of their own or moving the franchise. Other cities, anxious to lure pro football teams, smelled blood in the water and started circling. Birmingham, Seattle, Jacksonville, Memphis, and even Montreal were rumored to be interested. But with Tampa Bay, it went way beyond rumor and into an all-out and very public seduction that spanned a few years.

In November of '69, the Patriots were scheduled to play at Miami until the Dolphins moved the game to Tampa. And no housewife in Vegas tossing her room key on stage at a Tom Jones show was ever more blatant in her intentions than Tampa was toward the Patriots. A plane flew overhead pulling a banner that read "Welcome, Tampa Patriots." They had a presentation where they unveiled a team logo and uniforms. The governor of Florida met with Billy Sullivan and promised a year of free rent if he'd agree to move the team. Publicly, Billy was noncommittal, and in the understatement of the year called the whole experience "unnerving." And the pressure from the other owners to straighten out the stadium mess was about to get a whole lot worse.

The AFL was merging with the NFL, a huge break for the old Foolish Club and a financial windfall for them all. But the NFL wasn't going to mess up their own good thing by letting just any penny-ante operation in. The merger deal required any team joining the new NFL to have a stadium with a minimum capacity of 46,200, which seems like a pretty arbitrary number until you realize that George Halas' Chicago Bears were playing at Wrigley Field, home of the Cubs, which held (surprise!) 46,200. Even with the extra bleachers,

Fenway could barely hold 40,000, and even then only if you sold seats on the flagpole and bribed the fire marshal to ignore the death trap you were inviting the public into. Boston College's stadium had a capacity of 25,000. Harvard held 40,000, but any thought of expanding it was shot down when the aptly named university president Nathan M. Pusey started making high-minded public pronouncements about the "fundamental incompatibility" between amateur and professional athletics. Something had to be done and Patriots management knew it. The future of pro football in Boston depended on building a stadium. It had to be quick. It had to be big. And most of all, it had to be done on the cheap. Sports, politics, and revenge. And nothing brings all three together like a pro team looking to build a place to play.

This is another one of those situations where you have to give Sullivan his due. Whatever his shortcomings as a businessman and a realist, the man took a back seat to no one when it came to dreaming big.

By Sullivan's own estimate, at least 60 different stadium proposals were floated during those years. And officially, 28 of them were put up for a vote and shot down. The Patriots were trying to build within the city limits of Boston, which meant dealing with the Massachusetts State House and the Boston City Council, two organizations so historically corrupt that they make all other legislatures look like Plato's Aristocracy.

There was another governmental entity he had to deal with as well. In Massachusetts, there is no useful public service that can't be used as a means for sleazy politicians to grab power. And their preferred method of doing so is creating a state authority. Authorities are unelected, unaccountable, quasi-governmental agencies established to do . . . something. Anything. There's one that runs the Mass Turnpike. Another is in charge of the airport. There's one that allegedly handles conventions. But for the most part, they're tasked with the much more important business of providing patronage jobs to the friends, relatives, cronies, donors, and union thugs who support the politicians who set up the authorities. They're the self-sustaining perpetual motion machine of state politics.

So it was that in 1962 the Massachusetts legislature, seeing a state and a nation on the verge of political upheaval, social unrest, and war, decided to take swift and decisive action on the crucial business of getting sports stadiums built. And they approved the creation of the Greater Boston Stadium Authority.

You can accuse Billy Sullivan of being many things, but a political novice isn't one of them. Whatever promises he had to make, favors he had to grant, or palms he had to grease, he obviously did, because the solons named him the first chairman of the GBSA. Sullivan, the man most in need of a new stadium, was put in charge of the stadium search. It was the most obvious conflict of interest in state history. And the Red Sox, who were also supposed to be involved in the process, screamed bloody murder. But their protests fell upon deaf ears. The legislature reappointed Sullivan to two more three-year terms after that.

And a fat lot of good it did him. A huge part of the problem was the enabling legislation that established the GBSA in the first place. There were so many restrictions placed on the search that it made success almost impossible. For starters, the stadium had to be built within Boston's city limits. Second, by law it was required to have a dome. And last, the thing couldn't be backed by credit from the state. Besides those minor points, it was smooth sailing all the way.

After months of looking into possible sites, the one that seemed most plausible was in Boston's South Station area. It was in the city's financial district, near the Federal Reserve Bank. Accessible by mass transit. Just off the expressway. Though the area was a little congested, it made the most practical sense as a stadium location.

With one minor problem, which led to several major problems. That whole area of the city is landfill from the colonial days. At one time, Boston was not much more than a peninsula, until the hills around it were leveled and the soil used to fill in the harbor on both sides. And one of those sides was the spot upon which they wanted to build a massive stadium. It had been built up with loose landfill hauled down by mule teams and tossed in the water by guys with buckets and shovels. Putting the stadium in South Station would require drilling pilings down into the bedrock, which added $14 million to the cost. In addition, there was no parking in the area, so a garage, possibly an underground one, had to be included. And just for chuckles, the plans also called for a dome with a retractable roof. Why not?

Rather than be intimidated by the escalating costs and obvious implausibility of the project, Sullivan soldiered on. The less likely success seemed, the higher his expectations went. To help with the cost, he brought the Celtics and Bruins in and offered to build them an 18,000-seat arena to replace the decaying toilet that was Boston Garden.

That brought the total projected cost to 90 million bucks. Years later, Sullivan said he had the financing all ready to get the deal done, but at the last minute the Bruins scrapped everything. The Bruins owned the Garden and the Celtics were their tenant (which is still the case in the newly built TD Garden), and the Bruins didn't want to give up that arrangement. They demanded the right of first refusal on all scheduling conflicts, to (in Billy's words) "keep giving the Celtics the shaft, just like they'd always done." And the whole fiscal house of cards came down.

Every few months another potential deal came up, looked promising, then collapsed. In one, the city offered to build the stadium and asked only that the state build the roads leading in. The state refused. There was another where the state offered to pay for the stadium with revenue from adding racing dates at Suffolk Downs horse track. This time the city refused. Billy got word that the last deal had fallen through while he was out in Honolulu at the AFL team meetings. And he took it about as well as you'd expect anyone would take having his hopes and dreams treated like a soccer ball by competing teams of sleazy Massachusetts pols. The failure of this final deal hurt, especially because the proposed stadium site was a vacant lot near Sullivan's oil company office. "I'll be able to look out my window and see that rat-infested dump forever now," he said. He told the other owners that for all intents and purposes this meant the end of pro football in Boston.

But just then, fate stepped in. Fate in the form of a chubby, bearded little football writer from a suburban newspaper.

Ron Hobson was the Patriots beat writer for the Quincy *Patriot Ledger*, the paper of record for those on Boston's South Shore back in the days when suburban papers actually had reporters, and weren't just the place you went to for obituaries and school bus schedules. Every Saturday he did one of those gambling/prediction columns that are everywhere now. But Hobson did his in character, as a guy he called "The Humble Prognosticator," a football genius with a mansion and a butler. It was quirky and weird and hilarious, as were his Monday game recaps and daily Pats updates. It was Hobson who approached Billy Sullivan in Hawaii and made the suggestion that he take another look at putting his team in Foxboro.

The Foxboro site was something Sullivan had looked at back in 1958 when he was still scrambling for a franchise and before he signed his first lease with BU. The land was owned by E.M. Loew of the Loew's theater chain. Hobson's connection to the place was the horse track there, Bay State Racetrack, which was managed by his father.

It's important to note this wasn't just any horse track. To suggest it was a normal horse track would give the place more credit than it deserved. Horse racing has a time-honored tradition of gentlemen breeders, trainers, and jockeys racing thoroughbreds as generations of their forebears had done. It's the Sport of Kings. But Bay State Racetrack was something entirely different. It was a harness track. Meaning the horses pulled riders behind them on little two-wheeled, chariot-looking things. More importantly, they didn't run; they trotted. So it was the animal equivalent of walking races at the Olympics, the single stupidest sporting event ever devised by man. And every day, people drove to Foxboro to bet on it. Needless to say, they'd never be confused for the crowd at Churchill Downs on Kentucky Derby Day.

But what Bay State lacked in elegance, it made up for in abundant, cheap real estate. There was more than enough unused land next to the harness track to fit a football stadium. The site also had an accessible location, stuck as it was between Boston and Providence and between Interstates 95 and 495. It was everything the Patriots needed.

Sullivan didn't have anything close to the money he'd need to buy the land. But once again, to his credit, he didn't let a minor detail like that stop him. He talked Loew into donating the land to the town of Foxboro. In exchange, he'd get to keep the parking concession money and, theoretically, make a bundle as the value of the rest of his property went up.

As a general rule, Massachusetts towns are the not-in-my-backyard capitals of the world, so there was every reason to think Foxboro residents would never go for having an NFL team in town, screwing up their commute to church seven or so Sundays a year. So again, Billy figured out a way to pay off the locals without it costing him anything. He promised that the town would get increased property tax revenue and Foxboro residents would get first dibs on all stadium jobs. Then in 30 years, the stadium itself would become the property of the town. It was pure political brilliance from the old Irishman. And the resolution passed at a town meeting with 98 percent of the vote.

The futuristic $25 million domed palace in downtown Boston he had planned on ten years earlier was now an open-air prefab tenement next to a sleazy horse track in a town no one had ever heard of and was going up for $6.7 million. It was a shoestring budget in a down market for shoestrings. And to offset the costs further, Sullivan cut a deal to sell the naming rights of the place to the Schaefer Brewing Company for $1 million. Today, a shovel doesn't go in the dirt for a new ballpark without some corporation's name already attached to it. But at that time, when other stadiums were getting inspiring, lofty names like Soldier Field and Memorial Coliseum and Veteran's Stadium, it seemed tawdry. The Chicago Cubs played at Wrigley Field, but that was named after the owner, who also owned a gum company. This was an out-and-out sale of the name of the stadium, which, while a shrewd business move, made the Patriots franchise seem cheap and amateurish.

Frankly, it didn't help that the namers were manufacturers of a crappy beer. Today, a generation of hipsters have brought almost-defunct labels like Pabst Blue Ribbon, Schlitz, and Narragansett back and made them trendy again, while Schaefer is on the brink of extinction. And to show Schaefer was a product of its time, in the '70s their slogan was "Schaefer is the one beer to have when you're having more than one." Try getting a catch phrase like *that* past Mothers Against Drunk Driving.

It took 326 days of construction and a mere $200,000 over budget (well within the normal margin for error, but an amount Billy Sullivan flipped out about nonetheless) and Schaefer Stadium opened for business on August 15, 1971, for a preseason game against the New York Giants.

And as if to prove to the world that, new stadium and all, these were still the same old Patriots, that historic first game was an utter fiasco.

As anyone who ever went to a game at Schaefer will tell you, it was an ordeal even under the best of conditions. But that first preseason opener is the stuff of legend. People who went to that one pass down the story like old soldiers telling tales of an epic battle they survived.

For starters, the roads were gridlocked. The traffic crush was so bad and the road configurations were so poorly planned that thousands of people literally didn't make it to their seats until the second half of the game. Thousands more abandoned all hope, turned around and went home without seeing a snap. After the game, the roads going out were the exact same situation, in reverse. Traffic leaving the parking lots was at a standstill. Cars stuck in the line to leave ran out of gas where they stood. Thousands of other cars didn't even make it out of their spots until the early morning hours of the next day. The Roman Colosseum, which was completed in A.D. 80, held 50,000 people and was designed to empty out in approximately 12 minutes. If Titus' architect was as bad at traffic flow as the one Sullivan hired, the Empire never would've survived the first century.

Another thing the ancient Romans had was an aqueduct that brought them running water, which puts them *two* up on the Patriots. The stadium didn't have nearly the water pressure it needed to allow for 61,000 bladders filled with Schaefer beer. The toilets and urinals all over the stadium wouldn't flush and eventually filled up, then overflowed. The floors of the bathrooms were flooded with inches of raw sewage. Legend has it that stadium staff directed people away from the bathrooms and into empty storage rooms and told them to use those instead. And some who were there were eyewitnesses to the waking nightmare of a man taking a dump in a cardboard box. If there is a Hell on this Earth, it can't be any worse than a room filled with drunks peeing skunky, watered-down beer all over the walls and floors. I'm sure that for most of the guys there, those storage rooms were their Vietnam, though the trip home from Vietnam took less time.

The water situation was a crisis of major proportions. After that first game's septic catastrophe, the Foxboro Board of Health let it be known they were not keen on letting the public wade through ankle-high poop water. They made it clear there was no way the Pats were opening for business unless they could prove that the plumbing in the stadium worked. Additionally, the builders had never bothered to put in lower urinals for kids, which meant the kind of father-son bonding moments no one wants to remember. So with the home opener less than a month away, contractors scrambled to increase the pressure and change the urinals before the Patriots dream of having their own home went, a little too aptly, down the drain. After weeks of work, the board of health came back for the inspection. And in one of the all-time unique, surreal sports moments, the Patriots lined up every able-bodied volunteer they could for a demonstration. Front office people, coaches, players, stadium staff, even media members, fanned out around the stadium to every bathroom they could. When a horn sounded over the public address system, that was their signal to start flushing. Guys running along rows of urinals pulling the levers as fast as they could. Women racing from one toilet stall to the next, busting through the doors, flushing as they went. But the water pressure held. The inspectors signed off. Only the Patriots could've had their entire future riding on the prospect of crap making it down a drain. But it did. The Royal Flush worked, and at long last big-time pro football in New England finally had a home of its own.

The one thing Billy Sullivan felt uncomfortable about, though, was the idea of calling his team the Boston Patriots, given that they were now so far outside the city and as close to Providence as they were to Boston. So he brainstormed the clever and catchy Bay State Patriots, which not only reflected the fact that they were now a regional team, it paid homage to the racetrack and had sort of a nice ring to it. So they were officially the Bay State Patriots. At least for however long it took someone on his staff to break the news to him that everyone was going to be calling his pride and joy the "B.S. Patriots."

And thus, the New England Patriots were born.

By no means did having a new, bargain-basement stadium mean the end of the bizarre happenings for the Patriots, despite the true, luxury-like working plumbing. But as so often is the case when you've hit rock bottom—or spent most of your 12-year existence at rock bottom, as the Pats had—there's nowhere to go but up. And for the 1970s Patriots, the journey toward respectability began at home. Their own home.

Because if they did nothing else that year but embarrass themselves on and off the field, at least they finally got a stadium built and their troubles were over.

If by "over," you mean "just beginning."

7
GROWING PAINS

★ ★

Let me tell you something, my friend. Hope is a
dangerous thing. Hope can drive a man insane.
RED BOYD, *The Shawshank Redemption*

It's hard to say for sure what causes us to like the things we like. During our formative years, every human soul gets exposed to an infinite number of stimuli from the world around us. They mix together with our instincts, genetics, circumstances, and various outside influences. Some kind of biochemical reaction takes place that forms the cocktail our brains sip while they sort out our likes from our dislikes, our loves from our hates. Or something like that.

Some of the things we're exposed to, we ignore. Others, we despise. Some we take a passing interest in. Others imprint on us. And still more bore their way into our heads, wrap themselves around our cerebral cortex, and take control of us for life. What separates our loves from our hates really is one of the great questions of all time, one that greater minds than mine have struggled with. It's the whole nature vs. nurture thing. Heredity vs. environment. Which has not only fueled debate among great thinkers, it was the plot of at least half of the best *Three Stooges* episodes.

But if I had to pick one factor that influences what we love, and what we stay in love with for our whole lives, it would be timing. Timing, as they say, is everything.

I've never met a baby boomer who didn't think Bob Dylan was an unparalleled genius who touched their lives and forever changed the world. But to anyone who wasn't in Dylan's specific target demographic, he's just that guy with the nasally voice who convinced generations of no-talent subway musicians they could sing.

I happen to be part of what social scientists have called the "Baby Bunchers." We are that narrow band of kids who were preteens when *The Brady Bunch* dominated American television and who know every episode by heart.

But try to get a kid today to sit through one episode and he'll act like you've put him in the time-out chair (and not be wrong to feel that way). Admittedly, *The Brady Bunch* was garbage. But it was *our* garbage. And we'll take it to the grave with us.

It just so happened that I was at my most impressionable age at exactly the moment in time when the New England Patriots were finally hitting the big time. I was too young to appreciate just how amateurish the whole operation had been since before I was born. The whole decade they spent bumming around from one stadium to the next like vagrants didn't register with me. All I knew was that they now had a place of their own to play. They had a new name. They had the first pick in the 1971 NFL draft and used it to land a franchise quarterback in Jim Plunkett. That weird league they belonged to was now part of the actual NFL, the same NFL I was starting to like watching on Sunday afternoons. They mattered now. That, at least, was my little kid perception. Though the reality I was blissfully unaware of was that the Patriots were still the same clown show they'd always been.

UPTON BELL

In the midst of all this newness, Billy Sullivan put a new man in charge in 1971. Continuing the Patriots tradition of men with peculiar names, Sullivan's new general manager was Upton Bell.

In the mental calculus of a fan as young as I was at the time, the people running the organization meant nothing to me. Most kids can't even name the guys in the suits who make all the decisions. They just care about the ones in the jerseys with the numbers on them. So I'm certain that as the Patriots imprinted on me, Bell's name never registered. I only became vaguely aware of who he was years later.

There used to be a Boston sports radio show called *Calling All Sports*. It was the kind of old-school, super-serious talk show that thrived on people being pissed off about something. It didn't matter if it was the Red Sox pitching, the Patriots quarterback, contracts, owners, ticket prices, or fat-cat millionaire athletes who don't hustle. Whatever. *Calling All Sports* had two co-hosts; one of them, Bob Lobel, doubled as the sports guy on one of the local news stations, back when people got information from sports guys on the local news stations. The other guy was known for his terrible comb-over hair and the fact that he had once been the GM of the Patriots.

"Uppie" (Lobel's name for him) would sometimes mention his "time with the Patriots" and what sounded like a personal vendetta against Billy Sullivan.

Upton Bell—this angry, bitter, vindictive little media figure, this guy who made his living ripping everyone else in the city—was not only the Pats' GM, he was there during some of the worst moments and responsible for some of the most terrible decisions in the history of the franchise. For me it was like finding out the crazy old coot up the street who used to get mad when we'd hit a ball onto his lawn was once a general in a war. On the losing side.

Things went badly for Bell and the Patriots during his tenure, almost from "hello." And the divorce between him and Billy Sullivan was as public, rancorous, and drawn out as any you'll read about on the covers of tabloids while you're waiting for your groceries to get rung up. But as messy and contentious as things got, no one could blame Billy for wanting to hire Bell in the first place.

Upton Bell came with about as impressive a set of credentials as you could hope for in a general manager. He was only 32 years old, but had a reputation as a football boy wonder. He already had six years of experience as the defending champion Baltimore Colts' director of personnel, where he helped them win two Super Bowls. Bell was a football lifer, and no one could look at his résumé and not see a star on the rise. As a kid, Bell worked in the Colts' ticket office, and later as the locker-room attendant. He got promoted to equipment manager before moving to the scouting department, where he was eventually put in charge of negotiating contracts with all of Baltimore's rookies, and then finally was named personnel director. His story sounded like one of those inspirational tales self-made bazillionaires like to tell about how they started out shining shoes or sweeping up condoms in a brothel or something.

He also came with a pedigree. Bell's father was none other than AFL commissioner Bert Bell, the man without whose help Billy wouldn't have had a team to generally manage in the first place. So Sullivan was bringing in a guy who was not only young, bright, hard-working, and successful, but who also had that rare strain of Football Legend genetic code in his DNA. There was every reason to feel good about Upton Bell's hire.

Unless you happened to be Upton Bell.

For him, there were plenty of reasons for concern. For starters, he didn't have the best feeling about pro football in Boston, owing to the hours he'd spent as a kid in the 1940s listening to his father on the phone with the owners of the Boston Yanks. The older Bell was the then-commissioner of the NFL, and the calls to Boston never went well. It sounded to the impressionable young lad like the Yanks franchise was always on the brink of folding and that his dad was constantly running up there because the club wasn't making payroll or something.

Also, running the Patriots wasn't exactly anyone's idea of a dream job, especially someone with career prospects like Upton seemed to have ahead of him. The franchise hadn't been successful to that point. It was run by a board of directors who were constantly at war with one another. The front office had more infighting, power struggles, backstabbing, betrayal, and double-crossing than a summer's worth of Shakespeare in the Park. But there was reason for hope as well. The Patriots were finally getting their own stadium in Foxboro, due to open for the 1971 season. They also had their quarterback of the future, No. 1 overall pick Jim Plunkett, the Heisman Trophy winner out of Stanford. They also had a quality selection of high draft picks in the next few years, so the future looked bright. In the winter of 1971, Bell took the job.

As always with the Patriots, the mood of hope and confidence didn't last long. In fact, as had happened before, the cheer and optimism didn't make it out of the very first press conference alive. As Billy Sullivan introduced his new general manager to the assembled media horde, he gave a speech about the new era that was dawning on New England pro football. He waxed poetic about how this energetic young man would be just the shot in the arm the Patriots needed, and invited Bell to the podium. And just as Bell was about to say hello, a reporter from the back of the room yelled, "Don't touch the microphone!" Bell was dumbstruck. He had no idea why anyone would yell such a thing, but he launched into his speech anyway. When he was finished, someone pulled him aside and told him the story about how Clive Rush was almost done in by 120 volts of hot, zizzing death two years earlier.

Predictably, things went downhill quickly after that. Bell's first order of business was the NFL winter meetings in March. And to call it a major disaster would be an insult to major disasters. You'd have to come up with a brand new term for it, since no one yet has invented a word for when a brand-new general manager loses his entire team.

In those days, all players were under contracts that the club had to renew annually by sending the players a so-called "option letter." It was a routine, pro-forma thing all teams did with all players they intended to keep for the following season. Typically, the letters went out in early March. But a week or so after coming back from the league meetings, Bell took a call from the agent of Phil Olsen, a defensive end the Patriots had drafted the year before, and the younger brother of Merlin Olsen. Olsen was hurt his entire rookie year and never suited up for the club. But it was no secret he wanted out of New England in the worst way. And his agent sounded ecstatic on the phone.

"Thanks, Upton," he said, "It's wonderful that Phil's a free agent." Bell asked what he was talking about, since they had sent Olsen the option letter, along with everyone else. "No," the lawyer replied. "He never got his option letter, so I'm declaring him a free agent."

Bell was stunned. If Olsen didn't get his letter, then no one did, which meant his entire roster were now free agents and could sign with whatever team they wanted. The letter that they had all been sent wasn't an option letter, it was a general, rah-rah, "I'm the new GM and we're all gonna have a super season" job. More like the kind a college athletic director sends to boosters, but utterly worthless when you're trying to . . . y'know . . . have a few actual football players to send out onto the field when the season starts.

One of the better moves the Patriots did make during this time was to bring in veteran football front-office man Bucko Kilroy, who'd helped build the Redskins and Cowboys teams of the 60s. Picking through the wreckage in the wake of this monumental blunder, he came up with a plan. No one beside Olsen's agent had picked up on the mistake. Kilroy suggested that if they mentioned it to anyone, someone else would figure it out and they would risk losing the entire roster. So he and Bell quietly went about offering every player they could a new contract, complete with a small raise. That was unheard of by the Pats, who had earned their reputation for tightwaddiness. But they figured it would be cheaper than having to go out and buy an entirely new roster.

It was one of those plans that was just crazy enough to work, and it did. No one got wise and they managed to re-sign everyone they wanted to re-sign. But it took all of three months to do it, a time Bell later called, "Ninety days of getting up each morning wondering if this was the day the gaffe would blow up. But it never did."

To this day, the issue of who exactly dropped the ball on the contracts has never been fully resolved. What is known for certain is that Bucko's fingerprints weren't on it. He claimed the first thing he said to Upton on his first day on the job was, "Did you pick up all the options?" and Bell responded, "No, I didn't have to."

Billy Sullivan always insisted it was Bell's fault. Bell said he thought it was all set before he left for the meetings and implied it was a secretary's fault, then blamed the generally shoddy job Sullivan and his lawyers did drawing up the original contracts. He also kind of/sort of took responsibility for the fiasco, but not without adding this little bit of verbal gymnastics: "The letter sent to (Olsen) was not in the context of an option letter. What he got was (a letter) picking up his option, but it was not picking up his option technically because it was the wrong letter."

Glad we cleared that up. JFK said it much better, after the Bay of Pigs. "Success has many fathers. But failure is an orphan."

In Upton Bell's defense, he didn't create a mess in the Patriots front office, he walked into one. The family that adopted him was dysfunctional long before he got there. The partners Billy Sullivan brought in because he couldn't afford to own the team outright formed warring factions, with divided loyalties that were in a constant state of conflict. Bell couldn't walk down the office hall for a drink of water without one partner trying to get him to join his side against another. It was chaos. And at the center of it all was Sullivan, struggling to keep the team afloat while at the same time trying not to get Act-III-of-Julius-Caesared by his business associates. And Bell didn't have the power to make personnel moves without getting approval from all of them.

FRED "HUNTER" DRYER

Most of the bad personnel decisions were completely Bell's fault. And at least one made pop culture history. That was the case of Fred Dryer.

To most Americans who are fortunate enough to remember the 1980s—when every movie and TV cop was an aggressive, gun-toting badass whose number of cases solved was exceeded only by his body count—Fred Dryer was the star of NBC's *Dirty Harry* knockoff, *Hunter*. That same Fred Dryer was a six-foot-six defensive end drafted by the New York Giants with the 13th overall pick out of San Diego State in 1969. He was also kind of a mouthy brat who spent the better part of his time in New York ripping the Giants management, including, but not limited to, the time he called owner Wellington Mara "totally incompetent." Or the time he said, "If you had a race, every other team would be off and going up the track, but the Giants would blow the start." After the 1971 season, the Maras had stood all they were going to stand. So where did the Giants look to ship an underachieving malcontent?

The Patriots. Bell shipped their first round pick in the '72 draft and their third and sixth picks the following year to New York for Dryer.

Dryer was openly belittling to the Mara family, one of the most successful and respected owners in sports. You can imagine how the prospect of playing for the Sullivans sat with him.

Dryer didn't *literally* tell the Patriots that they could go fry ice and there was no way on God's green Earth he'd ever play for them. But he did imply it about as strongly as he could. Shortly after the trade he told the *Lodi News Sentinel*, "The only way I'd go to Boston is if they gave me a bean soup franchise or if Upton Bell came out here and told me, 'Here. Take all the money you want.'"[12] Dryer told both the paper and the Patriots that he was only interested in playing for one of the West Coast teams. After months of back-and-forth and attempts to try to change his mind, the Pats finally caved in. Finding themselves with zero leverage against a player who was willing to say or do anything to make them look like buffoons, the Pats took 50 cents on the dollar and traded

Dryer to the LA Rams for the following year's first-rounder and Cash. Which is to say, backup defensive lineman Rick Cash.

It was a great career move by Dryer. He not only developed as a football player, making the Pro Bowl in 1975, he became a celebrity almost overnight. The Hollywood Beautiful People crowd took to him like . . . well, like the Hollywood Beautiful People crowd takes to a tall, brash, good-looking quote machine who lives by his own rules. Media offers poured in. *Sport* magazine hired him to cover the Super Bowl in '74, playing a character named Scoops Brannigan, a parody of smarmy sports reporters. It was during this time that some television producers were casting the role of a Boston bartender named Sam Malone for a little pilot they were shooting called *Cheers*. Dryer was brought in to audition and didn't get the part. But he did play a recurring character on the show, Sam's old Red Sox teammate-turned-sportscaster Dave Richards.

That exposure led to Dryer getting the title role in *Hunter*, playing a tall, brash, good-looking crime-fighting machine who lives by his own rules. The show went seven seasons, aired over 150 episodes, and generated several made-for-TV movies, none of which would have happened if Fred Dryer had been willing to labor in obscurity for the worst-run franchise in football.

JOHN MAZUR

One major problem for Upton Bell that was *not* of his own making was the head coach he inherited, John Mazur, who had gotten the battlefield promotion, somewhat against his will, after Clive Rush's breakdown.

Not that Mazur was a terrible coach; no one was mistaking him for Curly Lambeau, but he was adequate. The problem Bell had with him was more along the lines of a personality conflict. Mazur was the Webster's definition of "old school." He wore his hair in a buzz cut. He was uber-serious. He had a low tolerance for nonsense. And he was from an older generation, something that Bell thought was significant, particularly in the early 70s. Bell saw himself as being the same age as the players. That they were all of the counter-culture generation and they could relate to him much more than they could to Mazur. And he did everything he could to use that fact to ingratiate himself to the players at his coach's expense. The semi-ironic thing is that it's not as if Mazur was a complete hardass. This wasn't Gunnery Sergeant Hartman in *Full Metal Jacket*, screaming and yelling at the hippie scum he has been saddled with in order to turn them into killing machines. He was a disciplinarian, but still a player's coach for the most part. When Mazur saw something that needed correcting, it was his common practice to pull the player aside and tell him to stop by later. Then he'd talk to the player in private rather than call him out in front of the entire squad. Bell of course, being a child of the 60s and trying to foster an atmosphere of harmony and togetherness, supported his coach's modern, enlightened approach.

Or rather, he did just the opposite.

Bell undermined Mazur every chance he got. Upton's office had a window overlooking the practice field, and whenever he saw Mazur pull a player aside and speak to him one-on-one, he knew what it was all about. So he took to finding the player that got pulled aside and telling him not to worry, that Mazur had no authority to discipline anyone and was getting fired soon anyway.

DUANE THOMAS

Into this already-toxic mix, Bell introduced the unstable compound that was Duane Thomas, the troubled Dallas running back he'd traded troubled New England running back Carl Garrett for in the offseason.

Thomas was the Cowboys' first-round pick in 1970, a running back out of West Texas A&M. By all accounts, he was highly regarded as a rookie. He averaged 5.3 yards a carry and was well liked by teammates and the people who covered the team. The problems with Thomas began, as they so often do, with a dispute over money.

Unfortunately for him, all the salary and bonus money he got in that great rookie year went, as they so often do, to his ex-wife in their divorce. So he went into his second year flat broke. He asked the Cowboys to renegotiate his deal, and they told him in no uncertain terms they were a great organization before he came, they'd be one after he was gone, and that essentially he could play for what he was signed for, or screw. His call.

The change in Thomas from year one to year two was noticeable to everyone. He was a completely different person. Even those who couldn't pick up on the change in his demeanor could pick up a paper and see that he had called out the Cowboys' Holy Trinity of Hall of Fame front-office legends. He called head coach Tom Landry "Plastic Man." Said general manager Gil Brandt was "a liar." And club president Tex Schramm got off relatively easy with "sick, demented, completely dishonest." (To which Schramm replied, "two out of three ain't bad.")

In *The New England Patriots: Triumph and Tragedy*, Larry Fox tells a story about talking to Thomas at a banquet where he'd been given a rookie award: "The words just spewed forth unchecked. We were interrupted. I left and returned. Thomas picked up his answer to the last question in mid-sentence at the exact word where he had quit several minutes before. It was weird."[13]

So Schramm and Billy Sullivan agreed to swap headaches. It was like an exchange of prisoners of war, except that the Patriots had to throw in a first-round pick and the Cowboys sent offensive lineman Halvor Hagen and wide receiver Honor Jackson. (Note: Getting *two* funny-namers in return *had* to make the Pats happy.)

By this time, training camp had been moved back to UMass Amherst. And Thomas had barely arrived before the entire Patriots organization was doing a collective Scooby-Doo "Ruh roh!" The first person to see him was Dr. Burton Nault, the team physician, who was stunned at Thomas' condition. He looked like death warmed over. He'd lost a ton of weight after going vegetarian in the offseason. Which would've been fine if the plan was to have Thomas drive around the country in a VW microbus following the Grateful Dead, but not to carry a football in the NFL.

And that wasn't the worst of it. The really bad news? "He was extremely difficult to communicate with." Ruh roh.

Thomas immediately demanded a new contract and promised management he wouldn't take the field without one. And the next day, he made good on his promise. With every other player in full pads running drills, he came to practice in a t-shirt and shorts, went down to the far end of the practice field, and began to work out on his own.

Upton Bell sat down with Thomas to talk the situation over. The conversation no sooner began than Thomas said, "You know, I'd feel more comfortable if we talked outside." Reluctantly, Bell agreed and followed his new superstar to the middle of the practice field, where they sat down to talk.

A local sports anchor was there, and he and his cameraman moved in for a closer shot because, after all, it's not every day you see a running back and a team executive conducting contract talks while sitting cross-legged in the grass. At least they started to move in closer. Thomas put a halt to that by standing up, shooting them a look that Bell called "the scariest, most demonic stare I've ever seen one human being give another," and giving them the old *Amityville Horror* "Get ooouttt!" Both of them spun on their heels and took off, and Thomas and Bell resumed negotiations.

After Thomas did agree to join the rest of the team, things got even weirder. It was summer in western Massachusetts, which oftentimes means the weather can change in a nanosecond, and on this day a storm rolled in. Dark thunderclouds came down from the Berkshires. The wind picked up. Rain came pelting down, followed by hail. The players and coaches scrambled to take shelter underneath the stands. All except for Duane Thomas. He walked out to the middle of the practice field and laid down on his back. A newspaper photographer who was there covering practice realized this was a moment not to be missed. So he grabbed his camera, put his head down, and made for the middle of the field. When he got there and started setting up his shot, Thomas said, "Don't. I'm communing with nature."

Thomas' new teammates could make no more sense of him than the medical staff, management, or dripping wet shutterbugs. One Pats player told a story about passing him in the hallways and offering one of those non-specific "Hey, how ya doing?" greetings. An hour or so later Thomas confronted him. "Why did you want to know how I'm doing?" he demanded. Ruh roh.

One guy in the picture who wasn't the least bit confused by Thomas was his head coach. Granted, Mazur was hardly unbiased. He was invested in Carl Garrett, both professionally and personally. And it was no secret he hated the trade. For all the bizarre stories about Thomas' career with the Patriots, there were witnesses to Mazur's dealings with him who said the coach had it in for him before he ever got on the plane for Boston. Wherever the truth lies, if Thomas and Mazur had been any more of a pair of polar opposites, they would've been cast as partners in a cop movie franchise.

According to Mazur, before Thomas had ever even suited up, players on the team were taking bets on how long this coach-player shotgun marriage would last. If anyone was holding a ticket marked "Less Than One Play from Scrimmage," he was the winner.

On the very first rep at the very first practice, Thomas was told to line up at halfback, behind the QB, which he did, in a slight crouch, elbows on his knees. Mazur stopped the play and corrected him, saying the Patriots offense calls for the backs to take a three-point stance, with one hand on the ground. So Thomas corrected his coach, informing him that he was strictly a two-point stance man. That's what he had run in Dallas; it helped him read the defense better.

The rest of the players were dumbstruck. This was a brand-new player challenging the authority of the head coach in front of everyone. It was a transfer student calling out the principal in front of the whole school on his first day. "Here we do things different," Mazur said. "Nah, coach. You gotta let me do my thing," Thomas replied.

"OK. That's it. Take it on in." And with that, Mazur kicked his new franchise running back off the field. After practice, the two had a meeting. Thomas showed up with a plastic bag full of trail mix which he kept munching on while Mazur tried to lay down some ground rules. Which Thomas responded to with "I'm me, man. You're you, man."

"Well, now that we've got that established," the coach said, "What the hell is the point?" And demanded Thomas be shipped out of town at any cost.

So the Patriots scrambled to try to undo the situation. Billy Sullivan called the Cowboys asking for a take-back. The Cowboys said no take-backs. He replied something like "Can too. Double stamp it, no erasies," to which they said, "Cannot. Triple stamp, no erasies. Touch blue make it true." Stymied by Dallas' clever maneuvering, he tried the old lawyer strategy of, when the law is not on your side, try to get them on a technicality.

Thomas had refused to take the follow-up part of the physical, the blood and pee tests to check for drugs. Sullivan played up that point, arguing that it made the deal null and void. It must have worked, because Tex Schramm agreed to reverse the trade. He gave a long, thoughtful explanation full of talk about "unique circumstances," "morals and ethics," and "undue hardships." But it can really be boiled down to "Boston is so bad and we fleeced them so much on this deal, we can undo and still come out ahead."

So Thomas went back to Dallas, where he won them Super Bowl VI that very season. No less an authority than Hunter S. Thompson said of him, "All he did was take the ball and run every time they called his number—which came to be more and more often, and in the Super Bowl, Thomas was the whole show." By everyone's account, Thomas was the overwhelming choice for MVP, but the editor of *Sport* magazine, who sponsored the award, was worried about him acting up at the awards dinner, so he just unilaterally announced Roger Staubach as the winner.

And the Patriots? They got back their divisive problem child who kicked his offensive line to the curb on his way out of town. But one guy who was ecstatic to have Garrett back was of course Mazur, and the two were close friends to the ends of their careers. In fact, one time, long after their time with the Patriots was finished, they met on the field and shared a tender moment. That is until they hugged, when Garrett forgot he was wearing a helmet and slammed into Mazur's face and almost knocked his teeth down his throat.

John Mazur was already on thin ice with Upton Bell, and the episode with Duane Thomas and the three-point stance was the straw that broke the camel's back. It convinced Bell that Mazur couldn't relate to the modern ballplayer and he had to go. But what Bell would find out soon enough was that firing his head coach wasn't that easy. And he'd find it out in the most ridiculously Patriots-ish way imaginable.

In November of '71 he was on a Boston radio show and was asked about Mazur's future. "I haven't made up my mind yet," he answered. It was a diplomatic if evasive answer that surprised no one.

No one except one particular listener named Billy Sullivan. Sullivan started coughing up his Jameson-on-the-rocks. Bell was on thinner ice with Sullivan than Mazur was with Bell, and this was a bigger straw than the one that broke his camel's back. It had gotten back to Billy that to Patriots' staffers, Bell would refer to Billy's office as the place "where I kiss his rings." That didn't help his standing with his boss any.

The next day, Bell was in his office when he got a call from *Boston Globe* writer Leigh Montville saying that Sullivan was on the same radio show. "Billy just said you have no authority to fire the coach, that it's up to him and the board of directors." Years later, Bell told *Boston Magazine*, "The next morning the controversy was all over the front pages: 'Sullivan Denies Bell Right to Hire and Fire Coach,' complete with editorial cartoons and follow-up stories. I ran into then-mayor Kevin White one day, and he said, 'What's going on? You're in the papers more than I am.'"[14]

The day after that was the kind of scene that couldn't have played out with any other franchise in all of sports. The Patriots board of directors called an emergency meeting at Anthony's Pier 4, the Boston waterfront restaurant that was a major hangout for everyone from politicians to cops to Irish mobsters. No Patriots GM had ever been invited to a meeting of the board, but Bell talked his way into this one. When he got to Anthony's, Bell had to fight through the mob of media outside. In the meeting, Sullivan made no bones about wanting him fired. Bell pleaded his case that, if he'd known coming to Boston meant he wouldn't have the authority to hire and fire his own coach, he never would have left the Colts. He argued that there was a decent amount of talent on the team, but they'd underachieved. And Mazur's coaching was to blame.

It's unclear how exactly things played out after that. Hopefully it was a lot of guys in suits, sitting around a giant conference table smoking cigars, firing down Jameson-on-the-rocks, and yelling "Harumph!" at each other, with special emphasis on the whiskey; they had to have been drunk out of their minds to come up with the solution they agreed on.

There was one game left in the season, against the defending Super Bowl champion Colts, Upton Bell's former employer and a team that needed to win the game in order to secure home field advantage in the playoffs. The Patriots were 5–8 and going nowhere. The plan was that if the Patriots upset Baltimore, Mazur would be brought back for another season. If they lost, Bell would be able to fire him and choose his replacement. Bell later called it "an agreement that is unique in the annals of pro football," which is true. He also called it "a travesty," which is probably more accurate, since this deal ensured that a general manager would be forced to root for his own team to lose. Simply put, if the Patriots lost, Bell won. If they won, he lost. It's entirely possible those weren't cigars they were smoking in that meeting room.

They were at least smart enough to keep this ill-conceived, harebrained scheme to themselves. Because the press, the fans, and the league would've gone bananas over a plan that forces a GM to root against his own team.

And possibly the FBI too, since it has got to be a violation of RICO statutes.

Things started off badly for Bell, which is to say, good for the Patriots; at halftime they had a 14-3 lead. But in the second half, the Colts came back and took the lead. Baltimore led 17-14, and things were looking good for Bell/bad for the Pats when they found themselves pinned on their own 12-yard line with less than two minutes remaining. But in what is probably the most significant play in team history to that point, Patriots rookie quarterback Jim Plunkett hit fellow rookie wideout Randy Vataha for an 88-yard touchdown and the win. Apparently Bell didn't have his poker face on. Because while the rest of the team's staff was going ballistic, the *Globe*'s Will McDonough walked by him and said, "Hey, Upton, that's a mighty long face for someone who ought to be pretty happy right now."[15]

So Mazur returned for the 1972 season, but by the middle of November, with the team 2-7, he was fired. Bell was only slightly more fortunate, in that he survived to the end of the season before he was canned too. And in 1973, Billy Sullivan made a clean sweep of his organization and finally, at last, brought in people who would bring the one thing he hadn't had in his first dozen years in pro football.

Respectability.

8

DARKEST BEFORE THE DAWN

★ ★ ★ ★ ★ ★ ★ ★ ★ ★ ★ ★ ★ ★ ★ ★ ★ ★ ★ ★

*Have you ever gotten the feeling that you aren't completely embarrassed
yet, but you glimpse tomorrow's embarrassment?*

JERRY MAGUIRE

After a decade of futility, the franchise known as the Boston Patriots
had a fresh start in just about every way imaginable. They, along with the rest
of the old American Football League, had been folded into the NFL the year
before. They were now calling themselves the New England Patriots. And after
years of being the pro football equivalent of carnival workers, moving from
place to run-down, inadequate place, they were finally moving into a place of
their own, Schaefer Stadium. They had pressed ctrl+alt+delete on their entire
existence.

And the one saving grace of the disastrous 2–12 season the year before is
that it gave them the first overall pick in the 1971 draft, and the chance to add
that marquee, game-changer player they had always so desperately needed in
order to become a legitimate franchise.

JIM PLUNKETT

In retrospect, if you were trying to gin up interest in a team no one much
cared about by landing a face-of-the-franchise-type cornerstone player, you
couldn't have done much better than drafting Jim Plunkett. He was already
a household name. He had an inspiring life story filled with adversity he'd
overcome. He was bright, thoughtful, and soft-spoken. Looking back all these
years later, Plunkett must have seemed like the perfect sports figure, the
football version of Joseph Campbell's The Hero with a Thousand Faces. Jim
Plunkett must have seemed like Luke Skywalker before Luke Skywalker was
Luke Skywalker. The kid with the humble beginnings who would finally bring
balance to the Patriots' Force.

Plunkett grew up in East San Jose, California, which wasn't exactly Tatoo-
ine ("If there's a bright center to the universe, you're on the planet that it's far-

thest from"), but it was close. His parents were Mexican-Americans, though the family name came from an Irish-German grandfather. Jim's mother was blind, and his father supported her and their three kids by selling newspapers. But in an incredibly cruel twist of fate, he too was stricken with progressive blindness. So Jim helped make ends meet by working odd jobs after school.

But Jim was also a multi-sport athlete. By the age of 14, he'd won a football skills competition by heaving a ball 60 yards. After his sophomore year of high school he transferred to James Lick High and played quarterback and defensive end. By the time he graduated, he was six foot three, got the attention of the major college programs, and accepted a full ride to Stanford. Once at Stanford, Plunkett wasted no time establishing his whole "overcoming adversity" persona, which would become his trademark. As a freshman, he had thyroid surgery, which weakened his arm, and almost lost his spot on the QB depth chart. Head coach John Ralston talked to him about switching to defensive end full time, but Plunkett would have none of it. To work his arm back and show his coaches how serious he was about quarterbacking, Plunkett threw hundreds of balls every day in side sessions. Eventually, they were convinced and kept him at QB.

Plunkett got his shot at starting in his sophomore year. In his first game, he threw 13 passes, completed 10 for 277 yards and 4 touchdowns, and never saw the bench again.

It was the late 60s, and the AFL was, in general, playing a more advanced, wide-open passing style of offense than the more run-dependent NFL was, thanks to pioneers like Sid Gillman. And that pass-first style was beginning to filter down into the college ranks. The Pac-8 in particular was getting away from power running attacks in favor of a more pro-style passing offense, utilizing extra receivers and throwing to backs coming out of the backfield, which suited Plunkett to a T. Washington State coach Jim Sweeney called him the "best college football player I've ever seen," so you could say people were impressed.

Just as impressive was the kind of guy Plunkett was off the field, spending much of his off time mentoring underprivileged and at-risk Latino youth. Because he'd red-shirted as a freshman, he was actually junior eligible to enter the 1970 NFL draft, where he was a mortal lock to be a top pick and cash in. God knows his family could've used the money, but Plunkett passed up the chance because he felt it would set a bad example for the kids he was working with. So instead, he returned to Stanford for his senior year. It was, as it turned out, a good move. The 1970 season cemented Plunkett's legend. He led Stanford to a victory in the Rose Bowl, where he was the MVP. He was the UPI,

Sporting News, and *Sport* magazine College Player of the Year. In a season that featured great performances from quarterbacks such as Notre Dame's Joe Theismann and Ole Miss' Archie Manning, Plunkett was the runaway winner of the Heisman Trophy.

The year wasn't as kind to the Patriots. They were 2–12, and this was the season their stands were catching fire and a half-drunk player was paged over the PA system and put into a game. And the power-struggle battle lines were being drawn in the front office. What the team did have going for them was the AFL-NFL merger, which meant only one draft, and they were holding the first pick. Since their team leader in touchdown passes was the immortal Mike Taliaferro, with a whopping four, their choice was the biggest no-brainer in the history of brains. The Patriots needed a quarterback. They needed a leader. They needed an identity. They needed hope. They needed someone to sell tickets to help keep the lights on in their new stadium. And Jim Plunkett gave them all those things. The team and player were the perfect match.

Whatever else history might say about the Plunkett-New England marriage, there's no disputing they made great newlyweds. By almost any standard, Plunkett had a phenomenal rookie season. He became the first rookie quarterback in the history of pro football to play every offensive snap. He won the NFL's Rookie of the Year award. In the last week of the season, he was the league's Offensive Player of the Week. He threw 19 touchdown passes, the last of which was the 88-yard game winner to Randy Vataha against Baltimore that saved John Mazur's job and cost Upton Bell his. And Vataha was another phenom that had Pats fans loving their future. He was not only Plunkett's teammate at Stanford and his favorite target, the two were friends. Heading into the draft, Vataha was not regarded as an elite prospect and dropped all the way to the 17th round, where he was taken by the LA Rams, on the 418th overall pick. He'd put up good numbers for Stanford, but scouts had doubts about his size for the pro game. He was small enough, in fact, to have once worked at Disneyland, playing, of all things, Bashful from Snow White and the Seven Dwarves.

The Rams cut Vataha in camp, and the moment he became available, Plunkett talked Pats management into bringing his buddy in for a tryout. The chemistry between the two was unmistakable. Whatever psychic connection exists between a quarterback and a wide receiver that makes them great together, they showed they had it almost immediately. Vataha not only made the team, as a rookie he started in 13 of 14 games, led them in receptions with 51 and in touchdowns with 9. They were a perfect pair. Polar opposites that fit together in the way only polar opposites do. Plunkett was big and quiet.

Vataha was small and highly articulate. The Plunkett-to-Vataha combination was exactly the kind of thing that makes coaches go all misty-eyed and fuels the wildest fantasies of a team's marketing department. The quiet superstar and his undersized, overachieving sidekick, bringing high-octane modern football to a region and putting a franchise on the map. Looking back through the prism of history, you could call them the Tom Brady/Wes Welker or Brady/Julian Edelman of the Moon Landings Era. They were the Patriots' Batman and Robin, minus the unmistakable gay undertones.

They were instant fan favorites and gave the Patriots the identity they'd always lacked, those marquee names that the TV networks love to promote. Unfortunately, there were bad omens that maybe, just maybe, Plunkett wasn't cut out for the hero business. There was a reason no rookie QB had ever played an entire season. Leading an NFL team is a huge undertaking, and not many kids right out of college can handle it. Especially not a shy, awkward kid with disabled parents who grew up poor.

The first warning sign came on the first day of Patriots training camp. In the oldest hazing stunt of all time, Pats veterans made the rookies stand up in the cafeteria and sing their school fight song. It's a ritual that began the first time Walter Camp drew a rectangle on a field and rolled a ball onto it, and it'll continue until civilization outlaws football. But Plunkett was thoroughly unprepared for it. He'd either never heard of the tradition, or just hoped to be spared the humiliation. When it was his turn to sing, he stood up, mumbled something about not knowing his school song, and sat back down. For a few awkward moments, no one said anything. Finally, a ball boy named Mike Cataldo broke the silence. "Well, do you know the words to 'Jingle Bells'?" Plunkett said he did. "Sing that then." So he stood back up and painfully croaked his way through "Jingle Bells" to a roomful of surly, badass, trained killers.

In the middle of July.

Then retook his seat.

The fact that Vataha was Bashful was colorful and endearing. That Plunkett was literally bashful wasn't ideally what you wanted in a quarterback, but the way he was playing nobody objected.

Patriots fans embraced Jim Plunkett from the beginning as the player who gave them visions of a future filled with all the wonders that pledging loyalty to a football team can bring. Passing records falling. MVP awards and Lombardi Trophies sprouting up like corn crops and unfurled Super Bowl banners raining down from Heaven. A week 14 home matchup with the Dolphins fell on his 24th birthday, and before the kickoff, the Schaefer crowd serenaded him with "Happy Birthday." He paid them back with two touchdown passes to

Vataha and a 34-13 blowout. He finished his rookie season on another high note, that 88-yard game winner to Vataha that beat the world champion Colts, saved coach John Mazur's job, and eventually cost GM Upton Bell his. And all was mostly right with the Patriots world.

Not that these new-look Patriots were completely without the same kinds of oddballs they'd had in their first decade of existence. Most notable was Steve Kiner, a linebacker whom I guess you could consider their Larry Eisenhauer: The Next Generation. That generation being the one that experimented with lots of pharmaceuticals.

STEVE KINER

In the early 70s, the NFL was one probably one of the last institutions in America to start feeling the effects of the whole 60s counter-culture revolution mess. And it's very possible that Patriots linebacker Steve Kiner was the league's Jim Morrison. Kiner was one of those guys who in the 70s was thought of as a "free spirit," in the 80s they'd call "a character," and today we'd probably call "someone with substance abuse issues." Coming out of college, though, he was anything but; Kiner played at the University of Tennessee, where he played well enough for Dallas to spend a third-round pick on him. And while he was eventually inducted into the College Football Hall of Fame, he didn't pan out with the Cowboys, and after his rookie year they cut their losses by flipping him to the Pats for a fourth-rounder.

In Boston, his teammates noticed right away that Kiner wasn't right in the head. It wasn't uncommon for someone to address him, only to have Kiner stare back, not say a word, and then walk away. During training camp, he didn't live in the dorm with everyone else. He stayed in a trailer nearby, and he'd regularly fill a cafeteria tray in the mess hall and bring it back to his place. What no one noticed . . . or to put it more succinctly, never bothered to check . . . was that Kiner was sharing his trailer with a roommate and bringing food back to feed them both. Whether the roomie was a freeloading buddy of his or a girl he was getting his swerve on with right under his coaches' noses is a mystery I was unable to solve through research.

One off-season, Kiner was in Tennessee, driving home in a rent-a-car, when a sheriff stopped him for speeding. The sheriff asked for his license and registration, which Kiner gave him. But when the cop ran his record, something didn't check out, so he asked Kiner to follow him to the station. The two got in their vehicles, the linebacker following along behind the police cruiser, but as the sheriff turned into the police station parking lot, Kiner drove right on past. So the cop went in pursuit, hit the siren and pulled him over. "Didn't I tell you to follow me to the station?" he said. "Sure," Kiner replied. "But you didn't say anything about stopping."[16]

Then there was the time in the early 70s when Kiner showed up for practice with a squadron of police cars trailing behind him. Their issues with him were twofold: one, for some reason that wasn't immediately clear, he was driving a bus. And two, he'd just blown through every toll booth on the Massachusetts Turnpike without so much as slowing down.

But without a doubt, the signature moment of Steve Kiner's Patriots career came in a 1973 game at Houston. The Oilers broke their huddle and came to the line. Kiner took a linebacker's stance, slight crouch, elbows on his knees, head up. At the snap of the ball, Kiner didn't move. The Houston quarterback went back to pass, released the ball, and still he didn't move. The Patriots intercepted the throw and still Kiner remained in a catatonic trance. Twenty-two bodies on the field, twenty-one of them flying around after the ball, and one frozen in place for the entire play. After the whistle, Pats linebacker Edgar Chandler came over and asked if Kiner needed help. "I . . . I think I better leave the field now," he said.

No one ever said for sure what kind of pills Kiner was on, but we can safely rule out Flintstone's Chewables.

The '71 season was, by Patriots standards, a success. They finished a respectable 6–8, good for third place in the newly formed AFC East Division. As was always the case with the Pats, though, the success didn't last. In 1972 they took a giant step backwards to 3–11, and Plunkett threw a measly 8 touchdowns to 25 interceptions, both among the worst in the league. After the team fell to 2–7 with a 52–0 loss, Mazur was fired and replaced by short-timer Phil Bengston. In fact, the only thing the '72 season is notable for is that it contained, in its entirety, the career of the guy known as "Superfoot." Which is bizarre in and of itself, because the man never actually did anything notable.

"SUPERFOOT"

The whole Superfoot phenomenon was a gimmick cooked up by the guys on a goofy local radio show called *The Sports Huddle*. This was the time when straight-ahead, American-style placekickers were being replaced by the European, soccer-style kickers we know today. So the *Huddle* guys came up with a radio bit where they would hold auditions in England to find a soccer-style kicker for the Patriots. They got the UK's *Daily Mail* on board and organized tryouts in places like Goole, Maidstone, and Pontypridd. Reading from the promotional material the *Mail* put out gives you an idea of how little they understood about what the job entailed. They described American football as "a rough and tumble game where the players turn out like spacemen in helmets and pounds of padding."[17]

Remarkably (or maybe not, given how the team had been run up until this point), the Patriots went along with it. Maybe they saw it as free publicity on both sides of the Atlantic. Or maybe they realized that their own scouting hadn't done them any favors and they had nothing to lose. But they sent a team representative over to England to go along for the ride.

Though apparently they didn't send the right guy. *Sports Huddle* co-host Mark Witkin told a story about a limo ride to one of the tryouts during which the Patriots rep was so boring, the driver fell asleep at the wheel, went off the road, and nearly killed the whole bunch of them.

Eventually, the tryouts came down to a dozen hopefuls, kicking in a rainstorm at a U.S. Air Force base in Oxfordshire. Mike Walker, a bricklayer from Carnforth, Lancashire, boomed a pair of 55-yard field goals to win the contest and a check for a thousand bucks, which he said was more than double what he made in a year.

Astonishingly, it didn't end there. The Patriots could have just said, "Well, that was all in good fun," enjoyed the positive press they got out of it, counted the British pounds they made selling t-shirts, and called it a day. But they kept this thing going. Fans all across New England couldn't stop talking about this mysterious Superfoot figure, the kicking sensation who was going to come over here and revolutionize the art of the field goal. The Pats were asking the NFL to let Walker wear a uniform jersey with a giant footprint on the front and back instead of a number.

More incredible still, he actually got a spot on the roster. One of Bengston's first moves as head coach (probably *not* without a little push from management looking to drum up interest) was to replace kicker Charlie Gogolak with Walker. Yet for all that effort and hype, Superfoot was two-for-eight on field goals and was let go at the end of the year, never to kick again. His legend, however, lives on.

As for Plunkett, the season wasn't considered a disaster. It was generally regarded as your garden variety second-year setback, the sophomore slump so many future greats suffer. The consensus was that the Pats would get a new coach: someone with the temperament to mentor the young superstar and the wisdom and talent to teach him the game of football, the spirit to inspire the best out of him, and the patience and kindness to guide New England's shy, reserved, franchise player down the path to glory.

And to do so, they hired a man singularly incapable of doing any of those things.

CHUCK FAIRBANKS

Billy Sullivan had reached that point that the owner of every sports franchise reaches sooner or later. That moment when it's time to stop dicking around trying to develop the next great coach and time to hire a coach who's already great. The problem, of course, is that already great coaches command great salaries. But the Patriots were long since past the point when they could afford to play it cheap.

Billy realized this better than anyone, and he wanted nothing less than the best college football coach money could buy. But this being the Patriots, it wasn't that simple. ("But this being the Patriots, it wasn't that simple" is a registered trademark of the New England Patriots, all rights reserved.) His first choice was the obvious one: he wanted Joe Paterno of Penn State, who even then was a legend. A couple of weeks after the '72 season ended, Sullivan went to the Sugar Bowl, where he watched Paterno's team lose to Oklahoma 14-0. But despite the score, Billy still only had eyes for Joe Pa and came after him hard. He offered Paterno complete control over the Patriots' football operations and a five-year, $1 million deal, which was a king's ransom at the time. Paterno went home after the meeting and said to his wife Sue, "Well, how do you like the idea of going to bed with a millionaire?"

However Sue felt about it, Paterno's first night of sleeping with a millionaire's wife wasn't the easiest of his life. There was more to consider than just a guaranteed million bucks. He spent the night weighing the pros and cons of his decision. For starters, while he was making a relatively paltry $30,000 a year at Penn State, he was also a tenured professor, and therefore virtually unfire-able. Job security is no small consideration in the transient world of football coaching. Secondly, the Paternos had five kids, all approaching college age, and the free education they'd all get was a huge financial consideration. Lastly, Paterno had enormous power at Penn State. Billy Sullivan could offer him the keys to the Patriots' kingdom, a million bucks, and the chance to be an NFL coach, but for all pro coaches, control is only temporary. Every NFL coach is hired to be fired. Only in State College, Pennsylvania, could Paterno have the kind of clout where (as it would transpire many years later) even outrageous and criminal indiscretion on his watch was ignored.

In the morning, Joe Pa woke Sue up and said, "I hope you liked your night with a millionaire, because it's the only one you're going to have."[18] Then he called Sullivan and told him the deal was off.

The problem for the Patriots was that news of the offer to Paterno had gotten out. So it was now publicly known that, for a franchise that was desperate for legitimacy, not even a million bucks was enough to get a top-shelf college coach to take their offer.

Billy's choice for sloppy seconds was USC legend John McKay. McKay danced around with Sullivan for a few days, but he was pretty much in the same situation at USC as Paterno was at Penn State. He was making good money. He was worshipped there. Trojan alumni had just put up the money to build him a swimming pool. Eventually it became clear that he was just stringing the Pats along to sweeten his deal at USC, which he did. So Sullivan turned to his Plan C, Bob Devaney of Nebraska. And where the Pats had been embarrassed in their pursuit of Paterno and McKay, this one lapsed into all-out humiliation.

Devaney had retired as the Cornhuskers head coach and been promoted to athletic director. But he was still willing to listen to offers to return to a football field's sidelines. He accepted an invitation to fly out to Foxboro to meet with the Patriots, and the team wasted no time turning this one into a public-relations nightmare. As a matter of fact, they did so before Devaney even made it to the stadium.

Clark Booth was the sports anchor on WCVB Channel 5 in Boston. In a TV world filled with chuckling buffoons, he was the uber-serious, erudite, report-erly type. He'd received an anonymous tip from a viewer who said he'd just spotted former Nebraska football coach Bob Devaney at Logan Airport. The team had made it clear to Devaney that they were trying to keep this a secret in order to avoid the kind of embarrassments they'd suffered in the talks with Paterno and McKay, and he was to keep as low a profile as possible. He agreed.

The subtle clue that gave Devaney away to Booth's sharp-eyed anonymous tipster was he came off the plane wearing a bright red Nebraska Cornhuskers hat with a red feather sticking out of it. Whatever Devaney might have brought to the table as a football coach, apparently the whole traveling incognito thing was lost on him. So Booth called the Patriots' office for a statement, and they gave him a vague non-denial denial. After they hung up with Booth, someone —apparently undeterred by how their efforts at spycraft were going so far— came up with a brilliant plan. They'd have someone in the office whose voice Booth wouldn't recognize call the station and report that they had spotted Devaney at the *Providence* airport, wearing a *blue* hat. That would discredit the first, actually true report, and throw the press off their trail. The job went to Billy's son-in-law, Mike Chamberlain. Chamberlain got on the phone with Booth and gave him the phony story. Unfortunately, either no one had properly coached Mike or adequately assessed whether he was smart enough to pull off the ruse, because the very first question tripped him up. When Booth asked him, "Where do you think Devaney was going?" Chamberlain replied, "Oh, I think he was coming here, to the stadium," while the entire New England brain trust face-palmed.

Devaney arrived in Foxboro for interviews. In order to assess what kind of team he'd be inheriting, he and the Pats management team went over some game films. After a while, one of the assistant coaches, a guy who was likely not to be retained under a new head coach and anyway was not at all welcome, came into the film room uninvited and sat down. Part of the discussion went something like this:

Bob Devaney: "Who's that at right end?"
Assistant Coach: "That's Rick Cash."
Devaney: "He's not very good, is he?"
Assistant: "If you think he's bad, wait till you see the rest of them!"

The Patriots brass admired many things, but honesty about how bad the team was while they were trying to woo a coaching candidate wasn't one of them. The assistant was let go that very day. Devaney apparently didn't appreciate it any more than they did, because he broke off talks and went back to Nebraska.

Metaphorically speaking, Billy had asked out three different girls and still didn't have a date to the prom, and the entire school knew about it and was laughing behind his back. So in his desperation, he turned to the guy who had fixed him up before. A call was placed to his old pal at Notre Dame, Frank Leahy, for advice.

Leahy's advice was something along the lines of (and I'm not so much paraphrasing as making this up completely) "Hey, Dumbass. You were at the Sugar Bowl, right? Did it ever dawn on you to hire the guy who kicked your boy Paterno's nuts all over the field that day?" Or words to that effect.

The Oklahoma coach who shut Joe Pa's Nittany Lions out that New Year's Day was Charles Leo "Chuck" Fairbanks. At 39 years old, Fairbanks was considered a bit of a wunderkind in the college ranks. He had been an assistant at Oklahoma under head coach Jim Mackenzie. But Mackenzie died suddenly in 1967. And despite the presence of several more experienced candidates already on the Sooners staff, the athletic director saw something special in Fairbanks and offered him the battlefield promotion. The move didn't sit well with the school's regents, who looked at the other coaches and saw that any one of them was more qualified (and therefore a safer pick), and questioned the logic of going with this nobody. So, in order to get the board to sign off on the hire, Fairbanks was hired only on an emergency basis, with a special two-way-out clause written into his deal. Meaning either side could opt out on the contract at any time without penalty.

It was a smart hire by the Sooners; Fairbanks was an immediate success. In his six years at the helm in Norman, the Sooners won three Big Eight championships, and in each of his last two seasons they went 11-1. Just as impressive as Fairbanks' record was his reputation for innovation and flexibility. One year he was dissatisfied with his offense, so he scrapped the entire playbook and installed a Wishbone offense in its place. As a matter of fact, at a time when the nuclear arms race that is big-time football had been dominated by defense, the Wishbone began to swing the balance of power back to offenses. The famed 5-2 Defense (which featured five down linemen occupying each of the offensive linemen, thus freeing up the two linebackers and the strong safety to make tackles) had stifled offenses for a generation. The Wishbone countered that by letting some D-linemen go unblocked, then optioning the ball away from them. That left unoccupied blockers free to pull in order to outnumber defenders at the point of attack. The Sooners ran it so well under Fairbanks that in 1971 they averaged an unimaginable 470 rushing yards per game, a record that still stands.

So calls were made. Interest was expressed. And meetings were set up. According to Billy Sullivan's sworn testimony in a civil suit years later (that's what creative writing teachers call foreshadowing, in case you missed it), the meeting between him and Fairbanks began like this:

Sullivan: "Are you under contract to Oklahoma? If you are, there's no point in proceeding any further."
Fairbanks: "Not exactly."

Sometimes it takes years for business associates to start misleading each other and setting up grounds for a lawsuit. Billy and Chuck had their first deceit out of the way in the first 17 words. "Not exactly" would turn out to be huge. Not since "Et tu" would two words lead to so much turmoil, conflict, strife, and bloodshed. But the two reached an agreement. On January 20, 1973, Fairbanks was introduced as the head coach of the Patriots, with complete control over the football operation. And he wasted no time cleaning up the joint. Chuck came in with a system that streamlined all the operations and got everyone on the same page. Scouts worked alongside position coaches, watched them work and got a sense of their philosophy so they could better find players that fit what the coaches wanted.

The dividends came almost immediately. The first draft under Fairbanks in '73 was not only perhaps the Patriots' best one ever, you could argue it was one of the great drafts by any team in league history, even to this day. They went into it with an embarrassment of riches, three picks in the first 20. And they struck gold on all of them:

* ★ 4th pick: Offensive guard John Hannah, who is widely considered the best offensive lineman of all time
* ★ 11th pick: Running back Sam Cunningham, who to this day holds several team rushing records
* ★ 19th pick: Wide receiver Darryl Stingley, a tremendous route runner with great hands

In the 14th round, they added pass-rushing defensive end Ray Hamilton. They claimed offensive tackle Leon Gray off waivers from the Dolphins, and paired him with Hannah on the left side to anchor their offensive line for a generation. And they picked up Mack Herron, a five-foot-five, 170-pound ball of pure entertainment, to return kicks and punts and see spot duty at running back.

Fairbanks stockpiled a wealth of talent on the sidelines as well. He put together a coaching staff filled with future NFL coaches: Ray Perkins, Ron Er-hardt, Red Miller, Hank Bullough, and Ernie Adams, who would go on to be a shadowy, mysterious figure behind the scenes for the Patriots' championship teams 30 years later. The Fairbanks coaching tree would later sprout limbs, branches, and offshoots that included future Super Bowl winners Bill Parcells, Bill Belichick, and Tom Coughlin. A virtual redwood forest of coaching trees, with Fairbanks as the first sapling.

And like any truly great coach, Fairbanks was an innovator. The SparkNotes version of his career would say he brought the 3-4 Defense to the pros (a pri-marily run-stopping scheme that had taken hold in the college ranks, in which a down lineman is replaced with a linebacker, providing 3 linemen and 4 line-backers, thus the name), but that's not entirely accurate. The 3-4 had been in use at Oklahoma since the 40s, but Fairbanks wasn't the first to adopt it in the pros. The '72 Miami Dolphins (the only unbeaten team in NFL history) used it to win the Super Bowl, but that was only out of desperation, when injuries left them short of linemen. (In fact, they referred to it as the "53 Defense," which was the number worn by emergency fourth linebacker Bob Matheson.)

But Fairbanks and his defensive line coach Bullough did install the 3-4 as their primary defense prior to the 1974 season, helped in large part, oddly enough, by a player's strike. NFL Players Association members weren't al-lowed to work out with their teams during the '74 offseason; fortunately for the Patriots, their roster was loaded with rookies who hadn't yet joined the union, and Fairbanks and Bullough took advantage of the time to bring the newbies up to speed. By the time the labor dispute was settled and training camps had started, they'd completely overhauled their defense.

While Fairbanks brought to the Patriots organizational skills, talent evaluation, and coaching schemes, he was lacking in one area: human relations.

Not that he came off like a bad guy. It's just that he didn't come off as . . . well, as anything. He was just sort of bloodless. Fairbanks was one of those people that made you feel like you could spend an entire year listening to him talk and not learn a single damned thing about who he was.

Not that anyone cared. The general consensus around New England was that, for the first time ever, it felt like the Patriots were being run by competent adults who knew what the hell they were doing. The fact that the guy running the show wasn't charming didn't matter to anyone. In fact, Fairbanks' extreme lack of anything resembling a personality was kind of a running joke. Not at all unlike the man who would hold the same office three decades later, Bill Belichick. Howard Cosell referred to him on *Monday Night Football* as "Chuckaroo," in the way that he called Don Meredith "Danderoo."

Fairbanks was boring. He was bloodless and dismissive. And probably nasty as hell to work for. And no one outside of the locker room cared.

But the guys inside the locker room did care. They cared a lot, actually.

To this day, the players who played under Fairbanks will tell you how terrifying the man was. Not that he was a screamer, because he was anything but. But the fact that he was a man of such few words was his most powerful weapon. What he had was a stare. They called it The Half Eye, and they describe it like it was a Marvel Comics villain's superpower. A vicious, piercing squint. A look of disapproval that would drill a hole into your soul and let you know what he thought of your efforts. To hear the old retired Patriots describe it, The Half Eye could kill a grown man where he stood. And the only thing worse was the dreaded Double Half Eye, that could lay waste to an entire army.

Maybe they exaggerate.

But they'll also tell you that they liked playing for Fairbanks, because he had the one trait you want most in the person you work for: they knew where they stood with him. Fairbanks' lack of personality also meant he lacked the ability to play head games with anyone. There was no agenda hidden behind sarcasm or cleverness or pithy quotes in the media. His focus was entirely on making the team better. And most players appreciated that much about their coach, anyway.

Most, but not all.

Fairbanks was exactly the wrong kind of coach for Jim Plunkett. They were like ammonia and chlorine: two useful, stable compounds until mixed together. Then they form a volatile, noxious fume that poisons the atmosphere and everyone around them. The reticent quarterback and the icy coach were a bad combination from the very beginning.

As much as anything, it was a matter of style. Fairbanks was the kind of coach who told you what you were doing wrong and demanded you correct it, while Plunkett was by nature a guy who struggled with confidence and responded better to positive reinforcement, which isn't a knock on either of them. It's not like Fairbanks was a monster or Plunkett needed Robin Williams telling him to stand on his desk and shout *carpe diem* all over the place. Nor was Plunkett soft in any way; God knows the things he overcame in his life prove his toughness. It's just that at Stanford his coaches had always accentuated the positive, and that style of coaching suited him best. And he was now getting the polar opposite in Foxboro, and it wasn't doing his self-esteem any good.

Things came to a head in the 1974 season. The pressure on Plunkett was building. It didn't help any when Fairbanks swung a trade that had him looking over his shoulder. Jack Mildren was Fairbanks' old Wishbone quarterback at Oklahoma, who'd been drafted by the Colts and converted to safety. When Fairbanks pulled the trigger on a deal to bring him to New England, it fueled rampant speculation that he planned on introducing the Wishbone Offense to the pro game, just as he'd done with the 3–4 Defense. He installed it in the middle of the season with the Sooners, and there was no reason to think he wouldn't try it in Foxboro.

The problem with that is the Wishbone is a run-heavy scheme that employs three running backs in addition to a run-first quarterback, which did not fit Plunkett's skill set at all. There is no way the Pats would go to it unless Fairbanks had lost total faith in his quarterback and wanted him gone. There ended up being no truth to the rumor, but the damage to Plunkett's already shaky self-confidence was done.

Plunkett's agent was Wayne Hoope. He flew out from California to sit down with the Patriots' de facto general manager Peter Hadhazy, ostensibly to talk about a new contract. Plunkett's rookie deal had one year left on it, and they met to discuss extending it. But the meeting went completely sideways. Not only did the QB not ask for an extension, he demanded a trade. He insisted he couldn't play for a coach who, after Plunkett threw seven straight completions, would say nothing, but would jump down his throat in front of the whole stadium if he threw an interception. Or worse, give him the dreaded Half Eye.

"The guy hasn't spoken to me in two years," Plunkett complained. And in no uncertain terms he wanted out.

Hadhazy was stunned. He had no idea his Hope of the Franchise was so unhappy. Neither did Fairbanks, until Hadhazy told him about the meeting. He hadn't the first clue his own QB, the guy he worked with 16 hours a day, hated him and wanted out.

Which helps prove Plunkett's point about the whole "hasn't spoken to me" business.

So Hadhazy had an idea, one born out of a million buddy comedies where a pair of mismatched goofballs go on an adventure together where they grow and learn and bond, and eventually come back as lifelong pals. His idea was that the two of them spend a weekend together. Fairbanks owned a vacation house on the water in northern Michigan, so Hadhazy suggested he invite his young QB up for some fishing, with no outside distractions. They'd be able to talk man-to-man and get to know each other, and come back friends for life.

And the plan worked, to a point. As soon as he got back, Plunkett marched into the GM's office and said, "I wasn't sure before whether I wanted to play for this guy, but I know now. After this weekend I definitely want OUT."

The thing Hadhazy didn't count on is that in the genre of Buddy Fishing Trip comedies—say for instance, classics like *The Great Outdoors* with Dan Akroyd and John Candy, or *Gone Fishin'* with Joe Pesci and Danny Glover—the mismatched duo on the trip always have something Fairbanks and Plunkett lacked: Personality. The stoic coach and the self-conscious QB basically stared at each other the whole weekend and barely spoke a word. So what was supposed to be an exercise in male bonding ended up being one of the most excruciatingly uncomfortable ordeals in the history of social awkwardness. Plunkett was more determined than ever to leave, and was willing to shoot his way out of town if necessary. His agent again sat down with Hadhazy and asked for a ridiculous amount of money in order to force a trade.

Oddly enough, the disastrous fishing trip didn't change Fairbanks' opinion one bit. With him, nothing was personal, it was strictly business. Plunkett was his QB, he was trying to build a team around him, and he wanted to keep him. He told his GM to pay whatever it took to get Plunkett's contract extended. But no amount, save possibly the deed to Schaefer Stadium and the Writ of Prima Nocta with all of the Sullivan family brides, would get a deal done.

If it was true Fairbanks valued Plunkett and wanted him to be the quarterback of his future, he had a funny way of showing it. It was true he wasn't converting the Patriots to a Wishbone team. But Plunkett was starting to get mangled on a regular basis. He was never the most mobile quarterback to begin with, and the constant pounding he took made him even less so. And as common sense would dictate, the more physically beaten up he was, the worse the team played.

In 1974, a 6-1 start degenerated into a 1-6 finish. In fact, the highlight of the season came on another one of those "Only the Patriots" moments that became part of the oral history of the team, passed down through the ages in song and story.

JOHN TARVER

Running back John Tarver had been with New England since '72 and managed a serviceable career, with 155 carries for 554 yards and 7 touchdowns. But his one transcendent moment came during a game in Oakland, when he was handed the ball with the Patriots pinned deep in their own end zone. Tarver ran left and saw he had nowhere to run, so he reversed field. With the Raiders defense in hot pursuit, he tried to make it around right end, but again saw he had no daylight. Tarver was just about to be tackled at his own one yard line, when he had an inspiration. He threw the ball out of the back of the end zone.

Everyone was dumbfounded. No one had ever seen it done before. After the game, Tarver explained his reasoning by saying he thought the Pats would get the ball at the 20, "You know, like a touchback." So someone explained to him that if that were the case, why wouldn't every team in football, inside their 20, just chuck the ball out the back of the end zone and get it at the 20 every single time? "Oh. I guess I didn't think about that."

The 1975 season began, more or less, on the same low note that the '74 season ended. For starters, there was a little training camp issue that set the entire team on edge.

THE LONE GUNMAN

This story comes, like legends often do, with no names attached, due to the fact that no Pats beat writer ever wanted to piss off a guy nutty enough to bring a loaded gun with him to training camp. But it seems that at UMass camp in 1975, a couple of concerned veterans came to the coaches to warn them a certain defensive end kept a handgun in his room. The club was understandably horrified, not only about the gun, but also because the player in question was the kind of unstable nutjob no one wanted to mess with.

So they hatched a plan. The next day they called for a full pads workout to get the players good and distracted. One coach was assigned to keep an eye on the perp while two others snuck into his dorm room to find the piece. Just in case, they all carried walkie-talkies, so the coach on the field could warn the other ones if trouble approached. It took them a while to case the joint, but they finally found the gun in his closet. They grabbed it, covered their tracks, left, and spoke of it no further. The next day, the player in question went to management complaining someone stole a gun out of his room. Assistant GM Peter Hadhazy drew the short straw of lecturing him about how dangerous and insane it was to bring a loaded weapon to camp, that it was against club policy for him to have had it in the first place, and that the team had no intention of paying for it.

"OK," he said, "but how about the five hundred bucks I had that also got stolen?" Of course there was no five hundred bucks, but since he'd already established that he wasn't the kind of guy you argue with, they gave him the money.[19]

The beginning of the regular season, while free of deadly weapons, was not much better. The club stumbled to an 0–4 start, largely due to the fact that Jim Plunkett was under attack from opposing rushes seemingly every time he dropped back to pass. Out of desperation, the coaches started asking their banged-up, six-foot-three, 230-pound quarterback to leave the pocket and throw on the run in order to buy himself more time.

Plunkett had played the entire '74 season with a severely sore shoulder that required regular cortisone shots. He also played through torn cartilage in his right knee that needed surgery as soon as the season was over. Still, he never missed a game. And yet, Fairbanks opted to install roll-out plays and even some run options that were better suited for a smaller, more agile running QB. In a preseason game against San Diego, Plunkett rolled out only to get pancaked by defensive tackle Coy Bacon. The hit separated his left shoulder, which required surgery to put a pin in to hold it together. In a regular season game against San Francisco, he ran the halfback option twice. After the second attempt, 49ers linebacker Dave Washington, in an excess of professional courtesy, told him "You better stop running that play." The next time the play was called, Plunkett ran it anyway. The Niners sniffed it out and covered the halfback, forcing Plunkett to keep the ball and run. Washington pursued him, came full speed, lowered his pads, and pummeled him with a clean hit that was so violent it dislodged the pin that held his shoulder together. He'd been warned. The shoulder had to be cut open again, this time to remove the pin. Fairbanks was asked about the wisdom of forcing his severely injured QB to put himself in harm's way. And his answer spoke volumes about how little he understood Plunkett's physical state. Or his heart. Or his psychology, for that matter. "Sure, we sent the play in," he said. "Jim said all week he didn't want his condition to inhibit our system."

It was awful to watch, as painful and awkward as a Fairbanks-Plunkett buddy trip if they had fished Cocytus, the frozen lake at the center of Hell in Dante's *Inferno*. Pats fans were coming to realize that the hope that Plunkett had represented a couple of years earlier was just another false promise. There was plenty of sympathy for the man, whom everybody liked and respected. But fans were human beings second and football fans first. So they did what any fan base does when things go south in a hurry: they took it out on the star. Pats fans turned on Jim Plunkett like the rabid dogs they were.

In week nine of the '75 season, the Patriots hosted Dallas. During the pre-game introductions, a frustrated, fed up and no doubt drunken Foxboro crowd booed Plunkett's name so mercilessly that even longtime Boston sportswriters couldn't believe the vitriol. They actually felt bad for the guy. And most of these writers would've mounted the heads of failed athletes on their walls if it was legal.

Plunkett actually responded well to the abuse. He threw for three touchdowns and ran for another. The Pats lost, but he led the offense to 31 points, threw two fourth-quarter TDs to Stingley, and stuck it in his critics' faces. But the damage was done. And irreparable. He demanded a trade, vowing that if he wasn't given one, he wouldn't report to Patriots training camp in '76. This time, the Pats were agreeable.

There is nothing a Bostonian resents more than an athlete who'd rather be playing in some other, nicer city. We like to think of ourselves as a tough region filled with tough people who live tough lives, and we demand our athletes to be likewise. When we're presented with a guy who we perceive would rather be surfing or golfing on his off days in December instead of suffering miserably alongside us with our lousy quality of life, it cuts us to the core. And there's no rooting for that guy ever again.

As it turned out, the accusations about Plunkett being soft and greedy and so on were unfair. But the one about him wanting to go back to the West Coast was 100 percent true.

A few teams were interested in trading for him. And as fate would have it, his hometown San Francisco 49ers were more interested than anyone. The Niners at that time were one of the worst franchises in football, fielding consistently bad teams and having a hard time selling tickets. The idea of bringing back their local hero to put asses in the seats made a lot of sense, both from the football and business sides of things.

Sensing the 49ers were desperate and had to get Plunkett at all costs, the Patriots did the decent and honorable thing: they took full advantage of the situation and took the Niners to the cleaners. They held San Fran's feet to the fire and screwed them out of two first-round picks in '76, a second-rounder in '77, and capable backup QB Tom Owen. It turned out to be one of the all-time great football trade hose-jobs, as Plunkett washed out of San Fran after only two seasons and the Patriots used the picks to shore up what was one of the NFL's most talented young rosters of the decade.

9 GROGAN'S HEROES

★ ★

*Everyone said I was daft to build a castle on a swamp, but I built it all
the same, just to show them. It sank into the swamp. So I built a second
one. That sank into the swamp. So I built a third. That burned down,
fell over, then sank into the swamp. But the fourth one? Stayed up!*
    KING OF SWAMP CASTLE, *Monty Python and the Holy Grail*

There comes a time in the life of every real sports fan when you fall
in love not just with a particular team, but with one particular edition of a particular team. That one, certain season that grabs yours heart, curls its fingers
around your aorta, balls its fist around your ventricles and holds on in such a
way that you know it'll never let go. It's like the distinction you make between
the blanket statement "I love Kate Beckinsale" and "I've been in love with Kate
Beckinsale since *Underworld*." Teams, like celebrity crushes, come across your
cultural radar in different ways. But typically there's only one that sticks with
you forever.

And for me, that one will always be the 1976 New England Patriots.

I can remember everything about that team and that season like it's playing
out in front of me in a Madden game on a high-def TV. I was just the right age
and, to be perfectly frank, had so little else going for me athletically, academ-
ically, or socially that I got completely caught up in the phenomenon that was
the '76 Pats. It was that 1976 Patriots season when I got introduced to live
pro sports for the first time. The game my brothers Jack and Bill, our cousin
Phil, and their buddy Tom took me to was the week 13 win over New Orleans.
The one that finally exposed me to what an amateurish, poorly run, third-rate
operation it was that was fielding the football team I had fallen in love with.

I suppose that while I had every right to be disappointed, I should not have
been surprised at how shabby Schaefer Stadium was. I mean, the whole journey to the stadium wasn't exactly a stroll up Main Street, USA, to Cinderella's
Castle. To get to Schaefer, you came down U.S. Route 1, a four-lane, traffic-
choked highway littered with liquor stores, parking lots, U-Store-It facilities,

117

used car lots, and crappy diners. As journeys to major sporting events go, no one ever confused the drive with turning down Magnolia Lane and heading into Augusta National. I have vivid memories of peering out the car window, straining to see the light towers and the tops of the stands, and even then I couldn't believe that an NFL team played on such a seedy-looking stretch of road. It just never seemed to fit.

But Route 1 was the Yellow Brick Road compared to the place we parked. Ringing the stadium was a collection of dirt parking lots without so much as a square foot of asphalt. The one we pulled into in was sandwiched between the stadium and the old rundown horse track next door. It pretty much had the topography of a World War I battlefield, with all of the trenches but none of the charm. There were massive potholes and ruts everywhere that seemed big enough to lose a half-ton pickup truck in. Though to be fair, they were probably only deep enough to get your tires stuck or to snap an axle. When it hadn't rained in a while, the lots were dust bowls. When it rained at all, they were mud baths. When it was cold, the puddles formed massive, frozen lakes. In any kind of weather, the parking lots were a disgrace.

The stadium itself sat on a hill high above us in the middle of it all. I think "loomed" might be the proper word. Like a fortress. Or better yet, like a prison.

At each corner of the stadium were paved pathways that led up the hill to the entry gates. As we trudged our way up the path to the part where everything bottlenecked and you had to force your way through the mob to get to the turnstiles, someone in the crowd started mooing. Like cattle getting herded into a slaughterhouse. Then a couple of other people joined him. Then everyone. Thousands of people all making cow noises. Jack told me they did it every week.

The area underneath the bleachers was wide open except for a few food stands that were offering unpromising hot dogs and cold popcorn, and others that sold beer. There were only a handful of souls brave enough to try the food, but the beer stands had lines hundreds deep across the concourse.

When the game was over, you had to make your way back under the bleachers, along that same fence, and through that same bottleneck to the ramp that led down.

Though not everyone bothered. I have a vivid memory of us back at our car, firing up the grill and polishing off all the burgers, sausages, and tips we didn't cook in the pregame. We'd left the game early so we could look up the hill to see people still filing out of the stadium above us. And every few minutes, someone with less brains than courage (liquid courage, to be sure) decided waiting in line to leave was a sucker's game, so they'd opt to scale the giant fence instead. It was the most entertaining part of the day, like watching an insect slowly crawl up your windshield, if the bug in question was a 225-pound drunken meathead from Quincy in a Patriots sweatshirt.

With one guy in particular guys were taking bets as to whether he'd make it over at all. He barely made it to the top, sat there straddling it for what seemed like hours before he swung his leg over, and slowly made his way down the fence. Finally, painstakingly, he got both feet on the ground, faced the parking lot and stood at the top of the hill, which had to have been a good 45-degree angle steep. He wobbled for a second (what the cops in drunk driving arrests like to call "appeared to be unsteady on his feet"), got his balance, and took his first step down the hill. Unfortunately for him—but really, really fortunately for the dozens of us watching—that first step caught nothing but air. The next body part of Drunky McStumbles to make contact with the ground was the crown of his head, and he somersaulted all the way down the embankment like Bullwinkle rolling down the ski slope, until he came to a stop at the edge of the parking lot. One of us yelled, "I give him an 8.5!" Someone else said "9!" And from behind us came "The Russian judge gives him a 6! Boo!!!" Then the poor buffoon got to his feet, regained his bearing, and staggered off to a smattering of applause and pats on the back.

Another unforgettable part of the fairy-tale day was noticing that a guy parked a few spaces away from us decided he didn't want to leave his hibachi grill out in the elements, so he slid it under his car for safekeeping. We later surmised that was probably not a good plan, evidenced by the fact that when we came back after the game, his car was a smoldering, burned-out shell. Which told us two things. First, that he put still-burning charcoal under his gas tank. And second, that his car was engulfed in flames without anyone bothering to do a damned thing about it.

Those were magical moments. Ones I've always cherished. It was losing my "Welcome to Patriots Football" virginity.

I can remember the 1976 *Sports Illustrated* Pro Football Preview issue like I'm sitting here with it on my lap. For every division in the NFL, they had a cartoon illustration. The AFC East's was an angry (Miami) Dolphin being chased by a fast-moving (Baltimore) Colt. Chasing them was a smallish, over-matched Buffalo (Bill). In the rear was a sad, pathetic-looking (New York) Jet. Between Buffalo and New York was a stupid, befuddled, hapless-looking Patriot. That, in graphic form, is how the world saw the Pats and their prospects in the division. Two powerhouse franchises, a middle-of-the-road team, a former champion turned also-ran, and the Patriots, who just kind of sucked.

The accompanying text was no kinder to them. The section on the Pats began with some claptrap about how Steve Grogan was a yokel from the Midwest who, when he went to a big city, craned his neck to look at the tall buildings. The rest was all about how bad the '75 season was and how there was no reason to expect improvement. The Pats were coming off a 3–11 season. With Plunkett gone and the team facing a tough schedule in a strong division, neither SI nor anyone on the national scene was giving them much of a chance to do any better than that.

STEVE GROGAN

The quarterback who replaced Plunkett in those last few games in '75 was no one's idea of a superstar in the making. You didn't watch Steve Grogan or listen to him give interviews and expect you'd be seeing him doing guest spots on *The Brady Bunch* in a couple of years. Grogan was a middling draft pick (5th round in '75, 116th overall) who didn't blow anybody's skirt up throwing the ball at Kansas State (12 TDs and 26 INTs over two seasons). But you got the sense early on that he'd be someone easy to root for, provided he proved he could play the game.

For starters, Grogan benefited from the old football axiom that the most popular guy in town is the backup quarterback—or at least he is when the starting QB is struggling the way Plunkett was. The New England public had turned on Plunkett in a nasty way, and Grogan seemed like everything he wasn't. He had an easy-going, Midwestern way of speaking, but he was articulate and direct. He was undeniably tough, proving he could take a hit (as well as dish them out) at a time when Plunkett seemed (unfair as it was) fragile.

Mostly, he could run, something Plunkett definitely could not do. At KSU, Grogan had rushed for almost 600 yards (including a 100-yard game) and 36 TDs. The fan base was tired of the way the team was headed and anxious to move in the opposite direction, much like the way the electorate will vote in a conservative after eight years with a liberal, and vice versa. Steve Grogan was the Anti-Plunkett, and that was good enough, at least in the short term.

Until he proved that he wasn't the answer either.

The start of the Grogan Era didn't exactly have people storming the box office for season tickets. His first game he threw for 365 yards and a couple of TDs, but he also threw three interceptions. And in spite of putting 31 points on the board, the Pats lost by two touchdowns. In fact, they went 0–5 down the stretch with Grogan behind the wheel, while the offense averaged just over 17 points per game.

To be fair, Plunkett led the Patriots to wins with 33 and 31 points scored in his last two starts in that '75 season. But the divorce was final. And for a first rebound date after the breakup, Grogan seemed good enough. If not Miss Right, he could be Miss Right Now. There was some talk-show debate about whether he was the answer, or if they should look for a QB in the draft, but no widespread panic in the streets over the 0–5 finish that season. The general sense was that the jury was out on Grogan and he was likely to be granted a whole year in the system to get himself ready. And if he didn't work out, *his* backup would become the most popular guy in town.

RUSS FRANCIS

Drafted with the 16th overall pick in the '75 draft, the tight end out of Oregon was that rare guy who had everything possible going for him. He was bright. He was good-looking. He was a likable free spirit. He lived in Hawaii, where he ran his own business chartering and flying planes. Women wanted him and men wanted to be him. Francis also had a natural athletic talent gifted to him by the gods. In high school he took up javelin throwing, and five weeks later he was setting the national scholastic record. In his first round of golf he shot an 82. John Hannah was never shy about admitting he was jealous of Francis' natural abilities.

In '75, Chuck Fairbanks asked his personnel director Bucko Kilroy who the best athlete in the draft was. Without hesitation, he said Francis. But, he went on to explain, there was risk involved. The Oregon program he was coming out of was a mess. He had three head coaches in three years. It was a period Oregon alumni call "The Dark Days of Dick and Don," after coaches Dick Enright and Don Read. (Enright was so incompetent that he took Dan Fouts, one of the best pure passers who has ever lived, and tried to turn him into an option QB.) "Besides, he didn't play a down his senior year," Bucko cautioned.

"I didn't ask you about that," Fairbanks shot back. "I just asked you who the best athlete is." If Francis was the best, he wanted Francis.[20] What complicated matters and gave Kilroy a case of the booboo-jeebies about drafting him was that Francis was eligible for the draft, but still had academic eligibility as well. So in order to be draftable under NFL rules, he had to go through the formality of stating to Commissioner Pete Rozelle in writing that he was officially forgoing his senior year and declaring for the draft. By this time, Kilroy had been in touch with him and told him the Pats would take him with their first pick. But in order to keep him off the menu for teams with picks higher than those of the Pats, he convinced Francis to wait until the last possible minute to submit his paperwork to the league.

It worked. The rest of the league was too busy preparing their draft boards to pay any attention to a guy who hadn't played in a year and was entering the draft pool at the deadline, and Francis flew right in under their radar. It was probably tampering, but it was the kind of move you can only pull off when you're on top of things. "The fact is, nobody else did their homework on him," Kilroy later said.

JOHN SMITH

The Pats could have been forgiven if the Superfoot fiasco had sworn them off of British soccer players with zero American football experience for good. But they actually got right back up on that particular horse the following year, 1974.

John Smith was bright, erudite, and colorful, the quintessential Brit. And from the start of his Patriots career, TV was fascinated with the novelty of him and he was all over the airwaves. He'd come to the Patriots after a few visits to the States to work at a friend's soccer camp; the camp director had him kick a few footballs and a scout caught wind of it and offered him a tryout. But American football completely baffled him, and he had hopes of turning pro in soccer back home, so he declined and went back to England.

Still, the Patriots were interested. And persistent. They sent him an invitation to training camp as well as a plane ticket, which Smith accepted, figuring that at the very least he'd get a free trip to the United States out of the deal.

Smith and the Patriots coaches both found that he was a natural, born with a knack for kicking American footballs. The rest of the game, however, didn't come so easily. His first live action came in a scrimmage against the Redskins. Smith was warming up on the far side of the practice field when the call came for him to go in for a kick; they were waiting for him. Smith panicked. He ran across two fields, into the huddle, found his bearings, got set, lined up, and boomed it. Perfectly split the uprights. He raced over to the sidelines, delighted with himself, and found Chuck Fairbanks.

He was overjoyed. "Great kick, huh?!?" he said.

"Right," Fairbanks replied, not exactly sharing the moment. "But where's your helmet?"

Smith's first kickoff was a few weeks later, in the preseason opener, the hall-of-fame game against the San Francisco 49ers. As he approached the ball, he got halfway there before he realized no one else was moving, and the play was blown dead. He'd forgotten to signal the refs. So they teed the ball up again. Only this time, Smith took a look across the line at the massive front line of the return team and got so distracted that he booted the ball off the side of his foot. It barely made it to the 10-yard line and almost went out of bounds for a penalty. Not a great way to start a career, especially with the game on national TV. Howard Cosell gave Smith a little taste of instant celebrity by saying, "If he continues to kick like that, he can expect a seat on the next boat back to England."

Still, Smith became a fixture with the Pats. He lasted 10 years with them and was a central figure in some of the biggest and most bizarre, indelible moments in team history, which we'll get to later. He also had a nice little side job as the color analyst for whatever pro soccer team happened to exist in Boston at any given time.

While they'd only finish 3–11 in '75, there was at least the sense that, while they had a long voyage ahead, the ship was at last on the right compass heading. They were not all future greats, tough guys, matinee idols, and colorful Englishmen, all lining up behind the banner of a genius coach. This was still the mid-70s. The culture war behind modern athletes and old-school Greatest Generation coaches was in full swing on all battle fronts, and The Half Eye was indeed powerful. But like Superman's X-ray vision in the presence of lead, the half eye couldn't see through crazy.

Take Mack Herron. He was proving himself to be a versatile, all-purpose weapon. In one game against Minnesota in '74, he had 30 rushing yards, 51 receiving yards, 55 kickoff return yards, and 59 punt-return yards. Performances like that, plus the novelty of his five-foot-five size, were fast turning "Mini Mack" into a fan and media darling. And, not surprisingly, he wanted to be paid like one. By 1975 he was openly griping about wanting a new contract, and Fairbanks was none too pleased. For starters, he was still a part-time back/special-teamer. Second, the coaches felt like he was too delicate and wouldn't play through pain. The last straw was when he threw a huge party on a Friday night in the middle of the season. He was cut the next day. Herron eventually wound up playing in the CFL for a short time, approximately as long as it took him to get arrested on drug charges up there and be promptly waived.

Fairbanks was 42, but he was what some grandmothers like to call "an old soul." A generation gap existed between him and his players that widened even further under the seismic shift of a labor dispute that occurred just before the start of that '75 season. The NFL and the Players Association had been playing without a collective bargaining agreement for a year. There was some talk among the players about a work stoppage, but there wasn't widespread support and nothing really came of it.

Except, of course, in New England.

THE ONE-TEAM STRIKE
Randy Vataha was the Patriots' union rep. And while the rest of the NFL players weren't terribly put out about the lack of a CBA, he decided to go all

Norma Rae on everyone. Just before a preseason game against the Jets, he called a team meeting and urged that they hold a vote to strike. He got his wish; Patriots players voted to strike a blow for workers' rights, break free from the yoke of bondage, and fight for human dignity the world over by sitting out an exhibition football game. In doing so, they made history; it was the first professional sporting event in North America to ever be canceled by a labor dispute. So if you've ever wondered who began the unproud tradition that led to the shutdowns of Major League Baseball in '81 and '94, NFL games with scab players in '87, the NBA strike of '98, and a half dozen or so NHL work stoppages, there's your answer. The 1975 Patriots were the pioneers.

The honor of breaking the news to ownership that there'd be no game played fell, naturally, to Randy "Samuel Gompers" Vataha. Team VP Chuck Sullivan was sitting on the team bus waiting to go to the stadium and wondering where his players were when Vataha came on board to drop the bomb on him.

It went about as well as could be expected. Sullivan the Younger blew his stack. He begged Vataha to reconsider and failed. He got Commissioner Pete Rozelle on the phone. *He* begged Vataha to reconsider and failed.

For their part, the Jets had no idea what to do. They were willing to play the game. Like most teams in preseason, most of them were fighting for jobs that weren't going to be won sitting around making symbolic gestures about the rights of the working man. But the Pats players held firm and the game was canceled. There wasn't another one-team strike by the Patriots, but the damage on this one was done. As Vataha would put it to Patriots beat writer and talk-show host Mike Felger years later, "Everyone was shaking their heads, saying 'Only the Patriots.'"[21]

So yes, Fairbanks was losing the occasional culture battle. But starting the first full year with Grogan replacing Plunkett and most of his building blocks in place, he started winning the football war.

Immediately out of the gate, the pessimists looked like they were right on the money. They opened the season in Baltimore, against the Colts and their media darling QB Bert Jones. The announcers adored him and his pretty-boy good looks. Grogan, on the other hand, was all Adam's apple and bulging veins in his neck. Grogan threw four interceptions and the Colts rolled to an easy 14-point win.

Week two was a home game against the Dolphins of Don Shula and Bob Griese. The Pats dominated in all phases of the game. They picked Griese off three times, sacked him five times more, and ran for 278 yards on their way to a surprise 30-14 win. They followed up the surprise with a stunner over the Super Bowl champion Steelers in Pittsburgh, 30-27. Russ Francis had 138 yards receiving, including a 38-yard touchdown catch. Grogan followed that up with a 58-yard TD to Darryl Stingley and a rushing TD.

The next day, the Quincy (Massachusetts) *Patriot Ledger* summed up the pure fun of beating the champs on their home field perfectly, in an article with a headline that should've won them the Pulitzer: "Grogan's Heroes."

But if the Miami game was a surprise and Pittsburgh was a stunner, they followed that up with a week four game that could only be described as a total shock. A 48–17 dismantling of the Oakland Raiders in Foxboro. The Raiders of the 70s were one of the more unlikable teams in NFL history. With their self-promoted bad boys image, they prided themselves on things like cheap-shotting guys and leading the league in penalties every year. Their coach John Madden came across as a wild, raving, insufferable lunatic, flailing his arms in the air while spittle flew out of his mouth and his enormous man boobs bounced all over the place underneath his turtlenecks. So it wasn't without a great amount of joy that New England fans watched the Pats slap Oakland all over the Schaefer field. They manhandled the Raiders in every respect. It officially put the Patriots in the conversation as one of the best teams in the league.

It was a month into the season, and the Patriots had already beaten three perennial Super Bowl contenders. In the process, they'd made themselves into THE national sports story. There's nothing the country falls in love with faster than a Cinderella team. A previously downtrodden franchise that suddenly finds its way and starts challenging the big boys. And there's nothing the media loves more than a young, upstart team full of unknowns they can introduce the world to. The Patriots, for the first time ever, seemed like they'd arrived. They had finally become a legitimate NFL franchise. A team to be feared and reckoned with. And it seemed like Pats fans, after all those years of crappy venues, half-empty stadiums, and local TV blackouts, finally belonged in the Big Time along with their team.

It was a feeling that didn't last long.

MONDAY NIGHT MAYHEM

October 18, 1976: A date which will live in Patriots infamy. It was the day that the pro football fans of New England proved they were literally Not Ready for Prime Time.

It was the day the town of Foxboro found out the hard way that, while tailgaters typically start boozing it up for a one o'clock Sunday game at nine or ten in the morning, when kickoff is at nine o'clock on Monday night, they start hitting the sauce at . . . nine or ten in the morning. Or so it seemed.

The Pats were playing the hapless Jets, who were 1-4. And it didn't help matters any that the home team jumped out to a massive lead. Early in the third quarter they were up 27-0. Then it was 41-7. The people in the stands went through whatever group-dynamic shift occurs whenever "spectators" turn into "a mob." It wasn't so much a football crowd as it was a complete breakdown of the social order. It was *Lord of the Flies*, if the little British boys were big fat guys with hairy bellies and the conch shell was a stack of used Schaefer beer cups.

It was a perfect storm of drunken debauchery. The cold front of excitement over the Pats' sudden success met with the nor'easter of a prime-time game and they got whacked with the high-pressure system of a blowout win. So all hell broke loose.

There were fights everywhere. One fan got stabbed. A cop was attacked and his gun stolen. In all, there were over 60 arrests and 35 people were sent to the hospital for medical treatment. The mayhem was so widespread that even ABC's *Monday Night Football* crew couldn't ignore it, and Howard Cosell in particular stopped talking about the game to do a play-by-play of the pandemonium unfolding below his booth.

But one story from that night went beyond mere news reports and became instant legend. And that is the story of the fan who, in the midst of all the chaos, suffered a heart attack. And while the EMT was working to resuscitate the guy, he felt something on his back. He turned to find a drunk standing behind him, beer in hand, pissing on him.

The next day, Foxboro Chief of Police Daniel McCarthy gave a statement in which he asked residents to "hope and pray" there'd never be a Monday night game in town again. It would be another four years until the next prime-time game. And since that one would make the '76 game look like a state dinner at Buckingham Palace by comparison, Chief McCarthy would eventually get his wish.

While the football fans of New England were cementing their reputation as America's surly drunken uncle, the Patriots themselves continued to prove to the country they were for real. After a Halloween loss in Miami had them sitting at 5-3, they went on a roll, running the table the rest of the way to finish at 11-3, thus reversing the 3-11 record of the year before. It was the biggest one-year turnaround in NFL history. They were a talented and very young team establishing their identity, and it was obvious they realized they were part of something special. One of the ways they demonstrated it was by holding hands in the huddle, something common in high school or college football, but almost unheard of in the pros.

You can't be a great team without a lot of great individual performances, and the Pats had them all over the field:

* They featured a three-headed running attack led by Sam Cunningham, Don Calhoun, and Andy Johnson, each of whom could run outside, run for power between the tackles, block, and catch the ball. In fact, one more yard rushing by Johnson would've meant all three of them would've topped 700 yards for the season.
* Mike Haynes (a future Hall of Famer) put together arguably the best rookie season by a cornerback in league history, with eight interceptions, three fumble recoveries and two punts returned for touchdowns.
* Their offensive line was among the best in the league, anchored on the left side by John Hannah and Leon Gray. Behind them the team averaged 5.0 yards per carry and allowed only 18 quarterback sacks all year.

Steve Grogan had a breakout year. His passing was efficient, if not spectacular (18 TDs, 20 INTs), but he quickly established himself as one of the best rushing quarterbacks of his era. He came just shy of 400 rushing yards, had a 6.6 yards-per-carry average, and set a league record for QBs with 12 rushing TDs. (There a was a minor controversy when, at the end of the final game, facing the expansion 0-14 Bucs, Fairbanks called timeout on Tampa's one-yard line to give Grogan a chance to break the record. But no one in New England was arguing.) But first and foremost, the '76 Grogan's Heroes Patriots were a *team*. They tied with the Colts for the best record in the AFC East, but due to the tiebreaker formula they came in second and were the conference's lone wild card. For them it meant a trip to—where else?—Oakland, whose Raiders had rolled to a 13-1 record, the blowout loss in New England the only thing standing between them and a perfect season. And they were stacked with talent, legends like Ken Stabler, Cliff Branch, Fred Biletnikoff, Art Shell, Gene Upshaw, Dave Casper, Ted Hendricks, and George Atkinson. If you rearranged the busts at the Football Hall of Fame, you could replicate half their locker room.

Plus, they were out for revenge, and the costumed, wrestling-goon losers in the Oakland Coliseum stands were out for blood. The Patriots had to be ready for an environment that promised to be 360 degrees of pure hostility.

As it turned out, they *were* ready for the Raiders. And the Oakland fans. What they couldn't have been ready for, however, was the other crew that was against them that day: the officials.

THE ROUGHING-THE-PASSER GAME

There are differing schools of thought about what happened with the officiating in the 1976 AFC Wild Card Game. First, there's the view that the refs made a lot of mistakes. The second is the belief that they intentionally made calls in the Raiders' favor. The third is the theory touted by one referee in that crew, Ben Dreith, who spent the last quarter of the 20th century and all of the 21st century so far insisting that they got all the calls right. But since that is the insane ranting of a deranged lunatic, let's look at the belief of generations of Pats fans, as well as many people in the organization, that the game was rigged in favor of Oakland.

For years, Raiders owner Al Davis had been badgering the city of Oakland to build his team a new football-only stadium. And as leverage (or more accurately, blackmail), he was threatening to move the club to Los Angeles. It stands to reason the league wanted nothing more than one of their tent pole franchises playing in a free stadium paid for by the taxpaying suckers of the Bay Area.

That's John Hannah's theory anyway. Years after retiring from football, Hannah told Michael Felger, "I think there have been several games that have been fixed in the NFL. And that was the most flagrant of them all . . . The league didn't want them to move. They felt that if the Raiders won it all, they'd have a better chance of staying." Russ Francis won't go quite that far. But he did tell Felger, "That was the only game in my 14 years in the league where I felt something was wrong. There had to be something there . . . All I know is I've played hundreds and hundreds of games, and that's the one that sticks out."

Chuck Fairbanks was only a little more reserved: "The weakest officiated game I've ever been a part of. They did a bad job. Terrible."

Whatever your opinion of the officials' incompetence/corruption, no one will argue the Patriots came out ready for playoff football. They scored on their second possession of the game, a one-yard touchdown set up by two big Grogan throws to Francis and one to Darryl Stingley, and led 7–3 at the end of the first quarter. Then after two more touchdown drives in the third, they took a 21–10 lead into the fourth.

But the danger signs were there all game as well, not just with bad calls by the officials, but with some self-inflicted wounds by the Patriots. Holding a lead in the second quarter, the New England coaches caved into the pressure of the moment with some of your classic panicky, too-cute, in-over-their-heads overcoaching. They sent in a gadget play where Francis ran a tight-end-around-option pass that got picked off by Oakland's Skip "Dr. Death" Thomas. (Not a great name for a heart surgeon, but for an NFL defensive back it's an all time classic.) That ill-advised decision set up an Oakland touchdown. But the officials were doing their damnedest to keep the Raiders in the game, that much was obvious. Pats center Bill Lenkaitis, who hadn't been called for holding once all season, got flagged three times for it in this one. Raiders linebacker George Atkinson sent his fist through the gap in Francis' facemask, shattering his nose across his face. No call.

One series in the fourth quarter helps support *both* sides of the "Patriots Have Themselves to Blame"/"The Officials Were in the Bag" debate. New England took over at Oakland's 48-yard line, sitting on a six-point lead with under five minutes to play. They were a first down or two away from running the clock down and putting the game away. On second and 8 from the 35, they handed the ball to Sam Cunningham on an off-tackle run. Sam Bam turned the corner, angled toward the sidelines, and inexplicably ran out of bounds, not only short of the first down, but stopping the clock in the process. It not only made no sense, it was completely out of character for a six-foot-three, 230-pound power back who always displayed good field vision and awareness of the situation. Then again, there's one school of thought that believes that play was on the refs as well. John Hannah insists to this day that the official holding the first-down marker moved it one yard back, and Cunningham—instinctive runner that he was—ran for it, only stepping out after he thought he'd picked up the first.

Regardless, it left the Pats with a critical third down, needing only one yard to ice the game. Grogan, hoping the Raiders would be jacked up and coming with everything they had, changed the snap count from "On one" to "On three." What he hadn't considered was that his own linemen were also jacked up. They were more than that. They were Henry V's troops, "like greyhounds in the slips/Straining upon the start." Practically foaming at the mouth, ready to blow the Raiders off the line of scrimmage and seal a playoff win. Three of Grogan's line jumped offside before Oakland ever had a chance to. The refs stepped in again to make it third and 6, though there's no one alive who blames them for that one. To his credit, Grogan has always taken the rap for that one. "I should've known better," he says.

But the next play was all on the officials. Facing a third and 6, Grogan had the perfect play call. He made the perfect read. Delivered the perfect throw to the perfect target, hitting Russ Francis perfectly, right in the middle of his perfect chest. But the ball bounced off and landed on the ground, a perfect incompletion.

There's no disputing who's to blame for that one, and they were wearing black and white zebra stripes. Francis couldn't catch the pass because Raiders linebacker Phil Villapiano had him in a bear hug, with his arms pinned by his sides. It was so blatant, an illustration of it should be in the rulebook demonstrating the perfect pass interference penalty. An official stood a few yards away with his eyes locked on the play, but the flag stayed in his pocket.

Francis was incredulous. The entire Patriots sideline went berserk. But no call. The Pats knew they'd been jobbed. The Raiders knew it. The bloodthirsty morons in the crowd knew it. The only ones who even pretended it wasn't a completely bogus call were Dreith's officiating crew. But the Patriots had to settle for a 50-yard John Smith field goal attempt, which he missed. And the Raiders were still alive.

Oakland was trailing 21–17 with time for one final drive. A Patriots sack of Ken Stabler put Oakland at third and 18 with 57 seconds left. On the next snap, Stabler stood in the pocket, buying time, waiting for someone to come open upfield. Pats defensive end Ray "Sugar Bear" Hamilton, coming from his nose tackle position in the middle of the line, stunted around to Stabler's left and beat Hall of Fame guard Gene Upshaw. As he came in clean, the left-handed Stabler released the ball, but too late. Sugar Bear got a piece of it and the pass fell out of bounds. The Raiders were facing a fourth and long with their season on the line.

That is, until Dreith stepped in. He called a roughing the passer penalty on Hamilton. It was an outrage. Hamilton was clearly lunging after Stabler while he still had the ball in his hands. Even if you want to do revisionist history on it and claim the call was because Ray hit Stabler's helmet, you can't; there was no rule against hitting the QB's head at the time. It would be like charging someone for failure to wear a seat belt in 1950.

Instead of facing a fourth and 18, the Raiders had a first down. En masse, the Patriots came unglued. Fairbanks was on the sidelines doing the Charlton Heston "You maniacs!!!" speech from the end of *Planet of the Apes*. Defensive end Mel Lunsford got called for unsportsmanlike conduct and that yardage was tacked on as well. Sugar Bear completely lost his marbles. On the ensuing plays he picked up two more unsportsmanlikes and was ejected.

The last couple of minutes of the game felt like they took hours. At that point the end seemed inevitable. The Raiders were like a cat toying with a mouse before killing it. Finally, with 14 seconds left and the ball on the Pats 1-yard line, Stabler rolled to his left, tucked the ball away and dove across the goal line to put New England out of their misery, 24–21.

Linebacker Steve Nelson was the first one into the visitors' locker room and, to put it mildly, he went completely ape-shit, kicking over furniture, smashing equipment against the walls, and tearing the place apart. To a man they faced the press and made no bones about the fact that they thought they'd been robbed. Fairbanks called it "a tragedy" and added, "I'll never forgive Ben Dreith for the call he made."

The NFL, for their part, stood by their officiating crew. But it wasn't lost on anyone that they didn't assign Dreith to ref a Patriots game for another eleven years.

The following week, Francis went to the Pro Bowl, where he met Phil Villapiano and they talked about the non-call on the pass interference. Villapiano readily admitted he got away with one. "I was beat, so why not take the chance?" he said. "It would only have been a first down, right? I can't believe they didn't throw a flag."

Francis also found himself in a war of words with George Atkinson over the broken nose, conducted through the press. He was quoted as saying, "I don't believe in revenge. But I do believe in getting even." Atkinson was incensed. He claimed that the forearm shiver to Francis' nose was an accident because Francis ducked into the blow. Besides, he said, the two had walked off the field together after the game, and Francis had told him he hoped that Oakland won the Super Bowl. He didn't take the change of heart especially well.

"Fuck Russ Francis, that sissy," Atkinson told the *Miami News*. "I'm a little sick of Russ Francis, Russ Francis, Russ Francis. Coming on like he's some Muhammad Ali. He'll get his chance and I'll see how much of a man he is. He is ignorant. He continues to mouth off after all these months. Some people don't like to get hit. That's Russ Francis' problem. People who don't want to get hit shouldn't go on the football field."

It's hard to say whether Francis ever got back at Atkinson. He did exact some measure of revenge against Villapiano, though. A year later, Villapiano and his wife were visiting Hawaii, and Francis invited them up in one of his charter planes. And when they'd reached maximum altitude, he reached over, opened Villapiano's door, and started to push him out. "I got scratch marks all over my neck from his wife. She thought I was trying to kill him. I guess I was."

Oakland did, of course, go on to win the Super Bowl, and their two wins after the wild-card game weren't even close. It was miserable watching it happen, realizing the Pats had Oakland's number in a way no other team in the league did. And knowing . . . just knowing . . . if it weren't for those bogus calls, no one would've challenged the Patriots either.

I've seen plenty of teams and individuals I couldn't stomach win championships in my life. But none ever bothered me as much as watching the Raiders hoist John Madden onto their shoulders at the end of that game, his fat arms flailing, a big smile plastered above all his chins. More than anyone on that club, he was the face of that whole despicable franchise, and I couldn't stand him. It wouldn't be long before I found out the hard way how wrong I was about the guy.

The '76 Patriots season ended in hideous, soul-crushing fashion, but there was every reason to feel good about the future. That's the way it always is with Cinderella teams; you just assume the prince will be at your door the next day with your shoe, he'll whisk you off to the castle to marry you, your servants will love you, and in no time you'll have your whole wicked stepfamily chained in the dungeon and live happily ever after.

The one thing no one ever expects is what usually happens to these teams. Everything is all sunshine and rainbows until Princess Cinderella realizes that she's not cleaning out fireplaces anymore and starts expecting to be paid princess money.

LIAR, LIAR

The first person to be rewarded for the Patriots success was Chuck Fairbanks, who understandably got a contract extension and a raise. John Hannah and Leon Gray got rewarded with a trip to the Pro Bowl, where they got . . . the shaft. At least from their point of view. Hannah and Gray were the cornerstones of one of the best young offenses in the NFL and among the best linemen in the game. Of that there was no doubt. On passing downs, Gray protected Grogan's blindside like the Secret Service. On run plays, he could block down on a defensive tackle or kick out an end with the best in the game. And Hannah? He wasn't so much a football player as he was a force of nature. He blocked with a fury on every down. It was routine to see him lead a sweep, knock a defender on his ass, keep running at full speed, make a second helping out of another defender, then keep tearing upfield, still hungry for thirds. To this day he remains one of the best linemen of all time. But when they got to the Pro Bowl, met their offensive line peers from around the league, and found out what some of them were being paid, they were appalled. "I found out there were guys out here making three times what I was making," he said. And after a little digging, he found out that, on his own offensive line, there was a part-time veteran splitting time with a rookie who was getting paid $25,000 more than he was.

The issue for both players was that they felt they had been lied to by Pats GM Peter Hadhazy when they hammered out their current deals. Hannah had signed for a $38,000 bonus (every penny of which he'd donated to an Alabama Boys' Club) and a $65,000 per year salary. Gray signed for a $25,000 bonus and $55,000 per year. But both insisted promises had been made to them at the negotiating table. First, they claimed Hadhazy assured them these were top-of-the-market deals they were signing. Next, Hannah walked away believing he'd been promised that he would always be among the highest paid O-linemen in the game. Gray felt he was promised that if he ever made All Pro, he'd get a new deal and be paid All-Pro money.

The whole beef actually traces its origins back to 1974, when the World Football League started up. The WFL was a rival league with no real financial backing that somehow managed to scrape together enough money to sign away a few NFL stars, including Ken Stabler, Miami's Larry Csonka, and L.C. Greenwood of the Steelers. Rather than take the long view that the WFL guys were a bunch of thieving weasels who wouldn't be able to keep the lights on in a year or so, most NFL teams panicked, including the Patriots. They scrambled to lock up their core players, even if it meant overpaying them.

Or, in New England's case, over-promising them. At least that's how Hannah and Gray saw it. They felt Hadhazy was willing to say whatever it took to get them to sign on the dotted line, even if it meant lying through his teeth. They demanded new contracts and made it clear they were willing to hold out if necessary to get them.

The Patriots, naturally, saw it differently. Both players had been represented by agents. They could've found out what the going rate for O-linemen was. And besides, no one put a gun to their heads. They'd signed contracts under their own free will and the Pats damned well expected their employees to live up to them. Hadhazy left to go take the GM job for the Cleveland Browns, but his replacement, Assistant GM Jim Valek, was told no promises had been made, so there was no handshake deal he needed to live up to.

Caught in the middle of all this was Fairbanks. It was a textbook case of a coach and an owner having different agendas. All he cared about was winning, and he needed his best players on the field to do it. If the Patriots lost money and investors had to skip a vacation or lay off some domestic staff to make ends meet, well, that wasn't his concern.

The Sullivans, of course, were in it for the long haul. They felt they couldn't have players dictating to them to tear up their contracts and get huge raises any time they felt like it. And if it meant sacrificing the season to make the point, so be it.

For Fairbanks, it wasn't just business, it was personal. Billy Sullivan had two sons involved in running the club, Pat and Chuck. To boil both men down into overly simplified, easy-to-understand stereotypes (rather than to paint rich, detailed character studies of them), Pat was the outgoing, hands-on, football guy and Chuck was the quiet, introverted business guy. To dumb it down even further, Pat was the jock and Chuck was the nerd.

Early on in his Pats career, Fairbanks had seen Pat working hard, hustling around the field on ball-boy duty, and told Billy, "That kid is going to be a general manager someday." In Chuck Sullivan, he saw the bean counter who was always telling him why the club couldn't afford things. To him, they were the Goofus and Gallant of the front office. *Goofus says you can't have your best blockers. Gallant helps you break down game film.*

An ugly situation was made coyote ugly by Hannah and Gray bringing in super-agent Howard Slusher. He was one of those agents that everybody hates except the players they get massive raises for. Even the NFL Players Association hated him, because he was one of those crusaders who was always demanding more rights for the rank and file, thereby trying to mess with the deals the union cut at the bargaining table. Lord knows the owners hated Slusher. And the entire Patriots fan base despised him instantly. Even the root form of his name is synonymous with shady business funds and the worst thing about winter.

Hannah and Gray, through Slusher, went with the only leverage they had, vowing to walk out of training camp if they didn't have new deals in place by the final preseason game. Game day arrived, there was no new contract, so they made good on their threats and bailed. The Patriots claimed that they were stunned. Hannah and Gray were stunned that they were stunned, given that they'd been calling this particular shot for weeks now.

Then, to the surprise of no one who's familiar with contract negotiations and action movie sequels . . . this time, things got personal.

Billy Sullivan's wife Mary had met Hannah's mother at numerous team functions, and the two had hit it off. During the holdout, she placed a call to Mrs. Hannah. And depending on which side you believe, she was either just being a polite, courteous woman trying to keep things civil with her dear friend, or a greedy battle-ax trying to bully an old lady into pressuring her son into caving in.

"She told my mother, 'You've got to be ashamed of your son,'" Hannah said. And it got worse. In a town like Crossville, Alabama, there can only be so many Hannahs in the phone book. So it became a daily occurrence for his wife Paige to take irate calls from anonymous Patriots fans—the kind who aren't shy about using sailor talk around lady folk. Hannah was outraged, and it only caused him to dig in his heels even further.

Needless to say, the whole situation threw Patriots fans and the media over the edge. The talk shows erupted with angry callers. A few took the players' side, but most went ballistic against Hannah and Gray. It's funny how, whenever an athlete is in a contract dispute, everyone plays the class warfare card.

Everyone has a story about how they grew up with nothing and these ball-players should be thankful they can make a living playing a kid's game. This particular dispute was no exception. It seemed like every Patriots fan with a phone grew up as a Dickensian street urchin or in a log cabin or survived the Depression eking out an existence shining shoes for a penny a pair. One of the phrases that came up constantly was "What's Hannah gonna do? Go back to Alabama and swab hogs?" The point being that he couldn't afford to pass up sixty-five grand a year in NFL money. But nothing could have been further from the truth. That "hog farm" he was going back to was the Hannah family's thriving agri-business. In addition to their own farm, they owned six warehouses in Alabama and Georgia that supplied farm supplies, feed, and livestock medicines to farmers. The fact is, he didn't need Sullivan bucks. He didn't need to scramble people's brains every Sunday to make a good living, so he could stand on principle. Hawg had what you could call "Fuck You" Money.

The regular season came, and still no deal was in sight. The Patriots locker room was divided between the guys who took Hannah and Gray's side, the ones who just wanted them back so they could start winning games, and the ones who didn't give a shit. In week one, they squeaked out a win over a Kansas City team they should have mopped the Astroturf with. Eventually, the matter was referred to the Player-Club Relations Committee to decide. Fairbanks called Hadhazy to make a personal appeal. He asked him—just to help an old colleague—to please admit he'd made those promises to Hannah and Gray, which might have worked, if Chuckaroo had any sense of timing; the Pats next opponent just happened to be Cleveland. Hadhazy was incredulous. "Do you honestly think I'd help you get those guys back before we have to play you? Call back Monday."

Eventually, the mediation worked, and the players were each given four-year extensions. Hannah's was for $600,000 total, and Gray's was for $10,000 less. They reported back to the team, but whatever positive juju they had from that magical previous year was already shot to hell. They finished 9–5, which wasn't good enough to make the playoffs.

Granted, it wasn't a total loss. They'd added some gifted rookies in corner-back Raymond Clayborn, tight end Don Hasselbeck, and most of all, second-round wide receiver Stanley Morgan, who'd go on to be the most prolific wideout in team history. And Hannah, Gray, the fans, and the team had put the whole fiasco in their rearview. So the future was looking bright.

What nobody knew at the time was that there was some bad blood between Fairbanks and the Sullivans, and the Hannah-Gray affair got it pumping. As

Hannah put it later, "The Sullivans took Chuck's authority away and turned him into a liar."

Tragically, that wouldn't be the worst situation anyone would have to deal with. Not by a long, long, long road. Before the 1978 season even began, the team was confronted by the worst kind of calamity a sports organization can face: the real life kind.

DARRYL STINGLEY

Darryl Stingley was, along with John Hannah and Sam Cunningham, one of the mother lode of first-round picks the Pats came away with in 1973. In retrospect, it was less a draft than it was a heist.

Stingley came out of Purdue University by way of John Marshall High School and Chicago's West Side. A five-year veteran, he was averaging over 17 yards per catch for his career, an impressive number on a primarily running team in a run-centric era in pro football. He'd also returned punts and occasionally ran the ball. And more than anything, Stingley was a dynamic, articulate, and altogether likable fan favorite on a team full of them. With the explosive Stanley Morgan now Grogan's primary target, Stingley was now the No. 2 guy on a receiving tandem that we all thought could (or should) take their place as among the best in the league.

In the early evening of August 12, 1978, the Patriots traveled to Oakland for a meaningless preseason game. Yet what happened during that game is one of the seminal moments in the history of a football franchise and the life of one man. And no fan of sports who was watching it live can ever forget it. Nor should they, really.

Stingley, in his No. 84 jersey, ran a crossing route over the middle. Grogan tried to hit him in stride, but the pass was slightly off and led him by too much. Darryl sold out for the ball, leaving his feet, extending his arms and trying to get his hands on it. The local feed TV camera was a little behind, but caught up to the play just in time to see Raiders safety Jack Tatum come across, directly at Stingley. Tatum lowered his head, buried his shoulder pad and helmet directly into the crown of the defenseless receiver's helmet, and basically shattered Darryl Stingley's spine.

This wasn't going to be just some "stinger" or separated shoulder or something you bounce back from. As Stingley lay there in an awkward, twisted heap, Russ Francis came over to check on him, but he was totally non-responsive.

It was worse than bad. Darryl Stingley never took another step in his life. Paralyzed from the neck down, he spent the remainder of his days confined to an electric wheelchair.

No flag was thrown on the play, and a case has been made that there was no penalty on the play, that, by the rules of 1978, the hit was legal. And that's fair. What isn't, however, is how Jack Tatum handled the aftermath. He didn't have to say he was sorry. Breaking a man in two on a technically legal hit doesn't necessarily require an apology. But it does call for some compassion. For some amount of remorse. Maybe just a small amount of human sympathy.

Stingley got none of that from Jack Tatum. Instead, what he got while he recovered was the spectacle of watching Tatum use the episode to brand himself. He bragged about it. He wrote a book called *They Call Me Assassin*. He wore it like a badge of honor. He did everything except put a sticker of Stingley on his helmet, like a fighter pilot marking his kills. He did everything except visit Darryl even once—not until decades later, when he publicly offered to meet with Stingley, on the condition that the news media be there to cover it. The timing of that visit just happened to coincide with the release of another one of his books. Stingley, with the same pride he carried himself with his whole life, told Tatum where he could stick his book sideways.

John Madden, though, was a different story entirely. He was the anti-Tatum. He and Stingley had never met prior to that game. But with Stingley confined to a hospital bed in Oakland, and his teammates having to go back home to get ready for the season, Madden maintained an almost constant vigil at his side. Which is to say, with a complete stranger, 15 years his junior with whom he had almost nothing in common, Madden stayed at Stingley's bedside to offer him whatever comfort he could. Eventually, the tragedy was too much for Madden and he retired from coaching for good to become a broadcasting, video game, and foot-powder pitchman legend. Those who disliked Madden when he was coaching the Raiders had perhaps never been more wrong in their judgment of another human being than they were about him.

Stingley died of heart failure in 2007, at the too-young age of 55. Tatum, in a case of pure karma, also lost the use of his legs to diabetes before he died in 2010 at the age of 61. One of the other sadly ironic parts of the Stingley story is that, for all the Patriots' tightness with a buck with their players, he and the team had just agreed on a contract extension that was going to make him one of the best-paid wideouts in the league. The contract was going to be signed as soon as the team flew back to the East Coast. It never was.

LIAR, LIAR PART II: ELECTRIC CHUCKAROO

As great as that 1976 Patriots team was, you can make a case that the '78 squad was even better. Since we live in a time where the NFL has, for all intents and purposes, outlawed pass defense, and passing stats are so inflated that QBs are putting up 5,000-yard seasons like roided-up baseball players used to hit 40 homers a year, it's easy to forget how much fun it is to watch a great rushing attack. And in the Late Cretaceous Period of NFL rushing offenses, the 1978 Patriots were the T-Rex. They put up an astonishing 3,165 yards on the ground, a record that stands to this day. If fact, no team has even come close. Even the 2006 Atlanta Falcons didn't come within 200 yards of the '78 Pats, and they got 1,000 yards out of their quarterback, Michael Vick.

And it's not as if they put up those numbers on the legs of one super back. They spread the carries around like no one ever had. Sam Cunningham, Andy Johnson, Horace Ivory, and even Steve Grogan each put up over 500 yards. And Don Calhoun was only a few yards shy of 400. The offensive line was the engine that pulled this particular runaway locomotive.

In a season in which their ground attack moved the ball with the relentless unstoppability of the continents drifting, there was one game and one play that still stands out. The Patriots were playing the Cowboys for only the third time in the history of the franchises. And for the first and only time in the lifetime I've wasted watching football, most of the pregame hype was about a matchup between two interior linemen.

John Hannah was lining up against defensive tackle Randy White, the reigning Super Bowl MVP, future Hall of Famer, and one of the premier D-lineman to ever play. I can honestly say that in the Thornton house, we focused on their battle on every single down. And I can tell you in no uncertain terms that Hannah dominated White the entire game. His best moment came at midfield on a simple power run. Hawg fired out, hit White high, driving him to the ground and opening up a hole that Sam Cunningham ran through untouched for a 52-yard touchdown. Watching Hannah's entire career has been one of my great blessings, and this was him at his all-time best.

After a 1–2 start, the Pats strung together a seven-game winning streak. They went 6–2 in the AFC East, finished tied with Miami at 11–5 but won the tiebreaker, achieving two things they never had before: they won their division and earned the right to host a playoff game for the first time in team history.

More importantly, they experienced one other milestone that few teams ever do but was old hat for the Patriots: a complete psychotic break by their head coach.

Unbeknownst to anyone inside the Patriots organization, while the team was on this roll, physically dominating other teams, setting records, enjoying the good times and getting ready for the playoffs, Chuck Fairbanks was spending a big chunk of his time secretly planning his escape. Whether the Hannah-Gray mess started it or Fairbanks was just sick of butting heads with

Billy and Chuck Sullivan or he just didn't like pro football, all that is known for sure is he wanted out, and he didn't care what legally binding agreement he had to break to do it.

In December, with the Pats sitting at 10-3, Fairbanks had a secret meeting with a booster from the University of Colorado, Jack Vickers. Vickers came to Fairbanks with an offer of $45,000 a year to coach the Buffaloes, plus his own TV show and endorsements that would push the deal up to $150,000. Of course, there was the little matter of the fact that Chuck had just signed an extension with New England that still had four years left on it. But it never occurred to him or the fellas at the Flatiron Club that the Sullivans would have a problem with him wiping his ass with their contract and walking out the door.

As is always the case with highly secret, covert meetings that are held in the strictest confidence, word quickly got out. Rumors were all over the place about it. Fairbanks was starting to get questions about meeting with representatives from Colorado, first from the press, then from Billy Sullivan.

And he took the high road. He stood tall, looked the reporters, the cameras, the public, and his employer straight in the eye, and with all the courage and honesty he could muster . . . he lied through his teeth. He responded to every question with the coachspeak version of *Whaaa? Huh? Me? Colorado? Boosters? Meeting? That's crazy talk! Where you getting this stuff from?!?! You guysss . . .* The University of Colorado did the same. They denied any talks of any kind had taken place.

This went on for a few weeks, until things finally came to a head before the last game of the regular season. The Pats had already clinched the division, so they faced an essentially meaningless game against the Dolphins in the Orange Bowl. The day before the game, Fairbanks and Billy Sullivan met in the visiting coach's office, where Fairbanks came clean. He told Sullivan he wanted out of the last four years of his Patriots deal. He would coach the Pats through the end of the season, but then he was off for Boulder. In the meantime, he needed to get going on recruiting players, which is why he was bringing this up now.

To put it mildly, Sullivan didn't take it well. To put it accurately, he blew his stack. Billy was in bad health as it was, and this put him right over the edge. He told Fairbanks he couldn't serve two masters and that there was no way in hell he was going to allow an arrangement where his head coach was calling high school kids when he was being paid good money to lead the Pats to a championship. Sullivan suspended Fairbanks on the spot. He kicked him out of the locker room and had Orange Bowl security escort him out.

It was surreal. For 24 hours, no one knew what the plan was for the Dolphins game, never mind the playoffs. Not the press, not the public, not even the players. All anyone understood was that in the middle of the most success-ful season the team had ever had, the best coach in club history had gotten himself fired. It wasn't until just before game time that the world found out what the short-term solution was. And it was idiotic.

Just historically stupid, even by Patriots standards.

The obvious choice was to do what every team does in an emergency like this: give a battlefield promotion to one of the coordinators. But Billy couldn't decide between offensive coordinator Ron Erhardt or defensive coordinator Hank Bullough. So with Solomon-ish wisdom, he cut the baby in half. He named them both. For the first time in history, a team was going into a game with co-head coaches. Erhardt would worry about the offensive plays, and Bullough would take care of the other side of the ball. And for all the other 10,000 decisions in between that a head coach has to make over the course of a game? They'd decide amongst themselves. Or flip a coin. Or do Rock-Paper-Scissors or something. No one knew, really.

The players found out at the last minute. Billy went before them in the locker room and explained the arrangement. Then they were treated to not one, but three pregame pep talks, the first by Sullivan, then the others by both of his half-coaches. The only one anyone remembers is Billy's, since he spent his whole speech bashing Chuck Fairbanks, calling him an "asshole" over and over again.

To the surprise of no one, Sullivan's grand experiment in demi-coaching was an unmitigated disaster. The Dolphins dominated both Erhardt and Bullough in all aspects of their respective specialties, and won 23–3.

Which helps explain the continued popularity of the One Head Coach ap-proach in all levels of organized sport.

Fortunately, New England had earned a bye week to sort out the mess be-fore they were to host the Houston Oilers in the AFC divisional playoff round. Unfortunately, the week was utter chaos. Sullivan was still furious. He let it be publicly known that Fairbanks had been calling potential recruits from his Foxboro office. So the whole time the coach was lying about having any in-terest whatsoever in another job, he was using his Patriots time, his Patriots office supplies, and his Patriots long-distance phone charges to help make the Colorado Buffaloes better. It was not a good look for him.

Coaches just didn't bail on their teams in the middle of a championship run. It simply did not happen. The great teams had great coaches—Don Shula in Miami, Chuck Knoll in Pittsburgh, Landry in Dallas—and they all hung onto their jobs like popes. But the first time the Patriots had someone who seemed like he was about to get his membership in the Great Coaches Society and learn the secret handshake, all he wanted to do was blow town. It was like Wile E. Coyote slamming into a cliff wall just when he thought he had his paws on Road Runner.

Over the course of the bye week, somewhat cooler heads semi-prevailed. It was decided that, for the good of all involved, Sullivan would reinstate Fairbanks and the team would actually try to focus on winning a playoff game and fight it out later. For all the good it did, they might as well have made Fairbanks, Erhardt, and Bullough tri-coaches. Because it was a disaster from the jump.

In the first quarter, Houston quarterback Dan Pastorini threw a sideline pass to receiver Ken Burroughs. Pats corner back Mike Haynes, one of the great defensive backs ever to play the game, tried to jump the route to go for the interception, missed, and the pass was completed for a 71-yard touchdown. That was pretty much the end of New England's effort on that day.

The Patriots scored on a gadget play, a halfback option throw by Andy Johnson to wideout Harold Jackson, but that was the extent of the fight New England had in them after a week of distractions and insanity. Pastorini only attempted 15 passes, but completed 12 of them for three touchdowns. Grogan was only 3-for-12 for 38 yards and two interceptions before getting benched in favor of backup Tom Owens. A garbage-time touchdown from Owens to Russ Francis helped make it a 31–14 loss, but it wasn't even that close. As the game got completely out of hand, the angry, boozy Foxboro crowd rained chorus after chorus of "Goodbye Chuckie/We're glad to see you go" down upon the home team's sideline. As the game came to a merciful end, team security, officers from the Foxboro PD, and the Massachusetts State Police had to form a Spartan phalanx to get Fairbanks to the locker room in one piece.

But that wasn't nearly as ugly as things got after the season was over. Sullivan fired Fairbanks before the automatic closer shut the locker room door behind him. If the two said anything at all to each other, it was undoubtedly filled with lots of anger, swear words, and "See you in court."

Which is exactly where the brawl ended up.

Nothing can ruin a good millionaire fight story faster than the two sides lawyering up. We'd all rather they settle things in the parking lot behind the stadium with switchblades and tire irons, but life seldom gives us what we want. Chuck Fairbanks pretty much felt that he could break a contract any time he wanted. The whole thing came back full circle, to the very first words out of his mouth in that very first meeting five years earlier, when Sullivan asked him if he was under contract with Oklahoma and he said, "Not exactly." Of course he was. He just didn't think much of it and never did.

Fairbanks felt like he had the option to jump ship on the Pats any time it suited his mood. He testified that he'd had three different college jobs and left every one of them while he was still under contract. The judge was incredulous. "This court cannot consider his idea of a contract; cannot accept it." And he ruled in New England's favor. He was legally bound to the Patriots until they said otherwise.

Oddly enough, Fairbanks being embroiled in this mess up to his twitchy eyeballs did nothing to discourage the boys from the Flatiron Club one bit. He was still their guy, regardless of what it took to get him. So Vickers and the other 238 members foreclosed on some mortgages, drilled a few more oil wells, embezzled money out of some 401(k)s, or whatever it is that rich western football boosters do when they need to raise funds. They bought Fairbanks out of his contract for $200,000, plus Chuckie waived over $100,000 in deferred salary.

The whole tedious, sordid fiasco was over, which was good. So was the Fairbanks Era in Foxboro, which was bad. Just when it seemed like the Patriots had finally gotten it all together, that they were being run by competent, football-savvy grown ups (who knew what they were doing and had put together a deep, young, talented roster, with a great coaching scheme), everything went sideways, just like it always had. What felt like a dynasty in the making lasted all of three years. Because once Fairbanks left, the franchise went right back to its default setting of short periods of mediocrity followed by long stretches of abysmal failure.

William "Billy" Sullivan, the visionary who took the down payment on a vacation house and turned it into a pro football franchise.

All photographs courtesy of the New England Patriots

Ron Burton was the Patriots' first official player — and the inspiration for the community-service award that bears his name.

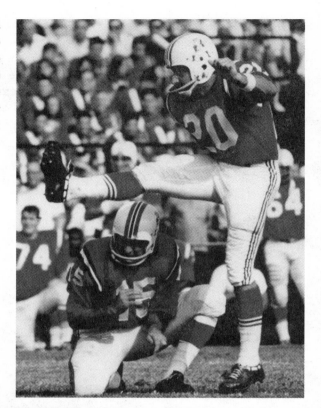

Babe Parilli, Gino Cappelletti, and Ron Burton: the early stars of the Boston Patriots of the upstart American Football League.

Defensive lineman Bob Dee was one of the great early Patriots and a member of the club's Hall of Fame. The former U.S. Marine's best play probably saved a child's life.

Linebacker Nick Buoniconti, the best player on the early Patriots, making a tackle. The team traded him to Miami — where he went on to a Hall of Fame career.

From 1963 to 1968, the Patriots' home field was Fenway Park which —
in spite of the chaos this caused — was a major upgrade from the college
stadiums the team had previously called home.

Billy Sullivan
announces a deal
to build Schaefer
Stadium. Unveiled
in 1971, it was
obsolete on the day
it opened. The man
on the right is Phil
Fine, a Boston lawyer
who assembled the
investment group.
The unidentified man
in the middle was
likely a Schaefer beer
representative.

After the team was nearly called the Bay State (B.S.) Patriots, a new name is announced.

Schaefer Stadium with the harness-racing track in the background.

Quarterback Jim Plunkett (16) was drafted first overall to lead the team to glory. Which he did. Unfortunately, that team was the Raiders, whom he led to two Super Bowl wins.

Chuck Fairbanks built the first very good Patriots team, but jumped ship before they could become truly great.

Coach Chuck Fairbanks demonstrating the dreaded Half Eye, which terrified his team.

Mike Haynes, one of the best cornerbacks of all time, was allowed to leave after seven seasons and went on to a Hall of Fame career with the Raiders.

Sam Cunningham was lead back in the most prolific rushing attack in NFL history. Unfortunately, due mostly to off-the-field chaos, that team would never win a playoff game.

Quarterback Steve Grogan hands off to running back Tony Collins in the mid-1980s. Grogan personified toughness while Collins became the face of a major drug scandal.

Schaefer Stadium at night. The crowds at prime-time games were so rowdy that, from 1982 to 1994, the Patriots were banned from hosting *Monday Night Football*.

Victor Kiam and Billy Sullivan: a case of one of the most cash-strapped owners in pro sports selling his team to one of the most reviled.

Bill Parcells came to the Patriots in 1993 and gave them instant credibility. But his divorce from the team would be one of the messiest chapters in franchise history.

Drew Bledsoe was arguably the first true franchise quarterback in team history and helped lead the Patriots to two Super Bowls.

Bill Belichick's bizarre defection from an archrival was the first step toward building a dynasty. Photo by David Silverman.

Gillette Stadium rises behind the remains of Foxboro Stadium. One of the best facilities in the sport replacing the absolute worst — a perfect metaphor for the team.

Tom Brady, the 199th pick of the 2000 draft,
turned a downtrodden franchise into a dynasty.
Photo by Keith Nordstrom.

10 BACK TO THE FUTURE— THE 80S

★ ★ ★ ★ ★ ★ ★ ★ ★ ★ ★ ★ ★ ★ ★ ★ ★ ★

You know, most people would kill . . . to be
treated like a god, just for a few moments.
COACH NORMAN DALE, *Hoosiers*

During my brief and un-noteworthy high school football career, I went out for the freshman team, and at the time I was too small to put anywhere but at safety.

I was also too small to ever see the field on game days, for that matter. Athletically, I wasn't a total loss. I was small and not particularly fast. But I can honestly say that at least I had an Irishman's ability to take a beating.

One of my proudest moments was the Saturday practice where maybe half the team had showed up. Saturday practices weren't mandatory, so the only ones who ever showed up were either the uber-dedicated team captain types or kids who simply had nothing better to do with their weekends. I'll leave it to you to decide which type I was. Short of bodies, I was picked to play middle linebacker for the scout team. To be more accurate, I was sent in as a meat puppet to be sacrificed so that our offense's guards—a 300-pound ninth grader and a future U.S. Marine—could practice double teaming the middle linebacker of our next opponent. I know the coaches didn't have a hell of a lot of respect for my football skills, and if I'd quit the team, they wouldn't have given it a second thought. But even a high school football coach doesn't want a death on his hands (what with all the paperwork, which is time spent away from game prep), so they were reluctant to put me in. But I said screw it. I wanted to try. It was a chance to prove that, if nothing else, I could take the worst they could throw at me and bounce back up. To prove it to myself as well as to them.

An hour or so into the practice, with me absorbing pummeling after vicious pummeling at the hands of these two behemoths, the offense broke huddle, came to the line, and I overheard Future Marine say to Huge Kid, "He *is* a gaybo. But at least he's tough . . ." At the end of the season, I went in to say

143

goodbye and thanks to the coaches, and the head coach shook my hand and gave me a speech about toughness and character and something about if he could put my heart into some of these other kids' bodies, blah, blah, blah . . . I was floored. I had no idea he'd felt that way. To this day, it's one of the proudest moments of my life. And it means more than any trophy, award, or competition I've ever won.

Little did I know it at the time, but the Jerry Thornton of the 80s shared quite a bit in common with the Patriots of the 70s; we both excelled at going out on a low note. I knew going out for varsity football the following year would be a waste of time, not to mention suicide. So I hung up the helmet and pads for good. Quietly. Eschewing the retirement press conference and all the farewell ceremonies the schools we visited would have no doubt have held for me. And that freshman team I retired from was the worst in our league. As the 1970s bled into the decade that would bring us acid-washed jeans, Rick Astley, *MacGyver*, and straight-to-video pornography, the Patriots would find themselves once again in familiar territory. They went from having ultimate triumph within their grasp to having it all crash down around their heads. They were the laughingstocks of the sports world once again. All in a matter of a few weeks.

The Patriots were back at square one, needing a coach to replace Chuck Fairbanks. It had been awhile—nearly four years—since they'd hired one, so they pulled out their old file marked "Searching for a Head Coach," flipped to the folder labeled "Recruit a Great College Coach Coming Off Tremendous Season," and found the name "Robinson, John."

John Robinson had been the head coach of the University of Southern California since 1976. Before that he'd been an assistant at Oregon, USC, and briefly with the Oakland Raiders, before returning to Southern Cal to take the head job. He'd just led the Trojans to the national title, so there was speculation all over the place that the Patriots were interested.

And you can see why. He had head coaching experience, pro experience, he was smart, innovative, and successful. To a person, all of New England thought he was the perfect candidate. But inside the Patriots' coach-hiring file was still that same old subfolder marked "Bungle the Hiring So Badly You'll Be Rejected and Publicly Humiliated." The one they'd used when they screwed up the hirings of Lombardi, Knoll, Paterno, McKay, and Devaney, et al. And once again, they followed that one to the letter.

In Robinson's case, Pats general manager Bucko Kilroy (a stand-up guy who was universally respected) was meeting with reporters to confirm that yes, the rumors were true. He could in fact proudly announce that the Patriots had offered their head coaching job to John Robinson of the National

Champion USC Trojans. What Bucko didn't know was that at that exact same moment, Chuck Sullivan was talking to a different group of reporters to say that the Patriots hadn't offered any job to anyone and everything they'd been hearing was a lie. In the "he said/he said" situation that ensued, Bucko had earned enough street cred over his career to get the benefit of the doubt. And whatever reason Chuck would have for contradicting him, only Chuck knew.

Whatever happened, John Robinson was not stupid enough to squander the mojo he'd built up at Southern Cal by leaving to go work for a team that couldn't decide if they'd offered him the job or not. He passed.

Rather than subject his family, his players, and his fans to another degrading coaching search like the one they'd suffered five years earlier, and for a job no qualified candidate would want, Billy Sullivan just decided to say "to hell with it" and promote from within. No one is sure what method he used to choose between Ron Erhardt and Hank Bullough, but Erhardt was the choice.

RON ERHARDT

You can see the logic behind putting Erhardt in charge. He was smart. He was a decent, honest guy. He had the respect of everyone. He was the coach of a record-setting offense. He wasn't the sexy pick, but it made sense on a lot of levels.

Ron Erhardt's only real problem seemed to be that he was Ron Erhardt, not Chuck Fairbanks. Whatever abstract, indefinable quality makes one man a natural leader and not a second banana, Fairbanks had it and Erhardt didn't. He was simply coming after an act too tough to follow. Think George H.W. Bush taking over for Ronald Reagan. His players liked him; he just lacked that moral authority that made men admire him, fear him, and bend to his will. And it didn't help one bit that Erhardt's bosses didn't fear him either. They showed deference to Fairbanks that Erhardt simply didn't get, and the players picked up on it right away. He was undermined on a regular basis, such as when Billy Sullivan publicly complained that the team lacked discipline. And he had to put up with some downright meddlesome behavior from ownership, like the time when Billy busted into the coaches' booth in the middle of a game and demanded they get on the headsets that were connected to the ones on the sidelines and tell Erhardt to make a quarterback change.

Not that it was all bad. The pieces were still in place for a solid ball club. They narrowly missed the playoffs by going 9–7 in Erhardt's first year. And again the next year, when they went a respectable 10–6. But in each of those years, the club faded down the stretch, losing five games and four games, respectively, in the second halves of those seasons.

It was one of those workplace environments where the employees pick up on the fact that the middle manager doesn't have the support of the higher-ups and it leads, as such things so often do, to dissension in the ranks. It's the kind of thing that's natural in a strong-willed group of athletes, but something that a strong-leader type like Fairbanks can crush before it affects winning and losing. A trait that Erhardt, for whatever reason, lacked. When the bitching and moaning got too much to take, Erhardt called a team meeting to get his troops in line. He stood up in front of them, looked them in the eye, and told them he'd had enough. It was time to come together, knock off the infighting, and start to focus on winning as a team. If anyone in the room didn't want to be a New England Patriot, he said, they could come see him in the morning.

The next day, there was a line of players outside his office.

ROCK BOTTOM

There was plenty of talent left over from the Fairbanks years. In fact, it was pretty much the same roster, playing in the same scheme. But the great, unwashed Patriots fan base had the general sense that the team was on the decline. On the surface, everything looked the same, but it didn't feel like it. It was the same entropy they probably felt in the Roman Empire post-A.D. 330. All the infrastructure was still there. You still had the Colosseum and the aqueducts and the baths and all that. And while no one was saying Emperor Constantine wasn't a swell ruler in his own right, even as he was moving the capital way to the east and converting everybody to Christianity, he was no Caesar. And like then, the prevailing wisdom in the Erhardt era was that the glory days were probably gone.

To be fair, Erhardt was put in an impossible position. He had virtually none of the say on personnel matters that Coach Half-Eye had enjoyed, and this was during a time when Pats ownership was trying to save a buck or two million by jettisoning a lot of their best talent. Eventually the money problems led to ownership trading away cornerstone players and team leaders, which demoralized everyone even further. Leon Gray was traded after that record-setting 1978 season. Russ Francis was shipped to San Francisco after the 1980 season. Others who took to the lifeboats included offensive guard Sam Adams, defensive lineman Mel Lunsford, and others. But the harder they bailed, the faster the ship took on water and the deeper they sank.

The lowest point of the low points, the absolute Mariana Trench of the Patriots of the era, was the '81 team. More specifically, the defense. They weren't bad in all statistical categories, but that's only because they didn't have to be. They were so bad at defending the run that no opponent saw the need to do anything else but cram the ball right up the middle, because the Pats were helpless to stop them. They had the second fewest pass attempts against them in the NFL, but the most rushing attempts, a league-high 2,950 yards. You knew it was bad because, while the NFL didn't keep track of tackles as an official stat until 1994, safety Tim Fox was the team's leading tackler. By far. And having your safety—who by definition is the last line of defense—making all your tackles 10 yards deep into your secondary is never a good thing. For his heart and effort, saving the D from being an even worse disaster than it already was, Fox was also dealt right after the season ended.

The single best thing about that unit was the name they were given: the Red Sea Defense. They parted down the middle so badly the Israelites could've walked right through them. That is one of the all-time great team nicknames, and its genius has never been fully appreciated.

The 1981 Patriots were the worst team in football, but it wasn't easy. They had to fight for the title. The Baltimore Colts weren't about to just let them take it; they had to earn it.

Statistically, the Colts were actually far worse than New England. They were near the bottom of the league in every offensive category, and on defense they were even worse. The Colts gave up a mind-boggling 33 points a game, 125 more in total than the second-worst team, the Patriots. But when it came to utter ineptitude, the Patriots would not be denied.

The Pats and Colts duked it out all season, matching each other loss for loss, suckpill for suckpill. Fortunately for fans of atrociousness everywhere, due to a quirk in the schedule, the two were set to face each other in the final week of the season. As the losses piled up for both clubs, it meant the loser of that game was going to finish last in the league. It was shaping up to be a showdown of wretched proportions. The prize to the loser was the No. 1 pick in the draft, and the consensus best player was a massive, run-stuffing defensive end out of the University of Texas named Kenneth Sims. For either team, with their historically bad defenses, the addition of Sims would be a godsend. The game, quickly dubbed The Stupor Bowl, was to be played in Baltimore, so the Patriots enjoyed the all-important Road Field Disadvantage. The loser of that final game was going to get Kenneth Sims. And with fans from both teams pulling as hard as they could against their own, the Pats managed to fail better than Baltimore did. Despite one final, desperate fourth-quarter touchdown that almost snatched victory from the jaws of defeat, they successfully cocked the game away. As the old saying goes, the Patriots simply wanted it less. They succeeded by failing, and the reward was that coveted No. 1 overall pick.

Having led his team to the very bottom, Ron Erhardt was fired, along with the entire coaching staff. Anxious to rebuild from the ground up, to the surprise of no one, Billy looked to the college coaching ranks for a new head coach. Even less surprisingly, he screwed it up about as badly as he could have.

RON MEYER

Ron Meyer was the hot new college football coaching commodity out of Southern Methodist University, having just led the Mustangs to a National Championship. Meyer also had some experience in the pros, having spent two years on Tom Landry's staff in Dallas. He was the genius who allegedly masterminded SMU's legendary "Pony Express" rushing offense that made stars out of running backs Eric Dickerson and Craig James. And earlier than that, he coached the University of Nevada, Las Vegas to an undefeated season in Division II. So there was no arguing with his *curriculum vitae*. But possibly Meyer's best asset was his communication skills. He had a reputation as a tireless recruiter who visited more high school players than any coach in the country. The conventional wisdom was that he had built the Mustangs program up from nothing to a national power by convincing the parents of the best recruits in America to send their sons to SMU just through the sheer force of his charm, personality, and likability.

And it was true. Or would be, if you replaced "charm, personality, and likability" with "guarantees of massive, regular cash payouts." What no one knew at the time, because it didn't come out until years later, was that Mustangs football under Ron Meyer (and his successors) was up to its ten-gallon hat in widespread, shameless, blatant payouts to their players. ESPN's 2010 *30 for 30* documentary, *Pony Express*, recounts players being handed envelopes of cash in the open, with no effort to hide them, despite the common knowledge that the program was under scrutiny from the NCAA. Ron Meyer literally won his national title with a professional team.

By the time the NCAA posse caught up to the SMU bandits, Meyer was long gone, even from the Patriots. In 1987 they gave the Mustangs the "Death Penalty" that shut the program down for the next two years and effectively destroyed it for the next twenty. The biggest gripe the powers that be seemed to have with SMU wasn't even so much the payouts, but the obvious, half-assed, ham-fisted way they went about it. It was like they didn't even *try* to hide what they were up to, even after repeated warnings from the NCAA. It was the crooked football program equivalent of carrying a giant flat screen out of a store without paying for it. The security guard feels more insulted by the lack of respect than mad about the TV.

By the time the investigation into SMU's player payouts was finished and the Death Penalty was handed down, Meyer was already part of New England's glorious past, the Pat's having long since figured out what a buffoon and a phony he was. That part actually only took a few months, when all those great communication skills gradually gave way to the realization that the man was completely full of shit.

Meyer had this way of talking in folksy little bromides and memorized catch phrases that he'd picked up along his personal journey, in order to make himself sound thoughtful and wise. Most of them are lost to history. But one he used repeatedly in interviews was, "Proper planning prevents poor performance"; he was obviously delighted with it. Essentially, he came across as forced and contrived. He had that kind of style that you realize might work great on some 17-year-old halfback trying to decide between SMU and Texas A&M, but on a naturally cynical, jaded population of Massholes, Maniacs, and New Hampsters, it didn't fly for a minute.

It took little time for his players to realize what a fraud he was. John Hannah, for example, hated Meyer with the white-hot intensity of a million pizza ovens. He openly admits he once chased Meyer around the stadium, trying to kill him. Hannah had caught him in a bald-faced lie while bad-mouthing some coaches Hannah actually respected, so he went after him. Meyer took off, running for his life. And once he'd made his successful getaway, he stayed out of sight the rest of the day.

Worse than the phoniness was when it became painfully obvious to the players that the man couldn't coach. He didn't run any meetings. He pretty much let coordinators Lew Erber and Jim Mora run the offense and defense. And on the rare occasions he did speak up, he came off sounding clueless. Eventually, the only meetings he really ever even went to were for special teams.

So it would make sense then that the one memorable thing that ever happened on Ron Meyer's Patriots watch was a special teams play. And that it was ridiculous. As in "Immortalized in Blooper Reels and 'Most Ridiculous Moments Ever' Shows From Now Until the End of Eternity"-caliber ridiculous.

THE SNOWPLOW GAME

It was December 12, 1982, and the Dolphins were in Foxboro for what was only the sixth game of the season due to a labor dispute. Miami was 4-1 and still a perennial Super Bowl contender under the legendary Don Shula. The year before, while the Patriots were hitting rock bottom, Miami finished 11-5 and won the AFC East. In the playoffs they lost an overtime heartbreaker to San Diego, despite clawing back from an early 24-0 deficit. They were still among the first class of NFL teams, while the Pats were limping along at 2–3.

The night before the game, the region suffered a severe rainstorm, which quickly froze over and then by game time turned to heavy snowfall. So, unsurprisingly the turf field was basically a frozen pond covered with snow, and the play of both teams reflected it. The footing was so bad, neither team could get any kind of passing game going. The Dolphins only attempted 18 passes, and the Pats threw 5 times for a total of 13 yards.

Under the circumstances, the NFL did make one accommodation, in that they allowed the officials to stop play periodically so that grounds crews could at least clear the five-yard lines and the sidelines. So at the very least, the players and 25,000 souls hearty or dumb enough to brave the conditions could have some idea what was going on in the game. Which meant every available Patriots employee and a few guys hired as per diems were standing by with shovels, snowblowers, and plows.

Predictably, neither offense could put anything together, and the game was still scoreless deep into the fourth quarter. The closest either team came to putting points on the board was one missed field goal by each team's kicker, neither of whom could get traction on their plant foot.

Late into the fourth, the Patriots somehow managed to put a drive together that stalled on Miami's 16-yard line, setting up a 33-yard attempt by John Smith. While Smith and the field-goal unit were furiously digging away at the ice with their cleats, trying to chip away enough ice to expose enough of the turf underneath to give him a decent chance to make the kick, Ron Meyer came up with an inspired idea. An insane idea. And tantamount to cheating. At the very least beneath the dignity of the league and one that cemented the Patriots' reputation as the biggest laughingstock franchise in all of pro sports. But inspired.

Meyer spotted a member of the grounds crew sitting on a ride-on lawn tractor outfitted with a spinning brush attachment for snow removal. Gesturing wildly, he motioned to the guy to drive out onto the field and clear a patch where Smith was digging. And he did. While the Pats special teamers dove out of the way, the plow came through and cut a curved swath of turf in the middle of the field.

To say Don Shula was angry would be the understatement of the 20th century. After decades in coaching developing a reputation as a calm, cerebral, taciturn figure on the sidelines, Shula completely lost his shit. No manager in the history of pro wrestling ever went nuttier than he did at that moment; gesturing wildly, screaming at the officials, his legendarily cool demeanor be damned. Of course, the more nuts he went, the funnier it was for the frigid, drunken sots in the stands. And Shula only screamed louder and the crowd only laughed harder when the kick was good.

Shula's protests fell on deaf ears. The refs apparently answered him with the same logic the umpire gave the manager of the Greenville Goons in that Looney Tunes cartoon where Bobo the elephant got to pitch for the Sweetwater Schnooks because there's nothing in the rulebook saying an elephant can't pitch. To the best of anyone's knowledge, there was no NFL rule specifically banning the home team from using a snowplow to help themselves; the play stood, and the Pats held on to win, 3-0.

It was the story of the year in the NFL. And it only got more press as the details came out. As it turned out, the snowplow belonged to Pats' GM Bucko Kilroy, who'd brought it from home. The driver became a celebrity overnight once the world found out he was out on work release from the state prison in Walpole. His name was Mark Henderson, and after that game Henderson would forever be a part of New England sports lore.

In the days that followed, the game was a national joke, but no one in Miami was laughing. Shula took his protest to the league office, but got no more satisfaction. "I called the commissioner [Pete Rozelle] and told him it was the most unfair act that had ever happened in a football game," he said. "He agreed. I asked him what he was going to do about it. He said, 'Nothing.'"

Back in New England, Ron Meyer was celebrated for his genius move, one that outsmarted the alleged smartest coach in football history. Years later, John Smith admitted that he felt he had the kick with or without the extra help and didn't appreciate being made to look like he needed to cheat to win. If anything, he was ripped at Meyer for taking forever to decide whether to kick or go for it on fourth down and damn near costing him the chance to win the game on the level.

Around Foxboro, the Snowplow Game is still celebrated as a triumphant moment in the Patriots' glorious past. The plow itself hangs from the ceiling of the Patriots Hall of Fame, a cherished artifact, like the Saturn rocket engine hanging in the National Air and Space Museum. And when the Pats held a ceremony to commemorate the closing of Foxboro Stadium in 2001, they brought it onto the field with Mark Henderson riding it. To anyone who was around in 1982, neither it nor he needed any introduction.

"GAME DAY"

Another New England legend made his ignominious debut in 1982 as well: Kenneth Sims, now a Patriot following the previous year's Stupor Bowl. At six foot five, with a chiseled 272 pounds on his frame and the pedigree of playing for a powerhouse Texas Longhorns team, he looked like the prototype of a stud defensive end who would anchor the Pats D and make the Red Sea defense a thing of the past.

At training camp in his rookie year, all the buzz was about Sims. Everyone wanted to know about the new savior of the franchise, and for that initial week or so all the news stories were glowing profiles and interviews. He seemed like a fairly bright, articulate, and nice kid, and an elite physical specimen.

And confident. When a reporter pointed out that the Patriots only had 20 sacks as a team the previous year, Sims vowed he'd have more than that by himself in the next season. It was a bold prediction, but after the defense had been so bad, it was refreshing to have a guy with a little attitude, even if it bordered on cockiness.

At least he looked that way until he hit the field.

After a few practices, it came to light that the one thing you never heard about him was how well he was playing. And that, as it turned out, was because he wasn't. Then you started to hear how truly terrible he looked in practice. That he was getting stuffed on a regular basis by undrafted, slim-chance offensive linemen who very soon would be driving trucks for a living. Concern grew into worry. Worry became fear. Fear evolved into a sort of panic that their defense's messiah was already a total bust. Finally, one reporter with perhaps more balls than manners asked Sims to explain how it was that—if he was the consensus best player in the draft—he could look so bad in practice?

"Don't worry about me," Sims said. "I'll be ready on game day."

Whatever message he was trying to deliver, the entire population of New England all heard it the same way. Their takeaway was that Sims—the player on whom the future of the franchise depended and a guy who had never played a down in the NFL—felt like practicing was unnecessary and a waste of his time, because he'd just be able to turn it on when it counted. And from that day forward, the nickname "Game Day" was his.

Sims played in all of 14 games in his first two seasons, and started in only 11 of them. And he fell short of his prediction of 20-plus sacks, finishing with only 17. Finishing his career with a total of 17, that is. Apparently, what he meant to say was that he was saving himself for "Game Day" of his NFL career in his *next* life, whenever that was.

The Patriots actually made the playoffs that year, but if any playoff appearance ever came with an asterisk, it was this one. The work stoppage shortened the season to only nine games. To mitigate the unfairness of it and to placate the fans, the league allowed a ridiculous 16 out of 28 teams to qualify for the playoffs. And on the "strength" of a 5-4 record, New England slipped in. But in an ironic twist, they were sent where no snowplow could help them: Miami. The Dolphins won 28–13, which was a measure of revenge, just not the revenge Shula probably would've preferred. But by then the league had put in a "No driving a lawnmower across an opposing coach's face" rule.

For Ron Meyer, that would pretty much be the peak of his coaching tenure in New England. As time wore on, it became more and more obvious that he had less and less respect in the locker room. "Fraud" was a term that kept coming up. For instance, one image Meyer tried to sell that no one was buying was him as the colorful, larger-than-life Texan. He drove around in a big, fully loaded, oil-tycoon Lincoln. He wore pounds of jewelry. And went around talking in a Texas drawl that J.R. Ewing would've said was too much. But everyone saw right through it. The harder he tried, the more ridiculous he came across. "For goodness sakes," said somebody in the organization, "he's from Westerville, Ohio."

Even when he tried to accommodate the players, it exploded in his face like a shaken-up beer can. One day, a local TV reporter tried to set up his equipment for some interviews before practice, a minor inconvenience in that it would cut into the players' warm-up time. No one considered it the hugest problem in the world, but some of the players brought it to the coach's attention. But Ron Meyer was never above swatting a fly by dropping a nuke on it. And so to address the issue, he closed all practices to all media forever. The players were stunned. "We had come off a big win," an anonymous team spokesman said. "And all of a sudden all anybody is writing about is closed practices."[22]

In fact, he might have lost the locker room sooner than that. A lot sooner. As in before his first game, when he tossed decades of football tradition (and common sense) out the window and started putting offensive and defensive players on separate buses. Whether he segregated the special teamers too is lost to history.

Meyer's on-field decisions weren't winning anybody over, either. In 1983 the United States Football League had begun operations, in order to challenge the NFL. Among the stars they lured with big-money contracts were future Pro Football Hall of Fame quarterback Jim Kelly, Heisman Trophy winners Herschel Walker and Doug Flutie, and Meyer's running back from SMU, Craig James. Following the USFL's initial season, Meyer convinced Billy Sullivan to spend considerable amounts of time, money, and draft picks to pry James away from the upstart league. Eventually they succeeded in landing him—only to watch Meyer barely ever put him on the field. In his first eight games in New England and reunited with Meyer, James had four or fewer rushing attempts six times, and never more than 10.

It would be nine games before James worked his way up to starting running back and led the team in rushing. But Meyer wasn't around to see it happen.

Meyer led the Pats to an 8–8 season in 1983, and they were off to a decent 5–3 start in 1984. But by then things were coming to a head. The players were increasingly fed up with Meyer's act and were going over his head to complain to upper management. He had violated the Prime Directive of Coaching. You can be a tough, disciplinarian coach. You can be an easygoing player's coach. But the one thing you can't be is a phony, which is how Meyer's team perceived him. He'd lost their respect and no search party was going to find it.

Pat Sullivan was by then the Patriots' general manager, and he came to realize that Meyer wasn't working out. "He tried to portray this image as a taskmaster," he told Michael Felger. "But the players saw through it. I'm reluctant to call it an act, but that's the only word that comes to mind."[23]

In order to keep Les Miserables from revolting, Pat was forced to hold meetings with the players behind Meyer's back. Meyer might have been a total phony, but he wasn't dumb. No coach survives long in a situation like that, so he did the brave, courageous, and honorable thing: he shot his way out of town.

Or to put it differently, he forced the team to fire him. Pat Sullivan was at a league meeting in New Orleans when he got a call from *Boston Herald* beat writer Kevin Mannix asking for a reaction to the fact that Meyer had just fired defensive coordinator Rod Rust. It was news to Sullivan, because Meyer didn't have the authority to hire and fire anyone.

Except himself, apparently, because he was canned the next day, to the delight of his players. Larry McGrew said his reaction to hearing the news was "Yahoo!!!"[24]

As a postscript to his Patriots career, Meyer ended up landing on his feet with the Indianapolis Colts, coaching them for a few years with little success. One of his former Patriots players who was signed to play for him in Indy was none other than "Game Day" Sims, who apparently was one of the Pats who despised him and undermined him the most in New England. When a Patriots writer asked him how he could coach a guy who did everything he could to get him fired from his last job, Meyer answered with one of the all-time quotes ever about life as a football coach: "In this business, we're all whores to talent."

RAYMOND BERRY

This time there was no nationwide coaching search, no battlefield promotion; the Patriots just went and hired someone who was not only outside the organization, he was also outside of football. Any football.

Raymond Berry was announced as the interim head coach halfway through the 1984 season. He had been the Patriots' wide receivers coach under Chuck Fairbanks and Ron Erhardt. But since being let go along with all of Erhardt's staff in 1981, he had been out of football. It seemed like they just hired him because nobody else would take such a miserable, thankless job, the same way migrant farm workers are hired to work in produce fields. However bad the Pats job was, it had to be better than whatever the hell else Berry was doing.

Raymond Berry had experience as an assistant coach but was also a football legend. A Hall of Famer who spent his career catching passes from Johnny Unitas in the black-high-tops and crew-cut-hair days. But the first rumors about him as a head coach were not good.

News soon broke that Berry had babysat some of the Patriots players' kids. That was not welcome news; the impression was that Ron Meyer was a strict, tough disciplinarian, and these pampered fat cat modern athletes were too soft to hack him, so they staged an uprising and got ownership to bring in a patsy they could walk all over.

Of course, that was the view from the outside looking in. And as time went on, the second, third, and subsequent impressions of Berry were much better.

If nothing else, he wasn't a phony. He met reporters in jeans and denim work shirts. He answered questions truthfully, even if it meant admitting that he didn't know all his players' names. Without knowing the inside skinny on all that had been going on in the locker room with the last coach, it was hard to grasp how important it was that Ray Berry be the Anti-Meyer. This was a team that wanted to be led, and this was a guy they'd follow. As running back Tony Collins later said, "Raymond Berry earned more respect in one day than Ron Meyer earned in three years."[25]

One of the things that he quickly established was an attention to detail that seemed insane. At least for a while, until it started paying dividends. For instance, Berry started having them practice fumble recoveries, which sounded like lunacy. The roll of a football is the most random thing in the world, and trying to practice getting to a fumbled ball sounded like planning your bingo card by practicing where the numbered balls will fall in the rotating drum. But later on it paid off. Hugely.

Going into the 1985 season, the Patriots were coming off several mediocre years, but there was reason to be optimistic. Not just because of the new head coach. Or because the NFL was set up so that nondescript, middle-of-the-pack clubs like them always had a shot at the playoffs. But because there was some true, legitimate talent on the roster.

John Hannah was still anchoring the offensive line. Craig James was joined in the backfield by four-year veteran Tony Collins. On the outside was Stanley Morgan, the most productive wideout in team history, who averaged almost 20 yards per reception for his career. And replacing Steve Grogan under center was Tony Eason, whom the Pats took in 1983's legendary Year of the Quarterback draft. Six QBs were taken in the first round that year, including Hall of Famers John Elway, Jim Kelly, and Dan Marino. Eason was the fourth to come off the board, 12 spots ahead of where Miami selected Marino. Eason was a soft-spoken, cerebral, introverted kid out of Illinois. A kind of blond-haired, Midwestern version of what Jim Plunkett was a decade earlier. Fair or not, Pats fans had grown increasingly frustrated with Grogan. And the general consensus was that he had taken the team as far as he ever would, and they were not going to claw their way out of football irrelevance without a star at the quarterback position.

Eason had been brought along slowly in his first two seasons as backup. By '85, everyone was ready for the Tony Eason Era to begin, and he was the week-one starter.

On the other side of the ball, they had their best defense in ages. Veterans like linebacker Steve Nelson and end Julius Adams were on the downside of their careers, but were still productive and gave the unit leadership. Cornerback Raymond Clayborn was in his prime. And outside linebacker Andre Tippett, a physical freak with a black belt in karate and also an intelligent, high-motor player, was entering the third season of his Hall of Fame career. And Kenneth Sims was showing just enough flashes of brilliance to make you think that the game day he had talked about being ready to play might actually arrive.

But above all, there was one player who gave the team hope. The No. 1 overall pick in the 1984 draft, who was arguably the most athletically gifted player New England ever had.

And just to prove these were still the same old Patriots, he was the most troubled player as well.

IRVING FRYAR

Through a series of trades, the Patriots had managed to get hold of the Tampa Bay Buccaneers' first pick in the '84 draft, only to sit back and watch the Bucs sew up the worst record in the league. The consensus overall No. 1 pick was wide receiver Irving Fryar, a physical specimen of six foot, 200 pounds, out of Nebraska. The Cornhuskers were loaded that year, with Heisman Trophy running back Mike Rozier, quarterback Turner Gill, and Fryar leading them to the Orange Bowl, where they met the Miami Hurricanes for the national championship. The Huskers lost by a point when coach Tom Osborne famously went for the two-point conversion and the win, when settling for an extra point and the tie would most likely have given him the title.

But to Patriots fans who were tuning in mainly to get a look at the guy who would undoubtedly be the new franchise player, the game was memorable for one other play: Irving Fryar dropping a perfectly thrown pass at the goal line, one that probably would've put the game away for Nebraska.

Fryar was, to put it kindly, "troubled." Or to put it more accurately, "trouble." He was such damaged goods to people who knew what was going on inside Nebraska football that plenty of them believed he dropped that touchdown pass on purpose to throw the game. He was notorious for going on cocaine binges, including the night before that Orange Bowl. Then there was the time he busted the door down on his girlfriend's apartment and beat the crap out of her. Or the fact that he owned two Dobermans and was known to pick them up in a rage and fling them against the wall.

That was the guy the Patriots made the first wide receiver ever to be taken with the first pick in the draft. And the gamble paid off about as well as you would expect.

The 1985 Pats stumbled out of the starting gate. There was a week-two game against Mike Ditka's Chicago Bears in which defensive coordinator Buddy Ryan's historically good 46 Defense decimated Eason with six sacks and three interceptions. (Foreshadowing!) There was another loss at home against the then–Los Angeles Raiders (fat lot of good the NFL throwing that Roughing the Passer playoff game did—the Raiders left Oakland anyway). The Patriots stood at 2–3 until Eason went down to an injury in the week-six game against Buffalo. Grogan came off the bench, put up two second-half touchdowns, and led the Pats to the win.

Grogan's return to the starting job seemed to spark the team. They got on a roll and rattled off six straight wins and eight out of nine overall. The only loss during that time was an overtime loss to the Jets at the Meadowlands. The Patriots split their last two games, including their obligatory loss to the Dolphins in Miami, which marked the Golden Jubilee of Consecutive Orange Bowl defeats for them, 18 straight in all, going back to 1961. But a win over Cincinnati in the final game made them 11–5 and got them into the playoffs.

Since it was the Patriots, however, something good couldn't happen without something equally ridiculous happening to balance it out.

SHOCKING BEHAVIOR

There's an old expression in pro sports that when you win, you should act like you've been there before. Which is something that didn't apply to Pats fans. After that victory, a 34-23 win to earn the AFC Wild Card, the Foxboro faithful rushed the field to celebrate. The last time they'd made the playoffs in a real NFL season was 1978, so it stands to reason that they could be forgiven.

What they can't be forgiven for is anything that happened once they got on the field. They tore up pieces of the artificial turf. They tore down the goalposts. They dragged the goalposts off the field. They carried the goalposts up the ramps out of the stadium. And since no one told them not to, they carried one set of goalposts over the turnstiles, down the hill, out of the parking lot and up Route 1. Why the hell not, right? What's the worst that could happen from a huge mob of drunks hauling a 30-foot section of poles made of thin-wall steel up a trafficky interstate?

The answer to that question is physics.

Some of the boozy jackasses carrying the thing decided that the best thing for all involved was to stick the stanchion into a metal garbage barrel and raise it up. Which brought the uprights into contact with high-tension wires overhead.

Among the reckless buffoons involved were 31-year-old Jon Pallazola and 25-year-old Robert Abramson. Pallazola, a computer programmer who you'd think would have known better, was shocked and burned to the bone. Abramson allegedly reached up to keep the goal posts from crushing his (empty) skull and got burned on both hands. They sued the town of Foxboro and the Patriots' security firm Wackenhut Corp. for failing to stop their own stupidity, and won. A jury gave Pallazola $3.25 million and Abramson $1.4 million.[26] It was like hitting the Moron Lottery.

In the wild-card round, three days after Christmas, the Pats went back down to New Jersey to face the Jets. At some point down the stretch, Tony Eason recovered from his injuries and, despite a relatively mild debate between the "You Gotta Stick with the Hot Hand" crowd and the "You Can't Lose Your Job to Injury" crowd, he was put back in the starter's role for the playoffs. And it was here that the method to Ray Berry's madness started to reveal itself for the first time. The Patriots D recovered three Jets fumbles. They only committed one penalty as a team. Eason was an efficient 12-for-16 with no interceptions, and they came away with a convincing 26-14 victory. By the standards of the franchise in their 25 years of existence, the season was officially a success. Anything they did from there on out was just playing with the house money.

What followed next was even more impressive and more dramatic. That Jets game proved it was possible for them to win. The next week they proved their winning was no accident. And immediately after the game, they showed they had people in charge who still didn't know the first thing about winning.

THE PUNCH HEARD ROUND THE WORLD

For the divisional round game, the Patriots headed to Los Angeles for a rematch with the Raiders. The week leading up to the game was filled with exactly the buildup that makes life as a sports fan worth living. Bad blood. Old scores to settle. Trash talk and insults creating new scores to settle. Raiders defensive end Howie Long got the controversy week off to a great start by calling out Patriots fans as shameless bandwagon jumpers. Long grew up in Boston's Charlestown neighborhood and struck a nerve with comments suggesting that the Pats had zero support back home. Especially compared to the Red Sox, Celtics, or Bruins. "I don't think anyone back there bleeds red, white, and blue," were his exact words.

The game confirmed everything Berry had so unorthodoxically worked on with this team. The Patriots fell behind 17-7 early on, but were opportunistic. They forced five Los Angeles fumbles, recovering three. They intercepted QB Marc Wilson three more times. Eason did exactly what a quarterback should do when his defense is taking over a game—nothing. Which is to say he played by the QB Hippocratic Oath: do no harm. He played conservatively, throwing for only 117 yards, but didn't commit any turnovers. Patriots safety Jim Bowman recovered a fumbled punt to set up one touchdown, then recovered a fumbled kickoff in the end zone to score another one. That proved to be the difference in the game, as the defense shut the Raiders out in the second half, for the 27-20 win.

And in that second half, Pat Sullivan, the owner's son and general manager of the club, demonstrated for the world in that moment of triumph what had been the hallmark of the organization in all those years they weren't winning playoff games: amateurishness and buffoonery.

As the game wound down and the Patriots D held on, Pat patrolled the sidelines—the last place a team executive should be—chirping at Howie Long. "Hey Long, where were you!? What are you doing out there?! You can't do anything!" he was quoted as saying. As the teams filed off the field, with over a hundred people from both sidelines heading toward the stadium tunnel, despite all laws of probability Pat and Long ended up face to face. Then things escalated quickly from there.

Long threw a fake punch at Sullivan, not intending to hit him, but just to embarrass him. "I just wanted to see him jump because I knew he was such a wimp."[27] Pat responded by walking away from the childish situation, his dignity and the reputation of his whole organization intact.

Just kidding. He grabbed Long's face mask. And that's where it got interesting.

LA linebacker Matt Millen, seeing his teammate getting accosted by some random nobody in an Oxford shirt, reacted. "I didn't know who the moron was, so I swung at him." Millen put all 250 pounds of himself behind a punch that connected on Pat Sullivan's jaw. Fortunately for fans of senseless mayhem everywhere, a photographer caught the punch on film, and within hours the image of Millen's fist extended toward the camera and Pat Sullivan's face distorted by the blow was all over the world. Millen still didn't know whom he'd clobbered, until reporters told him it was New England's GM.

"Oh, then it was a good hit," he said.

Neither the insult nor the injury were enough to get Pat to slink away and try to salvage what was left of his dignity or put the focus back on his victorious team. Instead he stood before the TV cameras to talk about it. He blasted some of the media members. Long fanned the flames by calling Pat "a little twerp" and "a classless slob" who was born with a silver spoon in his mouth. "I've got more class in my pinky finger than this guy does," he said.

That was what everyone was talking about in the immediate aftermath of the biggest win in the history of the Patriots franchise. No one remembers what else was done or said that day, or how the players and coaches went into an archrival's house and beat them. The details of the game are largely forgotten. All anyone remembers is the dumb actions and even dumber commentary by the GM and the sock on the jaw he took that embarrassed the whole organization.

Even though the team's heroics were overshadowed, they'd shortly have an even bigger win to celebrate.

SQUISH THE FISH

Pat Sullivan's meaty head aside, fans were delirious. They'd waited their entire miserable, hollow, desultory Pats fan lives for even one measly playoff win, and in the span of seven days they'd gotten two. On the road, no less. We all had longstanding dreams of even some semblance of respectability, and now they were on their way to the AFC championship game, to face the Dolphins in Orange Bowl Stadium. The Patriots were in the NFL's Final Four. It was incredible.

And they responded pretty much the way every fan base does the first time their team goes on its first championship run: like yahoos.

For the first time in their existence, the Patriots were the biggest story in New England. They dominated the local newscasts. Anchormen were doing awkward banter with their female sidekicks wherein they referred to the Pats as "we." FM DJs who barely knew they existed before this were doing song parodies about them. And somehow, instantaneously, across the whole region, a catchphrase was born that would launch a million t-shirt sales: "Squish the Fish."

In the blink of an eye, it was everywhere. Emblazoned across every chest, forehead, and car bumper in a six-state area by the early part of the week. As rallying cries go, "Squish the Fish" was admittedly pretty stupid (we got that dolphins aren't fish; *you* try rhyming something with "aquatic mammal"), but you had to admire the way the region was able to mobilize its T-shirt Industrial Complex so quickly. It was the sports merchandise equivalent of us starting the Manhattan Project after Pearl Harbor and having the bomb ready to drop on Japan the following day.

So while we were all feeding our insatiable desire for novelty wear with dumb, aquatically incorrect slogans on them and feeling better about the team than we ever had before, Irving Fryar was celebrating in the most Irving Fryar way possible.

By this point, Fryar was married, with a lovely wife named Jacqueline, a former cheerleader for the USFL's Boston Breakers, who was five months pregnant with their first child. The common media cliché of the time was that he was "maturing." That marriage had calmed him down and his love of Jacqueline and his pending fatherhood had taught him responsibility and "grounded him." So it was a shock to everyone to find out on Wednesday that the team flight to Miami didn't include their mature, grounded, super-responsible family man wide receiver.

Fryar explained that he suffered a severe cut on his right pinkie finger while putting a kitchen knife away—no doubt while making himself and his bride a nice mature, responsible, life-turned-around goodbye meal before he left for Florida. There was one problem with his story; several, actually, and they came in the form of the people in the Boston restaurant who saw Fryar and Jacqui out the night before and having a major blowout. Apparently Irving had chosen that moment to tell her that if the Patriots were to make it to the Super Bowl in New Orleans, he wasn't taking her on the trip. Not surprisingly, she did not take it well. The two started screaming at each other in the restaurant before taking it outside to the parking lot. At some point Irving (allegedly) struck her across the face and Jacqui retaliated by pulling a knife out of her purse and trying to stab him with it. So he used his No. 1 draft pick pass-catching hands to protect himself, and that's how he got cut.[28]

By the time the real story came out, Fryar had joined the team in Miami. He denied the reports for as long as he could, but even he couldn't try to sell the world the fiction that he had hurt himself at home while puttering around in the kitchen. By Friday he finally had to come clean and admit the truth, and the team sent him home to deal with his marriage problems and, once again, "turn his life around."

So, even in their moment of triumph, the Patriots were still the Patriots. Only now they were bringing their dysfunctional family circus to a national stage. And they had a more practical concern to worry about: the Orange Bowl was a house of horrors for them. They'd lost 18 consecutive games in Miami over the previous 19 years. And this particular Dolphins team was stacked with talent. Dan Marino was the QB the Pats had passed up in order to draft Eason, and he already owned a slew of NFL passing records. He had a pair of Pro Bowl receivers in Mark Duper and Mark Clayton. This was at the height of Miami's famed "Killer Bs" defense. And running the show was the winningest coach in NFL history, Don Shula.

Logically, there wasn't much to be optimistic about. But when you're riding a high like the fans were, in the throes of a euphoria and in full-on yahoo mode like they were, you'll believe anything is possible. "I mean, sure they have the edge in talent, coaching, and home-field advantage, but we've got 'Squish the Fish!'" was the general mood.

And as it turned out, perhaps for the first time ever, the fans were right. Once again, Raymond Berry's weirdo emphasis on practicing fumble recoveries paid immediate dividends; on Miami's very first offensive play, Pats linebacker Steve Nelson stripped running back Tony Nathan, and defensive end Garin Veris recovered the ball. On the opening kick of the second half, Mosi Tatupu forced a fumble that set up a New England touchdown. Later, safety Fred Marion intercepted Marino in the end zone.

The Patriots were turning the ball over as well, but their errors weren't as costly. Their offense was taking advantage of the great field position the defense and special teams kept giving them, and they rolled to the 31–14 win. Eason threw for three touchdowns, but amazingly had only 71 passing yards total for the game, completing 10 of his 12 attempts. It was possibly the ultimate "caretaker" quarterback performance of all time. The defense held Marino to just 20-for-48 and forced six turnovers in all.

Incredibly, improbably, and damned near impossibly, the Patriots were going to the Super Bowl. The team that went ten years without a place to play. The ones who pulled drunk guys out of the stands to make tackles and drafted dead people and drove their coaches to nervous breakdowns. Those Patriots were playing in the Biggest Sporting Event on Earth. The word "surreal" didn't go nearly far enough.

11

THE WRONG KIND OF
SUPER BOWL RECORD

★ ★ ★ ★ ★ ★ ★ ★ ★ ★ ★ ★ ★ ★ ★ ★ ★ ★ ★ ★

*For over a thousand years, Roman conquerors returning from the wars
enjoyed the honor of a triumph, a tumultuous parade . . . A slave stood
behind the conqueror, holding a golden crown, and whispering in his
ear a warning: that all glory is fleeting.*
GENERAL GEORGE S. PATTON, *Patton*

The improbable, unfathomable Patriots run to the Super Bowl
came for my friends and me during that blissfully responsibility-free time in
our lives when you're not living under your parents' rule (even if in some cases
still under their roofs) but are not yet domesticated by a woman. For most
guys, it's a narrow window, but the 1985 Patriots managed to hit it right in the
sweet spot.

Details of that AFC Championship over the Dolphins are sketchy. But I have
a pretty solid memory of a massive table by the television at the Weymouth
(Massachusetts) Knights of Columbus covered with empty beer bottles. And
a much more vague memory of crashing in my buddy Duke's dorm room at
Southeastern Mass University (now UMass Dartmouth) after a failed attempt
to watch the Patriots plane land at T.F. Green Airport in Warwick, Rhode Island, just outside of Providence. But we will not speak of it here.

The point is, it was one of the great events in an immature young man's
life. Different people celebrated in different ways. Some went on pointless and
stupid road trips; most were smart enough to go home. But the one thing
the entire region did as one was get right to work on coming up with a goofy
slogan. It's how we rolled in the mid-1980s.

"BERRY THE BEARS"

The shameless boosterism that shook the region before the Miami game
was only a minor tremor compared to what followed. The Yahoo Richter Scale
was now measuring a 9.0 magnitude quake. In the span of three games, the
Patriots had gone from merely relevant to surprising to shocking, and were

now one win away from immortality. And the lameness of "Squish the Fish" was quickly replaced by the even more forced and cornball "Berry the Bears."

In the normal course of things, the plucky underdogs who are riding a wave of improbability onto the white, sandy beaches of immortality would be the compelling story. They'd be the Cinderella everyone wants to see. America's Sweethearts.

But not in this instance. Not even close.

Long before Super Bowl XX, the 1985 Bears had crossed over from the sports world and become a full-blown pop culture phenomenon. Even now, that team in that season is the standard by which all other teams are judged ("Team Blank's defense has been OK, but let's not make them out to be the '85 Bears"), and you can't overstate what a legitimately big deal they were that year. The whole roster had become household names. Walter Payton was already a running back legend. Jim McMahon was the pain-in-the-ass, outspoken, counter-culture rebel at quarterback. Defensive coordinator Buddy Ryan was more famous than half the head coaches in the league, having unleashed his revolutionary 46 Defense on the world, a defense anchored by names everyone in the country knew, like Richard Dent and Mike Singletary. But the craze that was sweeping the nation was William "The Refrigerator" Perry, a morbidly obese defensive tackle who burst into the national consciousness when the Bears started handing him the ball in short yardage and goal-line situations because he was so hard to tackle.

And running the show was head coach Mike Ditka, who was already well known among football fans as one of the best tight ends ever to play the game. But coaching the '85 Bears turned him into an all-out cultural icon. Ditka and his Bears were rock stars. Literally.

The '85 Bears might not have invented insufferable, unrepentant cockiness, but they did raise it to an art form. You can't have lived in America in the three decades since and not come across their cringe-worthy "Super Bowl Shuffle" rap video. It's awful, unwatchable, and strangely fascinating, all at the same time. It spawned a million imitators, but for sheer awkward terribleness, no one has ever come close.

Everywhere outside of New England, the Bears were the story of this Super Bowl. The world couldn't get enough of them; they were the ones everyone wanted to see and hear about. The Patriots were nothing more than the Washington Generals to their Harlem Globetrotters. Four days before the game, a helicopter was hovering above the Bears' practice, so Jim McMahon mooned it, and America went berserk. Then he allegedly gave a radio interview in which he supposedly called the women of New Orleans "sluts," which he later denied doing by saying that he didn't get up early enough to do morning radio. Again, the country lapped it up.

Back in the day, there was always a prime-time Bob Hope Super Bowl Special filled with corny football skits, cheesy musical numbers, and Bob swapping badly scripted jokes with the two quarterbacks. And it seemed like McMahon was already a star who belonged on the national stage next to an entertainment legend. Tony Eason, on the other hand, came off like an afterthought, the boom operator or the custodian who had just wandered onto the stage and interrupted the show.

Odds-makers installed the Patriots as 9.5-point underdogs, which in retrospect was an incredible show of respect. The 1985 Bears were not just good, or even great. They were historically great. As Singletary would put it years later in an NFL Network show about them, they applied pressure in a way that had never been seen before. While the Patriots were taking advantage of opponents' mistakes to get to the Super Bowl, the Bears were dominating the world. They went 15–1 in the regular season. They led the league in every significant statistical category. In two playoff games, they didn't give up a point. In their first game, they held the Giants to only 32 rushing yards. In the NFC Championship Game, they only allowed the Rams 130 yards *total*.

There wasn't much reason to believe the Patriots could compete with a team that was that dominant, but that didn't stop them. The thinking was that the Pats were pretty much playing with house money at that point, that in any football game turnovers are huge and they'd shown a knack for coming up with the ball. And besides, the Bears had shown they could be beaten, by the Dolphins late in the season. If New England could beat Miami and Miami could beat Chicago, then the logical syllogism was that New England could beat Chicago.

Except that the logic turned out to be more Rock-Paper-Scissors, and the Bears were rock. A very big, very hard, very dangerous rock.

The Bears' rock didn't crush the Patriots' scissors, it disintegrated them into individual molecules, then set fire to their paper. New England was destroyed, to use Singletary's phrase again, in a way that had never been seen before. Certainly not in a Super Bowl.

All the details really don't need to be recounted here. Suffice to say things started out great; Raymond Berry's fumble strategy worked its magic again, right off the bat. On the game's first series, Payton fumbled on Chicago's 19-yard line and Larry McGrew recovered the ball. All that was now required was a couple of plays to punch it in, and Destiny's Team would be shocking the world.

On first down, tight end Lin Dawson tried to catch a sideline pass and tore up his knee. On second down, Stanley Morgan dropped a pass in the end zone. Another incompletion and they were settling for a field goal without picking up a yard. They led 3–0, but that would be the high-water mark of their season. Or their low-water mark. Let's just say the rest was a disaster of epic proportions.

Strangely, nobody in New England really remembers what happened in that game from there on out. The game played out like a sports movie montage in which play after play goes perfectly right for one team to demonstrate how dominating they are. It was all a blur. Seemingly the only Bear who didn't score that day was Walter Payton, which Ditka says he regrets to this day. Eason was 0-for-6 passing, with three sacks. And an urban legend arose that John Hannah told the coaches Eason was being such a coward that if he was sent back onto the field, Hannah would refuse to go. Not long ago Hannah was on a Boston radio show and confirmed the story is true. "We'd be out there fighting, holding our blocks, trying to protect the guy, and as soon as someone would get within ten feet of him, he'd curl up in the fetal position," or words to that effect.

Hannah got his wish and Eason was replaced with Steve Grogan. By this point, those fans watching in bars and living rooms across New England— who'd waited forever for this moment—were now having debates over whether to see if there was something better on another channel or stick around and see how bad it could get, just out of morbid curiosity. Grogan didn't fare much better than Eason had. But at least he fought to the end. And after Chicago rolled up 46 straight points, Grogan managed to guide the Pats to a garbage-time touchdown that added a tiny bit of respectability to the game. It turned a 46–3 debacle into a 46–10 rout.

In this game, the Pats set a slew of dubious Super Bowl records including, but not limited to, worst defeat (36 points), most sacks (7), and fewest rushing yards (7), which didn't add to the stylishness of those "Berry the Bears" shirts. In fact, if you ever wore one in public after that day, you left yourself wide open to the worst kind of ridicule, and deservedly so. No one with an ounce of pride ever took their shirt out again, except to wax their car with it.

The way the season ended was a complete catastrophe, to be sure. But at least Patriots Nation took comfort in knowing that once the sting wore off, they could feel good about the big picture. It was still by far the most success- ful season the team had ever had, and in no time at all they'd be looking back fondly at this Cinderella team and their improbable run and thanking them for how proudly they represented the people of New England.

At least that's how they felt for about 36 hours, which is about how long it took for a disaster to strike that made Super Bowl XX look like Shakespeare in the Park.

SCANDAL

Patriots fans spent the Monday after the Super Bowl more or less sifting through the wreckage and trying to figure out how to laugh about what a debacle it was. By Tuesday morning, it stopped being funny, as that's when an explosive Page One article in the *Boston Globe* by beat writer Ron Borges detailing rampant cocaine use by Patriots players broke, including, but not limited to, a description of an all-night Drugapalooza a group of them went on in Miami after losing to the Dolphins in December. And while Borges didn't name names, he said at least six players had come up positive in league-mandated testing.

For a region trying to lick their wounds, this was rubbing salt mixed with napalm in them. Not that there was any ignorance surrounding hardcore drug use; it was 1986, after all, and it was always implied that rich guys in their twenties sometimes put more into their bloodstreams than Flintstones Chewables. Hell, Berry himself had seen it firsthand back in the 60s, when he was catching passes for the Colts and his teammate Big Daddy Lipscomb overdosed on heroin.

But this was a team the city had embraced. It was one of those feel-good stories that unites a region and gets everybody caught up in the fairy tale, and now everyone was finding out Cinderella had lost her shoe snorting lines in the palace ladies' room.

Ray Berry claimed the story was inaccurate, which is to say he pointed out that it was more like *twelve* players. But five of them had drug problems he called "serious," so the *Globe* got the benefit of the doubt.

The *Globe* defended the timing of the story by saying the sources wouldn't allow them to run it until after the Super Bowl. So after the initial shock wore off, the speculation about who leaked the story began. Most people assumed it had to be someone in Patriots management, someone disgusted by drug use who wanted to out the guilty parties but didn't want the news to affect their shot at a championship. And since straight arrows don't come any straighter than the old school, deeply moral Berry, all signs pointed to him.

The morning after the Super Bowl, Berry held a team meeting where he gave his players the heads up that the report was coming out.[29] To say they were stunned is putting it mildly. The guys who weren't using were furious that they'd be suspected along with those who were. No doubt the cokeheads themselves didn't want their names to be made public. At Berry's urging, they voted as a team to submit to voluntary drug testing. When the NFL Players Association found out, they flipped their lids. Drug testing in any line of work is covered under a collective bargaining agreement. Unions get huge concessions at the bargaining table for something like that, and the Patriots players were just giving it away for free. So the NFLPA immediately grieved it to the National Labor Relations Board.

On Wednesday, the names of the Cocaine Six were revealed: Irving Fryar (no surprise there), Kenneth Sims (that explained a lot), two-time Pro Bowl cornerback Raymond Clayborn, lead running back Tony Collins, defensive back Roland James, and wide receiver Stephen Starring. The naming of names just poured more petroleum on the napalm. Now the players who hadn't been using were incensed, because this meant that either management leaked the names in violation of confidentiality agreements between players and the league or worse, it was one of their own.

Borges protected his sources, but did let it be known that both Berry and team VP Patrick Sullivan confirmed them. So that made it all but certain that the snitch was indeed a player. For Pats players, the idea that there was a rat in their locker room made them far angrier than playing alongside guys who were high on the "bouncing powder" ever did. The speculation played out the rest of the winter, through the spring and summer, all the way into training camp. And so much time, effort, conjecture, and conversation was spent on figuring out who the traitor was, they could've printed up and sold "Search for the Rat Tour 1986" t-shirts.

It was insane. Players were giving interviews in which they openly said they didn't know whom to trust. Tight end Lin Dawson said, "This has been a very tense and emotional time, and the height of embarrassment. There's a feeling almost like, 'What's next?'" Offensive lineman Ron Wooten said, "This has been the toughest off-season I could ever imagine. And if there is a lack of trust, then I think that could stop us this year." Others, like center Trevor Matich, pleaded for everyone to move on, but a fat lot of good it did. By the time camp started, the prime suspect in this particular conspiracy was Pats tight end Derrick Ramsey, a notorious malcontent who'd been beefing with Ray Berry ever since the previous training camp, when he missed a bed check and morning practice the next day. He had all the classic clues you look for in a perp: the means, the opportunity, and most of all, the motivation.

At the Pro Bowl, John Hannah was asked about the possibility that one of his teammates might be the source, and he made no bones about the fact that he would beat the snot out of anyone he caught ratting on his teammates. Ramsey called any suggestion he was behind it "ludicrous," adding, "I haven't gotten where I have in the NFL by telling on people." Unfortunately for the Boston press, they missed out on the chance to ask him about it all summer, because Berry cut him in July. It had a little bit of Jack-Ruby-whacking-Oswald-to-keep-him-from-talking feel to it, but by that time most of New England was so drug-scandaled out, they were glad it happened.

"THE MESS"

All things considered, the Patriots managed to come through an offseason of turmoil surprisingly well. Whether it was because of his personal disgust at all the drug and snitch talk or (more likely) the multiple surgeries he had on his shoulder and knee, John Hannah retired. And while his loss left a void, Eason was now 27, entering his prime, and now had playoff experience under his belt. The defense was still young and talented, anchored at the line, linebackers, and secondary by Garin Veris, Andre Tippett, and Ronnie Lippett, respectively. They won their first two games, put together a seven-game winning streak in the middle of the season, and won the AFC East for the first time in eight years. They qualified for a playoff bye week and an AFC divisional round playoff game at Denver, where they lost to the Broncos, 22–17. A week later, John Elway would lead those same Broncos past the Browns in Cleveland with the legendary "The Drive," before getting drubbed by Bill Parcells' New York Giants in the Super Bowl. Not a great season for the Patriots, but competitive nonetheless.

And one Patriots player in particular who picked up right where he left off was Irving Fryar. In 1986, he was entering his prime as well. The prime of a time in his life that many clean and sober years later he would look back on and call "The Mess."

The trouble started for Fryar when he was arrested for allegedly assaulting someone in the lobby of a Boston hotel. It seemed like a pretty unstable thing to do, even by 80s Irving Fryar standards, until it came out that the "victim" in this case was a friend of Jacqui Fryar (pregnant at the time) who had told her she looked "as big as a house." Irving punched his lights out. A judge later dismissed the case and Fryar scored an even bigger win in the court of public opinion; everyone in New England agreed that he showed remarkable restraint by not killing the jerk with his bare hands. However, during a late November game against Buffalo, he managed to squander whatever goodwill he had earned by defending his wife's honor: Fryar made NFL history by becoming the first player ever to be knocked out of a game during halftime.

He'd gotten hurt in the first half, and rather than be treated by team doctors and try to get back in the game like every other player since time immemorial,

Fryar decided his day was over. He got dressed, hopped in his car, left the parking lot, and headed home. He didn't make it more than two miles from the stadium before he veered off the road and slammed his car into a tree. His excuse to the police was that he was talking on his cell phone and had gotten distracted. Since 1986 cell phones were approximately the size and weight of modern refrigerators, his alibi could have been true. But since he was the 1986 Irving Fryar, he was probably lying through his teeth.

The rest of "The Mess" years for Fryar were more of the same. More drug- and booze-fueled crack-ups punctuated by more fawning puff pieces by token network sports anchors about how he'd put his past behind him and grown up at last. But his actions proved far different. In 1987 he told police he'd gotten robbed outside a jewelry store. He said he had chased after his assailants, who fired shots at him. The police investigation found no evidence, no spent shells at the scene, and no witnesses who said they heard or saw anything. The next year, he got pulled over in Pemberton, New Jersey, on a routine traffic stop. Police found he not only had a suspended license, but a rifle with hollow-tipped bullets. The reason for the heavy firearms, he said, "Wasn't so much New Jersey . . . It was Boston."

In April of 1990, Jacqueline gave birth to a girl, baby Adrienne, who was born needing open heart surgery. This was another one of those life-changing events that made Irving grow up, mature, and gain perspective. Which lasted all the way until October, when he and fellow Pats wideout Hart Lee Dykes hit up the notorious Club Shalimar in Providence and ended up in a fight with five morons. Dykes got beaten with a pair of crutches, and Fryar forgot about his baby's struggle for life long enough to pull a Smith & Wesson and get arrested. He spent the night in police lockup with a nasty gash in his head, signing autographs for the cops while no one came to bail him out.

By Fryar's own account, that night was rock bottom for him, and the moment when he decided to turn his life around, for real this time. He did eventually find his way into a church in the Roxbury section of Boston, where the word of God finally did whatever the word of God does for some people. Only this time the change in his life ended up actually happening. In the long run, he would become Reverend Irving Fryar, play a remarkable 17 years of pro football, and be one of the all-time great NFL redemption stories. That is, until 2015, when he and his mother were convicted of mortgage fraud and he was sent off to serve a five-year prison sentence.

The years Fryar called "The Mess" were no box of chocolates for the Patriots, either. Some of the key players got old and injured. The drafts of the late 80s yielded just as many misses (running back Reggie "Two-Yard" Dupard in

'86) as hits (Bruce Armstrong, the best left tackle in team history, in '87). And the whole franchise just slipped into entropy and decline, first with a couple of seasons of mediocrity ('87 and '88), then with the Patriots' default setting becoming atrociousness and irrelevance ('89 and '90).

The Patriots returned to their status as the squashed bug on the sole of the NFL's shoe, and no one personified the deterioration in the team's fortunes more than Tony Eason. The promise he showed during the Super Bowl run and the division championship in '86 was way behind him, and it was now painfully obvious that John Hannah was right; Eason was made of glass. Over the next two seasons, Eason only started five games for the Patriots and was regularly replaced by Steve Grogan, who was in his mid-30s, with so much wear and tear on his body that he was playing with a giant, linebacker-like neck roll on his shoulder pads. Grogan's quarterbacking was a shadow of what it had been in his prime. He was gutting it out on pure toughness every week. In the middle of the 1989 season, the Patriots finally put Eason out of his misery and traded him to the New York Jets. But now the Pats were doomed to that purgatory of mediocrity teams live in for years while they search for a new franchise quarterback.

Fortunately, the Patriots front office was smart enough this time to strike quarterback gold in the fourth round of the 1987 draft, when they picked Rich Gannon, out of the University of Delaware. Unfortunately, they were too stupid to realize it. They took the six-foot-three, 210-pound Gannon with the idea of turning him into a running back. Gannon told them in so many words that they were out of their minds and that he had no intention of being anything but a quarterback, so the Pats dealt him to the Minnesota Vikings. Given that Gannon went on to an 18-year NFL career that included four Pro Bowls, three All Pro selections, a Super Bowl, and 180 touchdowns, we can safely say that's Gannon: 1, Patriots Scouting Department: 0.

"THE MIDGET"

For as long as quarterbacks have been the stars of pro football, which is to say ever since the forward pass came into vogue during the Bronze Age in 1906, teams that find themselves without a viable franchise QB and declining fan interest have always tried one of two things: either they go after a really good team's backup and hope he somehow brings their success with him, smuggled inside his body like a drug mule, or they try to excite their fan base by bringing in some local hero. The Patriots started with the latter.

Doug Flutie was from Natick, Massachusetts, via Boston College. He was not only the best college football player in New England history and a Heisman

Trophy winner, but it has been argued that he had the most successful career of any Division I quarterback ever, even before he threw the Hail Mary pass in Miami that made him a legend. If ever there was a local athlete who could live his whole life without having to reach for a dinner check, it was Flutie. But because he was only five foot nine and 180 pounds, NFL personnel departments didn't share the enthusiasm, and Flutie fell to the 11th round of the 1985 draft, where he was taken by the LA Rams. Not long after, he was traded to the Chicago Bears. In '86 he appeared in six games for them and started one, which the Bears won. But his stint in Chicago was notable for only one thing, and that was the open, public, and relentless amount of crap he got from Jim McMahon.

Despite the fact that he was sidelined with a bad shoulder, McMahon thought Flutie should never have been brought in in the first place, and he responded pretty much the way you'd expect someone who moons a helicopter *would* respond. Team chemistry be damned, he let it be known to anyone who'd listen. And most everybody did.

Mostly, McMahon made with the cracks about Flutie's height—lots and lots of them. Like the time a reporter suggested McMahon's jokes were going over Flutie's head and he responded with "Most of anything goes over his head." Flutie, for the most part, took the high road [insert lame height joke here], and Mike Ditka made it clear that he was the one who pushed for the trade to get him. But it was a QB controversy that wouldn't go away. Flutie didn't help himself any the following year when the NFL had another labor dispute, brought in scab players for one game, and he was one of the people who crossed the picket line. He said he felt like it was his one and only shot to prove himself in the NFL and had no choice, but the move damaged his reputation with a good percentage of the public.

The Patriots were desperate and needed to do something to generate interest, so they made a midseason trade to bring Flutie in. The move was, in all respects, a success; Flutie went 6–3 as a starter in 1988. His passing didn't set the world ablaze, but he found ways to win. And behind a bad offensive line, he showed an ability to avoid sacks, scramble, and extend plays that hadn't been seen since Grogan's prime. The fans loved him for it.

But the fans weren't calling the shots, and it was painfully obvious that Ray Berry had no interest in a non-traditional quarterback like Flutie. Irving Fryar gave a glimpse into how Doug Flutie was perceived in the Patriots locker room when he was traded to Miami. He and his agent called Flutie "The Midget," and he said, "It wasn't any use. The ball just wasn't going to gel there."

Unceremoniously dumped by New England, Flutie defected to the Canadian Football League. All he managed to do there was set passing records such as the highest single-season yardage total in any pro league ever (6,619), lead the CFL in passing five times in eight seasons, win the Most Outstanding Player award six times, and win three Grey Cup MVPs before returning to the NFL in 1998.

As for the Patriots, they went to the panic move every struggling team desperate for a quarterback tries: they signed the backup of a much more successful team, in this case the LA Raiders. They picked up an aging, decrepit, end-of-the-line Marc Wilson. It was a deal that excited exactly no one who wasn't working in the Patriots front office. Wilson finished his New England career with a record of 1–9 before they finally put him out to pasture. In between, they tried to make do with the flotsam and jetsam of QBs no one else wanted. In no particular order, there were various Tom Hodsons and Tom Ramseys and Jeff Carlsons and a bunch of others no one will ever remember.

And the Pats were so snakebitten that, even when they did manage to find gifted, productive players at other positions, things tended to go wrong.

JOHN STEPHENS

There were a few standout players, at least in the short term. In 1988 they used their first round pick on John Stephens, a tough, bruising, cerebral running back out of Northwestern State in Louisiana. Stephens had a tremendous rookie season, carrying the ball almost 300 times for over 1,100 yards, and he showed all the promise in the world—that is, until the terrible collision in his second season that damn near led to the permanent paralysis of another player. Stephens was never the same player after that. The man Stephens hit, 49ers safety Jeff Fuller, was left temporarily paralyzed and, while he could eventually walk again, the collision has limited his use of his right arm to this day.

Stephens did nothing wrong; Fuller had caught him straight on with a full head of steam. Both players ducked their shoulders and hit each other, but Stephens had the size and all the momentum and Fuller fell to the ground limp. Stephens was simply trying to dish out a hit instead of absorbing it, the way every coach teaches from youth football on up. But he was a bright and sensitive guy, and it left him shaken. He never recovered from it. From that day forward his running was so obviously tentative, everyone in the stadium could see it, like he was gun shy about ever hurting another defender. He was never close to being the same player, and only lasted four more seasons in New England, mostly as a back up. That hit he dished out on Fuller essentially ended two careers.

Ray Berry was fired at the end of the 1989 season, but for all intents and purposes his coaching career ended before the season even began, in the final preseason game, to be exact. That was the game when Garin Veris, Andre Tippett, and Ronnie Lippett, the key players at all three levels of the Patriots defense, were lost for the season. To use the cliché, it was The Perfect Storm of injuries. They'd lost three critical players before any of them had played a meaningful down of football. And every man, woman, and child in New England knew there was no way the Pats would be competitive that season.

And they were right.

It was no fault of Berry's, but no one gets into coaching expecting life will be fair. And Berry seemed to accept the fact that he was a dead man walking with the same unaffected dignity with which he handled everything. No hard feelings, no bitterness. No angry, insane press conferences like they had back in the old days. He just left as quietly as he had come in. And the first truly beloved coach the Patriots had ever had, the guy who led the team to their one real (though very brief) moment of triumph, was gone.

The Patriots' steady decline left them stumbling to 5-11 as the 80s ended. What they didn't know (but we probably could have guessed) is that things were about to get worse. Much, much worse.

And as badly as things had been on the field those last few years, off the field the team was a complete disaster. Even by Patriots standards, the ownership situation was a train wreck. And given what they'd gone through in their 30 years of existence, that's saying something.

The Sullivan family, who willed the Patriots into existence, owned the team, kept it afloat, built it a home, and ran it for three decades, were in danger of losing their franchise because of . . . Michael Jackson.

12

TOO HIGH TO GET OVER, TOO LOW TO GET UNDER

★ ★ ★ ★ ★ ★ ★ ★ ★ ★ ★ ★ ★ ★ ★ ★ ★ ★ ★ ★

The Boston gig has been cancelled . . . Yeah. I wouldn't
worry about it though, it's not a big college town.
   IAN FAITH, *This is Spinal Tap*

It's quite possible that if, at some time in the early 1980s I
was given a writing assignment that asked me to compose the goofiest, most
ridiculous nonsense sentence I possibly could think up, the first thing I would
have come up with would've been some form of "The Sullivan family was in
danger of losing its franchise because of Michael Jackson." And yet it actually
happened.

First, some background.

Long after the Sullivans settled in Foxboro and finally built the stadium they'd
always hoped would give them financial stability, they still flew by the seat of
their pants and teetered on the brink of ruin. They were in a perpetual state
of fiscal turmoil that was still making more news in the business section than
on the sports pages. Though to be perfectly honest, I wasn't paying attention.

I knew this much: in order to keep the team afloat in the early years, Billy
Sullivan had sold shares in the team. In the mid-70s, some of the people he
sold them to got sick of seeing their perfectly good money going down the
toilet because of what they perceived to be Sullivan's incompetence. At some
point they tried to wrest control away from him. They voted him out and replaced him with Robert Marr, the son of one of his original investors.

Billy's son Chuck, the one who used to shuttle players back and forth from
Boston to Amherst during that first training camp, stepped in to help his dad
regain control.

Chuck's plan was to buy out the voting shareholders, and he went to the
banks to finance the buyout, promising that the team would generate enough
revenue to pay back the loan. The banks were unconvinced and demanded that
they put up the team as collateral. In order to do that, Chuck would have to go
to all the non-voting shareholders to get permission. And by that I mean he

would have to go to all the people Billy had sold shares to back in 1960 to raise cash. All those Wall Street investors, overseas military personnel who saw the stock offering in *Stars & Stripes*, and fans who bought shares as souvenirs.

Eventually, they bought out the non-voting shareholders at $15 a share and the voting shareholders at $12 a share. It was a terrible business decision. They were so anxious to own the team outright, they gave up all fiscal sanity. The stocks weren't worth nearly that much. As one former business associate of the Sullivans later said, "The price was way above what anybody else would've paid. The Sullivans always paid too much."[30]

The Sullivans had won. Chuck was now the sole owner of Schaefer Stadium, now called Sullivan Stadium. Billy owned 100 percent of the Patriots. And by "won," I mean they had won the right to have grossly overpaid for a franchise that put them in a financial hole they could never get out of.

The Patriots franchise and the Sullivan family lurched forward, always on the verge of hitting a financial iceberg, fiscally splitting in two, taking on a sea of red ink, and sinking in a North Atlantic of debt. Even when times were good on the field, they were a nightmare off it.

From 1984 through 1986, they made it to a Super Bowl, won their division, and sold out every home game with the highest ticket prices in the NFL. And in that time they lost $14 million. In the Super Bowl season of '85 alone, they lost $9.6 million, $3.6 million of which was owed to the shareholders. In 1987 the *Globe* did an investigative report, confirmed by Billy Sullivan, that said the team was $75-100 million in debt and might be forced to sell if they couldn't climb out of it. It didn't help matters any that about $20 million of that debt was in the form of deferred money to players. The Pats had been playing those financial shenanigans for a while, signing long-term extensions with their veteran players to keep from losing them. So now they'd have to sell any new prospective owner on the fact that he'd walk into the building owing tens of millions of dollars to guys who were no longer playing for him.

The team was basically operating by running up a credit-card debt they'd never be able to pay. At one point, they re-upped their broadcast deal with WHDH, a five-year, $20-million contract, payable up front. And as soon as they got payment from the station, they used the money to pay off bills that were already long past due.

The Patriots franchise was in the kind of financial straits you get in where debt collectors are calling you every evening and the repo truck could show up in your driveway in the middle of the night. And the issue wasn't so much that the team itself was losing money, though it was. The bigger problems lay elsewhere.

By the end of the 1980s, the Sullivans owed $33 million on the operation of the football team itself and another $78 million on the dreaded "other business ventures." It was in that set of accounting books that the real fun was, and where Michael Jackson comes into our story, carrying financial ruin in his sequin-gloved hand.

SNATCHING DEFEAT FROM THE JAWS OF "VICTORY"

It's hard to overstate just how big Michael Jackson was in 1983. He was a star from the time he first hit the charts in 1968, singing lead for the Jackson 5, all the way up to his bizarre, scandalous death in 2009, but 1983 was unquestionably his peak. His *Thriller* disc had already set sales records and was still churning out No. 1 hits. He was the first true superstar of the music video era. He was coming off his legendary performance at some awards show or other where he had debuted the Moonwalk, which according to people who watched it was a more historic moment than the actual first moonwalk.

And he was about to get even more famous. Because it was then, at the peak of his career, that Jackson announced he was reuniting with his brothers. They were cutting an album together for the first time in years and announcing dates of their "Victory Tour." In entertainment and pop culture terms, this was news on the scale of Jesus reuniting with the Apostles and playing venues around the country.

Enter the Patriots. For the most part, Billy Sullivan's kids divvied up his struggling empire between them. Pat was the extroverted, hands-on football operations guy, and Chuck was the quieter, behind-the-scenes manager of the business side of things. Chuck was in charge of Stadium Management Corp., which ran the family's land holdings and the team facility, now renamed Sullivan Stadium. What Chuck didn't know about Michael Jackson's unique blend of soulful R&B and funky, upbeat, synthesized dance jams could have filled a library. By all accounts his musical tastes ran more toward classical or old standards. But the one universal song everyone dances to is money, and he saw the chance to make lots and lots of it if he could convince the Jacksons to book his stadium for the Boston stop on the tour. Chuck flew out to Los Angeles to meet with Frank DiLeo, who was the VP of the Jackson's record label, Epic Records, to pitch Foxboro as a venue. Also present was notorious boxing promoter Don King, who'd fronted $3 million of his own money for a piece of the tour promotion action.

DiLeo mentioned that the tour's promoter had backed out and that they were looking for someone else to run the thing. By that stage of his career, King had been sued by Muhammad Ali, Larry Homes, and others. So any businessman worth the digits in his bank account probably would've taken a look at this venture, done the mental math, grabbed his hat and coat, and run back to the airport.

But not Chuck Sullivan. For every 10,000 people who walk past a three-card monte game on the street without breaking stride, there's always that one stupid tourist with more cash than sense who stops and gets taken to the cleaners. Don King was the streetwise dealer, and Chuck was the country bumpkin dumb enough to think he could beat him at his own game.

Chuck didn't know squat about King or the Jacksons, but he figured he knew what he was getting into. For one, he'd actually put on a few concerts in his day, first when he was in school at Boston College and later when he was stationed in Thailand with the Army. And how much different could promoting the hottest concert act in the world be? And besides, he not only owned his own 60,000-seat stadium, he was pals with a couple dozen other NFL owners who'd also be interested in booking shows. The whole thing just seemed like a license to print money, something that couldn't possibly fail.

Somehow, he underestimated his own ability to produce failure.

For starters, Chuck had to win the bid for the right to promote the tour. So he brought in Edward J. DeBartolo, Jr., owner of the San Francisco 49ers, as a partner (that would be the same Eddie DeBartolo who was later involved in a bribery and corruption case with the governor of Louisiana and got kicked out of the NFL by his fellow owners), but the arrangement didn't last long. DeBartolo looked at the people he'd be doing business with, decided that even by his standards they were too sleazy, and backed out.

Undeterred, Chuck decided to go it alone. Not surprisingly, he cut a terrible deal. Outbidding everyone else, he offered the Jacksons and their partners an unheard of 83 percent of the gross revenue, which was 25 percent higher than the industry standard. He then guaranteed them $36.6 million in advance, one-third of it paid up front, with the balance payable two weeks later. To come up with the cash, he went to Stadium Management Corp. (the family equivalent of the proverbial mason jar buried in the backyard), borrowing the money with Sullivan Stadium put up as collateral. The plan was for 55 tour dates, with just under half of those dates booked at NFL stadiums. Chuck put the arm on various owners to give himself and the Jacksons as much special consideration as he could, like breaks on the expenses, extra amenities, more revenue, and the like. But even calling in every favor he could, the tour was doomed from the start.

In *The Art of War*, Sun Tzu says that every battle is won before it is fought.

By that standard, the Victory Tour was a debacle before the Jacksons ever sang a note.

For starters, Don King and family patriarch Joe Jackson came up with a way to outrage ticket buyers and alienated everyone before even a single seat was sold. Tickets were $30 apiece, which sounds like pocket change today but was an unheard of sum for 1983. Not only that, but they could only be bought in packages of four. And they would only be available by lottery. In order to get into the drawing, you had to send in a money order for the full price of the four tickets. If you didn't get tickets, the amount would be refunded to you. But in the meantime, the promoters would be holding everyone's money and pocketing the interest.

Chuck Sullivan thought it was a great idea, which makes him the only one. To the rest of America, it was a cynical Ponzi scheme designed to cash in on the loyalty of fans, many of whom were too young and/or too poor to afford it. It was a public-relations nightmare.

Again, this was 1983 Michael, who was apparently still normal enough to possess a shred of human decency and concern for his audience. He called a press conference in which he read a letter from an 11-year-old girl who told him how unfair this ticket scam was to fans like her and that he was being "selfish." He was devastated. So he not only vowed he would take steps to change the system, he announced that he would take his share of proceeds from the tour and donate them all to the United Negro College Fund, leukemia and cancer research, and a camp for terminally ill kids.

Don King, Papa Joe, the other Jackson brothers, and of course Chuck Sullivan stuck with their plan to grab the public by the ankles, hang them upside down, and shake as much money out of their pockets as they could, starting with selling sponsorships. The Jacksons swung a lucrative deal with Quaker Oats to sponsor the tour. But when they ran it by King, he told them he'd already signed a deal with Pepsi. It wouldn't bring in as much money as the Quaker Oats contract, and there was the little matter of Michael's religious beliefs as a Jehovah's Witness, which wouldn't allow him to drink the stuff, but a deal's a deal.

So in defiance of his own devout beliefs and smart business sense, Michael was forced to shill for a soft drink he didn't consume because King and Sullivan said he had to. It was then on the set of his first commercial shoot that a light exploded, raining down hot sparks on Michael and setting his hair on fire. He wound up being rushed to a hospital with second- and third-degree burns. The subsequent treatment involved the use of prescription painkillers, which he became addicted to. Ultimately, that addiction to pills led to his death.

So yes, Chuck Sullivan not only cost his family their fortune with that stockholder buyout, he indirectly abetted the demise of the biggest star in pop music history.

Then insult was added to hot, burning injury. It's true that Chuck Sullivan managed to book a lot of the shows in NFL stadiums. One he wasn't able to book was the one owned by Chuck Sullivan.

The one chance Chuck was going to have to pocket all the profits at a tour stop without having to split them with the venue was going to come at the Sullivan Stadium shows. They were going to be his real cash cows. Except they never happened. The Foxboro Board of Selectmen voted down approval of the concerts, mumbling something about "a bad element" or some such nonsense. It was quite the controversy, given that they'd approved every other kind of event imaginable, from concerts and soccer games to tractor pulls and flea markets, and in later years approved events like the Grateful Dead and Monsters of Rock concerts, which didn't exactly draw Mormon missionaries.

The most common accusation hurled at the town was that they were just being racist, which made a great deal of sense. Since Michael's audience was largely made up of adolescents and young teens (mostly girls), it was a stretch to suggest that they were going to cause widespread destruction of the town, unless their high-pitched screaming could shatter windows. So, it's possible they didn't want a huge crowd of "urban" kids descending upon their sleepy little bedroom community.

On the other hand, Foxboro, Massachusetts, wasn't exactly the Jim Crow South. It was more than likely that the town just wanted to stick it to the Sullivans, to get back at them for being lousy neighbors. The chaos that came out of those Monday night games wasn't forgotten. Everyone within a three-mile radius of the Pats 50-yard line had a story about some drunk peeing in their bushes or passed out on their lawn. The traffic jams brought the place to its knees. They may have been racist, but it seemed more likely that they just wanted to wield their power and authority to be dinks.

And they succeeded. The "No" vote cost the Sullivans millions.

Once the tour began, it was immediately apparent to all that it was not going to make money. For starters, the *Victory* album itself wasn't very popular. The songs all sounded like Michael's leftovers that weren't good enough to make the cut on *Thriller*. Second, the ticket scam simply priced out way too many of their younger and poorer fans. And third, it didn't help any that the Jacksons insisted on a stage that was roughly big enough to use as a blimp hangar. It took up hundreds of otherwise sellable seats in each stadium and tens of thousands of seats over the course of the tour. And each seat that was eliminated was thirty more dollars out of the gross sales.

If this were an episode of VH1's *Behind the Music*, this is the part where the voiceover would say, "But off stage for the Jackson family, things were falling apart . . ." And they most definitely were. Tension between the brothers grew. Against everyone else's wishes, Michael started bringing outsiders backstage, such as cute child star/flavor-of-the-month Emmanuel Lewis. While the thought of Michael being so chummy with a little kid didn't have quite the ick factor it would in later years, it still rubbed everybody raw. It got to the point where each brother was just hanging out in his trailer by himself, and whatever chance they might have had to develop chemistry was shot to hell. And the performances got worse as the tour dragged on.

As if Jackson's chemistry wasn't suffering enough, the unstable element known as Don King added himself to the mix, causing a dissociation reaction that further ruptured the band's uni-molecular structure. King gave an interview where he said, among other things, "What Michael's got to realize is he's a nigger. He's one of the megastars of the world, but he's still going to be a nigger megastar. He must accept that." Michael was understandably furious. He told his legal team he was through with King and wanted to "sue his ass." They talked him out of filing suit, but the damage that was done would not be undone. It just further eroded the relationships he had with everyone involved in the tour.

Things were not quite as bad between Michael and Chuck Sullivan. One thing the Jacksons had in common was that they genuinely felt bad for Chuck making such a terrible deal for himself. It was increasingly obvious the tour was going to bankrupt him and his entire family, while every Jackson brother (and Michael's charities) stood to clear $7 million apiece. So they agreed to add extra shows to try and help Chuck recoup some of his losses. They also forgave the $10 million that Chuck owed them. But even that wasn't enough. They could've done a hundred extra shows for free, and Chuck would still have taken a financial bath, so bad was the arrangement he'd brokered. In all, the Sullivan family lost $30 million on his idiotic get-rich-quick scheme.

There was one last hope for Chuck to make back at least some of the money he was going to lose on the tour. He'd not only secured himself the right to sell Victory Tour merchandise, he'd worked out a separate deal with Michael to market a line of Michael Jackson designer jeans. So what he couldn't make in ticket sales, he had a shot to recover by getting the youth of America to squander their parents' money on overpriced t-shirts and ugly pants. The problems with the plan were twofold. One, no one was interested in buying novelty clothes commemorating a tour no one was enjoying to promote an album no one bought. Second, and much, much worse for Chuck, this was right about the time that Michael starting morphing from a widely respected musical genius into a troubled, possibly tortured "artist." He began the cosmetic surgeries that completely transformed his face and changed the color of his skin so much that he was almost unrecognizable. The first bizarre stories about him sleeping in hyperbaric chambers, trying to buy the Elephant Man's bones, and saying his closest friend on Earth was his pet chimp Bubbles began to surface. This was when Chuck learned the Marketing 101 lesson that, when you're trying to sell an image, no one wants to wear the same pants as a guy the tabloids are calling "Wacko Jacko."

What happened to all the unsold merchandise and designer jeans was never made public. There were rumors about warehouses full of the stuff somewhere. Some even suggested there were storerooms deep in the recesses of Sullivan Stadium filled with boxes of it, like the warehouse where they hid the Ark of the Covenant in *Raiders of the Lost Ark*. Perhaps it all got shipped to needy kids in some third-world country who got to spend the late 80s in skinny jeans with badly silkscreened pictures of a dysfunctional family across their chest. What *is* known is what happened to the stadium Chuck lost in this particular high-stakes card game; it ended up in bankruptcy court. Several parties bid on it, and in 1985 it sold for $25 million. The winning bid came from a cardboard-box mogul and Boston sports diehard who'd been a season ticketholder since the Patriots' first season in Foxboro, 14 years earlier. No Pats fan had heard of Robert Kraft before that day. And the first impression was he couldn't be much of a businessman to spend $25 million on that dump.

It turns out we were wrong.

FOR SALE BY OWNER

In 1986, San Diego Chargers owner Gene Klein published his autobiography, in which he wrote the immortal line, "Billy Sullivan is the only guy I ever knew who parlayed his life savings of $8,000 into $100 million of debt."[31] And that was coming from a friend. But like most things your friends say that are funny and cruel and said to humiliate you in public, it was completely true.

Between the money they'd lost on the Jacksons' tour, the money they owed stockholders, the deferred money they owed to past players, and the loss of the stadium, they were in a hole they couldn't get out of, even with the kind of heroic efforts that are used to rescue trapped miners.

Chuck had bought land around the stadium with plans to build a retail development on it, and Stadium Management Corp started defaulting on those loans. Then the football operations even started bouncing payroll checks. To show you how bad the mess was, the same season the Patriots lost $9 million going to the Super Bowl, the Green Bay Packers, who played in a smaller stadium and charged less for tickets, turned a $3 million profit.

The mess would never be fixed as long as the Sullivans owned the Patriots. After all the begging, borrowing, and stealing, the hard work and high hopes, all the dreaming and scheming, ownership of the Patriots had the Sullivans standing in the bottom of a $100 million crater they were never going to climb out of. They were left with no choice but to quit while they were behind. And the team they'd founded, fought for, and owned since its inception was put up for sale in 1988.

As a fan, when your team goes on the market, you look for two things in a potential new owner: someone local with no interest in moving them to another city, and someone with obscene amounts of money at his disposal so he can buy you a championship. That was especially true with a franchise as unstable as the Patriots were.

There were various names rumored to be interested. Assorted rich guys were reportedly forming rival gangs, deciding amongst themselves who'd be the *caporegime* and who'd be his lieutenants. One group that seemed to be in the lead for a while was led by a restaurateur from Philly named Jeffrey Chodorow, who later went to jail for defrauding the government. But if there was a favorite among the names being mentioned, it was probably Paul Fireman, who was supposedly ready to go halfsies on the team with some other Philly guy named Fran Murray. He was the CEO of Reebok, which had a huge presence in the area; the headquarters was just off the Mass Pike. He'd just finished building a golf course down the Cape that was always attracting superstars like John Daly and Greg Norman. Reebok was trendy and fashionable, Fireman was something of a celebrity businessman, and having him own the Patriots would've been cool. But when the dust settled and a final deal was announced, we ended up with a different, far less cool celebrity businessman owner.

VICTOR KIAM

Fran Murray had somehow managed to work his way in as minority owner, but three days before Halloween of 1988, Victor Kiam, the CEO of Remington Razors, became the Patriots Big Cheese.

For its part, Stadium Management Corp. was dissolved and Sullivan Stadium itself went into bankruptcy. It had several bidders, not the least of whom was Kiam. But all were outbid by the owner of a paper goods company who had quietly bought a parcel of land adjacent to the stadium by the name of Robert Kraft. Kraft's winning bid of $22 million seemed exorbitant for the dilapidated slab of concrete. But the stadium did come with a lease that bound the team to play there through 2001. But we're getting ahead of ourselves.

Kiam was a household name nationally because he used himself as the pitchman in his own ads. In the 80s, his signature catchphrase, "I liked the shaver so much, I bought the company!" wasn't exactly "Where's the beef?" but pretty much everyone knew it and knew him. While he didn't exactly have the cachet of moguls like Steve Jobs or Richard Branson, he was at least well known, not just from his ads but from regular appearances on *Late Night with David Letterman*. And to the best of anyone's knowledge, Kiam didn't have any dopey kids who took humiliating punches in the head in front of the whole world or who ran his empire into ruin like Billy did. So he felt like a tremendous upgrade.

Strangely, though, when Kiam took over the team he did not clean house and put his own people in charge. It was an odd move, like buying a house that has been foreclosed on and telling the family they can still live there. Maybe Kiam just needed some time to evaluate the operation and find the people he wanted. Maybe it was a reflection of the fact that the team had just recently been to a Super Bowl and was still a playoff contender. Whatever Kiam's motivation, Pat Sullivan was still the general manager and Billy stayed on as club president.

ROD RUST

In fact, the first major casualty of the Victor Kiam empire was Ray Berry, and he didn't get put out of his misery until after going 5–11 in the '89 season. His replacement was Rod Rust, the 61-year-old veteran defensive coordinator. After six years with the team, his firing by Ron Meyer, subsequent un-firing by Billy Sullivan, and countless hours of quiet dedication toiling in the background for the team, the highly respected Rust was finally getting his chance to be in charge. To show the world what he was worth.

They could not have made a worse choice. Well, maybe they could have, but there aren't too many names on the list. In every way a human being can fail at coaching football, Rod Rust failed. Utterly.

These were the Patriots of Marc Wilson at quarterback. He of the 1–9 Patriots career record with a touchdown/interception ratio of 9/16. The 1990 Patriots were last in the league in points scored, by a wide margin. On defense they gave up the second most points. They surrendered 300 more rushing yards than any other team. The Pats lost their first game, won their second, then didn't win another game the rest of the year. And as the season wore on and the losses became a constant, the only thing that changed was the degree and the severity of the vicious beatings they took. They lost in week three by a score of 41-7. In early November, it was 48-20. There was a 37-7 mixed in there. In late December, it was 42-7. The 1990 Patriots were a blowout factory. And the worst team in franchise history, which is really saying something. In one short year, Rod Rust became the Patron Saint of Good Coordinators Who Aren't Head Coaching Material forever after. As the drubbings mounted, Rust started giving off the unmistakably foul stench of failure. And the press picked up on the scent like hyenas, circling in for the kill. Rust did not handle it well.

After losing to Pittsburgh in week 14, he infamously told the press, "I'm proud of my team's effort today." They'd been beaten 24-3. With perfectly coordinated timing, the entire population of New England (at least the ones who were still following the Pats at that point) said with one voice, "Let me get this straight. You're proud of a 24-3 ass whupping? Then what exactly would it take for them to let you down???"

For Rust, there was no coming back from that. It was the death knell to his head coaching career. He was allowed to finish out the season, and he'd eventually get hired back as defensive coordinator for the Giants. But his days of ruining teams as head coach were over.

Amazingly, going 1-15 and producing the worst season in club history wasn't even the 1990 Patriots' greatest failure. They were actually doing worse things off the field than they were on it. Then again, since this is the Patriots we're talking about, maybe there's nothing amazing about it.

THE BODY PART THAT SAVED THE PATRIOTS

As a football team, they'd reached rock bottom. But as an organization, they managed to keep digging, put a drill down in there, and go even deeper. To achieve the absolute lowest part of low. They were the worst team in the NFL with the worst coach. They had the worst stadium situation and no quarterback. The owner was a complete novice and management was in chaos. Rumors were everywhere in the press that Kiam knew he couldn't turn a profit with the situation as it was and wanted to move the team to Jacksonville (note: the Jaguars didn't come into existence until 1995), so there was no telling if the team would even stay in New England beyond that season. And there was no reason to hope things would get better any time soon.

But as is so often the case in the course of human events, when things seem their darkest and hope hangs by a thread, one small moment can profoundly change the world. In 1066, at the Battle of Hastings, a rumor spread among the Normans that William the Conqueror had been killed. The lines faltered and some men went into retreat. Sensing victory, Harold of the Saxons sent his cavalry in pursuit. But when William reappeared, the Normans counter-attacked and the cavalry was cut off. The battle, and the throne of England, was theirs. In the 13th century, Genghis Khan's son Ögedei, having laid waste to the Middle East and Eastern Europe, was poised to conquer Germany until he suffered a fatal heart attack. In keeping with Mongol tradition, Ögedei's army had to return home to elect a new leader. This not only saved Western civilization from annihilation, but the trade routes the Mongols had left in their wake remained open, inspiring the Age of Discovery in the West. At Gettysburg, the 20th Maine regiment, led by a school teacher named Joshua Chamberlain, desperate, outmanned, and low on ammo, repelled a Confederate attack at Little Round Top. By holding the Union flank, Chamberlain protected the entire army, won the battle, turned the tide of the war, and ultimately saved the United States. At the Battle of Endor, Chewbacca captured one of those Imperial two-legged walker things and helped Han Solo take out the shield generator. The Rebel Alliance then blew up the Death Star II, defeated the Empire, and brought balance to the Force.

And so it was, at the lowest ebb in club history, that one small incident caused a chain reaction that set in motion a series of events that did nothing less than save the New England Patriots. It took several years, involved dozens of key figures and an uncountable number of lucky breaks to make it happen, but what one ordinary, unexceptional player did with a certain part of his body in that 1990 season eventually turned the Pats from a perennial laughingstock into one of the most successful teams in the history of pro sports.

The man was Zeke Mowatt. And the body part was his penis.

Mowatt was a Patriots tight end. He'd previously been a starter for the New York Giants, but by the time Bill Parcells was leading the Giants to two Super Bowls, Mowatt was in New England backing up starter Marv Cook. There was nothing special about him as a player; over the four previous seasons he'd averaged less than 14 receptions. He was the dictionary definition of what Parcells always called "JAG," meaning "just another guy." But sometimes, due to bizarre twists of fate, history is changed by such men.

The year 1990 was still the early days of female reporters being allowed into NFL locker rooms. There had been a gender battle brewing in the country for some time over the role of women in sports, and the locker-room issue was a hot-button topic. Women were just starting to get the same access to players that their male counterparts had always had, but they were finding out there was a wide verbal divide between being "allowed" in the locker room and being "accepted." On the day after the Patriots' second game of the season, *Boston Herald* reporter Lisa Olson walked into that divide.

Olson had graduated from Northern Arizona University with a degree in journalism three years earlier, and was new to the Patriots beat. On this particular day she was one of several reporters milling around the locker room, interviewing players. But to some Patriots, notably receiver Michael Timpson, running back Robert Perryman, and Mowatt, she was doing more standing around and looking at them than reporting. So Mowatt, coming out of the shower and seeing her interviewing Maurice Hurst, took what he determined to be the mature, reasonable approach to addressing his concerns. He stood in front of Olson, grabbed his junk, waggled it in her face and said, "You wanna bite this?" while Timpson and Perryman howled with laughter.

The next day, the episode drew a few mentions. A line or two in the newspapers' football notes columns. It might even have made the "Sports Flash" segments on the radio or a quick aside on the local news. Something about "an incident" involving a Patriots player touching his private parts near a female reporter, with a statement from the team that they were investigating it. And there the story sat for a day, maybe two, with nothing being added. But it didn't go away, either. It kept getting brought up on sports talk radio. A Boston columnist or two weighed in on it.

Then in some odd kind of delayed reaction, it gained all sorts of traction. The story went national. It became an item on *SportsCenter*, then crossed over from sports to the news section of national papers, before eventually making it to the network newscasts at a time when people still watched network newscasts. In a matter of days, it was the centerpiece of a national dialogue on sex, sports, and gender politics. It was nothing less than the No. 1 news story in America.

And it was surreal. After decades of mostly laboring in obscurity, the Patriots had the entire country talking about them, albeit for all the wrong reasons. Not just the team, but their second-string tight end. No one had ever heard of Zeke Mowatt before, but suddenly his name was a household word across the country and everyone was talking about his genitalia. Speaking strictly metaphorically, his dick was on everyone's lips.

Both sides of the whole gender-roles-in-sports debate had already been at DEFCON 1 for years. And like the idiot he was, Zeke Mowatt inadvertently walked right into the middle of it.

Everyone was debating the topic. It crossed gender lines and generations. It divided families. Filled miles of newspaper column inches and hours of TV and radio. It was the "Lisa Olson Is a Professional and Has Just as Much Right to Be in the Locker Room as a Man" crowd vs. the "Athletes Have the Right to Not Have Women Staring at Them Naked" faction facing off on the battlefield of gender roles.

Like any vital social topic America gets preoccupied with, this one had a limited shelf life. Maybe because at the exact same time, America was in a buildup to an actual real war, Operation Desert Shield. Or maybe folks just got really uncomfortable talking about Mowatt's junk. Regardless, after a few weeks it played itself out, the public had bigger fish to fry, and everyone moved on.

Everyone that is, except Victor Kiam, who volunteered to a reporter, "I can't disagree with the players' actions," and suggested that by sending Olson into the locker room in the first place, the *Herald* "asked for trouble." Not only that, but according to what he'd heard, Lisa Olson was "a classic bitch." Just as the fire had burned down to coals and was about to go out, Kiam had dumped a gallon of gas on it.

The world went wild. Overnight, women's groups organized a boycott of Lady Remington razors, which were a huge part of the company's sales. It was a PR disaster, not just for Kiam personally and for his company, and threatened to hurt every owner in the league if something wasn't done, and fast. NFL commissioner Paul Tagliabue put pressure on Kiam to put an end to this, and pronto. So Kiam reached for that handy volume, *So Your Stupid Remarks Are Threatening to Destroy Your Career*, that every CEO keeps on his bookshelf for guidance. He simultaneously denied saying anything bad, apologized for saying it, took out a full-page ad admitting his mistakes, and later said that what he'd actually called Olson was "a classy bitch."

As the season dragged on and the public pressure mounted, Kiam decided it was not enough to just hope the anger would die down and his PR problem would go away. The situation called for accountability. For a bold leader to show the courage of his convictions enough to take responsibility for his own actions.

Which is to say he fired people.

The first one gone was Rod Rust, which was a surprise to nobody. His one season of 1–15 secured him a bit of immortality, living forever on "Worst NFL Coaches of All Time" lists. Slightly less expected was Kiam's canning of Pat Sullivan, who was finally out as general manager. Billy survived another year as club president, but it was still pretty much a ceremonial thing anyway, like being Queen of England, only with way less money and respect and practically zero bowing to him.

SAM JANKOVICH

Replacing Pat Sullivan as GM was Sam Jankovich of the University of Miami. Jankovich had been the Hurricanes' athletic director through their ascendancy from a largely overlooked sports program to a powerhouse. On Jankovich's watch, Miami became known for two things: winning national championships and allowing a culture of nasty, borderline-outlaw thuggishness.

There's no denying that Jankovich's football teams of the 80s were bad-asses. They prided themselves on nasty, physical play and running up the score every chance they got, without apology. They loved nothing more than knocking opponents out of games with vicious hits and breaking the other team's will. Luther Campbell, lead singer of the uber-controversial rap group 2 Live Crew, was a fixture on the 'Canes sidelines, allegedly handing out cash bonuses for knockout hits.

And they were universally despised for it. The epic 1988 game against Notre Dame is immortalized as "The Catholics vs. The Convicts" and in 2005 was voted by Fighting Irish fans as the biggest win in school history. The whole country outside of Miami hated the Hurricanes. But since the Patriots had spent most of their existence being used as a boot scraper by the rest of the NFL, they were open to being hated instead of just laughed at. If Sam Jankovich could bring some of that Miami badassery to New England, Kiam was all for it.

DICK MACPHERSON

Jankovich's first move was to replace Rust with Dick MacPherson, the head coach at Syracuse University. It's always risky hiring a guy who has never coached in the pros before, but MacPherson seemed like a decent enough choice. In fact, he was hard not to like. If you called central casting and said, "send me an actor who can play a lovable football coach," they'd have Dick MacPherson in your office that very day. He seemed like a cross between Coach from the early seasons of *Cheers* and Jerry Van Dyke on *Coach*. And he'd led the Orangemen—not exactly a football factory program—to an undefeated season in '87, so the general consensus was "Why the hell not? He couldn't be any worse than what we just had."

So for a while, Kiam's firings and hirings served as a distraction that managed to take the heat off. The whole mess forced a team that was heading nowhere to make fundamental changes, so we took it as a positive thing. Maybe now grown-ups were in charge and the Pats would get better on and off the field.

Not that it did much for Lisa Olson's personal life. Her tires got slashed, her apartment was broken into, and she had to put up with all manner of abuse and ridicule from nitwits posing as Patriots fans. But to the wider public, the story was played out.

Until just after the football season. In February, Kiam was speaking at a banquet in Connecticut. This was during the height of Operation Desert Storm, and he decided to wow the crowd with this little chestnut, a joke which was already about four months past its expiration date by then: "You know what the Iraqi Army and Lisa Olson have in common? They've both seen Patriot Missiles up close!"

Where before he'd poured gasoline on the dying embers of the story with that "bitch" comment, this was throwing a brick of C4 packed with detonators on it. Every other NFL owner hearing this simultaneously spit his Chivas all over the front of his butler's shirt. It was one thing for Kiam to get the feminists riled up at him, his dysfunctional football team, and his stupid razor company, but this latest boneheaded comment threatened them and their bottom line. And that could not stand. Together they all did the *Blazing Saddles* "We've got to save our phony baloney jobs, gentlemen!" thing, and with good reason. The same women's groups that organized the Remington boycott vowed to do the same to the NFL if something wasn't done about this woman-hating buffoon.

As the lawyers say, Kiam couldn't unring this bell. All the full-page ads and non-apology apologies and scapegoat firings in the world aren't enough when you've got 50 percent of the population lining up against you and threatening to take money away from your billionaire associates. He was past fail-safe, past the point of no return, and needed to be gone. So they basically put a contract out on him. They put pressure on Tagliabue to put the pressure on Kiam to sell the Patriots and get the hell out of their league before he started costing them money. Those yachts, country club memberships, and ex-wives don't pay for themselves.

It took some time for Kiam to line up another buyer. The Patriots were still a financial disaster and not exactly the most attractive investment in the world. There was also the matter of the stadium being owned by this Robert Kraft guy, who held a lease that bound the team to play in that run-down piece of crap. That meant that if you were buying the team in order to move it, you'd have to get out from under the lease, which could get expensive. And that's assuming Kraft was even willing to deal, and there was no guarantee he was.

Just over a year later, Kiam did manage to unload the team to James Busch Orthwein, heir to the Anheuser-Busch fortune. You know that old line about how the ideal woman is a rich girl whose father owns a brewery? He'd be the dad in that equation. The problem with that was that Orthwein's home, company, and fortune were all in St. Louis, which happened to be without an NFL franchise. So the writing was on the wall that he was buying the Patriots to move them.

But that was still years away, and for the time being the stadium was still owned by a local guy who was a lifelong Boston sports fan. That was the thin thread hopes were hanging on, but at least it was something.

In 1990, the team was going nowhere. They had a terrible owner, an awful GM, an abysmal coach, a horrible stadium, and a horrendous future ahead. The only thing that rectified the situation and forced the change that eventually brought stability and prosperity to the New England Patriots was a nondescript idiot of a player doing something stupid. All the success that came later on we owe to one man and his inability to keep his hands off his package.

Mowatt's perverse hassling of a woman just trying to do her job ultimately led to the NFL strong-arming a terrible owner out of New England. He was replaced by an owner who brought about the change the franchise so desperately needed. Change in the form of a Hall of Fame coach who gave the club instant, legitimate credibility and showed a downtrodden franchise how to become a winner. And none of it would've have happened without Zeke.

If Zeke Mowatt ever has any regrets about how his life has turned out, his guardian angel will come down and show him, *It's a Wonderful Life*-style, how much good he has done in this world. As Clarence tells George Bailey, "One man's life touches so many others." And when Zeke Mowatt touched himself, he touched us all.

13 FISHING FOR TUNA

★ ★ ★ ★ ★ ★ ★ ★ ★ ★ ★ ★ ★ ★ ★ ★ ★

Are you not entertained?!
Is this not why you are here?!
    MAXIMUS, *Gladiator*

My friends and I had a tradition of playing Sunday morning touch football starting with week one of the NFL season and going right through to the Super Bowl. We'd generally leave the field at about noon and hit the dive-y neighborhood pub our buddy owned to watch the NFL games over a beer or two (dozen). And during this particular period, the Pats games were an afterthought. It was almost a pleasant surprise to have them on TV. Mostly the bar would have the radio broadcast on in the background while we watched the much more relevant Dallas, San Francisco, or Buffalo games.

Personally, I could tolerate the Patriots being awful—almost. I'd gotten more or less used to it. What ran right up my spine was them making no one care. We were stuck with a carpetbagging owner who was taking the very profits of the beer I was buying from him in unhealthy quantities to take one of the things that was most precious to me out of my life. And with every empty seat in Foxboro Stadium and every game we watched that wasn't a Patriots game, we were all just making it easier for him move the team to St. Louis. Collectively, we might as well have been loading the moving trucks ourselves.

During the period when Victor Kiam was putting the "Franchise for Sale by Owner" sign out front and spending his weekends hosting open houses for prospective buyers, Sam Jankovich was taking over the worst team in the NFL, a team that needed to get better, fast.

The Patriots had the first overall pick in the '91 draft, but Jankovich's first draft move as Patriots GM was to trade the pick to Dallas for two later picks, defensive back Ron Francis and linebacker Eugene Lockhart. Francis never played another down in the NFL, and in two seasons with the Patriots, Lockhart never recorded a sack or forced a turnover. This was the Cowboys' second season under owner Jerry Jones and coach Jimmy Johnson, and they used the

Patriots' pick to grab defensive tackle Russell Maryland, who became part of the foundation of their three Super Bowl dynasty teams.

The trade was a move right out of the days of Billy Sullivan drafting Gerhard Schwedes and Ed McKeever taking Dennis Byrd from a hospital bed and almost picking a dead guy. It established Jankovich's bona fides as another in the long line of Patriots GMs who had no idea what they were doing.

The first order of business was to try to find a quarterback to build around. Unfortunately, '91 was a notoriously bad draft for QBs, so the safe route was to try to land one as a free agent. This was still the period when they were signing the rejects of other, more successful teams and hoping to strike gold. This time they tried another veteran, only they didn't even bother with one from a winning organization. They settled for Hugh Millen of the Atlanta Falcons, a team that hadn't been even remotely good in 10 years. Millen was notable for one thing, and that was that he was dating the director of cheerleading for the Patriots, Lisa Guerrero, a world-class beauty who later went on to a career as a TV sports anchor.

Jankovich did manage to find a few gems in his first draft. With the 14th overall selection he got running back Leonard Russell, a durable six-foot-two, 240-pound power back out of Arizona State. And in the fifth round he found a five-carat diamond in the rough in tight end Ben Coates, out of the unheard-of Livingstone College. The only QB he took was mid-rounder Scott Zolak out of Maryland.

In that first year of the Jankovich/MacPherson Era, the Pats improved to 6-10, with three wins in the first half of the season and three in the second half. Russell was the AP Offensive Rookie of the Year. MacPherson actually got some consideration for Coach of the Year. They were baby steps, due mainly to the fact that when you're 1-15 you can't do much worse. But after the way things had gone the year before, those meager crumbs felt like a banquet.

The lasting memory of those years has always been MacPherson's coaching style, which was, to put it kindly, unique. If you wanted to put it unkindly, it was borderline silly. In a league that for generations was dominated by stone-faced, squinty-eyed alpha males like Don Shula, Tom Landry, and Chuck Noll, or by angry, demonstrative maniacs like Vince Lombardi and Mike Ditka, MacPherson was a big, roly-poly, white-haired ball of affection. Just a human bundle of moral support and enthusiasm, perpetually running around the sidelines in his nylon jacket, hugging his players, and patting any back he could get his hands on. He not only looked the part of the lovable coach sent up from central casting, he played it to the hilt. He had the coaching style of your favorite hilarious drunken uncle organizing games at the family reunion. And while it was entertaining to watch, there was widespread doubt that it would work as well in pro football as it might at your family's Wiffle Ball tournament.

There was also optimism that Hugh Millen could become the quarterback that New England so desperately needed. At one point in the season he led a fourth-quarter come-from-behind victory, and this was such a rare occasion that the *Sports Huddle* guys asked callers to come up with a nickname for him; even one dramatic win in those days was enough to make you nickname-worthy. It should come as no surprise that 99.9 percent of the suggestions were corny and pathetic. But one was actually clever and worthwhile: "Hugh-dini." It just seemed to fit somehow. At least up until The Great Hughdini returned to form, making his passes disappear into defensive backs' arms, and was kicked down the front steps after posting a record of 0–7 in his second year as a starter; another potential franchise savior gone.

And so it was that after one promising year, the Patriots reverted right back to form. They began the 1992 season with nine straight losses and finished it with a five-game losing streak on the way to a 2–14 season. For the second time in three years, under two different owners, two different general managers and two different head coaches, they finished with the worst record in the league.

The good news was they had the top pick in the draft again. The even better news was that this time Sam Jankovich wouldn't be around to give the pick away for two lower picks and a bag of used footballs. James Orthwein had seen enough, and mercifully took both Jankovich and Dick MacPherson out behind the barn and put them out of our misery. Jankovich/MacPherson went down in the record books as a failure of epic proportions. A total of 8 wins and 24 losses over two seasons. But it was much, much worse than that. Practically every home game was not a sellout, meaning they were blacked out on local TV. It seemed that the time to relocate the team to St. Louis had finally come.

Ultimately, two things prevented the move from happening: one, there were still years remaining on the lease held by Robert Kraft that kept the team in Foxboro, and two, as it stood the Patriots had zero appeal for anyone—not even for a city that had gone without pro football for five years. Bringing the Pats to St. Louis with Jankovich, MacPherson, and Millen in charge would've been like opening a kosher deli in Riyadh. Orthwein couldn't expect there'd be much of a market for it unless he made drastic changes.

And God bless the man, he did. He made a clean sweep of everyone. No doubt he did it to maximize his own investment and not because he cared about Pats-fan lifers, but he did. And after a decade and a half of irrelevance, a hare-brained scheme to promote a disastrous concert tour, hundreds of bad personnel moves, a mediocre player waving his penis around in people's faces, and the constant threat of the team getting moved out of New England, we finally got an owner to bring in someone competent to run an NFL franchise.

Not just competent, but an actual legend.

On January 21, 1993, James Orthwein hired Duane Charles "Bill" Parcells to be his head coach. And the exact moment the deal was announced, the Patriots were relevant again.

BILL PARCELLS

It's pretty damned near impossible to overstate how great an impact James Orthwein's hiring of Bill Parcells had on the Patriots franchise. He gave them the kind of instant credibility that one man can rarely provide to any organization. So much so that it almost defies comparison.

The Pats were such an amateurish operation, run by incompetents, lunatics, frauds and liars for so long, and Parcells gave them such immediate legitimacy, that I struggle to find a simile that fits. Let me try this: it would be like if you and your loser buddies formed a band that rehearses in your garage and is still hoping for your first paid gig, and one day Eddie Vedder shows up to be your front man. It's not perfect, but it'll have to do.

While the Patriots had been struggling through the entropy of the tail end of the Raymond Berry era and the degrading humiliation of the Rod Rust season, Parcells was leading the New York Giants to two Super Bowl championships. This was especially tough for me, because I grew up despising the Giants with white-hot intensity. All through my otherwise happy childhood they cast a shadow long and dark across New England, a remnant of the pre-AFL days before the Patriots existed, and I resented them deeply for it. My buddy Kenny grew up in a Giants household, and I stood next to him at the Weymouth Knights of Columbus bar watching Buffalo's Scott Norwood miss a field goal at the final gun to hand them Super Bowl XXV, their second championship in five years. It was miserable beyond description.

But even at my resentful, jealous, loathing worst, I always liked Parcells. If you were a fan of football and of sarcastic, Northeast assholes, it was hard not to like him. Bill Parcells not only knew how to coach the game, he was a master of running the show.

His defenses with the Giants were among the best in NFL history. His first Super Bowl, after the 1986 season, was won with quarterback Phil Simms putting together arguably the best performance in the history of the game, an almost flawless 22-for-25 with three TDs (one thrown to future Patriots savior Zeke Mowatt) and no interceptions. His second Super Bowl, after the

1990 season, was won with a journeyman backup, Jeff Hostetler. In doing so, he cemented his reputation as one of the best coaches in the NFL—if not *the* best.

But Parcells' true genius was in all the other stuff. The off-the-field handling of things that so many otherwise brilliant X's and O's coaches fail at. He excelled at managing a football organization, motivating his players, getting the most out of his coaches, and controlling the message. The latter was probably where he excelled the most. Parcells couldn't have handled the allegedly difficult New York media better if he came in to the press briefings swinging a whip. He was pure New Jersey: simultaneously condescending, dismissive, funny, profane, and insightful. And they loved him for it. The same New York press that took pride in running lesser coaches out of town totally kowtowed to Parcells.

In New England, there was always a bit of we-could've-had-this-guy dynamic with Parcells because he had been the linebackers coach on Ron Erhardt's staff in 1980. That's where he picked up the nickname "Tuna," which he has always insisted he got because his players tried to put something over on him and he said, "Do I look like Charlie the Tuna to you?" But the truth is that it was because he was fat and pale and looked like a fish. And when he was a national icon a few years later, Patriots fans were left to wonder how the Sullivans managed to not recognize how good he could be and settle for a twit like Ron Meyer instead.

By the 1990 NFL season, Parcells was burned out, mentally and physically. He was having heart problems and had to walk away from the game. After two mostly forgettable seasons in the broadcast booth, he had a clean bill of health, an itch to get back on the sidelines, and an owner in Orthwein who was only too happy to pay him the big bucks to put his franchise on the map. And he succeeded.

As a region, as a fan base, and as people just starved for entertainment, fans could not have been happier if Vince Lombardi had come back from the dead to coach, with George Halas and Jesus as his coordinators. For the first time in forever, the Pats were going to be run by someone who knew what he was doing. Orthwein gave Parcells total control over all football operations. Technically, Charley Armey was given the title of "director of player personnel," but there was no question who gave it to him and who'd be calling all the shots. The Patriots were now a dictatorship, and everyone would be answering to Parcells. Emperor Tuna I. And just to make the reboot complete, Orthwein made a substantial, if symbolic change; for the first time since their second year of existence, the Patriots were making a major change in their uniforms.

The Pat Patriot they'd had on their helmets since 1961 was history, replaced by the Flying Elvis on a silver background they have to this day.

As cool as Pat was, this was a long time coming. For years the NFL had been trying to get rid of it because it was too hard to replicate. It was the only team logo in the history of sports to be taken from a newspaper editorial cartoon, and Phil Bissell's drawing was too full of details to mass produce on jackets and hats and whatnot. And to be fair, 90 percent of the time it did look like garbage. Still, the fan base resisted the change. One time, years earlier, the team did a halftime promotion where they put Pat up against a new design, something that looked like the U.S. flag but where the field of stars was the profile of a Minuteman's head. It wasn't terrible. But when the crowd was asked to choose which one they preferred, Pat got cheered like he was the Pope in St. Peter's Square and the Flag Head was booed off the field.

But the whole operation needed a do-over, and this change was symbolic of it. Besides, it had gotten to the point were the old logo no longer stood for history and tradition as much as it did losing and penises. So the timing was perfect.

Parcells was at the press conference where they rolled out the new uniform. Andre Tippett was modeling the new look and Tuna was asked what he thought of it. His answer was perfect. "I think it's great. But then again, when you've got a player as good as Andre Tippett wearing it, any uniform'll look great." He was being the good soldier, toeing the company line, and complimenting his best player all in one fell swoop. The man was a genius at this stuff.

The next order of business for Parcells was the much more practical matter of improving the gawdawful team he'd inherited, starting with the No. 1 overall pick in the draft.

THE FRANCHISE QUARTERBACK

Leading up to the draft, there was the same speculation you get every year about the first team on the board possibly trading away the top pick. But as is so often the case, nothing came of it. (Sam Jankovich handing Dallas the Russell Maryland pick being one obvious exception.) There was little doubt in anyone's mind that the Patriots were going to take a quarterback. There were two candidates, and the only debate was which one Parcells would decide to build his team around.

One was Rick Mirer out of Notre Dame. In his two years as the starting QB of the Fighting Irish, the six-foot-three, 210-pound Mirer led them to two 10-win seasons and wins both in the Sugar Bowl and the Cotton Bowl. Mirer was already 23 and had the polish, poise, and the big-school résumé of a pro-ready quarterback. The other option was Washington State's Drew Bledsoe. At six foot five, 238 pounds, he had the size advantage over Mirer and was believed to have a stronger arm. He was also only 21, and the Cougars were coming off seasons of 4–7 and 9–3, and their only postseason experience was a win in the Copper Bowl. Of the two, Bledsoe seemed like he had more upside than Mirer, but he'd need more time to develop.

After weeks of conjecture and debate, Parcells went with Bledsoe and, with the second pick, Mirer went to the Seattle Seahawks. (My proudest memory of that particular day was telling my friends I was surprised Parcells took Drew Bledsoe, given the history of drinking and drug abuse there. And after they stared at me dumbfounded for a second I said, "Oh, wait. I'm thinking of Drew Barrymore." Yes, it's a dated reference. But at the time it was perfect. Screw you if you can't appreciate it.)

The first impression of Bledsoe was that he came off like a bright, cerebral, level-headed kid—emphasis on the "kid" part, because he wouldn't have looked out of place hanging out outside a liquor store asking if you could buy him and his buddies a case of beer. But he was polished, polite, and well-spoken. He said all the right things about being excited about the challenge and looking forward to working with Coach Parcells. It was pretty obvious he had a good head on his shoulders, and shelling out 65 bucks for his Patriots No. 11 jersey would be a safe investment, because he wouldn't turn out to be a dink.

(One aside about those jerseys: the original design of the home uniform was red numbers on a blue shirt. And they were a disaster. No one beyond the first two rows of the stands could tell one numeral from the next and it drove everyone—especially the play-by-play announcers—up the wall. As soon as the season was over, they switched to white numbers with a red drop shadow, and order was restored to the galaxy.)

In addition, that first draft under Parcells yielded inside linebacker Chris Slade, guard Todd Rucci, and receiver Vincent Brisby in round two. And in an afterthought, with the 198th overall pick in the now extinct eighth round, they took a lightly regarded receiver/special teamer out of Marshall named Troy Brown. These guys would be the first of several picks made by Parcells that were a gigantic upgrade from the stiffs Pat Sullivan and Sam Jankovich had been bringing in. And it seemed like Parcells took delight in dumping the previous regime's high picks. Almost immediately after the '93 season began, he got rid of 1990 top pick (eighth overall) LB Chris Singleton; and 1992's No. 1, guard Eugene Chung (13th overall), lasted all of one season before Parcells canned him.

He did likewise with one of his own picks, fifth-rounder Scott Sisson, who might hold the distinction of being the worst placekicker in NFL history. Overall he hit on a pathetic 14 of 26 in his Patriots career before Parcells jettisoned the pod on him after 13 games. To replace him, Parcells brought in reliable veteran Matt Bahr from his Giants teams, but not before Scott became immortalized with the nickname "Missin' Sisson."

It was a message to the rest of his roster that no one was safe. Regardless of how you got there, you were on notice to get it together and pull your weight, or else you'd be sent packing too. For the first time since the Chuck Fairbanks days, there was someone in charge who used fear as a motivator.

After the Pats took Bledsoe, Mirer went with the No. 2 pick to Seattle. And for much of their rookie season, it seemed as though the Patriots had made the wrong call. Through a weird quirk in the schedule, the Patriots and Seahawks actually faced each other twice, which is practically unheard of for two teams in different divisions. And Seattle won both games.

Though you couldn't blame Bledsoe for that second meeting, because he didn't play.

Through some combination of being injured and being benched, Bledsoe sat out weeks six through eight. And when he was in there, the rookie growing pains were obvious. In his first 10 starts, the Pats only scored 20-plus points once, and that was in a game in which he only had eight completions. By the beginning of December, their record stood at 1–11. Mirer, meanwhile, was locking up UPI's AFC Rookie of the Year.

All but the most irrational talk radio trolls understood that it was way too soon to start panicking about Bledsoe becoming the latest in a long line of major draft busts. He still hadn't reached his 22nd birthday, and kids his age almost never got to start right away. Parcells had him learning on the job, oftentimes putting him out there to throw the ball 40-plus times. And they were seeing enough flashes of brilliance to keep the hysteria down to a minimum. Besides, 8 of those 11 losses were by less than a touchdown.

But while all this was going on, it was hard to feel great about things. The whole issue of Orthwein moving the team to St. Louis still hung over New England like the Sword of Damocles.

Finally at the end of the season, the team seemed to find itself. Their second win of the year came in week 15, an improbable 7–2 job over Cincinnati. Then they got on a bit of a roll. A 20–17 win at Cleveland. A 38–0 blowout of Indianapolis where Bledsoe had an almost perfect passer rating. Finally, in the last week of the season they pulled off their fourth straight win in overtime at home against Miami. On the final play of the game, Bledsoe hit Michael Timpson for a 36-yard touchdown, his fourth TD pass of the day, and a 33–27 victory. It was not a packed house in Foxboro and the game was blacked out locally, but the people who were there did themselves proud. After that game-winning play, they started cheering and refused to stop. What started out as celebrating a victory became a protest. No one left the stadium—they just stayed in place, chanting and holding up signs, letting it be known they didn't want the team to move.

For all the stupidity, debauchery, and flat out inhumanity Patriots fans have displayed in their history, this was their finest hour. The outpouring of emotion proved the Patriots had a place in the lives of their fans and that pro football in New England was worth saving. One season ticketholder in particular, Robert Kraft, whose stadium lease was the only thing keeping the team around, seemed to think so too.

THE SAVIOR

By January of 1994, I was more or less a grown man. I was married. I had something resembling a career. I had a growing stand-up comedy side job that was bringing me a fair amount of bookings. My Irish Rose and I were living in her rent-controlled apartment in the working-class section of Cambridge and starting to map out the house/babies/future-job-situation phase of our lives. But I wasn't yet grown up enough that I had bigger things to worry about than the fate of a football franchise.

Nothing was bigger than this to me. While the world was riveted to the Tonya Harding–Nancy Kerrigan sports soap opera of the ages, I was obsessively poring over the sports and business news for any sign of hope that the Pats would stay.

According to news reports, James Orthwein was offering Kraft $75 million to buy his way out of the lease. It was devastating news, as that was absolutely an offer Kraft couldn't refuse. Kraft bought the dump for $25 million in 1988, meaning that he would have tripled his investment in under six years and would still own the property. A profit of $50 million just for tearing up a piece of paper. There seemed like zero chance anyone would turn that down.

Then, on the morning of January 21, Patriots beat writer Will McDonough of the *Boston Globe* was on Don Imus saying it was a done deal. Orthwein had bought Robert Kraft out of his lease and the Patriots would be moving to St. Louis starting that very day.

It was the worst sort of nut punch imaginable for anyone emotionally attached to a team. It's worse than having a wife leave you, because you can have another woman right away; it was likely to be decades before the NFL would put another franchise in New England. (Of course I don't mean *my* wife, who's irreplaceable. Save on the rebound!) New Englanders were staring into the abyss of living a life without pro football—or worse, weighing the option of continuing to root for the franchise that just jilted us versus glomming onto the New York Giants. As much as that in-stadium rally represented the high point of Patriots fandom, this news was undoubtedly the low.

For a few hours.

ROBERT KRAFT

Hours is how long it took for the entire story to do a complete 180. It was soon announced that not only did Robert Kraft reject Orthwein's Godfather offer, he made a counteroffer of his own, which Orthwein had no choice but to accept. McDonough might have been football's Mr. Know-It-All, but on this one he turned out to be dead wrong. The Patriots were staying put.

Kraft had been bidding against other investment groups, including one headed by Walter Payton and Paul Newman. But he blew everyone else out of the water with an offer of $175 million, an insane amount at the time. No one had ever paid so much for any NFL franchise, least of all one with such an unprofitable, craphole stadium. As he subsequently said, he was a sports fan in Boston back when the Braves left town for Milwaukee in 1952, and he never got over the disappointment. This time he had the chance to prevent history from repeating itself, and he succeeded.

Plenty of experts thought Mr. Kraft was out of his mind to pay so much, not the least of whom was Mrs. Kraft. His wife Myra was not happy. He'd pulled the equivalent of bringing home a dog from the pound without checking with the missus, only this particular mutt cost $175 million. At least in his case he meant it when he said he'd do all the caring and feeding and clean up after it.

It's hard to imagine a more significant day, or one with a bigger emotional and psychological reversal in the history of any sports city, than January 21, 1994, was in Boston, Massachusetts. This wasn't about one game, or even one championship. It was a transformation from a future without any team to root for to one where they're staying in perpetuity. And it all took place between breakfast and dinner.

A few weeks later, the deal was finalized and the NFL announced that Robert Kraft was now the sole owner of the New England Patriots. Coincidentally, the very next day tickets went on sale, and the Patriots sold almost 6,000 season tickets. That number shattered the previous one-day total by a factor of six.

And that last game of 1993? That one where the fans stuck around chanting and protesting, trying to *will* the team to stay? That was the last non-sellout the team has ever had.

Heading into the '94 season, there was no reason not to be optimistic. Even if you weren't being realistic, even if your hopes exceeded any reasonable expectation for the talent level of the Patriots, you could be excused. As bleak as the future looked back in early January, things now felt like waking up safe in your bed after a horrible nightmare. It was OK just to be glad you weren't actually falling off a cliff, hunted by scary clowns, or naked at work. We had football. And for now, that was enough. For the first time in team history, the ownership situation appeared stable. The coach was a legend. The quarterback looked to be catching on. And the rest of the roster was young but coming together nicely.

In the first round of the 1994 draft, Parcells took a big, athletic linebacker/defensive end out of Southern Cal named Willie McGinest with the fourth overall pick. In the sixth round he grabbed offensive tackle Max Lane, who showed promise. And Ben Coates had impressed him so much at tight end that he let starter Marv Cook walk.

The team as a whole wasn't much better right out of the gate, or for weeks afterward. A three-game winning streak begat a four-game losing streak, and by mid-season they stood at 3-6. One thing we learned about Bill Parcells in that first half was that he was a master manipulator. He knew exactly when to smack his team on the nose with a rolled-up magazine and yell, and when to scratch them behind the ears and tell them what good boys they were. During that losing streak, he had every justification for telling the world how bad his team was. Lord knows reporters gave him plenty of opportunity. But he passed practically every time. It wasn't about going easy on them; it was understanding the psychology of a young team. It was about him grasping the concept that the right time to rip a team is when things are going well, so they don't start believing their own hype. And when they're struggling, it's best to lay off, so you don't crush their spirit. It was brilliant. Coaching on a level beyond anything we'd seen before. Parcells wasn't just playing chess while others played checkers. He was playing that 3-D multi-level chess Mr. Spock had in his cabin on the *Enterprise*.

And it worked. The following week, the Patriots seemed to find themselves, especially Drew Bledsoe. The week 11 game against Minnesota was the exact moment he arrived as a legitimate NFL franchise quarterback. It was his coming-out party, like something out of MTV's *My Super Sweet 16* (except Drew wasn't wearing a tiara and crying that his dad ruined his special day by giving him his Lexus before the party).

It was a game for the record books. The Vikings were rolling over New England, up 10-0 after the first quarter and 20-0 in the second. At that point Parcells, who had always had the reputation of being an old-school, keep-running-the-ball-and-impose-your-will-on-the-defense coach, the guy who is credited with coining the phrase "Smashmouth football"—did a complete turnaround. At some point he just seemed to say, "to hell with it," and just opted to let his young QB chuck it on every play. Bledsoe set two NFL records that day: most pass attempts in a game (with 70) and most completions (with 45). He finished with an impressive 426 yards and no interceptions. More importantly, he led the Pats to 20 unanswered second-half points to tie the game, and a 14-yard TD pass to fullback Kevin Turner in overtime for the win.

Even more importantly than that, it saved the season. Sitting at 4-6 wasn't pretty, but it was a damned sight better-looking than 3-7, which they would've been had Bledsoe not pulled it out (which would have for all intents and purposes ended their season). Now there was hope—albeit a thin one—that they could build on this win and actually make a run at a spot in the playoffs.

And that's exactly what they did. They not only went on a winning streak, they didn't lose again the rest of the way. That win over the Vikings jump-started a seven-game winning streak to finish the season at 10-6. They wrapped up the regular season with a 13-3 win at Chicago on Christmas Eve that clinched them a wild-card berth. It would be their first trip to the playoffs in eight years.

Left tackle Bruce Armstrong was named to the Pro Bowl. Ben Coates was named All Pro as the best tight end in the league, with team records of 96 receptions and over 1,100 yards. And Bledsoe also made the Pro Bowl after leading the NFL in several categories, including attempts, completions, and yards. Unfortunately, he also lapped the field when it came to throwing interceptions, with 27 to the second-place finisher's 19. But he carried a young and flawed team on his back and into the playoffs, so no one was going to quibble with a few lapses in judgment. Besides, the kid was only 22. Surely he wasn't going to be making mistakes like that five, six, seven years down the road.

Right?

It was on to Cleveland for the wild-card playoff. And although no one could've possibly known it at the time, a date with destiny.

THE GENIUS

There were a lot of similarities between the Patriots and the Browns. Both organizations had gone from some respectable seasons in the mid-80s to the bottom of the league in 1990. And both had rebuilt themselves by raiding the

Giants' coaching staff. Parcells' defensive coordinator on those championship teams had been Bill Belichick, the boy wonder whose Super Bowl XXV game plan—the one that shut down Buffalo's K-Gun Offense—is on display in the Pro Football Hall of Fame. He was hired to run the Browns within days after that game.

Belichick, like Parcells, had his new club back in the playoffs by 1994, though his road had a lot more potholes along the way. In his first three years in Cleveland, the Browns went 20-28. He alienated much of the fan base by cleaning house and getting rid of most of their has-been holdovers from the 80s teams. Clevelanders reacted as if Belichick had committed a crime against humanity when he benched quarterback Bernie Kosar, a hometown hero despite the fact that he was pretty much a stiff.

But by '94, Belichick had remade the Browns in his image. Also like Parcells, he'd brought in some former Giants he trusted, such as veteran defensive leaders Chip Banks and Pepper Johnson. They only gave up 204 points all season, by far the fewest in the league and one of the lowest totals in the 16-game era. Unbeknownst to anyone at the time, the most impressive thing Belichick had done was surround himself with future front-office and coaching superstars. His staff included future NFL general managers Ozzie Newsome, Scott Pioli, Thomas Dimitroff, and Mike Tannenbaum. His defensive coordinator was Nick Saban, who has since won three college football national titles. And among his assistants were future NFL head coaches Eric Mangini and Jim Schwartz, just to name a few. The Browns had a football Mensa meeting in their coaches' conference room every day. From a coaching perspective, they were the NFL's *League of Extraordinary Gentlemen*. But since no one saw that movie, perhaps a better analogy is the gridiron *Avengers*. And Belichick was the Nick Fury who assembled them.

But the way New England looked at it, Bill Parcells could outthink Belichick and his collection of superheroes all by himself. Lord only knows how many newspaper column inches were taken up by hack-y articles milking the old "The Apprentice vs. The Master" trope for all it was worth. But with the roll the Patriots were on and Parcells' track record in big games, there was plenty of confidence that Parcells would scheme a way to a win over his old minion.

The Browns won 20-13, which was surprising only because it didn't feel like a one-score game. Belichick, Saban, and the Browns' defense forced Bledsoe into too many mistakes. He threw three interceptions. Late in the game, needing to lead a comeback, Bledsoe was constantly pressured by Saban's D. In the fourth quarter, he ended back-to-back drives with interceptions, and on the Patriots' last possession he turned it over on downs with four straight incompletions. And even though he completed 21 passes, they were on 50 attempts. In contrast, Cleveland QB Vinny Testaverde had 20 completions on only 30 attempts.

Of course, it wouldn't have been a Patriots loss without a lethal injection of O. Henry-esque irony. The best player on the field for either side in that game, the Browns receiver who torched New England for 122 yards on 7 receptions, was named Michael Jackson.

There was no finding fault with Bledsoe, Parcells, or anyone on the Pats. Quite the contrary; it was a hell of a good Browns team they'd just lost to, and there was no shame in it. The Browns were tough, disciplined, smart, prepared, and extremely well coached. All anyone really ever said of Bill Belichick was that he was no Bill Parcells. That he tried to control the press like Parcells but didn't have Tuna's larger-than-life personality to pull it off. That he was too much of a control freak and had a smartest-man-in-the-room demeanor that was going to bite him in the ass someday. Belichick was a no-nonsense straight shooter with a total focus on finding ways to build a winning program. He wasn't interested in winning people over, polishing his public image, currying favor with the press, or trying to line up a cushy media job down the road. He was a football lifer with a knack for getting the most out of players as fixated on winning as he was.

He had qualities that Patriots fans would come to know—and love—quite well in just a few years. But in 1994, he was just the girl you saw at the party but didn't talk to, but who someday would change your life.

The Patriots were still a young team. They were further ahead of schedule than anyone had dared dream. They were a work in progress, but all the big-ticket items were in place: a stable owner, a great coach, a franchise QB, talent to build around, and a future so bright you almost needed welder's helmets. There was no way this team could take steps backwards.

That is, until they did.

Inexplicably, the 1995 Patriots threw the gears into reverse and stepped on the gas, in spite of a huge influx of talent. The draft yielded an elite cornerback in Michigan's Ty Law, a powerful, run-stuffing middle linebacker out of Colorado named Ted Johnson, and in the third round, Pittsburgh running back Curtis Martin.

CURTIS MARTIN
Martin would end up being one of the franchise's all-time draft steals. Initially there were some concerns about him. Scouts didn't question his talent,

but he'd dropped in the draft due to an injury in his senior year and because of the dreaded "character issues." There were reports he had been part of a gang growing up, something Martin was candid about. He spoke openly about growing up in a bad neighborhood and how he'd considered gang life as a career option, until one day he found himself pinned under a car with bullets ricocheting off the pavement all around him. The come-to-Jesus moment that resulted convinced Martin it wasn't the lifestyle for him, and he never looked back. Besides, it was impossible to spend 20 seconds listening to Martin talk without realizing that this was a special kid with a good head on his shoulders and a moral compass that pointed true north.

The injury worries didn't make it out of training camp. Right from the first time Martin carried the ball in preseason games, you could tell he was 100 percent healthy. And his ability jumped off the TV screen at you. He was fast. He had great moves. He could break tackles and make defenders miss. The first impression of Martin was that he could be one of the best running backs in team history, and nothing he did in the regular season dispelled that notion. He put together the best rookie season any Patriots back ever had, with almost 1,500 yards and 14 touchdowns. And more importantly, zero gang-related gun battles.

But somehow, Martin's breakout performance just didn't translate into a winning season. Things started out well enough; the Pats opened the season with a small measure of revenge against Cleveland, beating them 17–14. But they lost their next five in a row and four out of their final six on the way to a mystifyingly frustrating 6-10 season. Ironically enough, Cleveland imploded even worse, finishing 5-11, although they took a much more excruciating path to get there. Midway through the season, Browns owner Art Modell announced he was moving his team at the end of the season to Baltimore. The voters of Cleveland had refused to build a new stadium for a multimillionaire, so he decided he'd go get fat suckling at the teat of the Maryland taxpayer. Browns fans were devastated and furious, focusing their anger squarely where it belonged —on Modell—and also where it didn't, on Bill Belichick. Incomprehensibly, they took their frustrations out on Belichick as much as they did on the man who was actually getting filthy rich by moving the team. Not since the time Lake Erie caught on fire had the skies over Cleveland glowed like they did from the thousands of little Belichick effigies being burned.

In the face of withering abuse from Browns fans, Belichick somehow managed to keep his players and coaches focused just enough to squeak out five wins. He remained stoic, kept his disappointment to himself, and showed unwavering public support for his boss. As a reward for his loyalty, and for weathering arguably the toughest public-relations storm any NFL head coach has ever faced, Modell fired him as soon as the season ended.

Belichick wasn't out of work long. In less time than it takes to fill out your unemployment compensation paperwork, Bill Parcells hired him to be the Patriots assistant head coach/secondary coach. It would turn out to be a shrewd move.

Though not the biggest decision Parcells made that week. Not by a long shot.

MARRIAGE TROUBLE

The 1995 season had been unexpectedly difficult, borderline miserable. The Patriots' defense had gone from playoff caliber to atrocious in one year. They were third in the league in yards surrendered, sixth in most points allowed, near the bottom in forcing turnovers, and just all-around un-Parcells-ian. And as is almost always the case when an organization is suffering through a stinky dumpster fire of a season like that, people behind the scenes start blaming one another for igniting the blaze.

In the Patriots' case, there were only two men calling the shots: Bill Parcells and Robert Kraft. And while the public wasn't totally aware of how bad things were between them, they were starting to smell the smoke.

Like all relationships between successful, strong-willed people, their problems were complicated. In a nutshell, Parcells saw Kraft as a meddling, uninformed know-it-all who'd made his money making cardboard boxes and thought his money entitled him to tell a football lifer like himself how to run his team. Kraft considered Parcells to be an arrogant, entitled, self-important ingrate with no respect for his boss' ability to run a business, or the fact that he'd risked $175 million of his own money to save the franchise.

Increasingly, Kraft was getting frustrated with Parcells' personnel moves, which he perceived to be running the team into the ground. For every grand slam like Willie McGinest, there were ugly strikeouts like Kevin Lee, Ervin Collier, and Joe Burch, guys who didn't make it out of rookie camp or produced nothing. And the win-loss record reflected it. Orthwein had given Parcells complete control over all football operations, but Kraft made no such agreement. Earlier in the year he'd promoted scout Bobby Grier to the position of director of player personnel so that he'd have someone answerable to him, instead of allowing Parcells carte blanche to do what he wanted with no oversight.

Publicly, Parcells played along and said all the right things about Grier's hiring, but privately he resented it as just more of Kraft's meddling. The night before the last game of the '95 season, Parcells called a meeting of all his coaches concerning something that would affect all of them. He had two years left on his contract, and he told his staff he was going to offer Mr. Kraft $300,000 to buy his way out of the final year, 1997. If Kraft didn't go along, he said, he would quit on the spot.

Kraft jumped at the offer. He was only too happy to let Parcells see his way to the door. To him, Tuna seemed less and less interested in the job anyway. He was fat. He was surly. In a long, first-person account that appeared in the *Globe* a year later, Will McDonough recounted a conversation he had with Kraft. "I had it up to here with that guy," Kraft told him. "It just isn't any fun to go down there. I'm not having any fun. I own this team. He works for me. With me, it's a matter of respect. We give him everything he wants, and still he shows no respect for me."

There were plenty of rumors going around about bad blood between the two. One story involved Jonathan Kraft, Robert's son and the vice president of the team, climbing aboard the team bus and finding one of Parcells' cronies sitting in his seat. When Jonathan told the guy he needed to move, he was told in no uncertain terms he could go fuck himself.

There were also rumors that Parcells was in the habit of openly treating Mrs. Kraft like garbage, and thus the owner would be only too happy to take his money and tell him not to let the door hit his ass on the way out. Besides that, Parcells had impressed upon Kraft that Belichick was on his way out the door in Cleveland, and that the three hundred grand would go a long way toward hiring him to be his successor coach in 1997. In January of that year, the papers were drawn up by Kraft's lawyer, buying out the final year of Parcells' contract in exchange for $300,000. Tuna would stay on one final season, with the stipulation that he could always come back for another if it was deemed "mutually beneficial" by both sides. Both sides were happy. Everyone was getting along. The Patriots world was at peace.

For a couple of months anyway. On draft day, all-out war broke out.

"SHE"

If Kraft and Parcells were having problems in their marriage, they managed to hide it for the most part. Granted, that whole contract restructuring thing seemed suspicious, kind of like finding out your parents have a prenup. But publicly, they managed to put on a bold front and keep whatever turmoil they were having on a "we are not fighting, we're having a discussion, now go back to your room" level.

That is, until the 1996 draft. That's when mom and dad caught each other lying and cheating and they started hurling insults and vases at each other, and we all realized what a sham their relationship had been all along.

The Patriots were sitting on the seventh pick in the first round, and there was a huge debate raging about which direction they should go with it. About half of New England was calling for help for the abysmal defense, and the other half was demanding more "weapons" for Bledsoe. The sportswriters in town were having the same debate. In the days right before the draft, *Globe* reporter Ron Borges wrote that the pick would be Terry Glenn, a supremely gifted but certifiably crazy wideout from Ohio State. In the same issue, Will McDonough was saying the pick would be the best defensive lineman available, and they'd grab a receiver in round two. Both writers cited sources within the Patriots organization, so something seemed screwy.

It turned out it was. Very screwy. Just as the Patriots were about to pull the trigger on a D-lineman (either Duane Clemons out of California or Texas' Tony Brackens), Kraft came in the Pats' war room, where he asked to speak to Parcells in another office. Parcells was dumbfounded. "I didn't know what was happening," he said later. That's when Kraft and Bobby Grier told him the pick was going to be Glenn instead.

Parcells argued briefly that they'd all agreed on a defensive player, but the other two stood their ground. As he later told McDonough, "I was mad as hell. I said, 'OK, if that's the way you want it, you got it.'"[32] So it was left to Parcells to go up and announce a pick he didn't want on behalf of two guys who made it without consulting him. The consensus among Parcells' camp was that the whole thing was orchestrated to humiliate the coach. That may or may not have been the intention, but it was definitely the net effect.

Leave it to Parcells, even in his frustration, to turn it into one of his truly golden moments. Making no secret that he was angry and felt totally blindsided, he told reporters, "They want you to cook the dinner, at least they ought to let you shop for some of the groceries. Okay?" Boom. Instant catch phrase. And quite possibly his best in a career full of them.

Kraft defended his decision in a way that made equal sense, but without the snappy phraseology. "It wasn't as much a slap at Bill as an endorsement of our system. We spend $2 million a year on scouting and research, and when it came time to pick, Terry was the highest-rated player left on our board."

You'd think two million bucks should buy a lot of quality produce.

As fate would have it, the very next morning my buddy Duke went golfing at Pembroke Country Club, a semi-private course in our area. And in a billion-to-one shot, he got paired up with McDonough, whom none of us had ever met. McDonough was fuming about what had gone down. He told Duke Kraft had looked him right in the eye and told him they were drafting defense, how Kraft's lie made him look like an idiot and that he'd never forget it. That

Parcells was furious and there was no way he'd ever coach for the Patriots beyond next year.

Then he dropped a bombshell. He said Parcells was already talking to the New York Jets about taking over their operations as soon as his deal with New England was done. If true, it would be stunning news. The kind of thing that would change the fate of two franchises.

The rest of the story—all the bad blood and humiliation and talk about grocery buying—was self-evident. It was all anyone was talking about. But this business about the Jets being in the equation was news to everyone. And it was weirdly frustrating being in on the secret, because every time I tried to tell someone they looked at me like I was telling them I'd seen Bigfoot. To be fair, it did sound ridiculous. And any time you're trying to pass along a colossally huge major news story no one's heard yet and your source is one of your idiot friends who heard it from a famous, influential reporter he magically bumped into on a local golf course, people are going to be skeptical. But as we'd find out in the months to come, it was 100 percent true. And it proves the old adage that no one ever tells a lie on a golf course.

You might assume that Glenn was the most divisive draft move made that day. After all, it blindsided a Hall of Fame head coach and made him want to quit and start taking job offers from a division rival. And were this any other team, you'd no doubt be right. But again, this was the New England Patriots, who demonstrated their true genius for creating controversy five rounds later. With their second pick in the fifth round, the Patriots grabbed Nebraska defensive tackle Christian Peter, whose personal bio made Terry Glenn look like St. Thomas Aquinas.

While at Nebraska, Peter had been arrested eight times, for offenses ranging from minor ones like peeing in public and yelling at a meter maid (which seems to me more like a public service than an actual crime) to much more worrisome ones like grabbing a woman by the throat. But it was the things he didn't get charged with that set off alarm bells. Three different women accused him of sexual assault. One of them said he violated her in a dorm room. Another, a former Miss Nebraska, said he groped her in a crowded bar while telling her how much she was enjoying it. The third victim was a freshman who said Peter raped her twice in two days, the second time while a couple of his teammates stood watch.

Even by Division I football factory-school standards, Christian Peter was a monster. In an NFL where a few speeding tickets can get a prospect the dreaded "character concerns" label for life, this made him a pariah. He was considered virtually undraftable by a lot of teams. Which is why it was surprising (to say the least) that New England, with the whole Zeke Mowatt/Victor Kiam fiasco still visible in their rearview, would take a flyer on garbage like him.

As it turned out, the selection of Christian Peter made NFL history. After 48 hours of taking withering fire from all directions—from women's groups, editorial pages, talk shows, and most especially from his own wife—Robert Kraft renounced the rights to Peter, calling the pick "incompatible with our organization's standards of acceptable conduct." It was the only time in the history of the draft that a pick has been given his release before even going to a practice.

Whatever the moral implications of the decision, it did not sit well with Bill Parcells. After Kraft blamed the NFL for not providing enough background information on Peter, Parcells told Will McDonough that Kraft knew damn well what kind of a bad guy the kid was. "Bob sat right at the table. He heard everything there was to say about Peter. There was nothing about his past that wasn't discussed in detail. He sat right there and approved of what was done." So while Kraft got credit for taking the difficult moral stand (and no married man can begrudge him trying to keep the Mrs. happy), it just further widened the gulf between him and his coach.

Amazingly, for all the dysfunction in the war room that day, they still managed to strike gold in the draft. In the second round they got a tough, physical, hard-hitting safety named Lawyer Milloy. And in the third, an undersized but insanely productive defensive end/outside linebacker from Arizona named Tedy Bruschi. Not only would both be foundations of the resurgent defense, they were instantly starters on the Patriots all-time Great Names Team.

In the immediate aftermath of the '96 draft, Parcells was thinking seriously of quitting. He felt duped. He considered his owner to be a meddler who talked out of both sides of his mouth and couldn't be trusted. For Kraft's part, he'd only had the team for three years. He was in it for the long haul, investing his time and fortune trying to build a winner, get a stadium, and make the franchise stable in perpetuity, something he couldn't do as long as he was depending on a coach who was threatening to quit any moment.

Ultimately, Parcells decided he couldn't go out that way, coming off a 6–10 season where he admittedly had done a horrible job. He vowed to get in the best shape of his life, rededicate himself to putting together one last great season, and leave on his own terms. A few weeks later, ESPN broke the story about how Parcells had made a deal with Kraft to cut the last year off his contract. Tuna confirmed the story and said he gave up the $300,000 so Kraft could bring Bill Belichick in to be his successor. A short time later, Kraft gave an interview where he said the deal was completely separate and that the money had nothing to do with him signing Belichick. Parcells wanted a shorter deal, he was granted his wish, and that's all there was to it.

As the summer gave way to the start of training camp, it was obvious that the major plots in the soap opera of the season would be the messy Kraft-Parcells divorce and the forced marriage of Parcells and Glenn. The former went on the back burner for a while, but no time was wasted getting right into the latter.

Early on in the lead-up to a season that would be a referendum on Glenn, he pulled a hamstring, and Parcells didn't pass up the opportunity to get his "I told you so" comments in. As the days wore on and the missed practices started piling up, he pointed out that Glenn was taking longer coming back from a pulled hammy than it had taken Parcells to come back from his heart attack. In August, he added another instant classic one-liner to his catalog. At his daily press briefing, a reporter asked how Glenn was progressing. "She's coming along," he said.

It was pure Tuna. Just New Jersey ball-busting raised to an art form. Condescending, hilarious, and made his point. Granted, it wasn't the politically correct thing to say; 1996 wasn't the Dark Ages, and you couldn't exactly question a guy's toughness by comparing him to a girl without getting some blowback from feminists who were none too pleased. But at least it was in the glorious days before employer-mandated sensitivity training and teary public apologies written by lawyers. And it was said in a time when a football coach could still treat a player with utter disrespect without his agent and the Players Association threatening legal action. So he got away with it.

It certainly didn't hurt Parcells' argument that Glenn sat out the rest of training camp and the preseason games. He also missed a week-one loss to Miami in which the Pats struggled to put 10 points on the board, and the legion of Parcells loyalists who blamed Kraft for the civil war that was dividing the franchise howled with indignation.

And there was no counter-argument. The one person who could have redeemed Kraft and Bobby Grier's decision was sitting in a whirlpool bath or riding a stationary bike on the sidelines at practice. Until Glenn got on the field and produced, what else could anyone say except that he was soft and that drafting him had been a terrible move by a clueless buttinski owner who should stick to making boxes?

And that's exactly what Glenn did. She—*he*—finally made it onto the field in week two and made it abundantly clear that he was a special talent. He laid out to make a spectacular diving catch of a Bledsoe heave inside the Buffalo 5-yard line and rolled into the end zone for a 37-yard touchdown. He finished the day with 6 catches for 76 yards. And followed that up with 5-for-66 in a 31–0 crushing of the Arizona Cardinals. His best game was a midseason 42–23 win over Miami, when he led the way with 10 catches for 112 yards. In all, he shattered the NFL record for receptions by a rookie with 90 of them. Just as importantly, he gained everyone's respect. As the Pats made a run into the '96 playoffs, Bledsoe flat-out said they couldn't have made it without him. Robert Kraft cited Glenn's tough upbringing, where he had to overcome the murder of his mother, by saying, "Terry is as mentally tough as anyone I've ever met."

And Glenn himself surprised people by taking Parcells' abuse in stride. "Coach Parcells just wanted a defensive guy. I can understand that," he told WEEI Sports Radio's Gerry Callahan, then of *Sports Illustrated*. "[He] likes tough guys, and as a receiver, people automatically look at you as some kind of pretty boy who gets hurt all the time."[33] From the beginning, he showed a maturity level (at least in public), both on and off the field, that no one expected. Out of the public eye, there were a few warning signs that maybe this kid wasn't all there. For instance, there was a matter late in the season in which the Foxboro police were called to a trail deep in the woods to investigate a pair of abandoned snowmobiles. Police thought they might have been stolen. But after a little investigation they discovered that the vehicles had been purchased by Glenn only four days earlier. He and a friend had taken them along some trails, gotten lost, and then decided to make their way back on foot and just leave the snowmobiles where they'd stopped. They were in mint condition, with practically zero miles on them. Was it as bad as Christian Peter's one-man war on women? Hardly. But to use the pop music vernacular of the day, it was a thing to "Make You Go Hmmm . . ."—at least for the people who knew about it.

A KICKING LEGEND IS BORN

It took a few games for the Patriots to establish that they'd bounced back from that wasted '95 season. Despite Glenn's heroics, they lost the week-two game to Buffalo by seven points when Adam Vinatieri, their undrafted rookie free-agent kicker out of South Dakota State, missed three field goals. After the game, a frustrated Parcells threatened to cut him and bring back his old Giants kicker, Matt Bahr, but ultimately decided to stick with the rookie. And his faith was rewarded two weeks later when Vinatieri went five for six, including a 40-yard game-winner to defeat Jacksonville in overtime. He then didn't miss a kick over the entire second half of the season.

But the moment the rookie truly won the hearts and minds of his coach, his teammates, and his fans came in a late-season loss to Dallas. By this point in his career, late-80s Cowboys superstar Herschel Walker was back in Dallas as a kick-return specialist. In this particular game, Walker fielded a kick, broke through the first ten Patriots on the coverage unit, and was about to break it all the way when Vinatieri came up as the last line of defense, buried his shoulder into Walker, dropped him, and saved a touchdown. In the locker room afterward, Parcells singled Vinatieri out as a guy who had proved he was a football player, not just a kicker. That week the papers were full of stories pointing out that he was not only a former high school wrestler he was also a third cousin to Evel Knievel. And as far as we were concerned, he'd shown more balls than Knievel ever did. There wasn't a man among us who'd rather get in front of Herschel Walker with a full head of steam than take on a little thing like jumping over 20 Winnebagos on a motorcycle.

The jury was still out on Adam Vinatieri as a long-term solution to the kicker problem that had plagued the Patriots for years. But he seemed like a mentally tough kid we could count on in a tough spot.

Nobody had any idea.

THE SUPER BOWL RUN

★ ★ ★ ★ ★ ★ ★ ★ ★ ★ ★ ★ ★ ★ ★ ★ ★ ★ ★

I don't know how to put this, but I'm kind of a big deal.
RON BURGUNDY, *Anchorman*

As the 1996 season rolled on, the Pats strung together winning streaks of three, four, and three games, enough to secure at least a wild-card playoff berth. But the loss to Dallas left them needing a win over the Giants in New York in the final game of the season to win the AFC East and maybe a playoff bye week.

The game got off to an ugly start with a Bledsoe penalty for intentional grounding in the end zone for a safety, followed by four straight Giants scores for a 22-0 halftime deficit. A 26-yard touchdown pass to Terry Glenn in the fourth made it a 22-10 game. Then Dave Meggett, a Parcells favorite for all the clutch plays he'd made on the Giants Super Bowl teams, brought the Pats to within a score with a monumental 60-yard punt return for a touchdown. Bledsoe then completed the comeback with a TD pass to Ben Coates in the final minutes, and New England became the AFC East Champs for the first time in ten years.

There was just one massive obstacle standing in the way of the Patriots' hopes of getting to the Super Bowl that stood a mile high. Literally. The Denver Broncos.

Over the years, Denver had been a haunted house to the Patriots. They'd lost nine straight games there going back to 1969. And even playing the Broncos at Foxboro was no picnic either. In mid-November they'd gotten trounced at home by Denver, 34-9. In all, the Broncos had rolled to a 13-3 record, which gave them home-field advantage throughout the playoffs. So the road to the Super Bowl was not only steep, it was slippery and had no guardrails.

Not that New England had zero hope. There was plenty to like about the club. Bledsoe had made the Pro Bowl, along with Ben Coates (9 TDs), Willie McGinest, and Meggett as the Special Teams selection. And best out of all of them was Curtis Martin, who'd established himself as one of the best, most durable running backs in football with over 1,100 yards and 14 touchdowns. But any thought that they'd go on the road and win the AFC Championship Game in Denver was a triumph of optimism over experience.

Nevertheless, the Patriots came out of the bye week hosting the Pittsburgh Steelers. And for that weekend, trying to win in Denver was the Jacksonville Jaguars' problem, not New England's.

Which they then proceeded to do. By a stunning semi-miracle, the Jags—in only their second year of existence—went into Mile High Stadium Saturday afternoon and beat the Broncos 30-27. It was just one of many huge upset wins in the career of Jacksonville coach Tom Coughlin, the former Patriots assistant and Boston College head coach on his way to gaining a reputation as maybe the best big-game coach, college or pro, in the history of football. A couple of decades later he would become "Death, Destroyer of Worlds" in New England. But for now, he was a hero. With the gigantic help of Coughlin and Jacksonville, the Pats would be playing Sunday for the right to host the conference championship.

Game time was scheduled for 4:00 p.m., which turned out to be a large advantage for the Patriots. A 4:00 p.m. game meant the ball would be kicked off right around the time the sun was going down in the Northeast, and the forecast called for the kind of nasty, windy, frigid, shitty conditions New Englanders typically call "not that bad out." But facing a team from Florida? It would be a huge edge. One of those ones where you look back later and say it was over as soon as the Jaguars got off the plane and took a testicle-shriveling breath. It was 23 degrees at the kickoff, and then the temperature plummeted to a tidy zero with the wind chill. The Jaguars weren't prepared for it. Jacksonville's first possession ended with a punt attempt from their 20-yard line, an attempt that ended when Larry Whigham sacked punter Bryan Barker at the 4-yard line. Two plays later, Curtis Martin ran it in for what would actually turn out to be the only offensive touchdown for either team.

To be fair, the game wasn't one of your all-time classics. In fact, the most memorable thing about it was the quintessentially Patriots moment in the second quarter when all the lights in the stadium went out. Super Bowl XLVII, on February 3, 2013, might be forever remembered as The Big Game When the Power Went Out, but the world needs to acknowledge that the Patriots were way ahead of the incompetence curve when it came to basic utilities.

While not a blowout, it was one of those games that just never felt close, even when it was a one-score game. Every time the Jaguars threatened, the Patriots defense stepped up. Marty Moore forced a fumble on a punt return, which set up an Adam Vinatieri field goal. With under four minutes to go,

Willie Clay picked Mark Brunell off in the end zone. And on their next possession, Chris Slade forced a fumble that Otis Smith returned for a touchdown. And rookie Tedy Bruschi closed the deal with an interception, for a 20–6 final.

They were going to New Orleans for another Super Bowl, this time against Green Bay, who'd blown out Carolina 30–13.

It was very 1985 Patriots-esque. The defense and special teams stepping up to force huge turnovers and even put points on the board. The offense was doing just enough to get the win. An improbable playoff run won them a trip to New Orleans to face a traditional NFL power franchise that was in the midst of a resurgence and had dominated the NFC. The similarities were uncanny, really.

And as in '85, this team was being led to New Orleans by a head coach who was going to be the biggest part of the Patriots' storyline. The major difference between Bill Parcells and Raymond Berry, of course, is that the Parcells drama not only owned the Pats headlines, it dominated all the press coverage of Super Bowl XXXI. Something no one was happy about.

Least of all the Packers.

THE SOAP OPERA

The '96 Patriots weren't the biggest long shot to ever make the Super Bowl, not by any stretch of the imagination. But if you want to give them a superlative, they have retired the trophy for Worst Front Office Drama to Play Out on Super Bowl Week.

The personality conflict/power struggle between Bill Parcells and Robert Kraft was the worst-kept secret in New England, as were the rumors that Parcells would be packing up everything in his office and heading to New York to run the Jets the minute the season was over. And his boss was happy to dig into his paper company's inventory to give him all the free boxes he needed, just to be rid of him.

Both sides said they would wait until after the season to make any decision, and the media played along with the fiction. To be fair to the people who covered the team, did the weekly radio sit-downs with Tuna, and interviewed Kraft, it's not like they could just address the elephant in the room with "Let's talk about how you guys hate each other's guts" and expect it wouldn't be a serious conversation killer. So everyone in the region pretty much did what you do any time you know your friends are having marital problems: pretend everything is normal to their faces, then talk about it incessantly behind their backs. This is what the entire period from the 1996 draft to January of 1997 was like in New England.

But the national press had no skin in that game. Super Bowl Week is a feeding frenzy of media predators so starving for any story to talk about, they'll pick the carcass of even the most boring, mundane scrap they can, rip it off the bone, and crap it out as "news." To them, the messy Kraft-Parcells divorce was a frigging banquet.

And in no way was the unhappy couple ready for scrutiny. For months they were able to avoid talking about the breakup, but now the whole world was digging around looking to air the dirty laundry. Kraft vs. Tuna was the sports equivalent of a celebrity couple ("Kruna?") getting hounded by TMZ and *The National Enquirer*. It had everything but paparazzi shots of Parcells doing the early morning walk of shame from a hotel after an all-night tryst with the Jets. Neither man could do an interview without being asked about their marital problems, and all the "We're just focused on the game" and "I've already answered that" comments in the world didn't stop the questions from coming.

It was the same for the players. Everywhere they went in New Orleans, they were asked about the situation. And no matter how much they tried to deflect the questions, someone else just came from another angle, dogging them with another question about it because nothing else mattered. They were like a teenager trying to get his parents to talk about *anything* beside the joint they found in his gym bag. It was the subject that would not be changed.

As *Sports Illustrated* put it, "Parcells sucked up more media attention than any coach in Super Bowl history." And given the way some coaches have been fawned over, worshipped, and treated like they hung the frigging moon over the years, that is saying something.

All year long Tuna preached "No distractions," and now he himself was the ultimate distraction. Here the Patriots were, management and players alike, getting the shot to play in the game they'd dreamed about their whole lives, sports heroes in the one city in America that has no rules for governing human behavior and where there was no sin you couldn't indulge in for a couple of bucks worth of plastic beads, and not one of them was having a lick of fun.

Someone else wasn't exactly enjoying all the attention that the "Kraft and Parcells are Splitsville" story was getting: the Green Bay Packers. They quietly seethed about it. They were a team that was stacked with talent. Future first-ballot Hall of Famers like quarterback Brett Favre and Reggie White. They had All Pros like safety LeRoy Butler and center Frank Winters. They had a young stud wide receiver in Antonio Freeman and a former Heisman Trophy winner turned special-teams beast named Desmond Howard. They set an NFL record with seven wins by 25 or more points, and were the first team since the undefeated '72 Dolphins to lead the league in most points scored and fewest surrendered.

But the only Packers stories getting any attention involved Favre, who was still in the peak of the Tough Guy Good Ol' Boy with Three Straight League MVPs stage of his career and not yet the Self-Absorbed Serial-Retirer Who Throws Interceptions in Big Games and Texts Photos of His Junk Around to Female Employees stage. Plus, his name had already been a household word for years because he had come out and publicly admitted that he had an addiction to painkillers and was being treated under the NFL's substance-abuse protocols. That became a big story because the league's treatment program prevented him from using any kind of substance, including alcohol, which set off a national debate between Favre, the NFL, treatment professionals, and power drinkers from coast to coast.

So sure, Favre was a compelling and sympathetic figure, for all the good it did him or his team. All that got them was a report that the NFL was going to allow him to booze it up on Bourbon Street during Super Bowl Week which, sadly for those of us rooting against the Packers, turned out to be fake. And then there was the interview his old college roommate gave in which he detailed how Favre's farts "could bring tears to your eyes," which sadly, turned out to be true.

But beyond Brett Favre's liver and gastrointestinal distress, Green Bay might not have even been there given the lack of press they were getting. The Parcells-Kraft drama was the black hole whose gravitational pull was so powerful that no other story could escape it.

As much as anything else the Packers had head coach Mike Holmgren going for them. He was your classic relatable, regular guy, players' coach, a man for whom his team was willing to run through the wall of the locker room, and they resented all the attention the Parcells story was getting at Holmgren's expense. LeRoy Butler later spoke for the whole team. "What really pisses me off," he said, "is that no one gave Coach Holmgren his due. Everything was 'Parcells, Parcells, Parcells.' I know Coach Parcells wants attention, but next time he should have more respect for Coach Holmgren."[34]

And that wasn't the worst of it. Kraft and Parcells decided to try to defuse the situation with a little comedy and throw in some humor to lighten the mood, the way Ronald Reagan used to. Like the time Reagan looked old and doddering and people were worried, so he said he wouldn't exploit his opponent's youth and inexperience and everyone laughed. Boom. Controversy over.

So the two went before the press and said they had a major announcement:

they had just reached agreement on a new contract. Kraft had just signed Parcells to a 10-year deal to [snicker] . . . wait for it . . . run his paper mill.

Instead of going over like Reagan's "youth and inexperience" joke, it went over like his classic "I've signed the order to bomb the Soviet Union" gag. Only the little bit by the comedy duo of Kraft and Tuna incited more outrage. Particularly, of course, among the Packers. Again, Leroy Butler: "Parcells jinxed his team by starting all that shit. Mike [Holmgren] is really pissed."

That he was. And if sports history has taught us anything, it is to beware the wrath of any group of talented, well-led, ego-driven, ultra competitors when they have a legitimate gripe to play the "no respect" card. Holmgren had ordered his team not to say anything negative about the Patriots in public, no matter how furious they were, and they complied. But finally, in a team meeting, Wayne Simmons got tired of keeping his anger bottled up and finally blew a gasket. "I'm tired of saying how great [New England] is! I've been watching film on them and they look like crap!"

His coach responded in the perfect players' coach manner. "Wayne, I appreciate your restraint. To tell you the truth, I'd like to tell the world I'm going to kick Parcells' ass!" It was the kind of thing that makes a team want to run straight through the locker room wall, leaving only a hole shaped like a silhouette of themselves holding hands with their coach, Roger and Jessica Rabbit–style.

Not that you could blame Green Bay for being cheesed off. As odd as all of this was, New Englanders were used to it. This was exactly the kind of silly, bizarre drama that unfolded any time the Patriots happened to stumble their way into the national spotlight. But to Green Bay, it was the worst kind of slap in the face, and it understandably galled them.

So Holmgren grabbed that Academy Award for Resentment, climbed onto the Stage of Disrespect, and waved it in his team's faces. Sometime during the buildup to the game, Parcells had been quoted as telling his players that when they got to the Super Bowl, he would "show you what to do" in order to win. In his pregame speech, Holmgren threw those words to his players like a zookeeper throwing venison steaks to his lions. "I don't have to show you how to win this game," he began. "You don't need me to hold your hands. Now go out and do it!"

The Packers went out and did it.

Patriots fans, for the most part, bought what Parcells was selling. The Vegas line opened with the Packers as 14-point favorites and didn't budge off that number for the entire buildup to the game. Not just the degenerate gamblers, but the nation as a whole looked at how the two teams stacked up and agreed that Green Bay far outclassed the Pats in every way. But most of New England was convinced that Parcells would find a way. He was going to use his sarcastic, uber-confident, paunch-bellied New Jersey magic to scheme, game-plan, motivate, and *will* us to a win. Just like he'd done those two times with the Giants.

And for a while there, it looked like we optimists were right.

SUPER BOWL XXXI

New England's opening possession resulted in a punt. Receiving that punt was Desmond Howard, who was the undisputed best special-teams player in the league. He returned three punts for touchdowns in the regular season, and added another one against San Francisco in the playoffs. For two weeks, Patriots coaches singled out Howard as the one guy they had to contain to prevent him from taking over the game. And despite that point of emphasis, he returned the punt 32 yards to set Green Bay up close to midfield. Then, on the second play from scrimmage, the Packers broke the huddle with the play intended to be a short, safe, quick one out to the tight end Mark Chmura. Instead, Favre came to the line and spotted the New England safeties inching up toward the line of scrimmage, tipping their hand that they were coming with an all-out blitz. It was exactly the look Green Bay had prepared for. It was so obviously the call the Packers had anticipated that the TV mics picked up Favre letting out an "Oh, shit!!!" before changing the play. Instead of the safe pass, he audibled to a deep post by wide receiver Andre Rison, who caught Patriots safety Otis Smith flat-footed and beat him clean for the 54-yard touchdown. Green Bay 7, New England 0, just like that.

On the subsequent New England possession, Drew Bledsoe got picked off by Doug Evans to set the Packers up at the Patriots' 28-yard line. The defense held Green Bay to a field goal, but it was starting to feel like a play-for-play reenactment of the humiliating Super Bowl XX teabagging at the hands of the Bears.

Instead, the Patriots surprised everyone by not only staying in the game, but by the way in which they went about it. There wasn't a man, woman, or child alive who didn't think Parcells would play it conservative, hand the ball off to Curtis Martin, keep it on the ground, and try to minimize mistakes. Instead, he went in the complete opposite direction, putting the ball in Bledsoe's hands, letting him chuck it all over the field, and trusting him to win the game.

In the first quarter, Bledsoe set a Super Bowl record with 15 pass attempts. At first, they kept the passes simple, to get the offense into a rhythm and keep Green Bay off guard. A running-back screen to Keith Byars picked up 32 yards. A dump-off catch and run to Martin got another 20. A pass interference penalty put them at the Green Bay 1-yard line and set up a Bledsoe-to-Byers touchdown pass to make it 10–7 Packers.

On the next possession, the Patriots opened it up. Bledsoe unleashed an absolute artillery shell down the deep middle of the field that Terry Glenn caught up to, dove after, laid out for, and hauled in with an incredible fingertip grab that would've been one of the all-time memorable Super Bowl plays, if only they'd won. But like the saying goes, history is written by the victors.

Still, Glenn's catch set them up at the Green Bay 4-yard line, and a play later Bledsoe connected with Ben Coates to give the Pats the lead, 14–10. Those 24 points were the most ever scored in the first quarter of a Super Bowl. More importantly for the Pats, they had the Packers reeling. Leroy Butler admitted, "We were completely baffled . . . No one had pushed us around all year, and they were killing us, doing stuff we hadn't seen before. It was a *great* game plan."

Packers defensive coordinator Fritz Shurmur—who was in no mood to congratulate Parcells or the Pats on their brilliance—was less complimentary. He told his charges to "get your heads out of your ass and do what you're supposed to do!" Specifically, he demanded that his defense get after Bledsoe and threatened to blitz every down if he had to.

But just when Patriots fans were starting to allow themselves to believe their own pregame hype, Green Bay answered right back. Once again the Packers' offense found a mismatch in the Pats' pass coverage and exploited it. The Pack came out in a three-wide set, and Favre immediately recognized that Lawyer Milloy had drawn the short straw and had to cover Antonio Freeman. No knock on Milloy, who was tough and physical, but athletically it was no contest. As Freeman said after the game, "A safety on me? Playing bump and run? I liked my chances."

So did Favre. He audibled to a "max protect" call on the line to buy himself time, waited for Freeman to split Malloy and Willie Clay's coverage, and hit him in stride for the 81-yard touchdown that put Green Bay up 17–14.

The Pats would never have the lead again. Green Bay scored 10 more unanswered points in the second quarter to take a 13-point lead going into halftime. It has been a common theme in the history of football that when one team finds themselves back on their heels and starts doubting that they ever belonged in the game (or just in a good old-fashioned panic), they often can't calm themselves down to get something going and the game turns into a hideous, unwatchable blowout. This was starting to feel like one of those games.

To their undying credit, the Patriots kept fighting. Even the smoke-filled stench in the air from a halftime show that featured "The Blues Brothers 2000" (with the late, great John Belushi replaced by his talentless brother Jim, John Goodman, and some little kid, God help us all) wasn't enough to crush their spirit. Late in the third quarter, a 52-yard drive capped off by a Curtis Martin 18-yard TD run made it a one-score game. This was *not* going to be a repeat of the Bears Super Bowl XX debacle. There was still a quarter and a half of football to be played and New England had the momentum back.

Of all the short-lived happinesses ever in the world, this was among the shortest. It lasted precisely one commercial break. In the time it took the soft-drink companies and fast-food chains to do their part to keep America diabetic, disaster struck.

The kind of phony intellectual, Ivy League snots who like to compare sports to Greek tragedies (i.e., before they started winning championships, the Red Sox were Sisyphus pushing a rock up a hill or some such pretentious nonsense) have always described what happened next as an act of hubris on Bill Parcells' part. That his excessive pride caused him to arrogantly do the one thing he shouldn't have. And ultimately it was his undoing.

But it wasn't Parcells' ego that made him kick the ball off straight to Desmond Howard. He simply got out-schemed. It wasn't a character flaw. It was what Aristotle called *hamartia*. A mistake. It wasn't Marty McFly being unable to walk away from a fight every time Biff Tannen calls him "chicken." It was Marty leaving the *Sports Almanac* back in 1955 for Biff to find.

And credit goes to the Packers for outthinking the Patriots on this one. The Green Bay scouts detected a tendency by the New England special teams to kick the ball off toward the return team's right, away from Howard. So, for the subsequent kick after Martin's touchdown, they flipped returners and lined Howard up on the right for the first time all season. The Patriots never noticed it. Rookie Adam Vinatieri's kick came down to Howard on the right hash mark at the 1-yard line. He caught it clean and split the Patriots' coverage. One Patriot you could normally count on to make a play in a situation like that was Troy Brown, but he was injured and didn't dress. One Patriot you could not count on was Brown's replacement, Hason Graham, who had the angle on Howard but whiffed on the tackle. Howard received the one block he needed from his up man, took it right up the middle, and ran it untouched all the way for the score, putting Green Bay up by 12. And when he got to the end zone he did a robot dance, just to add nut-punching insult to heartbreaking injury. A two-point conversion made it a 35–21 game.

Those would be the last points scored by either side. The point spread that had opened at 14 and stayed there for two weeks would turn out to be spot on. For the final 20 or so minutes, the Patriots could get nothing going. They took their running game, folded it neatly, packed it away, and sent it back to Foxboro early because they wouldn't be using it. Bledsoe, forced now to throw on every down, saw the blitzes Fritz Shurmur had threatened to pull out earlier and the Pats had no answer for it. Particularly overmatched was right tackle Max Lane, who was barely even a speed bump in the path of Reggie White. White tortured him for three sacks, including two in the fourth quarter. In all, Bledsoe attempted 48 passes, completing 25 of them for 253 yards and two TDs. But he also threw four picks and was sacked five times. The running backs had only 12 carries combined. Parcells' plan to let his young QB win the game for him did succeed in surprising everyone for a while. But it wasn't the winning formula.

Desmond Howard won the game's MVP, the first special-teams player ever to do so. After the game, he claimed he'd told Brett Favre at halftime that he was going to run a kick back all the way.

Once again, the Patriots had reached a height they had always dreamed about. Again they'd turned themselves from laughingstocks to respectability. Again they'd gone from afterthoughts to national prominence. Again they were young and talented and were going to be a force to be reckoned with for the foreseeable future.

And again, it was all going to hell.

15 PICKING UP THE PIECES

★ ★ ★ ★ ★ ★ ★ ★ ★ ★ ★ ★ ★ ★ ★ ★ ★

There can be only one.

CONNOR MACLEOD, *Highlander*

The whole region went to bed on Super Bowl Sunday wondering how long it would take for the ugly situation to turn really, truly butt-ugly, for it was a foregone conclusion that it would. As it turned out, the ugliness beat everyone else out of bed Monday morning.

The morning papers and talk radio shows were all fixated on one thing: the news that Bill Parcells skipped out on the team flight back to New England. Instead, he took a separate flight with his agent. In a lot of ways, it was like the drug scandal story that hit right after the loss to the Bears in Super Bowl XX. Once again, we never got to enjoy the party because all anyone could talk about was how we got drunk, told everybody off, and passed out in the seven-layer dip.

Parcells had a fair number of supporters among the Patriots' fan base, the ones who saw him as the football genius and Robert Kraft as the meddling, rich-kid bad guy in all this. But when Parcells ditched the team like that, it cost him a ton in the court of public opinion. At best, he came off as petty and vindictive, like a kid refusing to get in the minivan because his mom wouldn't get him something out of the gumball machines. At worst, he came off as disloyal to his players, like a general abandoning his post and telling his troops it's every man for himself. It made it hard for the people on Team Tuna to argue that he had his heart and soul completely in the game, since he already had his exit strategy planned. It came across as a slap in the face to the very players who respected him, played hard for him, got him to a Super Bowl, and, by the way, were not involved in this little wang-measuring contest he was having with his boss.

Not that Kraft was getting a free pass by any means. There was still plenty of animosity over the fact that he'd only been there a couple of years and had already driven off the coach who turned the franchise around. But then the team let it be known that over the course of the 1996 season, Parcells had made over 50 phone calls to Hempstead, New York. Which just so happened to be where the Jets headquarters was, making it unlikely that he was calling 1-900-HOTCHAT.

For fans old enough to remember Chuck Fairbanks 18 years earlier, making those same calls to the U of Colorado from the same office on the same damned phone, it was unbelievable. Or it would have been, were this any team but the Patriots. Running up the owner's long-distance minutes while ditching the team to further your career was becoming something of a team tradition.

And like the Fairbanks Affair of '78, once again the Patriots found themselves in a protracted battle of executives and lawyers, fighting it out to the death with pens and briefcases to keep a coach who'd screwed them over. Kraft dug in his heels to enforce the clause in Parcells' contract saying the Pats owned his rights. The Jets were willing to offer compensation to pry Tuna loose. They just happened to be sitting on the first overall pick in the upcoming draft, and Kraft told an interviewer that if they really wanted Parcells, they better hang onto that pick, because the bidding would start there.

From the Jets' point of view, one of the problems with that position was that the top prospect in that class was a blue-chip franchise quarterback out of Tennessee named Peyton Manning. And there was zero chance they were going to part with the chance to draft him with that top pick. They'd consider a package of other picks, but not that one.

Four days after the Super Bowl, Parcells ended the lack of suspense by formally announcing that he wouldn't be back to coach the Patriots. His entire Patriots coaching staff followed suit. As a group they were immediately hired in New York. The Jets had gotten the band, but still couldn't land the lead singer. To put it in terms of the times, they'd signed the Funky Bunch to their label, just without Marky Mark. As the negotiations over Parcells dragged on, the Jets tried to force the Patriots' hand with a ridiculous dog and pony show where they declared that Parcells was, in fact, joining them, but not as head coach, because the league hadn't decided if he could or not. Instead, he was coming aboard as a "consultant," and Bill Belichick was in fact the guy they had wanted all along; Parcells, to continue *The Godfather* analogy, would be his wartime consigliere. They even held a surreal press conference in which Belichick was introduced to the media, spoke for a few minutes, then handed it over to Parcells on the speakerphone; all the reporters took turns talking to his disembodied voice. And everyone just pretended like this wasn't an embarrassment to all involved. To Belichick, most of all.

It was the NFL version of the Hundred Years' War, a protracted and costly engagement fought on multiple fronts, filled with epic battles, espionage, heroes, treachery, arranged marriages between royal families, and massive casualties on both sides, but ultimately resulting in a stalemate. It dominated the sports pages and the talk radio debate in the weeks that followed. The "Parcells vs. Kraft: Who Ya Got?" argument that started on draft day the year before raged on, even on days when there was no news from the front.

Eventually, people began to get sick of it. Fortunately for all involved, one of the first to do so was the one person who could do something about it: NFL commissioner Paul Tagliabue.

Tagliabue decided that the whole mess was bad for business, so he stepped in to do the Lord's work and decided to broker the peace for the good of all involved. He allowed Parcells to coach the Jets in exchange for four draft picks: their third- and fourth-rounders in '97, their second-rounder the following year, and their first-rounder the year after that. That was a motherlode of picks, reflecting Parcells' stature in the game and the loss to New England. But the Jets would get to keep their No. 1 overall pick.

Unfortunately for them, Manning decided to go back to Tennessee and play out his fifth year of eligibility, and they traded the pick away.

Somewhere out there on another dimensional plane is the alternate world in which Bill Parcells' Jets managed to land Peyton Manning.

It took just over a week after the Super Bowl for Kraft to end the non-speculation about his next head coach by introducing the guy everyone knew would get the job all along: San Francisco 49ers defensive coordinator Pete Carroll.

PETE CARROLL

Carroll made a lot of sense for Kraft. The choice represented going back to the Hire a Guy from a Successful Franchise Well that had been a staple of coaching hires since time immemorial. Carroll had some head-coaching experience, albeit with the Jets (and he'd gotten fired after one year). But mainly it was the classic "replace a stern taskmaster with a player's coach" move that had been so successful in all team sports so many times before. And Carroll's reputation as a laid-back player's coach was no joke. When he was with the Jets he did things like put a basketball court in the parking lot and organize three-on-three tournaments for himself and his coaches in their free time. That's a whole other level of "easygoing." That's being the anti-Parcells. In fact, it's hard to imagine two guys in the same line of work who were such polar opposites. Folks from the Northeast tend to be turned off by the whole handsome, well-adjusted California persona, which Carroll had; anybody who is that pleasant and enjoys life so much is not to be trusted. But the players loved that quality in him.

At least they said they did. There was a lot of talk about them being "grown men" and "professionals" who didn't need to be screamed at all the time. Reading between the lines, you got the impression that they were as resentful of hearing about how great Parcells was as the Packers were. Now they'd finally get their chance to be treated like the men they were, instead of the children their former coach thought they were.

They did get that chance. And pretty much proved that Parcells was right all along.

The harsh discipline they were used to now gone from their lives, the Patriots were, on the whole, not ready to handle it. They more or less treated Pete Carroll like a substitute teacher. At every turn he gave them an inch and they took a light year. Guys started showing up late. Nodding off in meetings. One veteran would later describe how "the sight of [rookie first-rounder] Chris Canty wearing sunglasses with his feet up on the desk was all you needed to know." And how Carroll would constantly have to interrupt meetings to say, "Guys, shush, quiet down!" Those same players had been so terrified that Parcells would disintegrate them with lasers from his eyes for pissing him off, they'd show up 15 minutes before meetings began.

One guy who in particular did not respond to Carroll's laissez faire approach was Terry Glenn. A psychology student could probably do a dissertation on why Glenn responded to Parcells' harsh, sarcastic, and usually demeaning style of human interaction, but there's no question he did. Maybe Tuna was a father figure, or the mean, fat aunt he never had. But the kid straightened up and flew right under his coaching in a way that he just did not do for Carroll. There was one report that surfaced from an anonymous Patriot saying Carroll was forgiving to a fault, to the point that he once ordered Glenn to run laps for some rules infraction, at one of the fields out of sight of everyone else. He then allegedly caught up to Glenn, told him he didn't have to run but to tell everyone he did, even pouring water on his shirt to make it look like he'd sweated through it. Even if that story is apocryphal, there's no questioning that Glenn treated Pete Carroll like he had "WELCOME" written across his chest.

Also not helping one damned bit was Bobby Grier, who was handed the general manager job when Parcells defected to New York. In the same way that hiring Pete Carroll made sense on a certain level, it also seemed logical to put Grier in charge of "buying the groceries." The thinking was that Parcells had too much power, that when one guy is in charge of everything the organization is too beholden to him. If he fails or just decides he doesn't want to work for you anymore, the whole franchise is screwed. Besides, Grier seemed like he knew what he was doing. The pick of Terry Glenn was a grand slam. And he'd built a Super Bowl team in his first year of taking power. It seemed to make sense at the time.

There's an old Boston saying about the Red Sox, about how their players used to go "up the back stairs" to ownership to complain about the managers. In the Patriots locker room in Foxboro, there literally was a "back stairs" up to Grier's office. And by all accounts, Terry Glenn gained more yards vertically going up it than he did horizontally on the field. The few times Carroll did try to discipline Glenn, Glenn would go "up the back stairs" to undermine him to Grier. And since Grier owed his career to Glenn's success, it was in his best interest to take the side of his crazy, mercurial meal ticket over his affable, hardworking coach every single time.

When he wasn't sabotaging Carroll behind his back by taking the players' sides in everything, Grier was torpedoing him with terrible personnel moves. In his first draft at the helm, Grier demonstrated a peculiar fetish for guys with alliterative names who couldn't play football. In addition to Chris Canty (one of the worst busts in franchise history) he took Sedrick Shaw, Chris Carter, Damon Denson, and Ed Ellis. Thank God that the following year Rod Rutledge turned out to be a fairly productive player with enough juice in his career to end the Bobby Grier double-initial losing streak.

But the guy in the hot seat that first year was Pete Carroll, not Bobby Grier.

The Patriots spent the better part of the 1997 season saying all the right things about how they respected their coach and appreciated being treated like men. And as it turned out, it was said with all the sincerity of an 18-year-old telling mom and dad they could go away for a night and leave him in charge, because he's mature enough to handle things on his own. Because that's about how well their newfound sense of trustworthiness worked out.

On November 13, 1997, the Patriots sat at 6–4 and were firmly in the playoff hunt. They were headed to Tampa for a Sunday game against the Bucs. And on Thursday night, Drew Bledsoe, backup quarterback Scott Zolak, and tackle Max Lane went to the Paradise Rock Club on Commonwealth Avenue to see Seattle grunge band Everclear.

In its defense, the Paradise wasn't exactly a bucket of blood. But it was one of those clubs that as a general rule you should stop going to once you hit 23. Bledsoe, Zolak, and Lane were all between 25 and 30 years old, and were easily recognized pro athletes who between them weighed just shy of 800 pounds. They might as well have been wearing t-shirts with targets and the words "I dare you to sue me!" emblazoned on the front.

And yet, when the band invited them up on stage, they accepted. No problem there. Then they danced around for a while. No harm, no foul. Then, in one of those "it seemed like a good idea at the time" moments, they opted to do what everyone who's not an uber-sue-able millionaire athlete with everything to lose did at 90s grunge shows: they dove off the stage into the mosh pit below.

Granted, that was part of the culture. It was common knowledge that such things went on at every single alternative rock show back in the day. Knowledge common to everyone except a 23-year-old, 100-pound woman named Tameeka Messier of Maynard, Massachusetts, who apparently never saw the massive flying missiles of human flesh coming. She got crushed under the weight of the highly paid airborne men, bruised her back, and got rushed to the hospital in an ambulance, presumably with dozens of tort lawyers trailing behind in hot pursuit.

The next day the media was all over the story. It was a perfect way for them to demagogue the hell out of rich, drunk, out-of-control athletes who've been pampered their whole lives and think they can get away with anything. A young, innocent woman, victimized by their utter disregard for others. And to cap it all off, Bledsoe's wife had just had a baby three weeks before. So the righteous indignation on this one was off the charts.

There was no reasoning with the women of New England once they found out that Bledsoe had left his wife and newborn baby at home to be there. Of course, the one this reflected most poorly upon was Pete Carroll, who looked for all the world like the guy who couldn't keep his players in line because they didn't fear or respect him. The one thing that no one could argue was that no matter how you viewed the Mosh Pit Incident, it never would have happened under Bill Parcells; the players knew they would've ended up in a landfill somewhere in Jersey if they pulled a stunt like that during his tenure as coach.

All that really mattered was Sunday's game at Tampa. If they stepped up and played a good game and came out with a win, the whole episode would be chalked up to harmless hijinks. Men being boys. Blowing off steam in the midst of a long, grueling season. The game would be a referendum on Carroll's coaching style.

And the early returns were not good. It was a debacle. The Buccaneers rolled up on them early and often to a 27-0 lead. They ran the ball at will through the defense, 41 times in all. Bledsoe was terrible, completing just 14 passes for only 117 yards, with five sacks, a lost fumble, two interceptions and zero points before being pulled for Zolak in the fourth quarter. The final score was 27-7. And the players had some explaining to do, starting with the quarterback.

To his credit, Bledsoe faced the tough questions and stood his ground. "The only thing I'll have to say about this is that Thursday night had absolutely nothing to do with the preparation for this game," he said. "It wasn't a distraction."

But no one was buying it, including Pete Carroll, judging from his postgame remarks. "I have no idea where we are. Right now we have no direction," he said. It was pretty damning stuff. And you got the feeling that he was starting to question his team's commitment.

One thing you couldn't question, though, was Carroll's knowledge of the game. Whether his team respected him as a leader or not, the man could coach tackle football (something he proved definitively later in his career). For all the distractions, he led the club to first place in the AFC East, a 10-6 record, and the second round of the playoffs. Included in that record were three wins —twice in the regular season, and once more in the playoffs—over the Jimmy Johnson/Dan Marino Dolphins. The Pats beat them in Miami—which was a tall order back in those days—on the last week of the regular season, which earned them the right to face them again at home the following week in the wild-card playoff. In those two games, Carroll's defense held the Dolphins to 15 total points and only one touchdown. He was getting almost no credit, but he was managing to X&O up some big wins.

In the divisional-round playoff at Pittsburgh, Carroll's defense again came up huge, holding the Steelers to seven points, but that wasn't enough to win the game; the Patriots had been playing without Curtis Martin since he went out with a knee injury in week 13, putting the offense very much on Bledsoe's shoulders. It wasn't too much to ask when you consider that he had been the No. 1 overall pick, had been the starter for five seasons, and was theoretically entering his prime. Still, the chorus was growing more and more critical of Bledsoe.

This game against Pittsburgh gave Drew the perfect opportunity to silence the critics. Late in the fourth quarter he had the ball, with plenty of time on the clock and only needed to get the Pats into field-goal range to win the game and give his career that signature clutch moment that every quarterback needs to be considered elite in this highlight-driven, *SportsCenter* world.

And he failed. On the final drive, he got the Pats close to midfield when he went back to pass, got strip-sacked, fumbled, and lost the ball to Pittsburgh. Getting the sack and forcing the fumble was an obscure rookie backup outside linebacker named Mike Vrabel. It wasn't the last time he'd show a knack for making huge plays in big moments of games that ended the Patriots season.

THE POISON PILL

Not to be lost in the shuffle here are two huge games against Bill Parcells and the Jets early in the year. The Jets were vastly improved under the Patriots old coaching staff, going 9-7 after finishing 1-15 the year before. The two teams ended up splitting their home-and-home series in two excruciatingly close games. And had one or the other swept, it probably would have meant the difference in the division.

But as huge as the games were, they were infinitely bigger as events, each of them a three-ring media circus. Never mind sports stories, they were the top news stories of the weeks leading up to them. Every *Morning Zoo* radio show had their own lame "T-t-t-tuna and the Jets" song parody. Taiwan textile mills were working double shifts to meet the t-shirt demand. It was chaos.

And the games were epic. In the week three game at Foxboro, New York scored a late touchdown to tie it up before the Patriots won it on a Vinatieri kick in overtime. In the week seven game at the Meadowlands, the Jets came back from a nine-point deficit late in the third quarter to win 24-19.

The standout performer in both games was Curtis Martin. He was solid in the second game, with 87 yards on 21 carries. But in the first one, he was transcendent. He racked up 199 yards on an incredible 40 rushing attempts, and basically carried the Pats to victory. Not lost on anyone was how much it meant to Martin personally. He and Parcells made no secret of their admiration and respect for one another during their time in New England. And when the two were seen jawing at each other along the sidelines during the game, it was obvious that Parcells going all Benedict Arnold on the Patriots didn't put any kind of damper on their bromance.

And like the original Benedict Arnold, Parcells had something of value to offer the enemy: he knew the Patriots' secrets.

Specifically, he knew the Pats' salary-cap situation better than anyone in the league. Curtis Martin was coming up on the end of his rookie contract and Parcells wanted him badly. So he came up with a plan that was part Machiavelli, part Gordon Gekko, and part Ellis from *Die Hard*.

Martin was a restricted free agent, meaning the Patriots had the right to match any offer that came his way. So Parcells simply offered him a deal he knew the Pats would want no part of. It was a six-year, $36 million contract that also gave Martin the right to opt out after the first year as an unrestricted free agent, meaning he would end up with the Jets the following season anyway. It was a hostile takeover with a nasty poison-pill provision.

To tip New England's hand further, if they were to let Martin walk right away, they'd get the Jets first- and third-round picks as compensation. Sign him and have him leave a year later as a UFA, and they'd get nothing. This put the Pats in a bind, since they loved Martin as a running back, as a person, and as a team leader. But internally they were looking at how he hadn't finished the season and dropped in the draft due to injuries in college, and wondered if he was durable enough to take the punishment of being an NFL bell-cow running back. So they let him go.

To review, the Patriots now owned six of the Jets' picks over the next three drafts, all of them in the first three rounds. And here's the treasure trove of talent that Bobby Grier mined out of that motherlode of picks. See if any of these names sound familiar to you:

- ★ 1997: Running back Sedrick Shaw and guard Damon Denson
- ★ 1998: Running back Robert Edwards, wide receiver Tony Simmons, and running back Chris Floyd
- ★ 1999: Linebacker Andy Katzenmoyer

The only remotely memorable names out of that group are Edwards and Katzenmoyer, and not for good reasons. Katzenmoyer made the cover of the *Sports Illustrated* College Football Preview issue after his stellar sophomore year at Ohio State, which was almost unheard of. He then proceeded to almost get suspended from the team for academic reasons, which was made more interesting by the fact that: a) both of his parents were college professors, and b) you can imagine how bad his grades had to be for Ohio State to even *consider* suspending an All-America caliber player. Talk about "unheard of."

But he saved his eligibility by taking makeup classes, one of which was "AIDS and Society," which was taught by professor Randi Love.

Andy Katzenmoyer showed some promise as a rookie. But halfway through his second season he suffered a neck injury and retired.

Edwards was a much more interesting pick, as he was the heir apparent to Martin and had a monster rookie season that totally validated the Patriots decision to let Martin walk.

At least until he suffered perhaps the most Patriots-like injury in the history of the Patriots.

ROBERT EDWARDS

At five foot eleven and 218 pounds, the solidly built former Georgia Bulldog proved he could take whatever the NFL could dish out to a running back. He played in all 16 games, with over 1,100 yards on an impressive 291 carries. He looked for all the world like a guy who'd be a staple in the New England backfield for a decade.

He just had one weakness that the Patriots never anticipated, the proverbial easiest thing in the world: a day at the beach.

Edwards was one of a group of rookies who got invited to the Pro Bowl to take part in a touch football game in the sand. It was one of those things that seemed like a great idea at the time. It was fun for the players. They got to go to Hawaii. It got them exposure. Gave the fans a chance to get better acquainted with the NFL stars of the future. And besides, it was touch football played on sand. What's the worst that could happen?

The Pats found out in short order. The worst that could happen was, for all intents and purposes, the end of their franchise running back's career.

Edwards went out deep for a pass . . . thrown by Peyton Manning, no less . . . got his feet tangled in the legs of a defender and in the sand, and one of his legs dislocated at the knee. Worse than your garden-variety knee sprain, break, or ligament tear, Edward's dislocation meant that the major arteries to his leg were blocked off, stopping the flow of blood to his foot. Writhing on the ground in agony, he was rushed off to the hospital in an ambulance to reset the leg, and doctors later estimated that he had been about 45 minutes away from having to get his leg amputated.

To his everlasting credit, Edwards worked tirelessly for years to fight his way back into the NFL, and in 2002 eventually caught on with the Miami Dolphins in one of those feel-good stories that unfortunately never seem to last as long as you'd like them to. He managed only 20 rushing attempts over 12 games before the Dolphins just couldn't afford to carry him any longer, and he never played again.

There's an old definition of "ironic" that uses as an example the story of the Nantucket whaling ship *Essex*. It's the ship that Herman Melville used as the inspiration for *Moby-Dick* because it is the only known instance of a ship being rammed and sunk by a whale. Anyway, as the survivors were adrift in life rafts, they considered heading for Tahiti, but there were rumors of cannibals on the island, so they decided against it. The irony was that Tahiti was a paradise with a peaceful population, and in order to stay alive, the *Essex* crew had to resort to cannibalism.

The irony when it came to the Patriots and Curtis Martin was that the Patriots let Martin go because they were worried about his durability. The guy they tried replacing him with gave them one season, and Martin went on to play in 95 of the Jets' next 96 games, finished his career fourth on the all-time list in touchdowns, fourth in rushing yards, eighth in yards from scrimmage, and was voted into the Pro Football Hall of Fame on his first ballot. As ironies go, that is a hundred times more ironic than rain on your wedding day.

And for the Patriots, way more tragic.

In the much more immediate sense, what Bill Parcells' swindle represented was a total shift in the balance of power in the AFC East. The margin between the two clubs was razor-thin in 1997. But Curtis Martin was the super weapon that fell into enemy hands, and it made all the difference. The Pats won the division with him in '97 and the Jets won it the following year. Not only that, he carried them to the 1998 AFC Championship Game, where he scored a touchdown that had the Jets up 10–0 over Denver. Only a second-half rally by the Broncos to win the game averted a total nightmare scenario. But it would be years before that damage would be undone.

Not that the loss of Martin was New England's only problem. In that first season without him, they xeroxed a page right out of the desperate franchise playbook by replacing offensive coordinator Larry Keenan with Ernie Zampese. Zampese was a veteran of Don Coryell's "Air Coryell" system in San Diego and the great Cowboys teams of the 90s, with a precision and timing offense uniquely ill-suited to Drew Bledsoe, who could throw a ball through the armor of a tank (and in fact preferred to throw that way). It also meant having a new OC for the third time in three years, with a different offense, different nomenclature, and a different playbook. Bledsoe compared it to learning to think in a foreign language and hoping everyone else on the team was thinking along with you.

There was a growing concern as to whether Bledsoe would ever make the jump and "take his game to the next level," a concern that every quarterback faces until he has won a Super Bowl. One issue the '98 season did settle was any questions about his toughness. In the week 12 game on *Monday Night Football*, he broke the index finger on his throwing hand whacking it off a pass-rusher's helmet, but nevertheless led a fourth-quarter comeback gripping the ball with just his middle, ring, and pinkie fingers. He managed to suck it up and play three more games, even with a pin inserted in the finger to keep it straight (in hopes that it would heal by itself). The pin had a wire that stuck out the tip of the finger, which according to Bledsoe made it impossible to put on a sweater without tearing holes in it, but it didn't stop him from beating Buffalo and Pittsburgh, before his own team finally shut him down.

That put Scott Zolak in charge. Ordinarily, that would be a tough spot for any backup quarterback. But since Zolak had been there seven years, there was every reason to think he'd be able to handle it. He was the football equivalent of a vice president who has served almost two full terms when the president is suddenly taken out by an assassin. The thinking was, if he wasn't fit to lead, what had he been doing kicking around the White House all those years?

While Zolak was OK, he didn't exactly inspire anyone to put him at the top of the ticket in the next election. He led the Pats to a win against San Francisco before losing to the Jets in the final game of the regular season, completing 42.7 percent of his passes, with three touchdowns and three interceptions. But it was enough to bring the team to 9–7 and they squeaked into the playoffs, where they got drubbed 25–10 by Jacksonville in a game that was never competitive. It would be Zolak's last game in a Patriots uniform, and proved that the team as constituted would only go as far as Drew Bledsoe could carry them.

It didn't help either quarterback that Ben Coates was starting to wear down. He had been an unstoppable, game-changing force years earlier, but his skills were obviously on the decline. It seemed like every game he was having catches called back on his own pushing-off penalties; at first it seemed like the officials were unfairly targeting him, until it came to light that he was pushing off because it was the only way he could get open anymore.

As the 1999 season rolled around, it was obvious that it would be, as it is with all teams that are trending downward, a referendum on the head coach and the quarterback. It had been excruciating to watch the Jets come within one half of going to the Super Bowl with New England's old coaching staff and beloved former ball carrier. And no one was in any frame of mind to cut Carroll any more slack.

Early in the season there was every reason to like his chances. Through a quirk in the schedule, the bye week sat right in the middle of the calendar, with the final game of the first half of the season coming right on Halloween. They'd played well to that point. Drew Bledsoe was having arguably the best year of his career, and was the consensus MVP of the league through the first half of the season.

The week eight game against Arizona was the Pats' best and most complete game so far that season. They dominated from start to finish to win 27–3 and take a 6–2 first-place record into the bye week. There was nothing not to feel good about.

For about an hour or so.

In the postgame coverage, it came out that Ben Coates was extremely unhappy and didn't care who knew about it. His beef wasn't that his team hadn't played well, because they had. It was that he didn't have any catches. They'd rolled up on an opponent, done everything right, and seemed to be coming together as a team, and all he could talk about was his individual stats. It was exactly the kind of dispiriting, me-first, team-killing nonsense that only happens on loser teams. And it acted like a pin in the happy, helium-filled balloon of the '99 Patriots.

For the whole bye week, it was all anyone talked about. Coming out of the bye, it seemed to be all the offense could focus on. Whether it's fair or not, it seemed like Bledsoe started zeroing in on the guy he used to call "his security blanket," trying to keep Coates involved and forcing balls into tight coverage where they ought not to have been forced. As a result, Drew's numbers fell off dramatically, the offense dropped off noticeably, and Pete Carroll's coaching career in New England something-ed off adverbially. After going 6–2 in the first half of the season, they went 2–6 the second half. With a game still left to be played, it was no secret that Carroll's days with the Patriots were numbered. The team had gone from 11 wins in Parcells' last year to 10, to 9, and finally to 8. You didn't have to be in the Math Department at MIT to see the trend and know it all added up to the Green Mile for Carroll.

One person who did all he could to push Carroll toward the electric chair was Terry Glenn, who was fined $100,000 in the offseason for missing mandatory workouts, then completely checked out mentally as the season wore on. On Thanksgiving morning, he got a speeding ticket on the way to practice and still managed to show up three hours late. That Sunday, the offense only managed seven points (on a 45-yard garbage-time touchdown by Glenn) in a loss at Buffalo. And Glenn was his usual mature, stand up, face-the-music self after the game, telling reporters he didn't see what being on time had to do with being a champion. Two games later, he missed the last team bus to the game against the Colts. For the next-to-last game, Glenn didn't dress, due to illness. Which is to say, Pete Carroll got sick of him.

And by that point, so had every Patriots fan.

Pete's official explanation was that "there is too little communication here." Which was an odd way of saying that Glenn was a dog who was quitting on his team, blew off the Friday team meeting, and was told to stay home. Glenn claimed he was sick, but team rules require sick players to come in and be checked out by the team's medical staff. Besides, linebacker Willie McGinest openly doubted whether Glenn was sick at all, and declared that several Patriots players had been battling through major illnesses for weeks without missing any time. But by this point, Terry Glenn was such a selfish, childish punk, he was utterly incapable of being shamed.

Still, Carroll took the high road with Glenn. Even with the freedom of a man who knows he's on his way out the door and the luxury of having public opinion on his side, Pete refused to give the coach-killing Glenn the verbal flaming he deserved. "This was an attitude situation that wasn't right," was the worst insult he could muster.

But where he wasn't much for talk, Pete did take action. He suspended

Glenn for the season's final game, against the Baltimore Ravens. Glenn handled it with the same raw emotion and fiery passion that he brought to practices and games. When asked how he took the news, Carroll said, "Not much of a reaction. He didn't say much."

It would be Pete Carroll's last act of discipline, and it was about three years too late to do him much good.

By all accounts, Pete accepted the inevitable and took it with class and dignity. He allegedly had a private meeting with Robert Kraft, wishing him well and giving him advice on how he could help the team succeed in the future.

Bobby Grier . . . not so much. He basically told reporters that it was all Pete Carroll's fault, that there was plenty of talent on the roster, thanks to him, and that shoddy coaching was the reason the team was failing. It was your classic "shootout in the lifeboat." And astonishing to hear, because even if Grier believed it, which was hard enough to fathom, by saying it he was committing career suicide. He was making it impossible for his owner to ever bring in a decent coach; who would ever take a job working for a guy who would stab him in the back when things started to go south? Grier made it impossible to keep him around.

Within hours of the final, merciful end of the Post-Parcellian Era, Mr. Kraft fired Pete Carroll and made sure Bobby Grier was right behind him on the way down the stairs. And once again, the management of the New England Patriots was in total upheaval.

Fortunately for the Patriots, and for all of New England, the situation with the New York Jets was much, much worse. It was utter chaos down there.

Something for which Patriots Nation will be eternally grateful.

16

THE HOODED ONE

★ ★ ★ ★ ★ ★ ★ ★ ★ ★ ★ ★ ★ ★ ★ ★ ★

When I left you, I was but the learner. Now I am the master.
DARTH VADER, *Star Wars Episode IV: A New Hope*

Whatever Bill Parcells' faults may be, he is no dummy. He didn't survive growing up in New Jersey, the nomadic life of a football coach, and a million trips to the racetrack without being able to see a situation coming and plan several moves ahead.

Parcells recognized that Robert Kraft had a real affinity for Bill Belichick. That the two had struck up a relationship during their time together in New England did not go unnoticed by Parcells or anyone. That combined with the fact that the Jets' success had made Belichick the hot new head coaching candidate convinced Parcells that Kraft would without a doubt hire him as his head coach as soon as the Pete Carroll thing didn't work out. So, just as Parcells had done with Curtis Martin, he had shrewdly put a clause into Belichick's contract to make it virtually impossible for the Patriots to hire him.

Belichick was not only the Jets' defensive coordinator, Parcells convinced owner Leon Hess to pay him an extra $1 million to be assistant head coach, and put a clause in his contract that would automatically promote him to head coach when Parcells stepped aside. It was one of Parcells' more brilliant maneuvers, which is saying something. Hess and Belichick enjoyed mutual respect, and this arrangement gave everyone in the organization something they wanted. Belichick would get a second shot at running a team, his first since the Browns dumped both him and the city of Cleveland in 1995. Hess would get the continuity that had eluded Parcells' past employers when he inevitably got bored and wanted to move on to greener pastures (and spend more time at his beloved Florida racetracks). For his part, Parcells would stay on in a front-office role for as long as he wanted, still drawing a paycheck but without the grind of coaching.

There was also the added benefit of denying Robert Kraft his vengeance for the Jets stealing Parcells away from him. It was a perfect plan.

At some point on Sunday, January 2, 2000, the Patriots made their move, contacting the Jets and requesting permission to interview Bill Belichick for their head coaching job, a request that by league rules the Jets were required to grant, since it would be a promotion. Check. The Jets replied that Bill Parcells was resigning as coach effective Monday, January 3, thereby making Belichick their head coach. Permission denied. Check. And looking like Parcells had Robert Kraft at checkmate. Again, Parcells was five steps ahead of everyone else and it was paying off.

But there was another player in the game whom Parcells could not out-maneuver, the one that no man ever has: the Grim Reaper.

Leon Hess had died the previous May. The Jets were up for sale to several prospective bidders, none of whom were the man Belichick liked and trusted and had signed a succession agreement with. He had already lived through the pandemonium of Art Modell giving him an atomic wedgie and leaving him hanging from a coat hook in Cleveland, and he wasn't about to walk into the instability of working for someone he'd never met. Someone who'd undoubt-edly want to bring in his own people to run his brand-new toy.

The coaching profession is a pyramid with very steep and slippery slopes. Only an elite few make it to the pinnacle that is an NFL head-coaching job. Getting a second chance is even more rare. And the term for guys who mess up that second shot is invariably "assistant coach" (for the rest of their lives). Belichick was faced with a situation in which the man he'd signed his agree-ment with was now singing with the Choir Invisible, and he had no clue who he'd be working for in the future.

He'd signed a prenup, but his fiancée was long gone. If he went through with the ceremony, he had no way of knowing if, when he pulled back his new bride's veil, he'd find Jennifer Aniston or Danny Devito under there.

On Tuesday, January 4, the Jets were scheduled to introduce Bill Belichick as their new head coach at a press conference at Weeb Ewbank Hall. It was the same auditorium where, five years earlier, Hess had introduced Rich Kotite and famously declared, "I'm 80 years old and I want results now." He'd died waiting for them.

That morning, Jets assistant Carl Banks, who had been a linebacker on Beli-chick's defense with the Giants, found his new boss alone in a workout room, running on a treadmill. The two chatted for a bit. Banks asked Belichick if he needed anything before his big presser and was told, "No, Carl. Thanks, I'll be fine." They were the words of a man who was, well . . . fine. Confident that he'd made the right decision and comfortable with the chips falling where they may.

It just wasn't the decision anyone expected.

After his workout, Belichick showered, got dressed, went upstairs to Parcells' office and calmly broke the news that he was turning down the job.

Parcells was livid. He thought he had the situation completely under control. Everything had transpired exactly as he had planned. And now, with the assembled media about to celebrate the genius of his grand plan, it was imploding in front of the world.

Worse, he felt betrayed. The way Banks saw it, Parcells felt a genuine friendship with Belichick and was glad he'd had the chance to further his career. "Bill Parcells is a guy who does a lot for a lot of people. You'll never hear about it, but he puts a premium on helping people," Banks recalled. "In Parcells' mind, he said 'Bill's a guy that deserves to be a head coach and I'm going to give him the opportunity right here.'" So having that opportunity turned down not only ruined his best-laid plans and left the organization in turmoil, it also hurt on a personal level. Not that anyone would confuse Bill Parcells with Oprah Winfrey, but the man is not without his emotions, and this had to feel like disloyalty from a friend he'd tried to do right by.

Someone Belichick had no loyalty toward was Jets general manager Steve Gutman. On his way to the press conference, he detoured by Gutman's office and handed him the most famous handwritten note since a Union soldier found Robert E. Lee's Antietam battle plan wrapped around a bunch of cigars.

On a crumpled piece of paper Belichick had scribbled simply, "I am resigning as h.c. of the n.y.js." And, as with Lee's plans, the fate of the nation was changed forever with those words.

He gave the note to his now-stunned GM and walked off down the hall to face the media horde. No one was there to record the look on Gutman's face for posterity, but it was most likely the same expression as the one on Warden Norton's face when he peels back Andy Dufresne's girly poster and stares down the tunnel he has escaped through. Just open-mouthed, stunned, and completely dumbfounded by the deception.

Belichick strode to the podium and stood before a mob of reporters and cameramen who were expecting to hear the usual perfunctory remarks about getting to work to do whatever it takes to bring a title to New York.

What they heard instead shocked them into silence. He spoke for 25 minutes, and his remarks focused almost entirely on the uncertainty he faced in the wake of Leon Hess' death and how the arrangement was one he felt he couldn't afford to accept.

"I feel like I'm making a decision based on the circumstance and the situation as it is right now," Belichick said. "The agreement I had was with Mr. Hess, Bill Parcells, and Mr. Gutman, and that situation has changed dramatically. And it's going to change even further. There's going to be some point in time in the near future when the head coach is not going to be talking to John Hess [the late owner's son] and they may not be talking to Steve Gutman, and we know they may not be speaking to Bill Parcells. If I'm letting anyone down, I'm sorry. But the situation has changed and I have to do what's fair for everybody."

He added a few "I just can't do what I need to do here" comments, a couple of "there are a lot of unanswered questions," and a "I just can't do it with the conviction, confidence, and certainty that is needed to get the job done" or two. For good measure, he talked about his own history with unstable ownership. "I've been in the situation of head coach of a team in transition," he said. "Frankly, it wasn't a very good experience for me and my family." And he spoke a little bit about needing to pick up his daughter at school at four o'clock. He was also adamant that his decision had nothing whatsoever do to with trying to gain leverage for a new contract. He just couldn't, in good conscience, take the job with the organization in a state of flux like it was.

To say everyone in the room reacted like Belichick had lost his mind would be putting it mildly. Steve Gutman got up afterward and spoke as if that very moment orderlies from a rehab center would be strapping him to a gurney for his own safety. He described Belichick as a man with a lot of "internal turmoil" whom he felt sorry for. "I'm no psychiatrist," he said, "but I think we've listened in the last hour to a man who deserves our understanding and consideration."[35]

Belichick didn't respond to the comments until a few years later. In a moment of triumph, he was asked about them in an interview and said, "I'm going to say this one last time so that we can close the book on this: in all my years of football, I've never known a man who talked more and won less than Steve Gutman."

The New York press responded like Belichick had taken the podium in a gorilla costume and flung poop at them. The headlines on the tabloids the next day called him "Belichicken" and "Belichick Arnold," and screamed the Jets were better off without the "quitter." Depending on whom you heard from, he was "disheveled," "nervous," "rambling," "uncomfortable," or "a wreck, his voice cracking at his own gall." This from the same papers who days earlier ran headlines that greeted the news he'd be given the top job with "Jets Settle for Bill Belichick."

As for the team he left in his wake, the Jets were in a state of total chaos. Cornerback Aaron Glenn called it "about the craziest stuff I've seen."[36] Wide receiver Keyshawn Johnson talked about having four coaches in four years and added, "It kind of makes you wonder what's up with your future." A decade and a half later, ESPN would call it the worst day in Jets history. And given the fill-wash-rinse-spin-dry cycles of turmoil that franchise has been through, that is a bold statement indeed.

Despite the statements that Belichick had made about the ownership situation, the consensus opinion was that his real problem was with Parcells. The Tuna had vacated the coaching job but was far from gone. He would still play some amorphous, ill-defined role wherein he'd still be running the Jets, but on his own terms. He was President in Charge of Being Bill Parcells. And he was still a mythic, god-like figure in the eyes of the fans and the media.

So it followed that any coach who took the job after Parcells would have to deal with not only being way less popular, but the knowledge that every time the team hit a rough patch the whole region would be screaming for Parcells to fire him and get back on the sidelines. It was an impossible, no-win scenario. But Belichick insisted that it was never a factor, and has continued to do so ever since.

Belichick had walked away from a job in a move that astonished everyone but him. When asked, he said he didn't know where he'd end up coaching next.

But where he ended up heading astonished no one.

THE BORDER WAR

The same two franchises that had been locked in an agonizing stalemate in the battle for Bill Parcells were now back in the trenches, staring at each other over the No Man's Land of Bill Belichick. Only now they were dug in on opposite sides of the map they'd occupied before. This time it was the Patriots pinning their future on getting what the Jets had, and the Jets were demanding a fortune in order to get it. It had only been three years, but history was repeating itself with the irony meter dialed up to 11.

And like the Parcells War back in 1998, this one dominated the sports discussion as it dragged on through the winter. The Jets were demanding—at the very least—the Patriots' first-round draft pick, and the debate raged as to whether Belichick was even worth it.

We read and heard how he and Robert Kraft formed a bond during his time as a Patriots assistant, particularly during the social awkwardness of Parcells and Kraft barely speaking to each other. But even on a non-personal, professional level, Kraft was always impressed with Belichick's work ethic, his attention to detail, and his savant-ish understanding of the intricacies of football.

Most of the press and much of the public didn't share Kraft's affection. They pointed to Belichick's tenure in Cleveland as proof that he wasn't head coaching material, even to the point of ignoring the circles he coached around the Pats in the 1994 playoffs. They talked about how reviled he was in Cleveland, mostly for the heartless way he cut local hero Bernie Kosar. The press and public, however, ignored the little matter of Kosar being a really crappy quarterback, and the fact that Belichick had replaced him with Vinny Testaverde, who became an All Pro and played 20 seasons in the NFL. Mostly, the Boston media seemed to resent Belichick because in Cleveland he had been uncooperative with the press, didn't say much, and liked to control the message. And that was an unpardonable sin. Granted, Pete Carroll was the exact opposite, an expansive quote machine who'd give effusive answers for as long as anyone cared to listen to them (and they ran him out of town for his trouble), but the press didn't want another Carroll. They wanted another Parcells. Tuna also liked to control the media, but he did it in a decidedly hilarious, entertaining way. That Belichick presser in New York might have been great theater, but it was his only hit. Whereas Parcells churned out more solid gold No. 1's than Bruce Dickinson.

It didn't take long for some of the sports columnists in the region to condescendingly start calling Belichick "Little Bill" to Parcells' "Big Bill." As Belichick himself would later point out, if he had turned down the Jets' job to get out from under Parcells' "shadow," he was coming to the wrong team. Because even three seasons removed, it was still cold in Big Bill's shadow there in New England.

Several of the beat writers questioned Kraft's fixation on Belichick, suggesting he'd be much better off with Dom Capers, who had taken an expansion Carolina Panthers team to the NFC championship game in only their second year and more recently had been the defensive coordinator in Jacksonville, and who could be had for nothing. But Kraft was focused on getting his man, even if it meant giving the Jets compensation to get him.

Making the situation even more difficult was the rivalry between the two franchises, as well as the personal acrimony between Parcells and Kraft; those wounds were still pretty raw and profusely leaking bad blood. And the lingering resentment didn't make working out a deal any easier.

But then a peace between Parcells and Kraft was brokered by the most unlikely source imaginable: themselves.

It was actually Parcells who first lit up the peace pipe and offered Kraft a hit. On Tuesday night, January 25, he called Kraft in his office. "I told him it was Darth Vader calling and he said he knew who that was," Parcells said.

It was the first meaningful conversation the two had had since the Super Bowl three years earlier, and Parcells described it as "amiable." They talked for 40 minutes, mixed in a few laughs, admitted they regretted the way things ended between them, and "mended a few fences." They stopped short of taking their phones to bed and doing the "You hang up first / No, *you* hang up first!" thing. But it was a start.

Parcells told Kraft he had spoken to the Jets' new owner, heir to the Johnson and Johnson baby-powder empire Woody Johnson, and Johnson was adamant that they would not let Belichick go to New England for anything less than the Patriots' first-round pick. Kraft was just as insistent that the price was way too steep. One imagines they did the dance where Parcells said he had another couple ready to make an offer and Kraft said he'd go home and talk to his wife and Parcells said he'd go out back and talk to the manager. But the end result was that they hung up without a deal getting done.

Another factor standing in the way was that Belichick's lawyers were suing the Jets to get him out of his contract, thereby making him free to go wherever his heart led him. Things turned sticky when the judge denied a motion that was critical to their case, and the next day, while Kraft and his staff had Dom Capers in for an interview, Belichick's attorneys were dropping the suit. That night at 11:00 p.m., Kraft called Parcells back and they hammered out an agreement. It turned out to be one of those trades where picks from multiple rounds get swapped for other picks from other rounds, basically the draft-pick equivalent of giving you five dimes and two quarters for a buck and getting ten nickels for the dimes. The only thing worth remembering from all the horse trading is that the Patriots did cave on the first-round pick, sending the 16th overall pick to the Jets.

Unfortunately, the Jets subsequently traded the pick, costing the world the fun of saying the Patriots traded Player X for Bill Belichick, how'd that work out for ya? But suffice it to say that unless that player turned out to be the messiah, it was the best trade in Patriots history.

By Thursday the 27th, the deal was struck. At 10:00 a.m., Belichick "was flabbergasted" to get a call from Parcells telling him he was free to speak to the Patriots. By 6:00 p.m., he was in Foxboro being introduced as the Pats' new head coach and general manager.

"Hopefully, this press conference will go a little better than the last one I had," Belichick said.

It did.

Brian: "I am not the Messiah!"
Arthur: "I say you are, Lord, and I should know. I've followed a few!"
    Monty Python's Life of Brian

The German philosopher Arthur Schopenhauer said, "Talent hits a target no one else can hit. Genius hits a target no one else can see." And since he was smart enough to make himself famous by saying clever things that get quoted in books instead of working for a living like you and me, his point is well taken.

The whole history of the world has been shaped by people with brilliant ideas that seemed ludicrous to everyone but them. Columbus knew that he could sail west to find India, but had palace doors slammed in his face all around the Mediterranean before convincing the king and queen of Spain to "*Shark Tank*" his trip. Galileo proved that the Earth revolves around the sun, then spent the last 30 years of his life wearing the Roman Catholic Inquisition version of a GPS ankle bracelet for it. And to this day, a good half of America thinks Darwin just made up the whole evolution thing, no matter that *Inherit the Wind* is readily available on Netflix.

And so it was with the Patriots in the winter of 2000.

Bill Belichick arrived at Foxboro Stadium (as it was then called) the morning after that opening press conference and immediately established that he was in charge.

His first personnel move had nothing to do with any player. There were a few holdovers from past coaching regimes who were institutions in New England. One of them was strength and conditioning coach Johnny Parker, who was first brought into the NFL by Bill Parcells with the Giants in 1984 and had been working for the Patriots since Parcells took over. He was widely considered to be as good as anyone in the league at what he did, and was widely given the credit for the Pats players' relatively good health over his career.

Belichick's very first order of business was to fire Parker, who had apparently begun to believe his own hype. It delivered the message in all caps that no one was bigger than the team, and any attempts to put yourself first would no longer be tolerated, in that "sacred cows make the best hamburger" kind of way.

To further drive the point home in more of a positive-reinforcement way, he retained on his coaching staff Dante Scarnecchia, the respected, preparation-crazed workaholic who had been with the club since the Ron Meyer era. Scar had survived four different ownerships and would be working for his seventh head coach, and keeping him around demonstrated the point that if you're humble, work hard, and put winning ahead of your own self-aggrandizement, the new Patriots will be the place for you.

Most of the rest of his coaching and front-office staff were familiar faces to Patriots fans, because they had been in New England during the Bill Parcells years, went to the Jets with Tuna, and were some of the architects of the Pats' humiliations over the previous three years. His offensive coordinator was Charlie Weis. Romeo Crennel was named defensive coordinator. The new quarterbacks coach would be Dick Rehbein. And Belichick's right-hand man on all personnel decisions and the head of the team's scouting department was Scott Pioli, who—just because everything with the Patriots had to have some sort of Jets involvement attached to it—happened to be married to Parcells' daughter, Dallas.

The next order of business was a meeting in which Belichick would address the players and coaches to briefly explain what he expected of them. Again, think of Dalton and his "be nice until it's time to not be nice" speech. A couple of minutes into his talk, Andy Katzenmoyer came into the room, walked past him, and grabbed a seat.

According to Michael Holley in his book *War Room*, Belichick snapped at Bobby Grier's first-round pick, "Who in the hell do you think you are? Get your ass outta here! I'll talk to you after the meeting."[37] It was what parenting experts like to call "a teachable moment," and something that never would have happened under Pete Carroll.

Katzenmoyer would actually survive for one very forgettable season under Belichick, before retiring due to injuries at the age of 23, having played just 24 career games.

It would be shorthand to say that Belichick cleaned house in his first year running the show in New England, but it wouldn't be accurate. In fact, he kept quite a few of the holdovers from the Grier/Carroll era. While the following statistic isn't the most accurate way to illustrate this fact (due to injuries and other factors), his opening week starting lineup in 2000 had 13 of the 22 players who had started game one under Carroll the season before.

The first major roster move he pulled was getting rid of Ben Coates, which, given the fact that he had long been Drew Bledsoe's safety valve/security blanket, was somewhat controversial. Some argued for Coates' importance to Bledsoe and blamed his lack of production (he had half as many catches in 1999 as he'd had the year before) on bad coaching. But I was in the philosophical school that didn't forgive him for blowing up the team after their best win of the season just because he didn't get the ball as much as he would have liked. Anyway, it turned out to be the perfect decision by Belichick, as Coates went to Baltimore and became invisible, with only nine receptions in 16 games in his final NFL season.

While Belichick rode into town and established himself as a no-nonsense bouncer who wasn't about to let idiots act up in his club, he made one judgment call early on that surprised everyone. He announced that he was forgiving all the punishments levied on Terry Glenn by Pete Carroll. He was waiving all the fines the team had imposed on Glenn and starting with a clean slate. I mean, on one level it made sense. Following through on someone else's disciplinary moves would kind of be like getting married and continuing an argument your bride was having with her last husband.

On the other hand, Glenn had never really responded to any coach treating him like an adult, so we were all curious to see whether Belichick's leniency would appease him or just encourage him to be the same insufferable man-child he was before.

The thing that stood out most to me during Belichick's first few days was a statement he made somewhere in there about how his first priority was to improve his team's depth.

It sounded like lunacy to me. In fact, I was incredulous. Depth? The Pats had gone from the Super Bowl to ten wins to nine to eight. That they needed more talent across the board seemed self-evident. The no-brainer-iest of no-brainers. It was as if this team was barreling down out of the sky with the controls not responding and the wings falling off and the pilot was talking about replacing the beverage cart. It felt like that way lay madness.

And yet, to be fair, I had no interest in understanding the colossal mess Belichick had inherited from the previous management team. Bobby Grier had been handing out signing bonuses and guaranteed money like they were cheese samples at the supermarket deli.

The NFL salary cap at the time was $57 million, and yet just 13 of Grier's players put them $10 million over. Captain Belichick and Copilot Pioli weren't crashing the plane; they were jettisoning cargo to keep it aloft.

But the way the cap operates, it wasn't enough to just pitch high-priced players overboard. Since Grier had given out the financial goodies in the form of bonuses, the cap hits were spread out over the life of the contracts in question, meaning they still counted against the Patriots' cap, whether or not the players in question were still on the roster. The Pats had to get down to bottom of the league in payroll just to be cap-compliant.

By June, Belichick declared that he'd gotten the club under the salary cap "by about 20 bucks." By the time the season began, they were down to 29th in the league in payroll.

But ironically, the first significant personnel moves for the Patriots of the 2000s weren't even made by Belichick and Pioli. They were made a year before they got there. Under Bobby Grier, the Pats let linebacker Todd Collins, punter/backup quarterback Tom Tupa, defensive tackle Dwight "Wimpy" Wheeler, and offensive lineman Dave Wohlabaugh leave for free agency.

While the decision to part with those four replaceable, nondescript players didn't seem all that earth-shattering at the time, it did nothing less than change the course of not only the Patriots franchise but the whole sport of pro football.

When an NFL team loses players to free agency, the league employs a formula to mitigate their loss with compensatory draft picks. The formula is as complex and impossible to crack as the Windtalkers' code, and understood by very few people.

For losing Collins, Tupa, Wheeler, and Wohlabaugh, the NFL awarded the Patriots pick numbers 127, 199, 201, and 239 in the 2000 draft. Because the formula is so byzantine and secret, which player brought which pick is forever lost to history. So we can credit all four of them for bringing that 199th pick. That was the all-time game-changer, after which nothing would ever be the same.

THE MESSIAH

Generally speaking, the 2000 NFL draft looked to be a decent if forgettable one for the Patriots. The Belichick/Pioli brain trust didn't have a first-round selection, having used it to bribe the guards in order to escape from the Jets in the first place, so it was a problem that they really couldn't complain about.

The first pick of their regime was second-rounder Adrian Klemm, a guard who through a series of injuries would never amount to much more than an answer to a trivia question. Next was J.R. Redmond, a serviceable running back in a limited role. Then came Greg Randall, a massive right tackle who would start one of his three seasons in New England.

When the sixth round rolled around and most of America had lost interest, the Patriots were still holding five picks. With the first they took Antwan Harris, a defensive back who would be notable for having the 50th most popular spelling variation on the name "Antoine" and one gigantic special teams play (still more foreshadowing).

The scouting staff went into the draft in agreement that at some point late they would draft a quarterback. A few weeks prior, the team had signed Drew Bledsoe to a then-record 10-year, $103 million contract extension. But they were looking for a "depth guy," someone with upside they could develop behind Bledsoe and backups John Friesz and 1999 seventh round selection Michael Bishop. They decided that when it came their turn with the 199th pick, they would take the best QB left on their board.

It was considered a down year for quarterbacks in the draft, with only one going in the first round, Chad Pennington to the Jets with the 18th overall. Two went in round three: Giovanni Carmozzi to San Francisco and Chris Redman to Baltimore. Pittsburgh waited two more rounds before selecting Tee Martin. And then the sixth round brought a run on all the lower-rated quarterbacks, with several teams looking to take a flyer and hoping they found a diamond in the dog shit.

Marc Bulger went to New Orleans with the 166th pick and, as Spergon Wynn came off the board to Cleveland, the staff in the New England war room was holding a debate about which QB they should take. The candidates were Tim Rattay out of Louisiana Tech and a skinny, unimposing kid from the University of Michigan named Tom Brady.

Brady was coming off a college career in which he had struggled to hang on to the Wolverines starter's job for any stretch of time. Among the quarterbacks ahead of him on the depth chart at various times were Brian Griese, Scott Dreisbach, and head coach Lloyd Carr's own son.

New Englanders were way more familiar with the last guy he kept losing his job to, Drew Henson, because Henson had been drafted by the New York Yankees in the first round to be the superstar third baseman who we all expected would be mashing Red Sox pitching for the next 15 years or so. As a matter of fact, there was a widely held belief around Michigan that Yankees owner George Steinbrenner was trying to lure Henson with a promise to promote him to the majors right away, less to help out his own ball club than to help out his beloved Ohio State. Carr was therefore under more pressure to keep playing

Henson or risk losing him, because he had a privilege few college athletes ever enjoy: other options.

Brady felt he wasn't getting a fair shake, and that even when he outperformed Henson, it was doing him no good. It didn't help that Carr concocted the single dumbest on-field arrangement since the Black Power Defense. Or the Patriots' co-head coaches. Basically a repeat of Mike Holovak's goofy, discredited idea from 1961. Brady would play one quarter of the first half and Henson would come in and play the other. And Carr would then spend halftime ruminating on who he would anoint to be the second-half QB. It went about as well as you might think it would.

At the height of his frustration, Brady sat down with Carr and told him he'd had enough and was going to transfer to Cal-Berkeley. Carr told Brady that while he wouldn't stand in his way, he'd be making a mistake, advised him to sleep on it, and said that they'd talk in the morning. The next day Brady told his coach that not only was he staying on at Michigan, "I'm going to prove to you that I'm a great quarterback."

Brady was also coming off an NFL combine—the debutante's ball where league scouts rate all the worthy college player ingénues—where he did nothing to impress the scouts while running around in shorts and a t-shirt. He looked slow and unathletic for a position that many believed required more speed and agility than ever.

Still, quarterbacks coach Dick Rehbein, who'd worked Brady out personally, argued for him over Rattay. Whatever he'd seen in Brady carried weight in that room because he'd be the one in charge of trying to turn him into a pro quarterback. Rehbein got his way, and the Patriots made what would turn out to be—when you consider where they were picking and what they got out of it—nothing less than the single greatest draft selection in the history of pro sports.

A similar scene was playing out in the war room of the New York Jets. Bill Parcells, to use his metaphor, was not only shopping for the groceries, he was pushing the cart, carrying the store rewards card, using the self-checkout, and doing all the bagging himself. According to Gary Myers' 2015 book *Brady vs. Manning*, Jets midwest scout Jess Kaye did "everything but stand on the table" to persuade Parcells to take Brady, to no avail. The Jets had taken Pennington with their first pick and Tuna felt they were set at the position. It should be noted that Parcells doesn't remember it that way. Because, as JFK once put it, "success has many fathers, but failure is an orphan."

Brady seemed like a long shot to even make the club. Bledsoe was the Franchise. Friesz was a capable, veteran backup. And Bishop was a sensation. In preseason games he looked like the fast, elusive mobile quarterback people had spent a generation predicting was the future of the position. It had gotten to the point that the most popular topic on the Boston airwaves was whether Bishop should start over Bledsoe.

Brady's roster status wasn't even a thought, much less an afterthought. And yet when the team broke camp for the 2000 season, they made the unusual move of carrying four quarterbacks, with the rookie at the bottom of the depth chart: by default, the most dispensable player on the team. As origin stories go, you'd have to go back to Zeus almost being eaten by his dad Cronus before his mom Rhea saved him at the last minute (by feeding the old man a rock wrapped in a baby blanket) to find one humbler than Tom Brady's.

The 2000 season was your classic rebuilding year. The Patriots did nothing of note. They started with a four-game losing streak and then matched it by losing another four straight in the middle of the season. They were 25th overall in offense and 17th in defense. Drew Bledsoe threw for almost 3,300 yards, but that was the lowest total since his rookie season. And with his passer rating only 19th best in the league, the dissatisfaction with his performance and calls for him to be replaced were growing louder.

The Pats finished 5–11 and in last place in the AFC East. The one bright spot was that the lost year landed them the sixth pick in the NFL draft, their highest spot in seven years. With the team's passing offense in unquestionable decline, there was a consensus among the press and public that the team would draft receiver help. That they would, to use the cliché, "get Bledsoe some weapons."

Instead, they used the first-rounder to take Richard Seymour, a massive and powerful defensive end out of Georgia. With their pick in the second round, 48th overall, they nabbed Matt Light, a left tackle from Perdue.

To say those picks didn't go over with the pundits is an understatement along the lines of "*Star Wars* fans didn't embrace Jar Jar Binks." The *Boston Globe*'s Ron Borges blasted the Patriots on MSNBC.com for passing on top receiver prospects David Terrell and Koren Robinson. He said that Seymour "had one sack last season in the pass-happy SEC and is too tall to play tackle at six foot six and too slow to play defensive end. This genius move was followed by trading out of a spot where they could have gotten the last decent receiver in Robert Ferguson and settled for tackle Matt Light, who will not help any time soon." Borges' comments were some of the mildest, though as future events unfolded they'd become the most repeated.

In the run-up to the 2001 season, it became increasingly clear that Terry

Glenn was responding to Bill Belichick's benign, fatherly approach the same way he had to Pete Carroll's, by throwing a colossal hissy fit like the immature man-child he was. Glenn was apparently upset over . . . something. Or everything. Whatever it is that makes some really well-paid people who are gifted by God with supreme ability really miserable, Terry Glenn was running a surplus as the season approached. He had taken the clean slate Belichick gave him and written "I HATE YOU" on it in Sharpie, with dozens of frowny faces all over it.

It was in that atmosphere that I made my annual pilgrimage to the Patriots' training camp, which at the time was held at Bryant College in Smithfield, Rhode Island.

I was with my brother Jack and my then five-year-old son. And as we made the drive down, I was not feeling terribly optimistic. The team was coming off a terrible year. It felt like they hadn't made any dramatic improvements as far as personnel was concerned.

To Jack's undying credit, he did his best to snap me out of it. He was genuinely seeing diamonds where I only saw dog shit. He instantly rattled off a dozen free-agent signings the team had made that had gotten little to no rise out of anyone when they were announced. Offensive lineman Joe Andruzzi had been brought in the year before. For 2001 Mike Compton was added, as was defensive back Terrell Buckley. Running back Antoine Smith. Wide receiver David Patten. Linebackers Anthony Pleasant, Roman Phifer, and Mike Vrabel.

Vrabel was a particularly curious signing because he couldn't start for the Pittsburgh Steelers defense that was coached by Dick Lebeau, one of the great coordinators in the history of the game. But literally the minute the free-agent signing period began, Belichick called him and cited chapter and verse obscure plays that Vrabel had made in Pittsburgh that had managed to escape the attention of everyone else.

I'd love to lie to you and say I was convinced and immediately recognized the 2001 Patriots as the next big sports dynasty, but I want ours to be a relationship built on trust. As we walked the grounds and watched practice that day, all I was struck by were two things. How many fans were sporting $85 Michael Bishop jerseys (I counted at least two dozen) and the fact that Terry Glenn still hadn't taken the field the entire camp, claiming another hamstring injury. The day we were there, he spent the day riding a stationary bike. The Tour de Sideline.

If any of that made me feel good about the Pats' immediate prospects, I don't recall it.

FINALLY, WE CAN HAVE NICE THINGS

In the run-up to that 2001 season, there was one obvious, significant change that literally towered above the team: a brand new, state-of-the-art stadium was under construction in the parking lot adjacent to the old, still-crappy one.

The search for a decent venue had continued on unabated throughout the Kraft family's ownership. Through the late 1990s, they found themselves doing the same bizarre mating dance with the same sleazy politicians, kissing many of the same asses, and greasing some of the same palms that the three previous owners had, and with the same results.

The most promising possibility was a plan floated by Massachusetts governor Bill Weld, who proposed a multipurpose stadium complex down near the South Boston waterfront, a so-called "Megaplex" where all four Boston pro teams would play. To a lot of people the idea seemed like lunacy, on par with Billy Sullivan's old downtown plan. On a slow day, Boston traffic moves like the license-renewal line at the Registry of Motor Vehicles. And Southie is a static grid of narrow, one-way streets. The thought of getting in and out of there on a game day sounded like it would turn the entire city into one huge, constipated digestive system.

Still, the Megaplex was the brainchild of the governor of the state, who had pledged his support for the project. And Boston mayor Tom Menino was also on board. They both assured Robert Kraft that, if he pushed for it, they'd be right beside him every step of the way. So Kraft followed up by going to all the right meetings and talking to all the right people.

And of course, being Massachusetts politicians, at the first sign of trouble they cut and ran.

Almost from the outset, Kraft was portrayed by pols, community activists, and the press as a rapacious greed-head who planned to level neighborhoods and raid the treasury to build a palace for himself. Speaker of the House Thomas Finneran (who would go on to be one of three consecutive Speakers convicted on corruption charges) called him "a fat ass millionaire." As the rhetoric grew even nastier, Weld went back to playing poker with his Brahmin cronies at his old-money mansion in Cambridge and forgot the whole thing, while Menino more or less acted like he'd never heard the word "Megaplex" in his life.

The whole harebrained waterfront stadium scheme never got any further than a few artist's renderings, but the Krafts came out of it with what parenting experts like to call "a teachable moment" in what happens when you put your trust in a Massachusetts would-be solon.

The next possibility (a very real one) was moving the team to Connecticut.

UConn football was going to Division I and needed a stadium big enough to qualify under NCAA rules. The state's plan was to build an 80,000-seat venue for the Huskies entirely with public money and lure the Patriots there with a $1-per-year lease. Not only that, they were guaranteeing the Pats a minimum amount of revenue. Meaning that if ticket sales weren't up to snuff, Connecticut would pay the club the difference between what they actually made and what they would have taken in had they sold out. It was the sweetheart-iest deal in the history of sweetheart deals, with the added benefit of keeping the team in New England.

And yet, Kraft turned down Connecticut's offer and looked toward building a privately financed stadium on his own property in Foxboro.

It was a move that went against the advice of his financial advisers, sound business practice, and even the slightest bit of common sense. And it involved going "once more unto the breach, dear friends" with his home state's corrupt pols. But ultimately they hammered out a deal in which the Commonwealth picked up the $70 million tab for improving the roads, laying down sidewalks, and hooking up the utilities, as they would with any new business construction. A tax on parking would pay the state back, and Kraft would be on the hook for everything else. And he opted to do it with his own money, without charging season ticketholders thousands of dollars for personal seat licenses (i.e., charging them money for the right to spend even more money), which at the time was becoming all the rage in pro sports.

On December 6, 1999, the first shovel went into the ground for the new stadium. Because this was at the height of the Dot-Com Boom, the place was to be called CMGI Field, after one of those weird cyber-companies that went out of business before you could ever figure out what they did or how to use their products and services. By the start of the 2001 season, the name had been changed to Gillette Stadium, which made more sense, since it was at least a product everybody knew how to buy. And the new place began to rise above the old park, scheduled to open the following September.

Compared to Foxboro, the future home looked massive, modern, and beautiful. As had been the case back when the stands burned down in the middle of a game back in the 60s, it was a perfect metaphor for the team itself.

Training camp had barely gotten under way when quarterback coach Dick Rehbein died from a heart condition first diagnosed 13 years earlier.

Rehbein was by all accounts well-liked and universally respected, and the team took his loss hard. There were statements about how they were dedicating the season to him, though to be fair, there's no quantifying how much of an impact that had on the outcome of the season. Looking back, his legacy will forever be that he was the man responsible for bringing Tom Brady to New England. And there are few coaches in any sport with anything that significant on their résumés.

Rehbein's death would be the first real-life tragedy to affect the Patriots in 2001. It would by no means be the last for them, or for any other team.

A SILENT SUNDAY

The Patriots' 2001 season was a peculiar one before it even began. After Art Modell sucked the souls out of Cleveland Browns fans by moving the team to Baltimore in 1996, the NFL realized that, as much as it helped the local Bill Belichick effigy sales economy, it was still bad for business. So they quickly moved to create an expansion Browns team, which began operations in the 1999 season.

Which meant that for one of the few times in history, the NFL in 2001 was comprised of an odd number of teams. Therefore, at least one team had to have a bye during every week of the season (a situation that was rectified the following year when the Houston Texans were added). The Patriots were in the unique situation of having to play 16 straight games, then have their bye in week 17, whether they needed it or not.

The season opened innocuously enough, with a forgettable 23-17 loss at Cincinnati. Then two days later, America was shaken to its foundation by the terrorist attacks of September 11.

After the initial horror of the day's events had sunk in—once the literal smoke began to clear and the real dust actually began to settle—one of the first figures to emerge in the eyes of New Englanders was Joe Andruzzi. Pats fans who weren't familiar with their second-year right guard quickly learned all about him. And his family.

Andruzzi, we soon learned, was the son of retired New York City police officer Billy Andruzzi. And his three brothers, Billy Jr., Jimmy, and Marc, were all FDNY and among the first firefighters to reach the World Trade Center that day. For six hours neither Andruzzi nor his parents knew whether his brothers had made it out alive. It wasn't until Jimmy—who was on the 27th floor of the North Tower when the South Tower collapsed and was ordered to evacuate —convinced a stranger with a working cell phone to call his family that the Andruzzis knew their sons were safe.

For those of us looking at the events through the prism of New England sports, Joe Andruzzi's brothers were the face of the first responders who rescued so many people but lost so much.

The NFL, for their part, did the right thing and canceled the following week's schedule altogether, guessing correctly that America was in no mood for fun and games while we were still combing through rubble for human remains and doing a body count. Because of the Patriots' odd schedule, their game against the Carolina Panthers was moved from week 2 to week 17. And their first game back after the layoff would be, in an uncanny twist of fate, at home against the Jets.

THE GAME-CHANGER

For all their inconsequential, time-wasting silliness, sports are never better than at a time like September 23, 2001. It was one of those moments when pro football was more than a game. It was the rallying point for all of America. The campfire around which the whole culture gathered to come to grips with what had happened. Every NFL game featured some sort of ceremony intended to pay tribute to the dead and offer some comfort to the survivors. You can argue that pro sports don't matter in the grand scheme of things, and of course you'd be right. But on that day they were more important than ever.

Naturally, with all that had happened to New York, the Patriots-Jets game was drawing a lot of national attention. Players and coaches from each team unfurled a U.S. flag the size of the field. There were military flyovers. Service members from every branch of the armed forces were there. And front and center among the first responders were the Andruzzi brothers in their FDNY gear.

If you witnessed it and your eyes weren't welling up with tears, then you have an empty vacuum where your soul should be. It was absolutely heartrending. And it was almost assured that, while the ceremony would be burned into everyone's memory forever, whatever happened in the game would soon be forgotten.

The first part of that statement is of course true. The second part, not so much. Because something happened in the game that would leave an indelible mark on the future of pro football.

With the Jets leading 10-3 with five minutes to go in the fourth quarter, the Patriots were facing a third-and-10 from their own 19. Drew Bledsoe faded back to pass, but finding no one open and with his pass protection collapsing, rolled out to his right and tried to run for the first down. As he neared the marker along the sidelines, he was met by Jets linebacker Mo Lewis, running with a full head of steam, and forced out of bounds.

Laws of physics say that in a collision, the impulse encountered by an object is equal to the momentum change it experiences. The formula looks like this:

$$F \cdot \Delta t = m \cdot \Delta v$$

with F being force, t representing both players running at full speed, m equal to 260 pounds of Mo Lewis, and v standing both for Bledsoe's unwillingness to quit on the play and for how massive a hit he chose to absorb in an attempt to keep the drive alive rather than to step out of bounds for his own well-being.

But Bledsoe's refusal to take the coward's way out cost him more than anyone could know. Unbeknownst to the rest of the world, Lewis' hit, clean though it was, was nothing short of life-threatening. It actually sheared a blood vessel in Bledsoe's chest. You could say it was one of the really important ones, but aren't they all?

The viewers at home probably thought the collision wasn't that serious. As a matter of fact, everyone quickly forgot about it, because Bledsoe came back out for a series on the subsequent possession. It wasn't until he came back to the sidelines and seemed lethargic and incoherent that anyone realized how serious his injuries were.

Well, there was one person who realized right away, and fortunately he was the one viewer who needed to know. According to an interview in the *Boston Globe* days later, a thoracic surgeon from Mass General Hospital was on call, watching the game at home, and claimed that, as soon as Mo Lewis delivered Newton's Law into Bledsoe's chest, he turned to his wife and predicted that any minute his pager would go off telling him to get to the ER and do surgery on Bledsoe. I don't know if I believed that story, but we do know that the good doctor found that the quarterback had leaked half of his blood supply into his chest cavity.

By the grace of God and the good old American health-care system, the operation was a success. It was only weeks before Bledsoe was getting back to full strength and peak health, like nothing had ever happened. The only thing that wouldn't make a full recovery was his job as starting quarterback for the New England Patriots.

By the time of Bledsoe's injury, Tom Brady had moved up the Pats' depth chart as the No. 2 quarterback. And during Drew's convalescence, he played adequately. He wasn't setting the world on fire.

18 CALM UNDER PRESSURE

★ ★ ★ ★ ★ ★ ★ ★ ★ ★ ★ ★ ★ ★ ★ ★ ★ ★

Prepare for glory.

KING LEONADIS, 300

Brady's first start was a 44–13 blowout of the heavily favored Colts, although Brady didn't throw for a single touchdown and the defense picked Indy's Peyton Manning apart for the win. The next week was a horrible effort by the offense in a 30–10 loss in Miami, after which Bill Belichick brought the team out back behind the practice field to a hole he'd had dug in order to literally bury the game ball. But the Pats followed that up with wins over San Diego and another one over the Colts, and it felt like they were starting to build some momentum.

One thing that absolutely got some momentum going was the criticism of Drew Bledsoe. The old argument about whether he should be replaced came back kicking in the door and with guns blazing. Brady started with most of the Bledsoe critics in his camp anyway, and was beginning to win over more converts by the week.

The pro-Bledsoe loyalists argued that he was the best quarterback the team had ever had, the franchise player with the record contract, and that you shouldn't lose your job to an injury. Besides, they argued, Brady was just a "caretaker" quarterback, not someone who could carry a team as Drew had done.

The defectors to Brady's side fired back that the past didn't matter. Nor did salary. All that counted is what either guy could do going forward, and Bledsoe not only wasn't elevating his game to be among the elite QBs in the the NFL, he was actually regressing. And besides, Brady's "caretaker-ing" just meant that he was smart with the football, setting an NFL record with 162 attempts without an interception to start his career.

Whoever was right or wrong, the battle lines were drawn, the slit trenches dug, and everyone hunkered down for the conflict that would rage all season. For the first time since Bledsoe was drafted, a full-on Quarterback War was declared.

As odd as it sounds, the most crucial game of the entire season was actually a loss. In week 10, the Rams came to Foxboro for a nationally televised game. St. Louis was one year removed from winning a Super Bowl and at the height of their "Greatest Show on Turf" powers. They were 8–1 and former league MVP Kurt Warner was having his best season, leading the NFL in every quarterback stat worth keeping.

The Patriots were 5–4, but winners of four of their last five games and seemingly on a roll. The Rams were going to be a test of how legitimate they really were.

The Rams opened the Sunday night prime-time game with a 40-yard drive, but were forced to punt. After Tom Brady threw an interception that set St. Louis up for a touchdown, Bill Belichick was in front of the New England bench on his knee, telling his defense, "Slants and in-cuts! That's the game!" And the lesson took. Terrell Buckley stepped in front of a Warner pass at midfield and took it all the way for the tying score. Pats fans and the rest of the country were still skeptical they could hang with the Rams, but at least they were making a game of it.

A fourth-quarter Warner touchdown pass put St. Louis up 24–10. The Patriots responded with a quick five-play, 65-yard touchdown drive of their own to pull within a score with just under eight minutes to play, but they never touched the ball again. The Rams put on a sustained, clock-killing drive to end it.

Kurt Warner finished with over 400 yards passing, more than twice what Brady managed, and three touchdown passes. But the Patriots also picked him off twice, and the general feeling after the game was that they had an opportunistic, talented, and well-coached defense that was tough to quarterback against and could steal a game from even the best offense.

The Patriots had hung with the consensus best team in football with the whole country watching and, despite having a .500 record, proved that they were capable of making a run at the playoffs. Granted, you don't get to put anything in the win column for earning respect. But at least it's something.

Their next big test would be off the field, and it was coming right away. The Patriots were about to be caught in one of the worst situations any football franchise can deal with. The kind of thing that tears teams apart and has coaches springing out of their sweat-soaked beds with night terrors: a quarterback controversy.

THE BLEDSOE-BRADY WAR

Through the miracle of modern medicine and his own freakish, Wolverine-like recuperative powers, Drew Bledsoe came off the injured list after the

St. Louis game and was healthy enough to start. Which was what he fully expected to do. Not only because of the old sports adage that says you can't lose your job to injury, but because he felt he had been assured by the coach that the quarterback job was his as soon as he was ready.

Yeah . . . about that. The Patriots were 5–3 with Tom Brady as a starter. More importantly, Brady had the trust of the coaches in general and the head coach in particular. And that "adage" was always more of a guideline than an actual rule. So Bill Belichick announced that Brady would remain the starting quarterback. And to say all hell broke loose would be giving hell too much credit.

The region was split right down the middle on this one. Bledsoe was universally liked as a guy, but his job performance had become increasingly polarizing. At the same time, Brady had done some nice things, but had yet to actually carry the team as Bledsoe had so often done.

Add to all of this the fact that Bledsoe and Robert Kraft were famously close and had just agreed on the richest contract extension in football history. Bledsoe made no secret of the fact that he felt lied to by a coach who was reviled in Cleveland for benching their face-of-the-franchise QB and wasn't really winning any Miss Congeniality votes from the New England press either. He said publicly that he fully expected to be able to come back and compete for what he called "my job." All those factors joined together to form a massive Voltron of a controversy that crushed all other sports talk under its mighty feet.

Everyone had an opinion. Certainly the die-hard football fans, but also the seven-year-old kids with No. 11 Bledsoe jerseys and the old ladies who had never gotten over the mosh-pit incident. The one thing everyone did agree on was that it was a ballsy move by Belichick. You either thought he was a disloyal, two-faced liar or that he was making the right call in order to win. But everyone agreed it took guts. As Ron Borges put it, "Bill Belichick walked the plank this week. Now Tom Brady will decide if he goes off the end of it or not."

To put it in microcosm, like a Civil War family, my own brothers fought on opposite sides in the Bledsoe-Brady War. Jack was the first Brady-backer I knew, declaring from his first start against Indy that he was done with Bledsoe and never wanted to see him back under center. Jim was so Bledsoe-loyal that he was angry they were winning games without him, a stance he held on to long after the season was over.

I know they say the hottest places in hell are reserved for those who refuse to take sides in a crisis, but I was somewhere in the middle. Not to be all wait-and-see, but . . . I wanted to wait and see how Brady would do with the pressure of knowing he had to perform under the threat of Bledsoe challenging him for the job. When he was no longer just the temp, filling in while the real employee is out on sick leave. And if that meant eternal damnation for me, then so be it.

To me, Brady's real test would come the following Sunday at home against the New Orleans Saints. And the results were spectacular.

Brady was flawless. He completed 19 of 26 passes for four touchdowns, no interceptions, and a passer rating of 143.9. I was sold. For all my defenses of Drew Bledsoe, and as much as I truly did like him, I pushed all my emotional chips onto the table, bet my whole stack on Tom Brady, and decided I needed to keep letting it ride. The last thing I wanted to see was a situation where every time he had a bad drive we'd all be calling for a quarterback change.

The next-to-last thing I wanted to see was a lot of dissension within the ranks of the team, and that never happened. To the credit of everyone, Drew Bledsoe especially, they kept everything in-house. Not a word leaked out about who anyone thought the real quarterback should be. We didn't know it yet, but Belichick was establishing the talent that served him so well during Terry Glenn's nonsense and would be his greatest strength going forward. And that's the genius for keeping a lid on controversy, so it's deprived of oxygen and burns itself out.

Not that Bledsoe was happy. He just kept it to himself. Outwardly he said all the right things and appeared to be playing the good soldier. Inwardly he was probably still seething, but he veered onto the high road and stayed there. As did everybody else. So the kinds of issues that can fracture a team never materialized. And they kept winning, mostly by razor-thin margins.

Trailing 13-0 at the half in New York, they rallied in the second half and got a late interception from Terrell Buckley to win 17-16 and give Belichick his first win over the Jets. The following week they beat the Browns 27-16, thanks to an 85-yard punt return by Troy Brown. Then, against Buffalo, David Patten's bizarro non-fumble allowed the Pats to beat the Bills in overtime.

They went into week 15 on a roll, winners of their last four games. Facing the Dolphins at home, in a game expected to be the last one played in Foxboro Stadium, they held a pregame ceremony to honor all the great moments that had happened there. Given what a dump the place was and the gargantuan amount of failure fans had witnessed there, the main highlight came when they brought back the legendary snowplow, driven once again by Mark Henderson. When your most famous honoree is a former prison inmate who probably broke a rule to give a bad team a 3-0 win, it speaks volumes about your stadium. The whole ceremony was sort of the equivalent of looking through the yearbook of a high school where you got straight D's and someone gave you a wedgie every single day.

The Patriots took a 20-0 lead in the first half and barely held on to win by a touchdown. The victory made them 10-5 and gave them the tiebreaker over Miami, should it come to that. Afterward the players took a lap around the field to thank the fans for putting up with the dump that was Foxboro Stadium all those years.

This is where all the rescheduling caused by the horrifying 9/11 attacks weirdly worked in the Patriots' favor. Their bye now fell in week 16, giving them a full week off to prepare for their final game at Carolina. And the Panthers were a beaten, demoralized, 1-14 team playing out the string. Everyone knew that their coach George Seifert (who won two Super Bowls with San Francisco) was about to be fired. In fact, it would be his last game ever as a head coach, and he was the lamest of lame ducks. The Patriots rolled on to win a 34-9 laugher.

Just as important to them, and a much bigger surprise, was what happened in Oakland later that day.

With three weeks to go in the season, the Raiders were 10-3 and appeared to be a lock to at least earn a bye week in the playoffs, if not the best record in the AFC. But in week 15 they lost when Tennessee kicked a go-ahead field goal with under two minutes and Oakland's own kicker Sebastian Janikowski missed his third attempt of the game at the end of regulation. The following week they lost again on the final play at Denver; with Oakland trailing 23-17, quarterback Rich Gannon got picked off in the end zone.

Still, Oakland held the tiebreaker against New England as they faced the Jets at home in the last regular-season game. A win would give the Raiders the playoff bye and force the Patriots to play wild-card weekend, and it appeared likely, since they were 5-2 at home (with both losses coming by a field goal). So, no one was expecting any miracles. Especially late in the game, when the Jets were down two with just over two minutes to go. But we got it.

The Jets managed a drive that got them to the very edge of field goal range before it stalled. They had no choice but to line up for a 53-yard attempt, which John Hall nailed with a minute to go to win the game. So instead of earning a playoff bye, the Raiders had to host the Jets again the following week.

The bye went to New England, who'd be getting their second week off in three weeks, sandwiched around a game against the worst team in football.

The universe that had consistently conspired against the Patriots for four decades had, for reasons known only to it, decided to reverse itself once the new millennium rolled around. The 2001 Patriots got every conceivable break. This time, all the freakish occurrences, bizarre coincidences, and lucky breaks worked in their favor. Even when their one indispensable, franchise player went down to injury, it turned into a positive. They were the Bizarro World Patriots. And arguably no team in NFL history ever went into the playoffs under easier circumstances.

All those unlikely cosmic events that the Patriots benefited from led to one last game in their old, crap-tastic stadium. And it would turn out to easily be the greatest game ever played there.

THE SNOW BOWL

The Patriots, who appeared to be dead in September, found themselves in the postseason with a week off, sitting at home waiting for an opponent.

That opponent turned out to be Oakland, who had no trouble with the Jets in the wild-card round. Most Pats fans were pulling for the Jets, since the Raiders were by far the tougher challenge, so it appeared that maybe the run of good fortune had run out. But then nature stepped in, blew on the Patriots' dice, and kept the lucky streak alive.

For the 2001 playoffs, the NFL was trying something new. They were replacing the old Saturday schedule of games at 12:30 p.m. and 4:30 p.m. with a late afternoon game and another one in prime time. The Raiders at Patriots game was set for an 8:00 p.m. kickoff, and it was largely reported that Robert Kraft, who threw a lot of weight around on the league's broadcast committee, had lobbied hard for it. If true, it was a smart move on his part.

As Saturday rolled around, a major nor'easter whacked New England and had it looking like the region was inside a massive snow globe and God was shaking it with all His divine might. It was the kind of weather the Jets were used to, but not a team from the West Coast. Advantage: Patriots.

The invention of the prime-time Saturday night playoff game was an instant hit with football fans everywhere. It gave everyone the chance to get together with family and friends, throw house parties, congregate with like-minded people, and share the bond of fellowship that connects us with our fellow human beings. They loved it.

Or so I was told. Our first son had just turned five and our second one was still an infant horking down formula every three hours or so. Which meant the nearest sports bar might as well have been on Alpha Centauri for all the likelihood I'd be going there.

Not that I'm complaining. Well, I am complaining, but pay no attention. The scene on television, with the constant swirl of snowflakes in the stadium lights, the snow accumulating on the field, obscuring the yard markers faster than the grounds crew armed with leaf blowers could blow it off, was one of the most spectacular visuals I've ever witnessed.

But while it was nice to look at, like most games played in those conditions, it was a sloppy, low-scoring struggle. No one could find proper footing, and coaches on both sides were playing things conservatively. Oakland tried to throw the ball using a lot of short crossing routes, many of which were defended by New England defensive backs Ty Law and Otis Smith. The Patriots came out trying to establish the run and counter it with screen passes. Mostly they exchanged punts, and the game remained scoreless until the Raiders got on the board with a Rich Gannon touchdown pass that would have been perfect if he'd thrown it in practice on a sunny, 80-degree day. The Pats were down by seven points, but with offense in such short supply it felt like a thousand.

It wasn't until they opened the second half that New England was able to put any sort of a drive together. Offensive coordinator Charlie Weis scrapped the conservative play-calling in favor of passes to the Patriots' receivers and tight ends, who were getting open in the mid-range zones between Oakland's linebackers and safeties. The drive stalled when Tom Brady missed an open Rod Rutledge in the end zone, but Adam Vinatieri's short field goal made it 7–3.

Oakland hit on two more field goals to open up a 13–3 lead.

Early in the fourth quarter, the Patriots offense took over on their own 33 and began handling the conditions like a Snowcat grooming a ski slope. Brady completed nine consecutive passes, including a fluky first-down play at the Oakland 20 that ricocheted off David Patten's hands as he fell out of bounds and went right to an alert Jermaine Wiggins for a four-yard completion.

At second-and-goal from the Oakland six, Brady again went back to pass. Finding no one open, he pulled the ball down and ran it up the middle for the Patriots' first touchdown. I distinctly remember jumping off the couch screaming, but wearing socks on a bare tile floor, I immediately did a face plant, only to look up and see that Brady, while spiking the ball in the snowy end zone, fell on his face in the exact same manner. Now not only was he my new athletic hero, I decided that he and I were emotionally linked, like Elliott and E.T.

There were just under eight minutes to go and, with the score 13–10 and points hard to come by, it would be an exaggeration to say the Patriots needed a miracle, but they at least needed a magic trick of some sort.

The teams exchanged punts, and with Oakland running the clock down as the two-minute warning approached, the Pats started burning all their timeouts. The Raiders had the ball at midfield, facing a third-and-one. If they converted it, the game would be for all intents and purposes over.

The Raiders handed the ball to Zack Crockett, running behind fullback Jon Ritchie. But Richard Seymour cut through the line, met Ritchie head on, and stuffed Crockett for no gain. Seymour, the rookie defensive tackle whom practically no one outside the Patriots' war room wanted them to draft, ensured that New England would get the ball back with one final, desperate shot to keep the season alive.

It was on that last-ditch drive, with the Patriots on the edge of game-tying field goal range, that karma stepped in and forever changed the fate of a team, a league, a fan base, and one particular Patriots fan who bears a passing resemblance to me.

The Patriots had a first-and-10 at the Oakland 42 when defensive back Charles Woodson came in free on a blitz to hit Brady as he stood back in the pocket. The ball came loose, rolled on the snow until the seconds felt like hours, and the Raiders fell on it. The ruling on the field was that it was a fumble and Oakland's ball. The Patriots' season was effectively over.

Except that it wasn't. Not yet, anyway. The play was under review to see if perhaps, by some slim margin, the referee would determine that Brady's arm had been in a throwing motion when he was hit, making it an incomplete pass and still the Patriots' ball.

The season hung in the balance as those of us watching at home were treated to interminable replays of the hit, interspersed with cutaways of referee Walt Coleman with his head stuck into the shopping-mall photo booth that is an NFL replay setup.

There was a glimmer of hope. A fool's hope. But in my heart of hearts I didn't think Coleman would reverse the call. Not based on any special recall of the "Tuck Rule" play from the Jets game back in September or anything, because nobody remembered that. I simply assumed the fumble would stand because it was precisely the kind of thing that had happened to the Patriots my entire life. And this fumble happened at precisely the time it usually did. You could always count on it, like it was part of the natural laws of nature.

But not this time. Coleman stepped to the middle of the field and announced, "After reviewing the play, the quarterback's arm was going forward. It is an incomplete [inaudible] . . ." We assume the last word of that sentence was "pass," but it could have been "banana" or "fornication" for all anyone could hear through the 60,000 screams coming from the stands. The Patriots' improbable run of good fortune not only rolled on, it went to historic levels.

From the moment the call was reversed and ever since, it's been one of the most controversial calls ever made in the history of sports. Walt Coleman has been accused of making it up on the spot, as if NFL Rule 3, Section 22, Article 2, Note 2 never existed. It has been said the call had never been made before and hasn't been since, which is a lie. If the rumors are correct, Coleman's first reaction once he stuck his head under that review booth hood and watched the replay was "Oh, shit," because he immediately knew the fumble call was wrong and would have to be reversed.

The ultimate irony for Oakland, the one that poured road salt in their Snow Bowl wounds, is that if the Tuck Rule play had happened just 10 seconds on the game clock earlier, it would never have been reviewed in the first place. First, because the Patriots had used up all their timeouts on the previous defensive stand, so by rule they wouldn't have been able to challenge the call. Second, the play came with 1 minute and 50 seconds to go in the game, and in the final 2 minutes only the officials can call for a review. They did. And the fate of two NFL franchises turned on it.

The Patriots were still alive, but on life support and about to code if Brady couldn't stabilize their vital signs, stat. A 13-yard completion to Patten got the ball to the outer limits of field-goal range, but since the field still looked like the last five minutes of a Christmas movie, the Patriots needed more. They would get it. Two more incompletions and a quarterback keeper to put the ball in the middle of the field left them with a 45-yard field goal attempt.

Now it would take a miracle. For Adam Vinatieri, never the strongest-legged kicker in the league, kicking the ball in those conditions must have felt like kicking a butternut squash, and the footing must have felt like the surface of a frozen pond. He'd have to get a low trajectory on the kick and hope it found its way through the arms of the Raiders linemen and had the distance to make it over the crossbar.

It did. Just barely. All things being equal, it was one of the clutchest athletic plays any of us had ever seen. Set up by dozens of other crucial plays and one huge call the officials got right. But Vinatieri had made the one unforgettable clutch play. The game was tied at the end of regulation.

Overtime was an anticlimax. In the surest, most predestined 50/50 bet of all time, the Patriots won the coin toss. And through some combination of them being energized and the Raiders being demoralized by that final drive, the outcome was never in doubt. They sustained a 14-play march down the field in which they had only one negative play (a 1-yard loss on a rushing attempt) and Brady was 8 for 8 passing. It set Vinatieri up with a 23-yard field goal attempt. And after the entire offense scraped the snow off the spot under the ball with their cleats for what seemed like forever (no snowplows to be seen anywhere), he nailed the kick.

The players went all delirious on the field. Long snapper Lonnie Paxton was by far the most iconic, lying flat on his back doing snow angels. The Patriots had won the hardest-fought, most memorable, and simply best game ever played in the mostly sorry 30-year history of Schaefer/Sullivan/Foxboro Stadium.

And the last. Because once they thawed out, put on some dry clothes, and had some hot cocoa by the fireplace, they'd be heading to Pittsburgh to play the Steelers for the AFC title and a trip to the Super Bowl in New Orleans.

THE CHAMPIONSHIP GAME

There was plenty of drama, irony, and controversy in the AFC championship game to keep the 2001 Patriots' karma train rolling along at full throttle. As a matter of fact, in most seasons this would have been the game of the year. But coming as it did a week after an all-time classic like the Snow Bowl, it is largely overlooked. It's like Martin Scorsese following up *Goodfellas* with *Casino*. The title game against the Steelers will forever pale in comparison.

New England went into Pittsburgh as prohibitive underdogs. The consensus out of western Pennsylvania was that this was exactly the matchup they had been hoping for. The entire nation believed the Pats had benefited from a blown call on the Tuck Rule, denying everyone the Pittsburgh-Oakland matchup the world wanted, and this game was setting up to be a crushing bore.

Looking back, you can see why. The Steelers went 13–3, were 6–2 at home, had the most prolific rushing offense in the league, and gave up the third fewest points and the fewest yards by a margin of more than 300 over the No. 2 defense. Whereas, in the minds of most of the country, the Patriots had only gotten to the game through good luck and bad officiating.

During the week's buildup to the game, whenever anyone drew up one of those "Tale of the Tape" side-by-side comparisons of the two teams, the Patriots didn't get many checkmarks in their favor. One category where they did have a sizable advantage was in the kicking game. Adam Vinatieri's performance in the blizzard made him an instant legend. And Pittsburgh's kicker Kris Brown was notorious for missing field goals, particularly when kicking toward the open end of Heinz Field, which was tough on everyone. In fact, I remember reading that for the season he had missed 14 of 35 of his attempts from between 30 and 49 yards, which is so bad it made me think that I'd hate to see what the floor around his toilet looked like.

But virtually every other factor favored Pittsburgh. To the point that to open the local radio broadcast, Gil Santos referred to it as "the Cinderella New England Patriots against the big, bad Pittsburgh Steelers," adding, "I'm happy to report that, despite all the prognostications of doom, the Patriots *have* shown up here today and *will* take the field . . ."

In the early going, the game lived down to the lack of hype, though not because the Steelers were blowing the Patriots out. In front of a packed house twirling "terrible towels" (terrycloth snot rags that looked like a combination of something you'd hang on your golf bag and a penalty flag), the first quarter was mainly a puntfest. Until the New England defense stopped Pittsburgh on their third possession and Fate once again put her tongue in the Patriots' mouth.

As we'd later come to find out, the Steelers' punt team had one prime directive, which was not to let Troy Brown return a kick up the middle of the field. Their plan was to do whatever it took to force him to the outside, force him out of bounds, or bring him down going sideways. And this time it worked to perfection. Josh Miller's punt landed near the sidelines. Brown let it bounce, since it looked for all the world like it would go straight out of bounds. But instead it took a freakish kick and rolled before finally rolling out at the Pats' 23-yard line, for a 64-yard net punt that flipped the field on them.

Except that the Patriots caught yet another series of breaks, starting with a penalty on the Steelers that meant a re-kick. Secondly, the officials mistakenly put the ball on the right hash mark instead of on the left one, where the ball had been spotted on the original punt. Thirdly, the Pittsburgh coverage unit did exactly what they had been determined not to do.

Brown fielded this one at the Patriots' 45-yard line and proceeded to return it right up the center of the field. He never once had to step out from between the hash marks, instead roaring through the middle of the Steelers for the touchdown, like Mad Max straddling the double yellow line on a post-apocalyptic highway. Steelers coach Bill Cowher was incredulous. He got in the officials' faces and with spittle flying screamed, "You were wrong! How could you screw that up?!" It was hard to argue with his point. But even harder to argue that waiting until his team had given up a 55-yard touchdown return was the ideal time to broach the subject.

When whatever forces were guiding the Patriots' season decided that things weren't nearly surreal enough for their liking and it was time to intervene, Pittsburgh answered back with a field goal to make it 7–3. On a brilliant third-down pass from Tom Brady to Troy Brown that picked up 28 yards, Steelers' defensive back Lee Flowers came in on a blitz and wrapped him up around the legs just as he got rid of the ball. As Brady went down, his body twisted in that awkward way that often spells trouble. This spelled it in all caps.

Brady lay on the ground, writhing in pain and clutching his left knee. He had to come off the field. And in one of the most dramatic moments in a season full of them, the Patriots turned to Drew Bledsoe, who hadn't taken a snap since the life-threatening ones he took after the Mo Lewis hit back in the second game. The Brady injury was, as the gamblers say, a bad beat. But every last person in New England, no matter where they fell on the quarterback debate earlier in the season, acknowledged that Bledsoe was the best backup in the league and a luxury to have around.

And Bledsoe confirmed it on his very first play, delivering a textbook strike to David Patten for a 15-yard gain. This is when the surrealism kicked in. On his second snap Bledsoe dropped back to pass and, finding no one open, rolled around the right end on a quarterback keeper. Four yards later, as he stepped out of bounds, he took a vicious, full-speed hit by Pittsburgh's Chad Scott and was knocked on his earhole.

It wasn't just similar to the hit that almost killed him, it was practically identical. It was as if a group of those history buff guys who dress up in period costumes and recreate old battles did a reenactment of the Lewis hit. For a nanosecond, every heart in New England stopped. Which was how long it took Bledsoe to bounce back up and race back onto the field, clapping his hands and head-slapping his linemen like a man with a new lease on life. He looked happy just to be getting pummeled on the field instead of holding a clipboard by the bench. And it made your heart soar.

Bledsoe completed another pass to Patten to get it down to Pittsburgh's 11-yard line. Then he found Patten again in the back corner of the end zone, looking back into the sun and falling down backwards as he hauled the pass in for the score. Bledsoe was three for three on the drive, for 36 yards and a touchdown. You couldn't make it up.

The Patriots took a 14–3 lead into the half. Which was unfortunate for poor Sheryl Crow, who had the misfortune of being booked to do the halftime show for a crowd of shell-shocked Steelers fans who were in no mood to be entertained. She greeted the masses with a "How's everybody doing?!!!" as they sat in stunned silence, mini yellow towels covering their faces.

The rest of the game was anticlimatic. Pittsburgh put together a few scoring drives to pull to within a touchdown. Adam Vinatieri missed a long kick that would have put it out of reach, but Stewart, in his desperation to score quickly, threw interceptions on two bad overthrows as the Patriots put the game away.

In all, Bledsoe was 10 for 21, with 102 passing yards and the team's only offensive touchdown, but if you want to be critical, he was a mixed bag. It was all of the good and all of the bad we had come to expect from him. At one point he threw a short pass that hit Pittsburgh linebacker Joey Porter in the hands; had he hauled it in, he could have walked into the end zone. But he didn't. The Patriots' streak of good fortune continued. More importantly, the forgotten man had finally gotten to contribute to this incredible run that he had previously only been watching from the sidelines.

Even more importantly than that, the Patriots were going to the Super Bowl for the third time in their history. Once again with controversy dogging their steps. Only this time, instead of it being about a team filled with cokeheads or the head coach going to work for an archrival, the controversy was a football one: who would be the starting quarterback? And Bill Belichick wasted no time taking a fire hose to that one.

It would be Tom Brady taking the snaps in New Orleans. And once again, it would be against the St. Louis Rams.

A DYNASTY IS BORN

As good as it felt to see the Patriots make it to Super Bowl XXXVI, it seemed inevitable that they would draw the short straw of having to face the undisputed best team in football.

By 2001 all four Boston pro sports teams were mired in a horrific slump. It had been 15 years since any team had won a championship, and almost 30 years since a team not named "Celtics" had. And on the rare occasions that one of them made it to their league finals, they always managed to get stuck facing a powerhouse.

The Red Sox, for example, made the World Series once per decade in the 60s, 70s, and 80s, and each time they faced the best team of the decade, took them to seven games, and lost in spectacular fashion. The Patriots had been to two Super Bowls and faced the 1996 Green Bay Packers (one of the best teams of their era) and the 1985 Bears, who to this day are the standard by which all other great football teams are judged. Teams from New England sometimes got to play Cinderella, but they never got to play against her.

So make no mistake, the 2001 Rams were stacked. The "Greatest Show on Turf" had enjoyed its third straight year of scoring over 500 points. Kurt Warner had won his second Most Valuable Player award. Running back Marshall Faulk was the NFL Offensive Player of the Year for the third consecutive year. Wideouts Torry Holt and Ricky Proehl each topped 1,100 receiving yards. And the Rams defense, which had been 31st in the league the season before, improved to give up the seventh fewest points and third fewest yards in the NFL.

It's fair to say that most of the country was disappointed the Patriots had crashed the party and cost them the chance to see St. Louis go up against a real challenger, like Pittsburgh or even Oakland. And the pinkie-ringed goons who set the lines in Vegas concurred, installing New England as 14-point underdogs, just as they had been five years earlier against Green Bay.

In the buildup to the game, it was obvious that the NFL did arguably the best job in their history with regard to game presentation. And 9/11 was a constant presence. They changed the planned logo from the typical local-flavor New Orleans–themed one to a U.S. flag in the shape of the contiguous states. Pregame they trotted out the usual assortment of aging pop stars who are recognizable and non-threatening enough to appeal to advertisers, but this time they would all sing songs with a patriotic bent. And best of all, they booked U2 to turn the typical halftime schmaltzfest into a tribute to the victims of the attacks.

The first inkling we had that we were in for a special game was with the introductions. The Rams were designated the "road" team, so, according to protocol, they were introduced first and chose to have their offensive players announced to the crowd, with CBS play-by-play guy Pat Summerall on the mic. Next came the Patriots.

They came out at the end of the big inflated tunnel with their cheerleaders forming lines out to the field. "And now, ladies and gentlemen," Summerall began, "choosing to be introduced as a team, the American Football Conference champion New England Patriots!"

It took your breath away. Well, it took mine away. And that of any other New Englander still drawing breath. And I had to think that it resonated with most people watching across the country. If not for the sincerity of wanting to put the team first, then for the pure mindfuck of subtly making the Rams look like a bunch of selfish prima donnas by comparison. Which they were not, by the way. The individual intros had always been a Super Bowl tradition. It's just that the Patriots' gesture made the contrast so striking. It was like a politician running an ad where he says he loves America and so, by extension, implies that his opponent hates this dump and plans to turn it into Southern Canada.

Call it a show of solidarity or simple gamesmanship, it was effective. No Super Bowl team since has dared come out in any way other than being introduced as a team.

The game itself was a good one by Super Bowl standards. Had it been played in September, it might have been "Game of the Week" material on the highlight recap shows. But as Super Bowls go? It was a classic. We'd been cursed as a culture by so many tedious, one-sided blowouts down through the years, it was as if the football gods were giving us the one we deserved.

The Rams opened the game with great field position before the New England defense forced a punt that pinned them back on their own 3-yard line. Standing on his own goal line, Tom Brady's first career play from scrimmage was a completion on a quick slant to Troy Brown, who carried it to the 24-yard line and out of immediate danger. A run and another toss to Brown got the ball to midfield before the Patriots had to punt.

One Rams drive ended in a long field goal. The next ended on a long missed field goal try. Meanwhile, the Patriots could get nothing going offensively. The few Pats optimists among us had pinned our hopes on the defense's ability to force turnovers. It turned out that while we might have been naïve and delusional, we were not wrong.

St. Louis was leading 3-0 with the ball, on first-and-10 at their own 39-yard line. Not that anyone noticed, but just prior to the snap, left outside linebacker Mike Vrabel put his hand on the ground. It was the first three-point stance he was in all game. And by the complex, nuanced coaching points of pro football blocking assignments, it rendered him invisible to the Rams' offensive line. Vrabel was left unaccounted for and rushed in on Kurt Warner at a full sprint. Warner tried to hit Isaac Bruce in the flat, but had to rush the throw. The ball was underthrown, and Ty Law, reading it all the way, undercut the route, intercepted the ball in stride, and raced into the end zone for the score and a 7-3 New England lead.

With time running down near the end of the half, the Pats defense stepped up again. This time Ricky Proehl caught a ball at his own 40-yard line, but it was punched out by Antwan Harris and recovered by Terrell Buckley. Eight plays later, with just over half a minute to go in the half and out of timeouts, Brady hit David Patten (with Patten falling on his back) in the corner of the end zone; it was almost the identical route in the same spot as the one Patten had run to catch Drew Bledsoe's touchdown pass in Pittsburgh.

It was halftime of the Super Bowl and the New England Patriots had a 14-3 lead.

And then U2 came on. Behind the band these massive curtains were raised, and projected on them were the names of all the 3,000 innocents whose lives were taken five months earlier, while U2 played "Where the Streets Have No Name" and "Beautiful Day." It was chilling and haunting and oddly inspirational at the same time. That's a subjective opinion, I know. But objectively speaking, it was far more affecting than the "Blues Brothers 2000" show had been at the Super Bowl against Green Bay.

In the third quarter, the teams kept exchanging punts. Picture the montage from any *Rocky* movie where they cut from the fighters trading punches to the ring card girls to them sitting in the corner yelling inarticulate nonsense to the trainers while the music blares, and you pretty much have the idea.

Once again, though, the Patriots' defense came up huge. Otis Smith intercepted a Warner overthrow, setting up an eventual Adam Vinatieri field goal that made it a 17-3 game to start the fourth quarter. We were delirious, but the experienced Red Sox fan in all of us had seen too many championships evaporate before our eyes to celebrate. That was still an obscenely good Rams offense. And as badly as they had bungled everything to that point, they were still only two quick strikes behind.

To open the fourth quarter, St. Louis drove it down to the Patriots 3-yard line, which shockingly was their first trip to the red zone the whole game. Facing a fourth-and-goal, they went for it. Warner dropped back looking for someone open in the end zone and, finding no one, stepped up to try to run it in when Roman Phifer met him head-on and punched the ball out. Tebucky Jones fielded it on a hop and took it 97 yards the other way. Now all that careful doubt, Red Sox history, and gym class metaphors meant nothing. The score meant the game was hopelessly out of reach. The Patriots had an insurmountable lead and nothing could stop them from being world champions.

That is, until something did. There was a flag on the play. Holding on the defense.

Willie McGinest had, in no uncertain terms, wrapped his arms around Marshall Faulk, which is part of the reason Warner found no one open. We later found out that the Patriots' coaching staff had done careful study on the Rams and felt that the key to the offense wasn't Warner, it was Faulk. That the whole attack ran through him. Disrupt Faulk's timing, and it would mess up everything else. As the NFL Films narration would later put it, their game plan was "hit Marshall Faulk when he has the ball, and hit him when he doesn't."

Presumably they said nothing about bear-hugging him. The touchdown was called back. One play later, Warner ran in a quarterback sneak and instead of 24-3 and game in the bag, it was 17-10 and game on.

The Patriots had two more possessions sandwiched around a Rams drive and produced two three-and-outs. After a bad New England punt, St. Louis got the ball at midfield with no timeouts and not much time left. They didn't need either. Three plays and 14 seconds later, Proehl was crossing the goal line on a 26-yard catch and run. The game was tied with under two minutes to play.

It was sphincter-clenching time. After the kickoff, the Patriots were left with the ball on their 17-yard line, with 1 minute and 51 seconds remaining and no timeouts. For the vast majority of us, the great question was whether to just run out the clock and wait for a better shot in overtime, or whether to play for the win. For the tiny minority to which I belonged, the issue was whether to screw out of there to relieve the babysitter or potentially add hours onto her night. It was the kind of conundrum I never had to face back when I was irresponsibly stumbling around drunk trying to greet the Patriots plane when they were heading to the Super Bowl back in January of '86. But parenthood was the business I'd chosen.

Legendary CBS analyst John Madden had no advice for me on the babysitter issue, but he was firm on the Patriots' strategy. He made it clear in no uncertain terms that the Patriots should take a knee and play for overtime.

The same issue was being addressed on the Patriots' sidelines. Brady would later say that offensive coordinator Charlie Weis told him they would play for the win, but made it clear that the top priority was to "take care of that ball." But Brady also said, in a story that would be passed down into legend in stories repeated by tribal elders around a million campfires, Drew Bledsoe got between him and Weis and said, "Fuck that. Go out there and sling it." And sling it he did.

Though not right away. The first play was a pass to running back J.R. Redmond that only got the Pats out to the 22 and burned 24 seconds off the clock. Another pass to Redmond didn't move the ball much farther, while Madden got increasingly exasperated by how dumb they were being. On a short checkdown pass, Redmond not only managed to pick up 11 yards but also dragged a St. Louis defender to the sidelines like a husky pulling a sled and stopped the clock.

Now even Madden was starting to get on board the with the decision to go for it. In one of the biggest plays in franchise history, Brady found Troy Brown on a short slant over the middle, and Brown managed to angle his way to the sidelines for 22 yards and another clock stoppage. The Patriots were on the absolute edge of the acceptable field goal range, the Kuiper Belt on the outer reaches of the game-winning kick solar system. So they took one more shot at advancing the ball while the souls of everyone in New England left our bodies and hovered over us.

A completion to tight end Jermaine Wiggins got the ball to the Rams' 31-yard line as the final seconds ticked away. While the rest of us were in all-out panic mode, Brady gathered everyone to the line of scrimmage and, with a preternatural calm that made no logical sense, casually spiked the ball to stop the clock with seven seconds left.

It's possible I've watched that replay more than any other sports highlight of my life, and I can never reconcile the situation with how calmly Brady acts. There's a story about Super Bowl XXIII, when Joe Montana needed to lead his 49ers the length of the field to beat the Bengals, and he was so overly excited that he was hyperventilating and had to throw a pass out of bounds just to catch his breath. But having led the Patriots to within range of kicking a championship field goal, Brady spiked the ball, gently reached out his hand and softly caught the ball on the first hop, like a man feeling for raindrops.

In retrospect, Brady was the personification of keeping your cool while there's chaos all around you. Whereas I was dying a horrible death inside as the field goal unit took the field.

Adam Vinatieri lined up for a 48-yarder, which was a long kick under any circumstances. But with the championship riding on it and the weight of the football world on his shoulders, it felt like we were asking for the planets to align and make the impossible happen. The optimist in me was thinking that if he missed, at least the Patriots had a 50/50 shot to win in overtime. The voice of experience was saying you don't watch a 14-point lead evaporate only to win in OT.

Vinatieri's kick wasn't just good. It wasn't just a no-doubter. It was perfect. It split the uprights halfway between, bisected the goal post and had plenty of distance. And I'm not ashamed to admit I cried real tears.

The New England Patriots, the New England Patriots of my childhood and the once Boston Patriots of infamy, were the Super Bowl champions.

It wasn't just improbable. It wasn't an impossible dream. It wasn't even a miracle. This defied all natural laws. It was the stuff of an alternate timeline in a parallel universe where everything you know is wrong.

The team I'd inexplicably attached myself to for as long as I can remember, the bizarre, dysfunctional franchise who went ten years without a stadium, the ones who drafted injured guys, drove coaches to nervous breakdowns, set records for losses, arrests, turmoil, sexual harassment, and coaches quitting in the middle of playoff runs, the poorest team in all of sports with the worst ownership who lost their franchise because of a pop music superstar, was the best team on the biggest stage in all of American sports.

It made no sense on any level. But in the calculus of a lifelong fan's mind, that didn't matter. All I understood or cared about was that all of the bad, the futility, the embarrassments, and the failure had all been worthwhile.

A few weeks after Super Bowl XXXVI, NFL Films released their highlight package of the game. What we found out then was that in the pregame, Rams wide receiver Ricky Proehl had looked into the camera and said, "Tonight, a dynasty is born, baby!" What we didn't realize until a few years later was, he was right. He just had the wrong franchise.

The actual dynasty turned out to be the one that had endured all that darkness.

EPILOGUE

★ ★ ★ ★ ★ ★ ★ ★ ★ ★ ★ ★ ★ ★ ★ ★ ★ ★ ★

The 2001 Patriots winning Super Bowl XXXVI wasn't the first improbable, semi-miraculous championship I'd ever witnessed, and it wouldn't be the last. So it was no surprise when they topped the news cycle that winter, hit all the sports magazine covers, and dominated the media landscape the way surprising winners do.

The first inclination I had that this one would stand out even among the select few that are considered truly great, memorable championship teams was when Tom Brady appeared on the cover of *People*. Without looking it up, I can picture that issue like I'm holding it on my lap. Brady shirtless and clutching a football, with the headline "Those lips! That chin! That Super Bowl win!"

Staring at that issue in the supermarket checkout line, waiting for the cashier to ring up my six-pack and Weymouth Shrimp (what you would call cheese curls), that's when it hit me that this was no longer my same old Boston/New England Patriots. They were now breathing that rarefied air few sports teams ever get to. They were achieving crossover appeal beyond their sport and entering the world of pop culture.

What I had no clue of at the time was how much they'd dominate the national consciousness, both on and off the field, and for how long.

Two more Super Bowl championships quickly followed, in 2003 and 2004, seasons in which they went a combined 34–4, the greatest two-year stretch in NFL history. Over the next decade, they made three more Super Bowl appearances, including their fourth win after the 2014 season.

The franchise that set the standard for ineptness and futility for 40 years was now the great dynasty in a league that was structured to prevent just such sustained excellence. The team whose first owner had to borrow money just to start the team, borrow more money in order to keep it afloat, then borrow yet more money to pay off the original investors to the point that the team went bankrupt was now one of the most successful, profitable franchises in all of North American sports.

The team that was always on the verge of folding or moving—the one that could have easily become some long-forgotten footnote to history, like baseball's Cleveland Spiders (1887–98), hockey's California Golden Seals (1970–76), or basketball's Providence Steamrollers (1946–49)—was now a model franchise.

The worst facility in all of pro sports was replaced with a state-of-the-art stadium surrounded by a retail, dining, entertainment, and hotel complex.

And the management that was for decades the laughingstock of pro sports became the gold standard by which all others are judged.

But remarkably, it's possible that since that first Super Bowl win in February 2002 the Patriots have made more news off the field. The football club that imprinted on me during a time when almost no one cared about them have spent a decade and a half being one of the most divisive, controversial, and talked-about teams in the history of pro sports.

Scandals real (Spygate, 2007), imagined (false reports that they taped the Rams walk-through before Super Bowl XXXVI), and open to interpretation (Deflategate, 2015) have put them at the front of the nation's consciousness longer than anyone could have ever imagined when they were struggling for a mere semblance of credibility.

For me personally, during all this success and controversy I went from writing posts about the team on the website Patriots Planet, to blogging for an obscure, free Boston newspaper called *Barstool Sports* that exploded into a national phenomenon, to a full-time career covering the team for WEEI Sports Radio and WEEI.com's *Thornography* blog. One of the duties of the job is to interview Bill Belichick every week during the season. I guess the team and I have both come a long way since that first glimpse at Schaefer Stadium when I was 13.

It's not uncommon that I get accused of being partisan or a fanboy for the team, charges I don't reject. I defy anyone to name another organization that ever spent so much time at the bottom, only to instantly turn it around and manage to be so dominant for so long. When you look back at the dysfunctional clown show that the Patriots were for the 20th-century portion of their existence and see what they've become since, I'm not being a homer. I'm being genuine. It's what makes life as a sports fan worth living. I apologize for nothing.

I endured all the darkness. I'm certainly not going to miss out on enjoying the dynasty.

NOTES

1 Larry Fox, *The New England Patriots: Tragedy and Triumph* (New York: Macmillan, 1977), 21.

2 Sean Leahy, "How the Patriots Morphed from a Cape House into an NFL Titan," *USA Today*, June 22, 2009.

3 Michael Madden, "Patriots' Past-Catching Game: As First Coach, Saban Saw History—and Histrionics," *The Boston Globe*, October 2, 1994.

4 John Steinbreder, "The $126 Million Fumble," *Sports Illustrated*, March 14, 1988.

5 Robert Hyldburg, *Total Patriots: The Definitive Encyclopedia of the World-Class Franchise* (Chicago: Triumph Books, 2009), 88.

6 Fox, *The New England Patriots: Tragedy and Triumph*, 53.

7 Bill Pennington, "A Team's Ragtag Roots: Early Patriots Were a Comical Traveling Sideshow," *New York Times*, January 27, 2012.

8 Steve Sabol, "Football at Fenway," *NFL Films Presents* video, 4:55, 2012, http://www.nfl.com/videos/nfl-films-presents/0ap2000000118047/NFL-Films-Presents-Football-at-Fenway.

9 Will McDonough, "The Wild and the Wacky," *The Boston Globe*, February 10, 2002.

10 Fox, *The New England Patriots*, 82.

11 Hyldburg, *Total Patriots: The Definitive Encyclopedia of the World-Class Franchise*, 259.

12 "Will He Play for Patriots? Dryer Has Plenty to Say," *Lodi News-Sentinel*, February 22, 1972.

13 Fox, *The New England Patriots*, 109.

14 Upton Bell and David Chanoff, "Settling the Score," *Boston Magazine*, December 2001.

15 McDonough, "The Wild and the Wacky."

16 McDonough, "The Wild and the Wacky."

17 Richard Jones, "The Forgotten Story of Lancashire's American Football Ace," *The Guardian*, January 18, 2012.

18 Fox, *The New England Patriots*, 178.

19 McDonough, "The Wild and the Wacky."

20 Fox, *The New England Patriots*, 212.

21 Mike Felger, *Tales from the New England Patriots' Sideline: A Collection of the Greatest Patriots Stories Ever Told* (Champaign, IL: Sports Publishing, 2012).

22 Richard Hoffer, "The Real Thing: Patriots Coach Raymond Berry, Unlike Predecessor, Comes Across With Players," *Los Angeles Times*, September 27, 1985.

23 Felger, *Tales from the New England Patriots' Sideline*, 72.

24 Felger, *Tales from the New England Patriots' Sideline*, 72.

25 Hoffer, "The Real Thing."

26 "Patriots Fans Hurt in Goal-Post Mishap Are Awarded $5M," *Seattle Times*, December 14, 1991.

27 Felger, *Tales from the New England Patriots' Sideline*.

28 Rick Reilly, "Fryar and Brimstone: Irving Fryar, Former Hell-Raiser, Has Found Heaven as a Preacher and a Wideout in Miami," *Sports Illustrated*, June 5, 1995.

29 Craig Neff, "The NFL and Drugs: Fumbling for a Game Plan," *Sports Illustrated*, February 10, 1986.

30 Steinbreder, "The $126 Million Fumble."

31 Steinbreder, "The $126 Million Fumble."

32 Will McDonough, "An Inside Look at Parcells-Kraft: How They Came to the Breaking Point in a Tumultuous Year," *The Boston Globe*, February 16, 1997.

33 Gerry Callahan, "A True Survival Test: Don't Try Telling Patriots' Wideout Terry Glenn That There's No Greater Pressure Than Playing in the NFL's Ultimate Game," *Sports Illustrated*, January 27, 1996.

34 Michael Silver, "Return to Glory After Suffering Through a Week of Patriots Blather, the Packers Got on With the Business of Winning Their First NFL Title in 29 Years," *Sports Illustrated*, February 3, 1997.

35 Steve Gutman, public press conference, January 4, 2000.

36 Mark Cannizarro, *Tales From the New York Jets Sidelines* (New York: Skyhorse Publishing, 2011), 102.

37 Michael Holley, *War Room: The Legacy of Bill Belichick and the Art of Building the Perfect Team* (New York: Harper Collins, 2011), 24.

INDEX

Also by Jerry Thornton

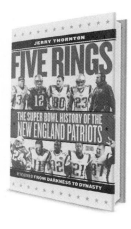

Five Rings
The Super Bowl History of the New England Patriots (So Far)

ISBN 978-1-5126-0271-5

*Five rings to rule them all!
A history of the modern Patriots
as seen through the lens of their
Super Bowl games*

"Jerry has done a great job capturing the details and emotions of the Patriots' five championship seasons. It has been an honor to be on two of those teams. I hope we can add a couple more chapters to the book."
—Julian Edelman, New England Patriots

"Jerry's passion for the Patriots, and his knack for capturing the story with both great detail and humor, make him the perfect person to capture the history of the organization in a way that has never been done before. From Boston to Foxborough, and from Boston to the Bay State to the New England Patriots, Jerry is bringing to life many of the tales that make the franchise one of the most compelling stories in all of sports—in a way that only he can."
—Mike Reiss, ESPN staff writer and coauthor with Troy Brown of *Patriot Pride: My Life in the New England Dynasty*

"Jerry does not deny his Patriots fandom. His ability to take a step back and have a realistic, in-depth look at both the wins and losses is what sets him apart. This book will tell you why the Patriots are able to sustain success and also point out the few missteps over the last fifteen years. You don't need to be a Patriots fan to enjoy *Five Rings*."
—AJ Hawk, Green Bay Packers, Super Bowl XLV champion